Political Vegetables?

Political Vegetables?

Businessman and Bureaucrat
in the Development
of Egyptian Agriculture

Yahya M. Sadowski

The Brookings Institution
Washington, D.C.

Copyright © 1991
THE BROOKINGS INSTITUTION
1775 Massachusetts Avenue, N.W., Washington, D.C. 20036

Library of Congress Cataloging-in-Publication data:

Sadowski, Yahya M.
    Political vegetables? : businessman and bureaucrat in the
development of Egyptian agriculture / Yahya M. Sadowski.
        p.   cm.
    Includes bibliographical references and index.
    ISBN 0-8157-7662-4—ISBN 0-8157-7661-6 (pbk.)
    1. Agriculture and state—Egypt.   2. Agriculture—Economic
aspects—Egypt.   I. Title.
HD2123.Z8S24   1991
338.1'862—dc20   91-21026
                                                                         CIP

9 8 7 6 5 4 3 2 1

The paper used in this publication meets the minimum requirements of the
American National Standard for Information Sciences—Permanence of Paper
for Printed Library Materials, ANSI Z39.48-1984.

035480

Foreword

IN THE EARLY 1980s many development experts believed that the key to promoting growth in the Third World was to reform government economic policies that inhibited the operation of market forces. After ten years of disappointment with this strategy, a growing number now argue that to be effective (or even to be implemented) reforms of economic policy must be accompanied by fundamental changes in a country's political structure. Until governments become more responsive and corruption free, economic policy reforms cannot in themselves ensure development.

In this book, Yahya Sadowski, a senior fellow in the Brookings Foreign Policy Studies program, documents how political factors frustrated recent efforts to reform economic policy in Egypt. Using case studies from the agricultural sector, he shows how businessmen and bureaucrats have learned to manipulate economic policy to maximize their personal benefits at the expense of national development. He argues that attempts by international development agencies to impose economic policy reforms on Cairo have actually reinforced the influence of these "crony capitalists." Sadowski suggests that fundamental political reforms to curb the prevailing pattern of corruption and rent seeking are necessary before Egypt can fully benefit from changes in economic policy.

Many persons who provided interviews, information, and documentation to the author were employees of the Egyptian government, the United States Agency for International Development, or the World Bank. Thus the author must thank them as a group rather than individually. But this in no way diminishes his debt to them, or his gratitude.

Scholars who shared their expertise with the author included

Mahmud Abd al-Fadil, Galal Amin, Ahmad Bahgat, Tahsin Bashir, Ken Cuno, Nicholas Hopkins, Saad Eddin Ibrahim, Rim Saad, Abd al-Mun'im Sa'id Aly, Mustafa Kamil al-Sayyid, Tim Sullivan, Elizabeth Taylor-Awny, and Joshua Walton. Fouad Ajami, Lee Feller, Ellis Goldberg, Ed A. Hewett, John Kerr, Afaf Lutfi al-Sayyid Marsot, John Parker, William B. Quandt, Ray Prosterman, Alan Richards, Delwin Roy, and James Toth contributed insights into Egypt or the development process. Tariq Jad and Nadia Anissa provided irreplaceable moral support.

Jean-Jacques Dethier, Sherif Elmousa, William B. Quandt, Robert Springborg, and John D. Steinbruner read early drafts of the manuscript and suggested revisions. Susanne Lane assisted the author throughout the project, serving first as research assistant, then as typist, and finally as copyeditor. Alice M. Carroll edited the manuscript; Marlin Dick, with Vernon Kelly, verified it; Donna Verdier proofread the pages; and Max Franke prepared the index.

Brookings gratefully acknowledges the John D. and Catherine T. MacArthur Foundation and the Rockefeller Foundation for providing financial support for this project.

The views in this book are solely those of the author and should not be ascribed to the persons or organizations acknowledged above, or to the trustees, officers, or other staff members of the Brookings Institution.

BRUCE K. MACLAURY
President

June 1991
Washington, D.C.

Contents

Tables

Figures

A Note on Transliteration

The transliteration system used in this book is a compromise between the demands of scholarly precision and typesetting simplicity. It is based in general on the system adopted by the *International Journal of Middle East Studies*. However, widely recognized Anglicized variants are used for Arabic proper names, such as Nasser, Sadat, and Cairo (instead of the technically accurate 'Abd al-Nasir, al-Sadat, and al-Qahira). Diacritical marks indicating vowels and emphatic consonants are dropped. The initial *'ayn* is dropped from all personal names. In Egyptian personal and place names, a *g* is used instead of a *j* to reflect colloquial pronunciation. The resulting transliterations, less jarring to Western eyes, should be easily comprehensible to scholars and Arabic speakers.

A Note on Currency, Weights, and Measures

Even for specialists, the vast array of distinct measurements employed in the Egyptian economy can be confusing. The currency is fairly straightforward: the standard unit of account is a pound (*ginayh*) divided into a hundred piasters (*qurush*). The value of the pound varies dramatically over time and because Egypt maintains multiple rates of exchange applicable to different commodities. As a rough measure, two Egyptian pounds can be considered equal to one dollar.

Egyptian agricultural measurements are especially complex. Wheat, for example, is often measured in *ardebs,* a unit of dry measure equal to 198 liters. (Corn is also assessed in *ardebs*, but as a unit of weight equal to 140 kilograms.) Seed cotton is measured in *qantars,* each comprising 157.5 kilograms. Other crops are often weighed in *ratl,* a unit of 449.2 grams. Wherever possible, these units are given in their metric equivalents. A *ton* in the text always means a metric ton (equaling 2,204 American pounds).

The unit of measure for land in Egypt is *feddan.* One *feddan* equals 4,200.8 square meters, or 1.038 acres. Most land measurements are given here in terms of *feddans.*

Political Vegetables?

CHAPTER 1

Introduction

AFTER THE OCTOBER 1973 WAR, EGYPT BEGAN TO CURTAIL ITS TIES with the Soviet bloc and forge an alliance with the United States. This reorientation made it eligible for massive economic assistance. Between 1974 and 1990 the United States Agency for International Development (AID) allocated $17 billion to promote Egyptian development.[1] Cairo hosted the largest AID mission abroad and Egypt received more American assistance than any country except Israel. The World Bank also expanded its operations in Egypt, investing hundreds of millions of dollars in new factories, power plants, and land reclamation schemes. And, the International Monetary Fund (IMF) began to attend seriously to Egyptian development, advising Egypt's government on macroeconomic policy and helping Cairo to qualify for billions of dollars in commercial loans.[2]

In the 1970s AID, the Bank, and the Fund—which together form the core of the official Washington development community—pursued independent agendas in Egypt. The World Bank and AID originally targeted their assistance on "basic human needs" through projects designed to improve water supply, irrigation and drainage, transportation, and energy supply. The Fund took a more conservative stance, trying to persuade the government in Cairo to reform its economic policies to create an atmosphere more conducive to development. But by the early 1980s the objectives of all three agencies had begun to converge and they increasingly coordinated and cooperated in their efforts to influence the Egyptian government.[3]

This convergence within the Washington development community was, in large part, the result of an intellectual counterrevolution. In the 1970s a group of neoclassical economists, including Lord Bauer, Anne Krueger, Bela Balassa, and Deepak Lal, articulated a devastating

1

critique of prevailing aid policies.[4] They argued that project aid, directed at building bridges or subsidizing credit for poor farmers, was misdirected and largely wasted. The real key to development, they claimed, lay in government economic policy. In most Third World countries, state intervention distorted prices by rigging exchange and interest rates, subsidizing consumption, and restricting trade. Price controls encouraged inefficiency and stifled entrepreneurship. So long as controls remained in place, infusing aid money into a developing economy would do little good. The real task of the development community, according to these neoclassicists, should be to press for changes in government policy that would "get the prices right."[5]

Egypt exemplified the stifling problems that agitated the neoclassicists. The government in Cairo required farmers to grow specific crops and sell them to the state at fixed prices. Since the officially mandated prices were so low that they made these crops virtually unprofitable, farmers did not work very hard at producing them. Yet since cultivation of these crops was required by law, farmers wasted valuable land and water in the attempt to produce them. The government also maintained an artificially overvalued exchange rate in order to reduce its own import bill. But this made Egyptian exports correspondingly expensive, discouraging the production of fruits and vegetables that might otherwise have found profitable foreign markets. The government had nationalized the manufacture of textiles, food processing, and other industries that were supposed to add value to agricultural products. Yet its poorly managed public sector firms were subject to rigid price controls and were chronically overstaffed. In many cases, processing in the public sector seemed to subtract rather than add value to crops.

The new orientation of the Washington development community brought about important changes in the way it dealt with the Egyptian government. The Cairo regime, which had been seen as an ally in the struggle for development, was now seen as part of the problem, not part of the solution. The annual economic report of the American Embassy reflected the new perspective in a catechism, repeated year after year, of the Egyptian government's sins: "The primary impediments to greater productivity are a tradition of centralized planning, reliance on an uncompetitive public sector, and government restriction of private economic activity. These date from the 1950s when President Gamal Abdel Nasser resorted to nationalization and land reform to accelerate industrialization. . . . The extension of government control throughout the economy discouraged individual initiative, and distorted resource allocation. The history of nationalization and the prospect of government interference discouraged private investment. Mandatory quotas on farmers for delivery at low prices of key agricultural commodities such as cotton encouraged inefficiency and neglect in the sector that had been the backbone of the Egyptian economy."[6] The new objective of the Washington development community was to roll back the tide of state intervention, to restore the role of the free market and private initiative, and to confine the state to its minimum essential role.

In the 1980s the elements of the Washington development community stressed this approach to Egypt with increasing fervor. They flew Cairo's technocrats and intellectuals to the United States for seminars on privatization and modern management practices. They flew Americans and other foreign experts to Egypt to study the problems of its policy environment and to devise plans for liberalization. Most effectively, they applied direct economic pressure on the Cairo government to change its ways. All three aid agencies switched to a strategy of conditional assistance, making release of their funds contingent on the reform of specific Egyptian government policies.

Egypt became, in effect, a gigantic laboratory for the new development strategy. The scale of American assistance and the severity of Egypt's economic problems gave the Washington development community unusual leverage in Cairo. Egypt's foreign advisers coordinated and reinforced each other's programs, each focusing on a specific aspect of reform. The Fund lobbied for changes in interest and exchange rates, the Bank urged a reduction of government subsidies, and AID pushed for decontrol of prices.

The Egyptian government appeared to respond to these pressures. In 1976 it proclaimed a green revolution, in 1978 an administrative revolution, in 1981 a war against excess consumption, in 1982 a war on corruption, in 1985 a liberalization of agricultural prices, and so on. Yet in 1990, after fifteen years of massive foreign assistance and voluminous advice, economic conditions in Egypt remained depressing.

Indeed, in some ways economic conditions had grown worse. Egyptian government statistics suggest that the growth of Egypt's gross domestic product slowed from 9.9 percent annually to 4.2 percent between 1982 and 1987. Even these figures are probably upbeat, and a March 1988 U.S. Embassy report concludes that "real gross domestic product fell in 1986/87 after having increased only marginally in each of the two previous years."[7] Egypt's current account deficit grew through much of the 1980s, peaking at $1,730 million in fiscal 1985–86. It then declined briefly to $545 million in fiscal 1987–88 as a result of the 1987 currency devaluation. By by fiscal 1988–89 it was growing again, reaching $1,457 million. A 1987 agreement with the IMF on the rescheduling of debt payments only put off the day of reckoning. Debt service for 1988 was reduced to $1.1 billion but payments were projected to climb back to $6.3 billion by 1992.[8] The most optimistic data (those Egypt supplies to the World Bank) suggest that between 1980 and 1987 agricultural output grew by 2.7 percent annually, which would be about average for a "middle income country."[9] Egypt's population, however, was growing at an estimated 2.8–3.0 percent annually, so agricultural output per capita was actually declining. Egypt was progressing, but at a glacial pace.

Why was Egypt's response to the new development strategy so disappointing? This book sketches some answers to this question through a study of Egypt's agricultural sector. Foreign experts and Egyptians alike believed that agriculture had greater growth potential than any other sector of the Egyptian economy.[10] Egypt enjoyed an ideal climate and rich farmland. Agriculture remained primarily in private hands, although government intrusions had stifled and distorted production. Hopes were high that if inimical government policies were changed, making farming profitable again, this sector would take off. Comparisons of Kenya and Tanzania and of India and Pakistan seemed to show that agriculture was particularly responsive to changes in government policy.[11]

This suggests that the disappointing response of Egyptian agriculture to pressure for policy reform may be especially revealing. The detailed discussion of Egyptian agriculture in this study is not intended to provide a comprehensive analysis of the country's agricultural system or a blueprint for its development. But the examples drawn from this sector's experience illuminate problems in implementing economic reform that are common to many sectors, and even to other countries. The analysis is not aimed at chickens or cotton, but at the problems that arise when the powerful agencies of the Washington development community attempt to impress their development philosophy on a recalcitrant society.

The Problem of Political Will

Superficially, the cause of Egypt's disappointing progress seemed obvious. Despite pressure from the Washington development community, policy reform never materialized. The mandated policy changes either were not made, or were watered down, or were delayed past the time when they would be useful. By 1990 some of the policies that were thought inimical to development had been tempered, but most were still in place and seemed unlikely to be altered in the near future.

Campaigns to reform Egypt's policy environment have been plagued by persistent and protracted delays. As early as 1977 the Egyptian government, acknowledging that its system of price controls inhibited the production of key crops, adopted a new strategy of steadily increasing prices. In 1982 President Husni Mubarak appointed a new minister of agriculture, Yusuf Wali, who promised to eliminate virtually all price and production regulations. But Dr. Wali was only able to launch his first serious attempt to repeal controls in 1985. He finally made this reform stick in 1988—after a decade of delay.[12] Compared to reforms in other areas, this was quite expeditious. The government's commitment to reduce its subsidies for key consumer goods and to reform public sector industries progressed even more slowly.

The reforms that were made were often offset or negated by new state policies. A key article in the reform program that Egypt negotiated with the IMF in May 1987 was to reduce state subsidies on kerosene, cigarettes, sugar, and other consumer goods. The government made many of the required changes, but to insulate citizens from the resulting price rises it also increased wages in the public sector by 20 percent.[13] Policy changes made to ease the pain of reform often had the effect of undermining reform.

Why did the Egyptian government engage in such apparently self-defeating behavior? Why were blueprints for reform so slow to be implemented? Why did reform efforts stall so easily or fail to gain momentum? These seem to be the critical issues in the Egyptian development debate today.

Officials at AID, the Bank, and the Fund offer similar answers to these questions. They blame the inadequate progress of reform squarely on the Egyptian government. They claim that Egyptian politicians have not embraced reform with enough force, commitment, or enthusiasm.

They accuse some Cairo officials of willfully sabotaging reform, by dragging their feet or inventing problems and obstacles. Unconsciously borrowing their rhetoric from the cold war theology of Reinhold Niebuhr, members of the Washington development community complain bitterly about the "failure of will" or "lack of resolution" among their Egyptian counterparts. They are convinced that the Egyptian government could have promoted reform but that it would not.

Foreign advisers offer a variety of distinct, but not mutually exclusive, explanations for the lack of will among Egyptian officials. One of their favorites is the suggestion that Egyptian officials refuse to surrender control over the private sector because they fear it will diminish their power and wealth. Ambition and venality prevent them from endorsing reform. One AID official whom I interviewed grumbled that every time he proposed a policy reform to his Egyptian counterparts they insisted on forming a committee to study the matter. Not only, he complained, did this slow down or arrest the reform process, it allowed Egyptian officials to collect special salaries for their committee service.

A more generous interpretation is that Egyptian officials resist reform because they know that initially it will mean hardship for their people. Cutting subsidies or devaluing the currency will raise the price of goods, a prospect that is threatening for the millions of Egyptians who already live on the margin of poverty. John Waterbury, America's leading expert on Egyptian politics, has argued that Egyptian leaders have been "unwilling (but in a technical sense not unable) to engage in a kind of primitive extraction of surplus from their populations through public policies and ideologies that promote forced savings, defer consumption gains to future generations, and maintain a societywide state of militant austerity. . . . Neither [Nasser or Sadat] felt that it was necessary or desirable to sweat significant segments of the citizenry for the sustained savings that might have made relatively autonomous growth possible."[14] According to this school of thought, Egyptian officials have consistently refused to aggravate the misery of their citizens, even after it has become clear that the price of failing to adjust and grow will have to be borne by future generations.

Other members of the Washington development community blame the inaction of Egyptian officials on ideological impediments. They view Egyptian officials as misguided paternalists, who cling to policies that damage their economy because they deeply believe that state intervention is necessary or desirable. Some blame this on indoctrination. Officials of AID in Cairo commonly allege that their Egyptian counterparts must have been trained in the Soviet Union. Others claim that the problem has deeper, cultural roots. Many Western officials in Cairo seem to have read Lawrence Harrison's *Underdevelopment Is a State of Mind*,[15] in which a career AID officer argues that development programs in Latin America have been crippled by local cultures that promote values that are "essentially anti-democratic, anti-social, anti-entrepreneurial, and anti-work."[16] A Western banker suggested to me that a combination of tropical climate and a history of foreign occupation had left Egyptians "lazy, nonconfrontational, and dedicated to the pursuit of something for nothing." One Washington official with responsibility for the assistance program for Egypt alleged that Egypt's failure to reform revealed "a genetic resistance" to change and hard work.

In the California vernacular I learned as a child, a person who seemed brainless, purposeless, and incapable of action was regarded as having "vegged out" or "gone vegetable." One hot afternoon in Cairo, while I sat listening to a Western aid administrator complain about the incompetence of his "native" counterparts, it occurred to me that he was in effect claiming that the Egyptians had "vegged out," that they were political vegetables.

Problems of Political Capacity?

The growing consensus that policy reform had been undermined by a failure of will had profound consequences for the way that the Washington development community sought to prosecute its program in Egypt. Aid agencies were fairly generous and cooperative so long as they thought that the Egyptians were trying to help themselves. But once they suspected that the Egyptians were willfully resisting reform, that officials in Cairo were not fully committed to the only strategy that offered a real hope of triggering development, Western advisers began to adopt a new approach.

This change of attitude was particularly evident in the United States. "Americans believe that a neighbor deserves help if, through no fault of his own, he is in temporary trouble. Calls for disaster relief therefore receive an enormous response from the United States, usually greater than from any other country. But most Americans also believe that over the longer run people and countries fundamentally get what they deserve. They are reluctant to confront the possibility that there may be deep structural causes explaining poverty or underdevelopment. In general, they tend to believe that the rich are rich because they have earned their wealth and the poor are poor because they have not tried hard enough."[17]

By the late 1980s many American officials suspected that Egypt was not trying hard enough. Newspaper articles began to highlight the apparent lack of results of the American aid program in Cairo. Congressmen, confronted with a growing budget deficit at home, asked why the United States should continue large-scale aid to Egypt. Even Lee Hamilton, chairman of the Middle East subcommittee of the House of Representatives' Foreign Affairs Committee, who had defended the AID program for years, began to lose patience. He complained that Egypt had not yet embraced significant policy reform and warned that the United States might have to be "much, much tougher and stronger in demanding and insisting" on economic changes.[18]

The Washington development agencies took an increasingly tough line in their negotiations with Cairo. They demanded ever more dramatic reforms. They threatened to withhold aid if Egypt did not cooperate. And they started to intimate that some reduction in the overall aid package was soon going to be inevitable. President Mubarak admitted that he could see the day coming when Western economic support for Egypt would evaporate.

Whether or not Egyptians possessed the "political will" necessary to reform, therefore, ceased to be an intellectual question and became an important, practical political issue. But did the Egyptians lack political will? Most of the Egyptian officials and technocrats I met with in Cairo were sincerely interested in economic reform. Many were patriots who thought that a market system held the key to their country's national development. Some were self-interested politicos who saw that their own careers and fortunes would prosper if they could play a role in promoting the private sector. They all saw the flaws in the existing system of state intervention quite clearly. They all wanted change.

Most had staked their careers on the success of economic reform and had invested long hours in its pursuit. President Mubarak asserted that he was at his desk by seven o'clock each morning, worked twelve to eighteen hours a day, and devoted 90 percent of his attention to domestic (mostly economic) problems.[19] Most of his subordinates shared the same work day. The upper echelons of Egyptian officialdom can be faulted for being unproductive or disorganized, but they are not lazy. (Similarly, foreign advisers may complain that Egyptian peasants use crude tools and obtain lower crop yields than they might; but no one who has seen the *fallahin* march to their fields at six in the morning and start hoeing the mud for twelve hours under the hot sun can seriously suggest that these men are lazy.)[20]

Like their Western counterparts, Egyptian officials were frustrated by the slow pace of reform. The minister of tourism, Fu'ad Sultan, constantly lectured his colleagues about the importance of a market economy and complained about the need for more decisive policy reforms. Since he spoke English, had worked at the IMF, and traveled frequently to the United States, he was recognized as a sympathetic figure by the Washington development community. But other Egyptian officials, who had poorer contacts in Washington, were also angered by the pace of change. Muhammad Abd al-Wahhab, the minister of industry, was thought by AID officials in Cairo to be unresponsive to their reform proposals and was suspected of being a "closet socialist." But in a May 1990 symposium of Egyptian officials, Abd al-Wahhab lost his temper and admitted that he thought Egypt's public sector industries were beyond rescue and that private enterprise offered the only hope for future development.[21] All too often, Western advisers' judgment of how committed an Egyptian official was to reform hinged on the Egyptian's command of English.

The reformist, pro-market orientation of most Egyptian officials was less surprising, considering where they had been trained. Few if any had received their education in the Soviet Union. Virtually all of the country's prime ministers had been educated in the West—Mustafa Khalil at the University of Illinois, Ali Lutfi at the University of Lausanne, Atif Sidqi in Paris.[22] Most of the cabinet ministers concerned with economic policy had been educated in the United States—Yusuf Wali, minister of agriculture, at the University of Arizona; Kamal Ganzuri, minister of planning, at Michigan State University; Sultan Abu Ali, minister of finance, at Harvard University; Atif Ubayd, minister of presidential affairs, responsible for supervising consumer subsidies, at the University of Illinois.[23] Among the younger technocrats charged with implementing economic reform, a training stint in the United States was almost universal.

Egyptian bureaucrats seem to be like bureaucrats in most countries, including countries that have developed successfully. Drive and imagination are most evident in the senior echelons, where officials tend to be "public sector entrepreneurs," among whom zeal for reform and personal ambition are indistinguishable. Below this level, most functionaries are decent people who turn petty, inattentive, slothful, and sullen once they sit behind their office desks. Neither in the upper nor in the lower echelons are there any cultural or ideological barriers that rule out the reform of economic policy.

But in Egypt, specific social conditions seem to conspire to frustrate and obstruct economic reformers. Obstacles to innovation and initiative are ubiquitous, afflicting both the most influential political elites and the humblest family enterprises. They thwart businessman and bureaucrat alike. An entrepreneur seeking to launch a new venture, a government leader seeking to promote a new project, and a recent university graduate seeking to build a career for himself are almost equally likely to fail. Most of the country's key institutions seem paralyzed or bankrupt. Even those spirits most ardently committed to championing reform eventually wither and acquiesce. Neither the political nor the economic elite seems capable of promoting development. In Fouad Ajami's memorable phrase, Egypt is a "stalled society."

All the evidence suggests that the will to reform is not missing in Egypt. Officials in Cairo want to adopt and implement new policies that will open the economy to private sector initiative. They want to, but they cannot. Political will, it seems, may be a necessary condition for economic reform but not a sufficient one.

Structure of the Study

The confusion over why policy reform programs are not implemented is one instance of a much wider problem. The Washington development community has achieved a much greater understanding of the economic policies that promote development than it has of the political forces that retard change.

The flowering of neoclassical economics supplied the development community with a common vision of the key conditions necessary for economic growth. Washington analysts generally concur that private incentives are the critical motor of technological change, that market mechanisms provide an efficient means for creating and allocating such incentives, and that state intervention (particularly interventions that distort prices) can cripple markets. The development community's advice, to Egypt and other Third World countries, has been to revise government policies so that markets can work their magic. The case for policy reform in Egyptian agriculture is outlined in chapter 2.

But implementation of a policy reform program is a political, not an economic, task. It involves persuading leaders to order policy changes, bureaucrats to implement them, and the public to accept them. The Washington development community, sadly, lacks the understanding of political conditions in the Third World necessary to achieve such reforms. Indeed, neoclassical thinkers, who did much to advance the economic sophistication of the community, probably weakened its grasp of political analysis. To the extent that the neoclassical school contemplated political forces at all, it clung to the proposition that (paraphrasing Orwell) "market good, state bad." It blamed politicians for creating and prolonging Egypt's problems by promoting their power at the expense of economic efficiency. It favored a wholesale transfer of economic tasks from bureaucrats to businessmen. It portrayed the state as the major obstacle to development. This view of the state as bad was not just an intellectual flaw in an otherwise elegant theory. It systematically undermined the Washington development community's efforts to implement policy reform in countries like Egypt.

This book outlines the major flaws in the development community's assumptions about politics in the Third World and shows how those assumptions have crippled the practice of reform. It presents an empirical critique, rather than an examination of failures in methodology or logic. The analysis relies on detailed description of cases, such as the production of cotton and the pricing of chicken. An anecdotal description of Egypt might be easier to digest, but reliance on anecdotal evidence was one of the factors that fostered the development community's misunderstanding of Third World politics.

One of the most comprehensive flaws in the Washington orthodoxy about development politics lies in its exaggerated assessment of state power in the Third World. The development community tends to assume that ruling regimes possess massive power, which automatically translates the ruler's intentions into social practice. In this vision, leaders declaring policy changes by fiat can quickly cripple or promote economic change. This is rarely the case, as examination of the history of Egyptian agricultural policy in chapter 3 makes clear. The state in Egypt and other developing countries is typically weak. As a result, the array of policy options open to leaders is limited and alterations of policy require careful anticipation of the reactions of the interest groups they affect, both among the public and among implementing officials.

Just as the development community often overestimates the power of the state, it has failed to appreciate the influence of the private sector in Egypt's economy. Chapter 4 shows that over the last twenty years the formulation and execution of government policy have increasingly been shaped by businessmen. But Cairo's business community does not consist of the market-oriented entrepreneurs envisaged in neoclassical economics. Egyptian businessmen pursue profits as eagerly as their counterparts elsewhere in the world, but they have learned that lobbying the state for various forms of rent may be a sounder way to do this than risking their capital in a volatile marketplace. Cabals that ally businessmen and bureaucrats often determine the operation of economic policy in Egypt today.

The weakness of the state and the strength of social forces, contrary to the expectations of the development community, played an important role in retarding economic growth in Egypt. Chapters 5, 6, and 7 examine how those forces have retarded efforts at policy reform. Chapter 5 examines three critical cases in which social forces frustrated efforts to reform agricultural price policy. The account of how fear of bread riots constrains government food policy will not surprise anyone familiar with the recent history of the Third World. The accounts of how businessmen sabotaged efforts to reform price controls on vegetables and poultry, however, highlight the flaws in the "market good, state bad" perspective.

Some development economists are aware that businessmen in the Third World often support monopolies and other price-rigging mechanisms. As an antidote to this condition, they have recommended massive liberalization of the financial system, which would make funds available for newer, more competitive enterprises. Chapter 6 analyzes recent efforts at financial reform in Egypt. In this sector too, cabals of businessmen and bureaucrats have derailed reform efforts and reinforced the prevailing pattern of monopoly power.

How might these alliances of public and private sector luminaries be broken up, clearing the ground for economic reform? Some of the more radical neoclassical economists have proposed a full-force assault on the state's economic functions by drastically curtailing its fiscal revenue. This, they hope, would both force the state to stop intervening in the economy and compel businessmen to reorient their interest toward the market. Chapter 7 suggests that such programs may do more harm than good for developing economies. Businessmen and bureaucrats do not always base their support of state intervention on personal calculations of power and profit; in a variety of areas, state intervention may be a legitimate and rational response to the demands of national development.

Chapter 8 sketches some broad conclusions revealed by analysis of discrete cases. Proponents of development need to study political conditions more carefully to see how they affect policy reform programs. They need to devise strategies that can neutralize or circumvent the cabals of businessmen and bureaucrats who obstruct policy reform. They need to set out criteria that will distinguish the kinds of state action that cripple market forces from those that augment or support market forces. Understanding of the political reforms that are necessary to sustain economic reform is sadly underdeveloped.

The prevailing contention of development experts is that powerful, interventionist states inhibit development, while weaker states with limited government promote it. The Egyptian experience suggests that the difference between success and failure may be much more subtle. Capitalist development requires that businessmen and bureaucrats collaborate, but not too much. Politicians must have the will to reform economic policy, but they must also have the authority to adopt and implement reforms in the face of external opposition. The political system must possess enough power to execute economic reforms, but not so much power that it can insulate itself from the demands of society. Striking a balance among these conflicting requisites of development takes time and effort in any society. In Egypt, it may require a revolution.

No one has ever suggested that economic development is easy or simple. This study suggests that it may be even more complex than has been imagined. The successful reform of economic policy may require dramatic political change too. Once the political component of economic development is acknowledged, the role of foreign advisers becomes more contentious. Thus, this study does not present a blueprint for changes that Egyptians should make in their political system. Not only is no such plan possible—given constant change in material conditions—it is not desirable. This study clearly indicates that choices about development are intrinsically political. Decisions among different land regimes, crops, and even cultivation techniques inevitably benefit certain groups at the expense of others. Taken together, these choices exert a profound influence not only on the future of the economy but on political and social structure as well. Foreigners, however well intentioned, should not presume to make such decisions for Egyptians. At most, they may hope to clarify the options and their implications.

CHAPTER 2

Policy Reform and Agricultural Development

EGYPT IS ONE OF THE MOST FOOD DEPENDENT COUNTRIES IN THE WORLD. In 1988 Egypt produced only 22 percent of its food needs (see figure 2-1).[1] Whatever it could not produce domestically, it was forced to import, including 32 percent of its sugar, 78 percent of its wheat, 79 percent of its cooking oil, and all of its tea.[2] In 1987 Egypt imported 9 million tons of wheat, making it the world's fourth largest importer, behind the Soviet Union (32 million tons), Japan (27 million), and China (15 million).[3] The degree of Egyptian dependence is even more striking when translated into per capita figures—for each of its citizens Egypt imported 180 kilograms of wheat, much more than the 14 kilograms per person imported by China and the 115 kilograms by the Soviet Union. Only Japan imported more wheat per person than Egypt (223 kilograms), and Japan enjoyed a large industrial base and hefty trade surpluses which Egypt lacked.

The Egyptian government financed the import of wheat, not as a public service but as a political necessity. For many Egyptians any serious increase in the price of wheat, much less a shortfall of supply, could make the difference between life and death. Wheat is the foundation of the Egyptian diet; the Egyptian word for bread, 'aysh, literally means "life." Wheat provides half the daily calorie intake for the average Egyptian.[4] Despite government subsidies that made bread cheaper in Egypt than anywhere else on earth (in 1988 a standard three-ounce loaf cost only 2 piasters—1 U.S. cent), in 1975 the poorest fifth of Egypt's urban population still spent 10 percent or more of its household income on bread and flour.[5]

Food shortages and price rises have been major triggers of protest and rebellion in modern Egypt. A package of price hikes in 1977 came close to igniting a revolution. Smaller increases in the cost of necessities

Figure 2-1. The Wheat Gap, 1965–85

Millions of metric tons

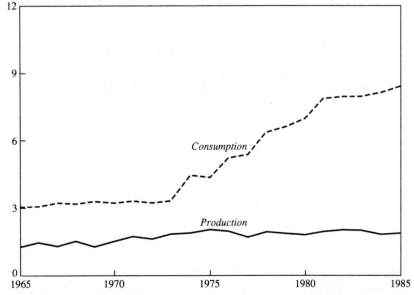

Sources: U.S. AID, *Egyptian Agricultural Data Base* (Cairo, 1987), p. 26; Agency for International Development, Grant M. Scobie, *Government Policy and Food Imports* (Washington: International Food Policy Research Institute, 1981), pp. 68 and 70.

have sparked riots or strikes every other year. In 1987 Egypt was still what the World Bank called a lower-middle-income country with a per capita gross national product of only $680—poorer than New Guinea, El Salvador, or the Congo.[6] The government in Cairo understood that economic hardship contributed to a rising tide of public unrest that in 1989 included violent strikes at Hulwan and a large-scale confrontation with Islamist demonstrators in the Fayyum. The Egyptian government worried increasingly that any crisis in the supply of food might fan otherwise limited political protests into a national bonfire.

At the outset of the 1980s, a survey of Egyptian leaders saw the problem of providing food security as the primary challenge confronting the government.[7] The issue, if anything, grew in importance over the ensuing decade. In the March 1987 parliamentary elections, one of the criticisms all of the opposition parties leveled against the government was that it had failed to make progress toward guaranteeing food provisions.[8] On any given day, major Egyptian newspapers, magazines, or intellectual journals include articles that touch on this problem.

Egyptians view food supply as a major issue of national security; any threat to imports or domestic agriculture exposes the country's Achilles heel. Food security problems are hotly debated in the officer corps. In private interviews Egyptian officers who resisted the idea of military intervention in the Iraq-Iran War or against Libya insisted that Egypt might have to use its forces against Ethiopia, whose dam-building plans threatened Egyptian water supplies. In the 1980s the Egyptian military diverted a growing share of its revenues to its economic arm, the National Service Projects Organization—particularly to the latter's Food Security Division.[9] The Food Security Division was created to make the military itself self-sufficient in food. It administers a major land reclamation project at Nubariyya, a network of dairy farms, potato cooperatives, and the like. Some claim that the division produces £E 488 million of food annually, equal to 18 percent of the value of all domestic production.[10]

The Egyptian government assigns the highest priority to ensuring wheat supply. The wheat subsidy is the first item calculated when the cabinet prepares the state budget, and it has always had first claim on the hard currency receipts of the Central Bank. The government finances wheat imports and administers and supervises their domestic distribution. Fearing the effect that speculation might have on prices, the government banned private trade in wheat until 1985. The foreign purchase and domestic marketing of wheat was managed instead by the General Authority for the Supply of Commodities (GASC), a special agency attached to the Ministry of Supply. The GASC trucked wheat and flour from the ports, stored it, doled it out to bakers, and retailed it through four thousand state-owned consumer cooperatives (*gam'iyyat*). Not only did the GASC ensure regular and ample supply of bread and flour, it spent millions of pounds subsidizing their price (see table 2-1). The government arranged imports and subsidized the sale of wheat to consumers by 20 percent or more. In 1988 the cost of the subsidy on these goods was at least £E 500 million.[11]

These operations cost the government dearly. In 1988 the government had allocated $900 million to finance wheat imports; in 1989 it expected to spend $1.4 billion.[12] In the mid-1980s a glut on the international wheat market made imports moderately cheaper, since wheat sold for $70 to $80 a ton. But at the end of the decade the glut had evaporated and officials in Cairo faced skyrocketing costs. In July 1988 Egypt paid $149 for a ton of wheat and the government worried

Table 2-1. **Food Subsidies in the State Budget, 1982–87**

Item	1982–83	1983–84	1984–85	1985–86	1986–87
	Millions of Egyptian pounds				
Government revenue	9,749.0	10,371.0	11,311.0	12,794.0	13,498.0
Total subsidies	2,053.7	1,986.6	2,006.7	2,908.8	1,653.0
Wheat and flour subsidies	757.8	862.2	614.0	474.1	190.1
	Percent				
Wheat and flour as a share of total subsidies	36.9	43.4	30.6	16.3	11.5
Total subsidies as a share of government revenue	21.1	19.2	18.3	22.7	12.2

Source: World Bank, *Egypt: Country Economic Memorandum* (Washington, January 1989), vol. 2, pp. 26, and 28.

that prices might rise as high as $240 within a year. Similar increases spread to many of Egypt's food imports. In the same period the price of corn climbed from $84 a ton to $132, forcing the government to allocate an additional $108 million to subsidize imports of this commodity. Cooking oil climbed from $458 to $790. Sugar, which had been $171 a ton, leapt to $270.[13]

There were strong reasons to expect the cost of food imports to rise. Increased cereal production in the 1970s had given the world a surfeit of grain for most of the 1980s. After 1981, however, the global area planted in grain actually began to decline. Many of the earlier increases had been obtained by overpumping and farming marginal lands that could not be sustained. By 1988 a leading expert noted that "in 1987 world carryover stocks of grain (the amount in the bin when the new harvest begins) dropped from 457 million to 390 million metric tons. This year, stocks could well fall below 300 million tons, a reduction that could easily raise grain prices to twice the 1987 level."[14] Even the conventionally optimistic U.S. Department of Agriculture expected that world cereal stocks in 1988–89 would be 38 percent lower than two years earlier.[15]

During the years of the wheat glut not only had prices been lower but financing was easier to come by. Between 1975 and 1987 the United States gave Egypt $2.7 billion in highly concessional loans to purchase wheat and other American agricultural commodities.[16] A 1983 trade war between France and the United States for the Egyptian wheat market led both countries to offer additional export subsidies.[17] But as the glut dried up, so did these subsidies. By 1989 Egypt was having difficulty arranging financing for imports of French flour even at $290

Table 2-2. Drain of Food Imports on Hard Currency Revenues, 1981–87

Item	1981–82	1982–83	1983–84	1984–85	1985–86	1986–87
	Millions of U.S. dollars					
Hard currency receipts						
Petroleum	4,669	4,164	4,532	4,781	3,995	2,679
Cotton	380	314	452	414	356	343
Suez Canal tariffs	909	957	974	897	1,028	1,148
Total government receipts	5,958	5,435	5,958	6,092	5,379	4,170
Workers' remittances	1,935	3,165	3,931	3,496	2,973	2,845
Tourism	611	304	288	410	321	376
Total hard currency receipts	8,504	8,904	10,177	9,998	8,673	7,391
Cost of agricultural imports						
Wheat and flour	1,130	834	1,056	1,013	983	718
Other commodities	1,550	1,559	1,877	1,698	1,583	1,293
Total	2,680	2,393	2,933	2,711	2,566	2,011
	Percent					
Cost of agricultural imports as a share of government receipts	45	44	49	45	48	48
Cost of agricultural imports as a share of hard currency receipts	32	27	29	27	30	27

Source: World Bank, *Egypt: Country Economic Memorandum* (Washington, January 1989), vol. 2, p. 10.

a ton.[18] Canada decided to completely phase out credit for wheat sales to Egypt.[19] Australia, to which Egypt already owed $800 million for wheat, planned to follow suit, but the Egyptians persuaded the Australians to continue wheat sales by making a $130 million good faith payment on their arrears and agreeing to pay double the 1988 price.[20]

Increasingly, the Egyptian government had to pay for its wheat imports in cash, without benefit of credit or subsidies. And the cash it had to advance was hard currency—not Egyptian pounds but U.S. dollars. The government's major sources of dollar income were oil sales, state-controlled agricultural exports, and transit revenues from the Suez Canal. Financing food imports cut deeply into all of these (table 2-2). In 1985 food imports totaled £E 2.1 billion, which was greater than Egypt's earnings from petroleum exports (£E 1.8 billion), and more than four times the total value of its agricultural exports (£E 475 million).[21] Indeed, as a result of global overproduction and price cuts by the Organization of Petroleum Exporting Countries (OPEC), Egypt's petroleum revenues actually declined in the late 1980s just when it needed them to pay for food.

Not only was the Egyptian government having a harder time assembling hard currency, it had to dole it out among a growing number of obligations. For example, to remain eligible for U.S. aid, Egypt had to honor its official and private debts to Americans. (The Brooke Amendment, an element of U.S. foreign aid legislation, prohibits any further assistance to any state that falls more than one year in arrears on its repayment of debt to the American government.) But repaying these debts was almost as burdensome as financing wheat imports. By 1989 the World Bank estimated that Egypt's total foreign debt (excluding military debts to the Soviet bloc) had reached $50 billion and its debt ratio (estimated total debt as a share of exports of goods and services) was more than 400 percent—one of the highest in the world.[22] In the same year Egypt was expected to repay $1.1 billion to the U.S. government and another $1.6 billion toward other foreign debts.[23]

Cairo clearly showed the strains of trying to juggle rising world food prices, decreasing hard currency revenues, and increasing debt service obligations. The government labored to ensure that wheat supplies remained ample, but the shortfall of cash was evident in the provision of other consumer staples. In March 1988 a cargo ship sailed into Alexandria with 18,000 tons of sugar under contract to the Egyptian Ministry of Supply. The ministry applied to the Central Bank for $4.5 million to pay for this cargo, but its request was rejected. Hard currency was in such short supply that it could not be released without a special appropriation by the cabinet. Before the ministry could assemble the political resources to petition the cabinet, the cargo ship, tired of waiting and overdue at its next destination, sailed for Aden.[24]

The government's fiscal problems quickly translated into real hardships for the man in the street. Early in 1988 sugar and edible oils disappeared from the shelves of government *gam'iyyat*. Whenever supplies became available, consumers rushed to the stores to wait in long lines. As supplies dwindled, prices on the open market began to soar. Sugar jumped from 30 piasters to 70 piasters a kilogram, cooking oil from 40 piasters to 80 piasters a kilogram. Even the price of a piece of soap rose—from 7.5 piasters to 55 piasters. Officials began to worry that brawls in the lines outside *gam'iyyat* and bakeries might ignite into rioting. Finally in April the government was able to assemble an emergency allocation of $75 million and the Ministry of Supply was able to restock its shelves.[25] The restoration was timely; it occurred just before the Islamic holy month of Ramadan, a period of daytime

Table 2-3. Population Growth in Egypt, Selected Years, 1960–90

Item	1960	1970	1980	1985	1988	1990
Population (millions)	26.0	33.0	39.8	48.5	53.3	54.7
Gross national product per capita (dollars)	n.a.	n.a.	580	610	760	650
Density (number of persons per habitable square kilometer)	686	869	1,047	1,276	1,403	1,458
Crude birth rate (births per thousand persons)	43.1	35.1	37.0	36.0	38.0	38.0
Crude death rate (deaths per thousand persons)	16.9	15.1	12.0	10.0	9.0	9.0
Rate of natural increase (percent)	2.6	2.0	2.5	2.6	2.9	2.8

Sources: World Bank, *World Development Report, 1982*, and *1988* (Oxford University Press, 1982, 1988); Population Reference Bureau, *World Population Data Sheet, 1988* and *1990* (Washington, 1988, 1990); and John Waterbury, *The Egypt of Nasser and Sadat* (Princeton University Press, 1983), pp. 41 and 46.
n.a. Not available.

fasting which Egyptians are accustomed to celebrate by eating all night.

Origins of the Food Security Crisis

The immediate causes of Egypt's food security difficulties lay in the international rise in grain prices and the government's fiscal crisis. But Egypt's vulnerability to these short-term changes was the product of three other factors: population growth, land scarcity, and modest agricultural yields. The interplay of these structural forces is what made Egypt dependent on food imports in the first place.

For foreign observers, at least, population is the most obvious culprit.[26] Egypt's population is growing relatively fast (table 2-3). Its rate of natural increase is 2.9 percent annually, which may seem moderate compared to that of Iran (3.6 percent) or Jordan (3.5 percent) but is distinctly speedy when contrasted with the rate in Europe (0.3 percent), China (1.4 percent), or even Indonesia (1.8 percent). In 1970, when the cost of Cairo's wheat imports was almost exactly balanced by the value of its cotton exports, Egypt's population was something like 34 million. By 1990 it had grown to at least 54 million, with another million being born every eight months. Barring some Malthusian holocaust, Egypt's population by the year 2000 will exceed 69 million.[27]

This growth puts a terrible strain on all of Egypt's resources—a trend immediately evident in the jammed streets of Cairo. Every year more workers cram onto the bumpers of buses, more children crowd into schools, more petitioners pack into government offices. Housing shortages, endemic since the late 1960s, compel the poorest strata to seek shelter in the medieval cemeteries that surround Cairo.[28] Demand for waterlines, electricity, and sewage treatment continues to skyrocket. Cairo alone generates 4,000 tons of new garbage every day, of which 600 tons or so passes uncollected and untreated.[29] With massive American assistance, the government successfully modernized the sewage and telephone system in the early 1980s, but these facilities will soon be swamped; the population of greater Cairo, which stood at 8.8 million in 1980, is expected to exceed 20.6 million by the year 2000.[30]

The most immediately threatening dimension of the population explosion may be the surging demand for new jobs. In the 1960s the government guaranteed employment to all university graduates and most military veterans. As time passed, it became harder and harder to find jobs for all these applicants, so public sector enterprises were ordered to hire certain quotas for which they had to "make work" with fictitious jobs. By 1989 the state had still not been able to find jobs for all the qualified applicants who had applied in 1982 and had had to create 450,000 jobs just to keep the rate of unemployment from rising. The rate of unemployment already stood at 20 percent, leaving 2.8 million citizens, mostly young, educated, and frustrated, wandering the streets. They form a nervous mass, anxious for a change in Egyptian society, many waiting to be mobilized by some political movement. They fill the nightmares of Cairo officials.[31]

Some Egyptians, including officials who direct the government's population control program, hope that Egypt will grow out of this problem. They argue that as incomes rise Egyptians, like people in already developed countries, will desire fewer children. In the long run this may be true, but in the short run the opposite may occur. Studies show that Egyptian families are carefully planned; people calculate how many children they want, and they do not just rely on God to sort out the numbers. In rural Egypt—where 57 percent of the population lives—families generally seek to have two boys. There are good economic reasons for this—to provide support for the parents in their old age, to help with farm labor, and so forth. But to reach this desired objective, rural families typically wind up with several girls too, so the average family has 5.2 children. Indeed, women actually give birth to an average of 7.5 children, since they expect two or three to die in infancy. Thus, although 89 percent of women in rural areas are familiar with modern birth control techniques, they have very little use for them. In Upper Egypt, where women have fewer children than they need to assure their two-male target, there is actually an interest in fertility enhancement.[32] As their incomes rise, many families will seek to have more, not fewer, children.

Egyptian officials and intellectuals recognized the dangers inherent in population growth decades ago, and when Nasser took power in 1952 he immediately launched a public relations campaign to encourage population control.[33] Partly as a result of these efforts, Egypt actually achieved a decline in its rate of natural increase between 1967 and 1973.[34] But this campaign stalled in the 1970s as the government became increasingly sensitive to criticism from the growing Islamist movement. The Islamists contended that the decay of family values was the taproot of most of the country's political and economic problems. Between 1979 and 1985 they attacked and succeeded in repealing personal status legislation that would have liberalized marriage and divorce laws. Although the Islamists differed among themselves over whether birth control was a legitimate or desirable objective, they were uniformly opposed to government attempts to influence family decisions on these matters.[35]

In the 1980s the Islamist movement grew into a major force in Egyptian politics. The Islamic current expanded to include not just radical underground groups seeking to overthrow the government but also the largest public opposition parties and a wing of the government's own party.[36] Under these conditions, the government did not feel it could afford to emulate the energetic population control programs of countries like Singapore and Indonesia, which have successfully limited population growth by assessing taxes that penalize large families. Instead, budgets for population control programs remained modest, forcing family planning advocates to pin their hopes on a series of colorful—but quite ineffective—television advertisements.[37]

Egypt desperately needs population control. But even if the government were to adopt a more forceful stance today, it would not actually ease Egypt's food crisis for decades. The baby girls born in 1990 will be having children of their own in fifteen to twenty years. It takes a full generation for the introduction of family planning to begin to influence the size of a country's population.[38] Those who want to manage, much less resolve, Egypt's food security crisis will have to look elsewhere for solutions. For the foreseeable future, local food production or imports will have to grow by 2.6 percent every year just to sustain existing levels of consumption.

A second factor underpinning the food security crisis has been the limited amount of land available for domestic farming. The great Sahara Desert covers most of Egypt; only the narrow valley of the Nile, a mere 2.8 percent of the country's land area, is suitable for cultivation.[39] As the population has grown, this relatively fixed area of arable land has had to support ever larger numbers of Egyptians. In 1960 each hectare of arable land had to feed 10.3 Egyptians; in 1988 it had to support 21.2.[40] The same population pressure eroded the area of land actually available to the average cultivator. In 1961 there were 1.6 million landowners in Egypt and their individual holdings averaged 3.8 feddans. In 1982 there were 2.5 million landowners and their individual holdings had declined to 2.5 feddans.[41]

All Egyptians dream that pressure on the soil may someday be eased by land reclamation, that new technologies might turn the desert green. Half of all government funds invested in agriculture flow into land reclamation schemes.[42] These programs do not operate in the Sahara; rather, most programs work to recover land along the fringes of the Nile Valley which has not been farmed because its soil is marginal or it is too far from water sources. Recently there has been talk about extending these programs to the Mediterranean coast and parts of the Sinai.[43]

The Egyptian government claims to have reclaimed 912,000 feddans between 1952 and 1975—equal to one-sixth of the traditional cultivated area.[44] It has publicly committed itself to reclaiming 3 million more feddans. But there is no reason to expect that it will be able to deliver. Existing land reclamation projects have been plagued by poor management and massive technical problems. Much more than piped-in water is needed to make marginal lands suitable for farming. Soil must often be trucked in, lavished with fertilizer, and planted under special land-stabilizing crops. It takes years for these techniques to make the land fertile enough to support conventional crops, and even then yields on reclaimed lands remain starkly lower than on "old lands."[45] Since investment costs are high and yields low, the margin of profit is always low and sometimes nonexistent. Alarmed by these problems, the U.S. Agency for International Development (AID) in 1979 commissioned a major report on the economics of land reclamation by Pacific Consultants. This investigation concluded that, even with the best management, technical constraints made investment in land reclamation of marginal value. As a result, AID phased out all funding for land reclamation.[46]

In the 1980s, however, new technologies that made land reclamation appear more viable became available. For example, giant pivot irrigation systems were developed which could actually distribute soil nutrients as they watered the land.[47] These were still quite expensive, but there were other, even more promising technologies such as "plasticulture." Cheap, easily constructed greenhouses (*subat zira'-iyya*), made from polyvinylchloride (PVC) plastic, limit water evaporation and soil erosion, making it economical to begin farming on land covered with only a thin layer of imported soil and watered by truck. When combined with drip-irrigation technology (in which small tubes provide a continuous trickle of water directly to individual plants, rather than over the entire surface of the plot), the greenhouses dramatically reduce the cost of farming on previously arid lands. Since the overhead costs of such operations are not high, Egyptian entrepreneurs began to erect such greenhouses in large numbers in the early 1980s. Other private firms opened up small factories producing PVC for use in greenhouses and pipeworks.[48]

New land reclamation technologies offer badly needed hope for Egyptians, but even if they fulfill their promise they will not make much of a dent in the food security problem. Despite massive public investment in the 1950s, 1960s, and 1970s, Egypt's cultivated area has remained essentially constant. As quickly as new land was made arable, old lands were taken out of production. Inside the Nile Valley—an area smaller than Rhode Island where population density is higher than in Bangladesh—property developers will pay more for an acre of land than farmers can afford. Much of what was once productive farmland is now submerged under Cairo suburbs. The construction of roads and warehouses, the expansion of villages, and urban sprawl all nibble away at the black soil of the Nile Valley. Farmland in Egypt is disappearing at a rate of 60,000 feddans a year.[49]

The government is doing what it can to slow the loss. It has legislated stiff penalties against the conversion of farmland into real estate. It is trying to lure people away from Cairo by building a series of new cities—10 Ramadan City, Sadat City, El Amiriyya, and 15 May—in the desert adjacent to the Nile Valley. Experts hope that with "proper planning and the construction of new housing and industrial work opportunities, 10 million Egyptians could be relocated to new desert areas within the next 15 years."[50] Building new cities, however, may prove much easier than creating jobs that will keep people there. Besides, even if the government achieves its objectives, the villages and cities within the Nile Valley will still have to grow to accommodate an additional five million to ten million people.

For the next twenty years, Egypt cannot expect any significant increase in the size of its cultivated area, nor any reduction of the population it has to support. Efforts to promote its food security, then, must focus primarily on the third structural component of the current crisis, agricultural yields, or the size of the crop that can be produced on a given unit of land. Happily, there are solid grounds for hoping that the yields of Egypt's land, and the productivity of its farmers, can be increased dramatically.

Egypt's farmlands are a natural wonder—one of the richest agricultural systems in the world. The weather is temperate and predictable, with ample sunshine. The Nile supplies 55 million cubic meters of water every year at a cost so low that the government has never bothered to charge farmers for water use. The concentration of the population within a single narrow valley keeps transportation costs low, and the proximity of Europe provides a large, viable export market.

With these lavish natural endowments, it is not surprising that agriculture may first have been invented in Egypt.[51] Already in antiquity Egypt was synonymous with fertility; classical Rome depended on the huge grain ships that sailed from Alexandria. In the Middle Ages Europeans got their first taste of sugar and first touch of cotton from Egyptian exports. (Despite Russian claims of priority, it even seems likely that beer was invented in Egypt.) The irony of the fact that the country Napoleon acknowledged as the "breadbasket of the Mediterranean" should today depend on food imports is not lost on modern Egyptians.

In country-by-country comparisons, agricultural yields for Egypt still rank high. For extra-long staple cotton they are the highest in the world; for sugarcane they rank second; for peanuts, third.[52] Egypt enjoys ideal conditions for rice cultivation; only Japan and South Korea have achieved higher yields.[53] But country-by-country comparisons are misleading. When Egyptian production is compared to the output of similarly irrigated regions in other countries, the potential for improvement becomes clear.[54] As the minister of agriculture, Dr. Yusuf Wali, noted: "In parts of the USA, with agroclimatic conditions similar to ours, the productivity is said to be 70% higher than in Egypt. For instance, improved varieties of tomato and strawberry introduced from California yield respectively three to eight times higher than the local varieties. Similarly, through introduction or development of least land-intensive varieties, productivity and profitability of the existing cropping patterns could be enhanced."[55] Thousands of Egyptian, American, and other experts have devoted years of research to devising means that could raise Egyptian yields. The result is a smorgasbord of techniques and technologies from which Egyptian farmers might choose.

Advisers from AID, for example, launched a massive program in the late 1970s to investigate how mechanization might raise the productivity of Egyptian agriculture.[56] They wanted Egyptian farmers to buy tractors and give up using livestock as traction animals, in hopes that this would free land planted in *birsim* (clover fodder) for planting with other crops. (*Birsim* takes up one-third of Egypt's cropped area.)[57] Unfortunately, more detailed studies suggested that Egyptian farmers raise livestock primarily for the value of the meat and cheese they produce, so that mechanization would not reduce the size of herds or the demand for *birsim*.[58] Still, mechanization research identified a number of specific niches in which specialized technology could prove valuable to Egypt.

Seed drills, for example, could both reduce the waste of seed typical of hand broadcasting and allow closer spacing of plants, permitting larger crops on the same acreage. Tractors equipped with laser gradiometers can be used to level land to produce a uniform slope that requires less water for flood irrigation and eliminates the danger of puddles and uneven absorption which can reduce yields. In the past few years Egyptian farmers have rushed to buy "Turkish threshers," an excellent example of appropriate technology. These cheap, rugged machines, which can be powered by any tractor engine, can thresh a variety of crops with greater efficiency and at a lower cost than hand threshing.[59]

Another promising technique is deep furrowing. Plowing land to a depth of sixty centimeters loosens the soil, permitting root penetration, aeration, moisture retention, and simpler weeding. On experimental farms this has resulted in dramatic improvements in yields. The Egyptian government has already launched a program to introduce deep furrowing on 5.25 million feddans by 1992, although there are complaints that the agency responsible for furrowing has done a lackadaisical job.[60] Still, in principle deep furrowing can even be done by hand; the technique originated in ancient China where farmers used simple spades.[61]

Even without changes in technology, farmers could increase their profits simply by changing the composition of what they plant. Many Egyptian peasants have already discovered that they can make more money by restricting their plantings of cotton and shifting their land into corn and *birsim* clover. A minority who have excess capital and enjoy access to marketing facilities have dramatically increased their profits by planting flowers, mushrooms, or strawberries—higher-value crops for which there is also an export market. Changes in the cropping pattern may not actually increase the yield for specific crops, but they maximize the economic return for each unit of land.

The prospect of such changes has triggered a major debate about the optimal cropping pattern in Egypt. Some scholars have suggested that to minimize its food dependence, Egypt should plant as much land as possible in wheat.[62] The price of converting to wheat would be stiff. In 1988 the average wheat yield in Egypt was 2 tons per feddan and consumption was 9 million tons. Complete self-sufficiency would have required devoting 4.5 million feddans, or three-quarters of all cultivated land, to wheat. Others have argued that Egypt should exploit its comparative advantages in agriculture. It would be more economical to shift most land into higher-value crops, promote their export, and use the resulting hard-currency revenues to finance wheat imports from countries like the United States and Australia where extensive, flat grasslands make wheat cheaper to grow and harvest.[63] Officials of AID consistently support this approach, citing a study that showed that by cutting the land planted in wheat, corn, and cotton by 5 percent, and increasing the area available for export crops like rice, tomatoes, potatoes, melons, oranges, peanuts, onions, and garlic, Egypt could decrease its agricultural trade deficit by 19 percent.[64] (The Ministry of Agriculture eventually split the difference between these two camps. Official policy called for efforts to achieve 50 percent self-sufficiency in wheat production and to promote the planting of high-value crops on land not needed for wheat. This would provide a moderate degree of food security while encouraging increased production of export crops.)

Perhaps the most promising strategy, however, for Egypt to increase its yields lay in joining the Green Revolution by adopting a new generation of high-yield variety (HYV) seeds. Specially engineered HYV seeds dramatically increase yields. In some varieties, like HYV wheat, the plant invests more energy in the production of grain than in stalk. In others, like HYV rice, plants mature more rapidly, permitting farmers to plant an extra crop in the course of the year. In Egypt, for example, farmers who tested Philippine HYV rice found that they were able to follow it with a crop of sunflowers in the same season. Farmers who planted HYV cotton were able to extend their growing season for *birsim* and make extra cuttings of the latter.[65] Experiments with HYV wheat in 1980—planted according to a precise schedule, at optimum density, with appropriate fertilizers—suggested that grain output could be doubled.[66]

Countries like India, Thailand, and Indonesia, once heavily dependent on food imports, became self-sufficient after switching to HYV seeds in the 1970s. But Egypt has not yet followed their example. In 1982 less than 1 percent of the rice area sown in Egypt used HYVs, compared to 48 percent of India's and 80 percent of the Philippines' plantings. Only 52 percent of Egypt's wheat acreage employed HYVs, compared to 76 percent in India and 84 percent in Pakistan.[67] Egypt developed its own versions of HYV wheat and tried to promote them after 1981, but by 1985 acceptance levels had dropped back to their earlier level.[68]

Green Revolution crops have not proved to be the panacea for world food problems that many hoped they would be. The HYV seeds are more fussy than traditional seeds and require special attention. They must be planted at just the right times, absorb heavy quantities of water and fertilizer, and are very vulnerable to disease and weather changes.[69] Often only wealthy farmers can afford to pay for the extra attention that HYV seeds require, so the Green Revolution has often worsened income inequalities.[70] Some of the Southeast Asian countries that adopted HYV seeds have found it difficult to maintain the supports they require and have seen their yields decline to earlier levels.[71] But in many ways, Egyptian conditions are ideal for the use of HYVs.

Egyptian cultivators of all classes are accustomed to using high volumes of fertilizer and intensive irrigation. Working on small plots, with the kind of plant-by-plant attention that North Americans associate more with gardening than farming, they can give HYVs the kind of attention they need.

Egypt's receptivity to a green revolution was demonstrated in the early 1980s by the Small Farmer Production Project (SFPP), which some observers have called "the single most successful AID-supported agricultural project we have seen anywhere."[72] The SFPP offered modest amounts of short- and medium-term credit to Egyptian peasants who were willing to adopt a package of new farming techniques. The package included HYV seeds, appropriate fertilizers (matched to local soil by scientific testing), improved management of irrigation, and precise planting schedules. Thirty thousand families participated in the project—with spectacular results. Farmers planting corn produced 2.4 tons to 3.4 tons a feddan, comparable to the highest regional yields achieved in Iowa or northern Greece. In the same districts the previous yield had averaged less than 1.5 tons; Egypt's national average was 1.7 tons. Other SFPP programs obtained increases of 70–100 percent in soybean yields, 90–110 percent in citrus, 200 percent or more in *ful* (broad beans, a staple of the peasant diet), 300–450 percent in tomatoes, and 500 percent in cucumbers.[73]

All of these techniques and technologies are available to Egypt; most have been proven economical for peasant agriculture. Several important studies have suggested sweeping programs, combining different technologies and crop mixes, to improve Egypt's food security.[74] Yet many are not being adopted, or at least are being introduced only very slowly, and as a result yields are not increasing nearly as rapidly as they might. During the 1970s the value of agricultural output in Egypt stagnated; food production actually declined by 7 percent.[75] In the 1980s output began to grow again but only by 2.7 percent annually— barely enough to keep pace with the growth in population. Agricultural growth in Egypt has been only modest by international standards; even other Arab states at comparable levels of development (particularly Jordan and Morocco) have grown faster (see table 2-4).

Officials in Cairo often blame this on the innate conservatism of the peasant, claiming farmers willfully resist adopting new techniques. Farm-level studies flatly contradict this. They suggest that Egyptian

Table 2-4. Agricultural Performance in Egypt and Seventeen Other Countries, 1965–87

Country	Population, 1987 (millions)	Gross national product, 1987 (U.S. dollars)	Average annual growth in agriculture (percent) 1965–80	Average annual growth in agriculture (percent) 1980–87	Average index of food production per capita, 1985–87 (1979–81 = 100)
Arab countries					
Kuwait	1.9	14,610	n.a.	23.6	n.a.
United Arab Emirates	1.5	15,830	n.a.	11.6	n.a.
Saudi Arabia	12.6	6,200	4.1	10.3	209
Oman	1.3	5,810	n.a.	9.4	n.a.
Algeria	23.1	2,680	5.6	6.0	103
Tunisia	7.6	1,180	5.5	4.2	114
Jordan	3.8	1,560	n.a.	4.1	108
Morocco	23.3	610	2.2	3.6	109
Egypt	50.1	680	2.7	2.7	106
Yemen Arab Republic	8.5	590	n.a.	2.3	115
Mauritania	1.9	440	−2.0	1.5	90
Sudan	23.1	330	2.9	0.8	100
Syria	11.2	1,640	4.8	−1.1	96
Non-Arab countries					
China	1,068.5	290	3.0	7.4	124
United States	243.8	18,530	1.0	3.5	97
Indonesia	171.4	450	4.3	3.0	117
Mexico	81.9	1,830	3.2	1.4	97
India	797.5	300	2.8	0.8	109

Source: World Bank, *World Development Report, 1989* (Oxford University Press, 1989), tables 1, 2, and 4.
n.a. Not available.

peasants are energetic and enterprising and will adopt any innovation that promises an increase in profits.[76]

Other experts have faulted the government in Cairo for not paying enough attention to agriculture.[77] There is some truth to this. There have been periods (especially the early 1970s) when the government cut back investment in agriculture. Egypt lacks an effective agricultural extension service; the agronomists of the Ministry of Agriculture in Duqqi rarely travel to the farms and their innovations often remain confined to the laboratory. Yet this accusation misses the point.

The Egyptian government pays very careful attention to agricultural policy and spends a significant amount of money on agriculture. It tells many peasants what seeds to plant, when, and with which pesticides and fertilizers. It maintains a vast network of agricultural cooperatives, banks, and machinery stations in the countryside. It is the sole legal purchaser for such major crops as cotton, wheat, and sugarcane and takes responsibility for their processing and marketing.

This lavish state attention to the agricultural economy has actually held back innovation and slowed the growth of yields. The primary obstacle to rural development in Egypt is government agricultural policy that has actually encouraged inefficiency and discouraged production.

Agricultural Policy and Incentive Structure

Food security first became a major issue for Egyptians in 1972. In that year the Soviet leadership, confronting a rising public desire for beef and a domestic harvest ravaged by frost, broke with its tradition of self-reliance and began importing grain—wheat, corn, and barley— from the West. American grain shipments to the USSR jumped from 34 million tons in 1971 to 82 million by 1975. The value of American agricultural exports climbed from $7.7 billion to $21.3 billion.[78] The Soviets began their massive purchases at a very sensitive moment for international grain markets. World cereal production was at a historic high, but global reserves were unprecedentedly low; during the preceding decade the global population had grown faster than food production. Moreover, in 1972 there were droughts in many parts of the world, perhaps as a result of the unusual Southern Pacific weather configuration known as El Niño. In Ethiopia and the Sahel these droughts triggered some of the worst famines since World War II. As a result, grain prices skyrocketed.[79]

During this "world food crisis," wheat prices soared from $60 to $250 a ton. In 1973 the cost of Egypt's wheat imports jumped from $147 million to $400 million, turning the Egyptian government's commitment to ensure local wheat supply from a nuisance into a trauma.[80] Over the following few years, high international prices and growing domestic consumption exacerbated the problem. The price that Egypt paid for wheat imports quadrupled in 1974 (from £E 55 million to £E 233 million) and then doubled by 1981 (to £E 531 million).[81] The rocketing of grain prices in the 1970s has left Egyptians insecure ever since.

The Egyptians were more fortunate than many countries; for them the crisis of cereal prices coincided with a sharp rise in international petroleum prices. This meant that Egypt's oil-rich Arab allies could afford to supply aid to help finance wheat imports. After 1975, when

Egypt recovered its Sinai oil fields which had been occupied by Israel, Egypt's own petroleum exports helped to pay the bill. Moreover, in 1973 Egypt began to realign itself with the United States and to receive a growing volume of American assistance, including Public Law 480 grain shipments. As an American ally, Egypt also found it easier to borrow funds from international banks (who were eager to recycle vast dollar reserves deposited by petroleum exporters). During the 1970s this wash of dollars eased the sting of rising wheat prices and made Egypt's dependence on food imports tolerable to the government.

Had the food crisis occurred when the government had fewer revenues, it might have been forced to raise domestic grain prices, or at least to ration the quantities it made available to the public. During the years of Egypt's active military confrontation with Israel (1967–73) government rationing had actually reduced per capita wheat consumption. But after 1973, with the challenge of war removed and the political legitimacy of the regime in doubt, President Anwar Sadat declined to impose such sacrifices on his people. Instead he froze grain prices and even allowed inflation to reduce their real cost. Low prices (and rising incomes) encouraged Egyptians to increase consumption.

In the 1950s and 1960s annual wheat consumption in Egypt hovered just above 100 kilograms a person. But by the end of the 1980s it had rocketed to 200 kilograms—one of the highest levels of wheat consumption in the world. In Saudi Arabia it is only 154 kilograms, in Jordan 104, in Mexico 70, in India 57.[82] Up to a point, this is laudatory. In India, a country that is statistically food self-sufficient, millions live in hunger. In Egypt, hunger and malnutrition are comparatively rare and famine is unknown. But by the 1980s most Egyptians agreed that government-subsidized prices for many goods actually bred an excessive level of consumption.

Sadat's successor, President Husni Mubarak, regularly pleads with his people to reduce their consumption and thereby ease the drain on Egypt's resources. He complained that "in our country people fill their glasses to the brim, even if they do not intend to drink it all."[83] He admonished his countrymen that they actually devoured more sugar per capita than Americans. In one speech he groaned: "Cairo is a swallower. It eats. If you bring it 1 million loaves of bread every day, it will consume them. The discharge of the sewers will increase."[84] Some of his advisers thought that reducing consumption to normal levels was the best way out of Egypt's food security crisis. They argued that if Egyptians could limit their wheat intake to 120 kilograms, an amount they had lived on in the recent past, national demand would be reduced by a third and Egypt's dependence on imports cut by almost half.[85]

Speeches and public relations campaigns, however, had no discernible effect on levels of consumption. So long as prices remained low, there were no material incentives for Egyptians to tighten their belts. Grain and other subsidized goods were easy to come by; Egyptian consumption reflected not only the legitimate demands of diet, but a scandalous degree of waste.

"Waste is a large problem in Egypt because consumption subsidies have kept the prices of basic foodstuffs so low that people have little concern over waste at all levels of the marketing chain."[86] Experts who have observed the domestic operations of the GASC (General Authority for Supply of Commodities), the agency responsible for distributing wheat to Egyptian consumers, tell horror stories about imported wheat mildewing in antique warehouses and flour blowing out of the back of trucks. Government handling of the domestic crop is also sloppy; most fertilizers, and all grains and animal seeds, are stored in open-air facilities where they are exposed to heat, sunlight, moisture, insects, birds, and rodents. In 1989 the World Bank joined with Egypt's Principal Bank for Development and Agricultural Credit (PBDAC), which handles domestic crop procurements, to invest $103 million in the construction of new storage facilities, a program expected to save $22 million a year.[87] Egyptian officials themselves complain that because of improper transportation and storage, perhaps 30–40 percent of local wheat production vanishes before it reaches the consumer.[88]

This pattern of waste extends down to the farm level. Irrigation water is free; even the cost of pumping it is partly covered by government subsidies on fuel, so peasants tend to flood their fields. Peasants also use government-subsidized fertilizers and pesticides in volumes that are excessive by international standards. One Western agronomist observed that peasants have to lavish fertilizer on their crops because much of what they apply is washed away by irrigation inundation.

Overconsumption and waste are only two of the myriad and far-reaching effects that government subsidies and price controls may have on the functioning of an economy. Constant vigilance and careful planning are required to minimize the insidious consequences of such interventions. Even when a government launches a subsidy program with the noblest of intentions, its consequences may be quite the opposite of what was intended.

For example, early in 1989 the Egyptian government faced its worst nightmare, bread shortages. In January production of 'aysh baladi, the 2 piaster bread that formed the mainstay of the diet, began to decline. Cairo bakeries often sold off their available stocks by midmorning, forcing consumers to take time off from work to stand in long lines leading to the neighborhood oven. In central Egypt many village bakeries had only enough flour to operate for two hours a day, compelling hungry peasants to flood into cities like Minya where bakeries were still functioning.[89] On February 4, after weeks of dealing with shortages and crowds, the people of Minya and Bani Suwayf turned to public protest. They assembled at their mosques to demonstrate and chant antigovernment slogans. The government responded with a police sweep to arrest the suspected ringleaders of the demonstrations.[90]

As the bread crisis persisted into April, it took on the flavor of a siege. The newspapers began to carry human interest stories about people who died of heatstroke while waiting in line, and even hinted at murders being contracted so that certain people could move to the head of bread queues. The government mobilized the police to keep order in lines. Students who tried to distribute leaflets protesting the situation were promptly arrested. In an attempt to impress the public, the Ministry of Supply publicized its arrests of bakers caught profiteering on the black market. Special sections of Cairo's chief prison were set aside for bread offenses.[91]

Government officials understood what had triggered these shortages. They claimed that Egypt faced a "second world food crisis."[92] In the winter of 1987–88 drought sharply reduced the American and Canadian grain crops. The projected loss in the American harvest was 78 million metric tons, leaving less than 200 million—the lowest total since 1974. Internationally, grain reserves were projected to fall from 402.3 million tons to a mere 251 million—enough to meet global demand for fifty-four days.[93] Naturally prices rose. In January 1988 the Egyptian government had been able to import wheat for $2.90 a bushel; by July the price had risen to $3.89.[94]

But initially officials did not understand how changes in international prices had translated into shortages of bread. The increased price was being absorbed by the government, which did not allow the volume of wheat imports to fall. If the same quantity of wheat was available, why was cheap bread so hard to find? The answer was evident inside any bakery; the price increase created incentives to redirect wheat away from bread production toward other uses.

As part of its bread subsidy program, the government subjected bakers to lavish regulations, specifying how much wheat of which grade they were supposed to use in baking a specific quantity of loaves to be sold at a fixed price. Unfortunately, these directives were based on outdated assumptions about how much bakers would pay for wages, electricity, fuel oil, water, yeast, salt, machinery depreciation, delivery, and so forth. The real cost of baking a loaf of bread was about 2.8 piasters, but bakers were only permitted to charge 2 piasters.[95] For years bakers had sought to reduce their losses on bread, but their rising wage bill in the late 1980s made this imperative.

There were a number of subterfuges by which bakers could reduce losses. For example, in the cities they could sell bread to hotels and restaurants for more than 2 piasters a loaf. More imaginatively, they learned to take advantage of the fact that most baking employed three different kinds of flour sold by the government—82 percent extraction (used for *'aysh baladi*, the coarse 2 piaster loaf), 72 percent extraction (used for the finer *'aysh fino*, a more expensive loaf preferred by the Cairo middle class), and pastry flour. Pastry flour cost nearly twice as much as *fino*, which in turn cost nearly 50 percent more than *baladi*. Clever bakers discovered that they could buy cheap 85 percent extraction, sift out its bran for resale as animal feed, and use it to bake *'aysh fino*, reducing their cost by more than one-third.[96] There were many opportunities for this kind of diversion of flour from low-profit to higher-profit activity. The government defined seven distinct prices for different kinds of flour, ranging from £E 11.50 to £E 30.00 a sack.[97]

This kind of diversion had been going on for years, but only in modest amounts since for most of the 1980s grain was cheap in international markets. The rise in grain prices in 1988 created much more powerful incentives for adopting such subterfuges.

In the cities bakers began to market a whole new variety of bread, the *tabaqi* loaf. This was larger (and typically cleaner) than any of the traditional loaves. As a new item, its price was not regulated by the Ministry of Supply, so it could sell for 10–15 piasters a loaf. Since its dough was mixed from subsidized flour, the bakers made a healthy profit.

The rise in wheat prices also created some incentive in the countryside to divert wheat for use as animal feed. In 1988 the squeeze on the government's hard currency resources had forced it to cut back on imports of corn, the key ingredient in poultry and cattle feed. Corn imports fell to 1.5 million tons, half the previous year's total.[98] This caused real hardship for Egyptian peasants, who typically earned more from their chickencoops or buffaloes than they did from raising major crops. They began to buy up alternative grains as fodder, causing local wheat prices to skyrocket. Before long, village bakers discovered that a sack of flour they bought from the government for £E 11 was worth £E 30 if they sold it to a farmer out the back door.[99]

For years Egyptian politicians, particularly those on the right who favored a reduction of subsidies, had complained that "subsidized bread leavings are commonly used as feed concentrate for poultry and sometimes larger animals. It is impossible to obtain even estimates on this, but the practice is widespread and nearly everyone admits it. As one farmer said, 'Why shouldn't I feed my animals some bread? The Cooperative (agricultural) never has enough feed concentrate for us, but there is always this bread . . . what does it matter whether I eat it myself or my animals eat it? Who cares?'"[100] It is difficult to determine how much wheat was actually diverted in this way. Some Egyptians claim only 30–35 percent of wheat is actually consumed by humans.[101] But a detailed study by the International Food Policy Research Institute concluded that less than 6.6 percent of the bread sold in rural areas was fed to animals.[102] How much is actually diverted must be determined largely by the economics of the moment. When corn and conventional fodder prices are high, the incentives to feed chickens flour or bread leavings grow correspondingly stronger.

The diversion of wheat for use as fodder reflected not only the effect of government grain subsidies but also other price interventions. In the late 1970s the Egyptian appetite for meat grew sharply, a trend encouraged by the government. To assuage consumer anger after the price riots of 1977, the government launched a program to import poultry. Shortages and inflation in 1980 triggered a similar program to import red meat. By 1981–82 the Ministry of Supply was spending £E 145.2 million to subsidize beef and poultry imports.[103] The government also created a series of subsidies and nontariff barriers to encourage local meat production. Most experts think that these programs have done even more to retard Egypt's development than wheat subsidies.[104]

Government incentives helped make raising a buffalo or a few chickens much more profitable than growing traditional crops for many peasants. Farmers began to alter their cropping pattern to reflect the increased value of fodder. The area devoted to cotton declined from 1.6 million feddans in 1970 to 1.2 million in 1980—a loss of 28,200 feddans annually. In the same period the land under perennial *birsim* increased from 1.5 million to 1.7 million feddans. While by 1984 fodder crops occupied 30 percent of the cropped area and fed 4 million animals, food crops occupied only 55 percent of the cropped area and fed 50 million people.[105]

This switch to meat production aggravated Egypt's food dependence in a number of subtle ways. Meat, of course, is a less efficient way to supply calories for human consumption than grains. In the United States "a cow must be fed 21 pounds of protein in order to produce 1 pound of protein for human consumption"—which means that "an acre of cereals can produce *five times* more protein than an acre devoted to meat production."[106] To raise more meat Egypt had to devote part of its farmland to this inefficient calorie conversion and increase its imports of fodder. This was particularly evident in the growth of demand for corn, the primary ingredient of chickenfeed. Imports of yellow corn soared from 136,000 tons a year in 1965–69 to over 500,000 tons annually in 1975–79 and reached 1,866,000 tons by 1985.[107]

The high price of feedstuffs had a ripple effect that touched many aspects of the rural economy. Egypt's wheat farmers discovered that the straw their crop produced was almost more valuable as a form of summer fodder than the grain they sold for human consumption. Peasants came to prefer wheat varieties that produced long straw— which discouraged them from adopting HYV seeds that produced short stalks. Similarly, to feed livestock they often stripped husks and tops off their green corn, even though this reduced their final crop yields.[108]

Egyptian peasants grow cotton and *birsim* in succession on the same fields. As a form of fodder, the value of *birsim* rose steadily; one feddan could produce £E 500–£E 600 per season.[109] So peasants delayed planting cotton so that they could take extra cuttings from their *birsim* crop. This trend was aggravated by another set of government

policies—mandatory procurement and price controls which left peasants with little or no incentive to cultivate cotton.

Cotton could only be legally marketed through the state which, as
a monopoly buyer, could set prices as it wished. Much of Egypt's
cotton is of the extra-long staple (ELS) variety, which fetches premium
prices on the international market. The government relied on cotton
exports as a major source of hard currency revenue, so to maximize
its profits it set domestic cotton prices as close to the cost of production
as it dared. Many Egyptian peasants would have abandoned cotton
production entirely, but for the fact that planting a certain quota of
cotton was mandatory for all members of government-controlled
agricultural cooperatives. Poorer peasants, in particular, could not
afford to withdraw from the cooperatives, which handled the redistribution of land under agrarian reform and were the official outlets for
government-subsidized fertilizers and pesticides.[110]

The government's effective tax on cotton was very heavy, averaging
around 35 percent annually. But similar systems of procurement and
administered pricing were applied to rice, wheat, and most major
cereals. Domestic price controls (intended to keep costs low for
consumers) were imposed on onions, beans, and many fruits and
vegetables. The overall effect of these interventions was similar to that
of a value-added tax of 30 percent levied on the agricultural sector as
a whole.[111]

There was one critical difference. A straightforward tax on agriculture would have affected all farmers equally. Farmers would remain
free to select which crops to grow in response to market incentives.
In contrast, Egypt's pattern of state monopolies and procurements
penalized certain peasants (such as those planting cotton) and subsidized others (those raising livestock). It also dictated certain cropping
choices to farmers. Those who were required to plant highly taxed
crops lacked any material reason to nurture their fields. If they could
not profit from what they planted, why should they invest more than
minimal amounts of labor and capital? The result, in all too many
cases, was yields that either stagnated or increased only very slowly.[112]

In the 1970s a growing body of studies demonstrated the iniquitous
effects of poor policy in Egypt and many developing countries. By the
1980s, the importance of policy reform had become a touchstone of
orthodoxy for development experts. Yet governments in the Third
World embraced policy reform only slowly and cautiously. Frustrated

by this recalcitrance, and charged by the weight of intellectual evidence on their side, development experts made increasingly more inflated and comprehensive claims about the importance of policy reform. Some began to portray it as a sufficient condition for economic development; all that was needed was to "get the prices right." Regressing toward ever more fundamentalist theories of economics, they began to claim that policy reform required the virtual abolition of state intervention in the economy.

Detailed studies of Egypt suggest that these claims are exaggerated. In countries like the United States, an increase in crop prices may trigger expanded production by making it profitable for farmers to bring fallow lands back into production or to extend cultivation to marginal lands. But in Egypt there are no marginal lands; land and water restraints set much tighter limits to price response. Moreover, changes in the price of individual crops may not have dramatic effects on Egyptian output because planting sequences link certain groups of crops together. For example, cotton and *birsim* compete for land in a linked planting cycle; so long as *birsim* remains relatively more profitable than cotton, an increase in the price of the latter may not induce farmers to actually plant more.[113]

The Egyptian government experimented with price reform in the 1980s (figure 2-2). Price reform will increase output, but initially only by modest amounts. Von Braun and de Haen estimated that in 1979–80, price distortions attending government intervention reduced agricultural output by the equivalent of 1.5 percent of national income or 7.5 percent of agricultural production.[114] Any change that might increase Egyptian output by 7.5 percent is well worth pursuing, but not nearly so revolutionary as some development experts dream.

Policy reform will have some positive effects on Egyptian agriculture that are not so easy to measure. The expansion of marketing mechanisms will make decisions about planting faster and more consumer responsive. The possibility of larger profits in agriculture will prompt greater energy among farmers and more investment by businessmen. A more liberal system will encourage the development of diverse institutions—storage depots, shipping agencies, exchanges, credit facilities—each of which will incrementally boost output. How far such development goes depends on many factors other than policy reform, but their potential contribution to agricultural output is substantial.

Policy reform, then, is best thought of as the keystone of a series

Figure 2-2. Agricultural Price Changes, 1973–85

Ratio of procurement price to border price

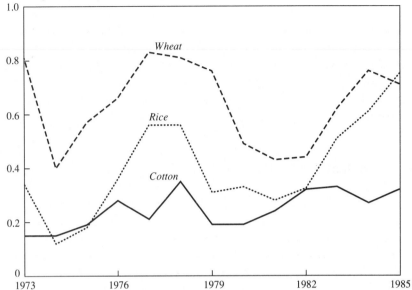

Source: Jean-Jacques Dethier, *Trade, Exchange Rate and Agricultural Pricing Policies in Egypt,* vol. 2 (Washington: World Bank, 1989), pp. 44–45, 53, 57, and 60–61.

of forces which, taken together, could spur major changes in Egyptian agricultural output. Policy reform is not a substitute for government action. "A removal of price distortions might be needed if agriculture is to grow more rapidly. But . . . it may not be enough. The rigid constraints on resources, deficits of public water and input supply management, and the inefficiency of the agricultural extension service tend to offset the incentives price adjustments give for growth. Price policy should not be viewed as a panacea for Egypt's rural development and national food problems."[115] Policy reform might even create conditions that would make additional state action desirable—to assemble funds for investment, to develop irrigation systems and other public works, and to sponsor agricultural research and extension programs. Effective policy reform is not the same as leaping to a laissez-faire economy.

These cautions do not diminish the importance of policy reform. If raising agricultural production is the key to ameliorating Egypt's food security crisis (and to other problems), reforming agricultural policy remains the key to increasing production. The current pattern of policy, despite its laudable objectives, has had the effect of encouraging consumption and discouraging production of certain commodities. Curbing the lavish subsidies that encourage waste of wheat, water, and agricultural inputs would encourage greater efficiency. Eliminating the trade protection that encourages meat production would liberate land and capital for cotton and grain cultivation. Terminating the price controls and mandatory procurements that reduce the profitability of key crops would restore incentives for productivity. Policy reform deserves pride of place in Egypt's economic agenda.

Agriculture and Development

The same kind of poor policies that suppress yields in agriculture hinder productivity in many other branches of the Egyptian economy. Trade has been distorted by a combination of overvalued exchange rates and myriad customs barriers. Industry has been hampered by public sector monopolies for certain products and a vast array of government licensing requirements. Thus, many of the problems (and solutions) that crop up in discussions of agriculture can be taken as parables for conditions in the wider Egyptian economy.

Yet agriculture also has certain special characteristics and occupies a pivotal position in the operation of the Egyptian economy. There are a number of reasons for believing that the reform and development of the agricultural sector may deserve priority, or even be a precondition for progress at the national level.

In 1989 the Egyptian Society for Financial Administration prepared a report that emphasized the centrality of agriculture. It showed that agriculture supplied 30 percent of the national income, employed 25 percent of the labor force, and provided 55 percent of nonpetroleum commodity exports.[116] Development in agriculture would benefit a large share of the Egyptian population, including small or landless peasants, the poorest elements of the population.

Another reason for assigning priority to agriculture is the instrumental role that agricultural development must play in resolving Egypt's food security crisis. Reducing dependence on food imports has become (with management of the foreign debt) one of the two most important economic preoccupations of the Egyptian government. Food security problems do more than threaten hunger; they hinder development in the nonagricultural sectors of the economy. A 10 percent rise in the cost of imported foods decreases Egypt's industrial output by 1–2 percent by consuming hard currency that would otherwise be available for the purchase of industrial inputs. Conversely, if government spending on food subsidies could be decreased by 10 percent, thereby reducing the government's budget deficit, the value of the Egyptian pound would increase by 3 percent and reduce the inflation rate by 5 percent.[117]

The way that the volume of food imports affects the availability of capital is only one example of the many links between development in agriculture and industry. This is an important point, because some Egyptians have tended to see industrialization as an alternative to agricultural development. For example, in the policy debates provoked by the first world food crisis in 1974, Ismail Sabry Abdullah, a leading intellectual who served as minister of social affairs under Nasser, argued that "Egypt's future lies in the export of manufactured goods and the import of foodstuffs. The worldwide rise in the price of food must act as an incentive to increase the rates of growth [of the economy] so that from the earnings on our industrial exports we can pay for our food."[118] While there are strong arguments for saying that Egypt's long-term future lies with industrial development, there are equally sound reasons to believe that in the short term this cannot be achieved without progress in agriculture.

Studies by the World Bank suggest that the areas in which Egypt enjoys the greatest comparative advantage for industrial development are (in descending order) food processing, textiles, metals, and chemicals.[119] Success in the first two sectors clearly hinges on the supply of inputs from agriculture. In addition to these forward linkages in which agriculture supplies inputs for industry, there are also backward linkages by which agriculture provides a market for the outputs of industry, such as fertilizers and chemicals, tractors and machinery. The stimulus that different sectors of the economy (or distinct economies) exert on one another forms the critical engine that sustains development; increased productivity in one sector helps to raise production in another, and vice versa, in a continuing cycle of growth.

In the past, some development experts scoffed at the importance of these linkages. The forward linkages attending the processing of agricultural outputs were generally thought to be weak. Many of the export crops characteristic of the Third World—coffee, jute, tea, for instance—receive only a minimum of processing before shipping. It was thought that they did not linger in the local economy long enough to generate strong linkages. Albert O. Hirschman summarized the conventional wisdom years ago: "Agriculture certainly stands convicted on the count of its lack of direct stimulus to the setting up of new activities through linkage effects: the superiority of manufacturing in this respect is crushing."[120] Certain studies of Egypt claimed to support this contention.

For example, the backward linkage between Egyptian agriculture and chemical manufacturing does not appear strong enough to translate a growing demand for fertilizer into impetus for industrial development. Egyptian fertilizer manufacturing is already highly mechanized and concentrated, so increased demand stimulated by agricultural growth would not stimulate the emergence of new firms or expand job opportunities. Egypt produces fertilizer in nine large factories, all of them overstaffed because of the government's public employment program, yet the largest of these plants employs only 2,400 people.[121] Worse, much of the technology needed to produce fertilizers must be imported, so even orders for expanded plants would not lead to new business for Egyptian firms.

Recently, however, development experts have had occasion to reconsider and reappraise such judgments.[122] A study of the role of cotton in the Egyptian economy, for example, suggests that links between agriculture and other sectors of the economy are much more powerful than was once thought.[123] For many years Egypt was one of only four countries (with the Sudan, Peru, and the United States) growing the highly desired extra-long staple variety of cotton; and Egypt farmed more of it than any other (40 percent of total world production). But in the 1980s Egypt exported the great bulk of its ELS cotton to Thailand raw, where it was processed for use in Asia's burgeoning textile industries. Egypt had a large textile industry of its own, but the irregular quality and relatively high cost of its product has confined most of its product to the domestic market. Thus, Egypt actually imported short-staple cotton to supply local mills, since it could fetch a higher price for its ELS cotton in exports.[124] If Egypt could raise local productivity in cotton, it could maintain its export revenues while creating a surplus for use by local industry. Because Egyptian firms have access to ELS cotton at low cost, expanding the local processing industry might give them a competitive advantage that would allow them to contemplate penetrating foreign markets.

The textiles industry in Egypt supplies 25–30 percent of the total value of industrial production, about one-third of industrial employment, and almost one-half of non-oil industrial exports. Traditionally the public sector dominated textile production, doing all of the spinning, 75 percent of the dying and finishing, 65 percent of the weaving, and so on.[125] But in the 1980s a new generation of small firms began to develop in the private sector. They specialized in weaving high-quality ready-made fabrics for Egypt's upper classes. They competed successfully against imported textiles and looked for ways to break into export markets. But entrepreneurs had to compete with the public sector to get enough cotton to meet their demand. They complained that local cotton prices had risen sharply in recent years and were climbing higher as Egypt's exchange rate became more realistic.[126] Raising cotton productivity would be a real boon to these firms, and their operations would generate employment and hard currency revenues that would stimulate the wider economy.

Not only are such forward linkages from the agricultural sector unusually strong in Egypt, there is also reason to believe that backward linkages—demand for inputs or goods generated by growth in the agricultural sector—is quite strong. This became evident in the 1980s when the rural economy grew because peasants who had left their villages to labor in neighboring oil-rich countries sent remittances home. Workers' remittances fueled a wave of demand for consumer durable goods—refrigerators, fans, television sets.

The economic effects of agriculture on small-scale industry are now well documented. Studies of Malaysia and Ghana suggest that even in fairly isolated districts, where fragmented, low-productivity farms prevail, every dollar of income created by agriculture generates 80 cents of demand for nonfarm activities.[127] When peasant incomes rise, so does peasant demand for dairy products, clothes, tools, and other goods that can be manufactured in the villages and towns of rural provinces. This is welcome news for a country like Egypt where, as of 1974, 80 percent of all private sector employment was in small firms employing fewer than ten workers.[128]

The great majority of small-scale firms in Egypt are very traditional enterprises—two-thirds are either home sewing operations or cheese-producing sidelines. But a handful are quite modern and dynamic.[129] Local shops that make tools, work metal, and repair and rent agricultural machinery have grown and show great potential for expansion. Provincial furniture craftsmen have not only captured a growing share of Egypt's urban market but have begun to explore opportunities to break into export markets. Some rural foundries have signed on as subcontractors for the public-sector automobile industry, producing bolts and small parts more cheaply than they can be imported. This resembles a pattern well established in Japanese industry, where small rural firms often do specialized subcontracting from large urban industries.[130]

Rural industries—and textile firms specializing in high-quality fabrics—form part of a burgeoning movement of small-scale firms that are energizing the Egyptian economy. In recent years small private firms producing leatherwork, shoes, aluminum kitchen utensils, stationery, and even plastic combs have shown themselves to be both profitable and competitive.[131] Across the Third World, firms of this kind are proving to be effective engines of development. Contrary to expectations, they are highly effective at assimilating advanced technology and sophisticated production techniques. In Hong Kong a third of the work force in electronic manufactures—one of the three largest branches of industry—is employed in firms with fewer than nine workers.[132] The old assumption that economies of scale are necessary for modern technology dies hard, but for many industries its corpse is quite cold. Small firms may be inappropriate for shipbuilding or automobile manufacturing, but for electronics assemblage, plastics, textiles, and similar branches of industry they seem quite appropriate.[133]

The example of greatest interest for Egypt may be Taiwan.[134] Here the roots of industry were small scale and rural. The first modern factories were built in rural areas to process agricultural products. Gradually firms in rural areas switched to subcontracting for larger, urban enterprises. Early industrialization in rural areas actually eased the growth of manufacturing in urban areas. The rural labor force did not crowd into the cities to hunt for jobs; peasant families simply began to switch their surplus members from farm work to employment in local factories. Even today small, family-owned, labor-intensive firms predominate. They supply 70 percent of employment in Taiwan.[135]

Small-scale industries should not be thought of as a crutch for use by backward nations or a utopia appealing to "small is beautiful" romantics.[136] Studies of already industrialized Western economies demonstrate that small-scale firms offering high-quality service to well-defined market niches may be not only viable but extremely competitive.[137] Robert B. Reich, a leading American economist, notes that "almost all of the growth in American manufacturing during the past few years has been in small-batch businesses aimed at specialized markets."[138] He proposes that the development of rural small-scale industries may hold the solution for the American farm crisis.

Small-scale industries may play an important role in the industrialization of Egypt. Some will remain traditional or contribute only to the local economy—although even they will help to create employment and value. Some may grow to be significant in the national economy and the export sector. Either way, their growth will probably be easier and more rapid if agricultural development spurs their linkage effects.

Historically, successful industrialization has typically been accompanied or preceded by a revolution in agricultural production.[139] An undeveloped agricultural system can cripple the industrialization of an economy by keeping the prices of wage goods (such as food) high, by keeping income levels low and the size of the domestic market small, and by depriving the economy of one of its most obvious sources of capital accumulation. This seems to be true no matter which precise industrialization strategy a country adopts. Jacques Loup notes: "In a strategy of import-substituting industrialization, agriculture plays a fundamental role, since productivity increases in the agricultural sector are necessary to stimulate the demand for industrial products. In the case of export-oriented industrialization, while agriculture may not play a vital role at the beginning, its modernization soon becomes necessary to prevent the development process from remaining confined to an enclave. In all cases, therefore, the development of the agricultural sector largely determines the eventual success of the industrialization process."[140]

Some scholars have suggested that countries like Egypt pursue a strategy of agricultural-demand-led industrialization (ADLI). This strategy treats agriculture as the primary sector in development and emphasizes promoting industries that have strong linkages to the agricultural sector. The ADLI approach "would stress the raising of agricultural productivity, especially that of medium-scale farmers, as a means of achieving industrialization. It would accomplish the industrialization goal by expanding internal demand for intermediate and consumer goods produced by domestic industry." Economic modeling suggests that this approach might lead to the same high rate of industrialization that characterized the export-led development strategies of South Korea and Taiwan, yet produce "a higher rate of labour absorption, a better distribution of income, better balance-of-payments results, less poverty, and a higher rate of growth of per capita gross national product."[141]

In certain countries (Denmark is perhaps the best known example) agriculture completely took the place of industry as the primary engine of development. This may not be an option for Egypt; its population may be too large, and too few of its people still work on the farm, for Egypt to support itself as the dairy of the Middle East. Yet agriculture remains sufficiently central to the Egyptian economy for progress in this sector to trigger growth in many others. Perhaps economic development in Egypt should end in industry, but it probably must begin with agriculture.[142]

Conclusion

Officials at the Ministry of Agriculture offer yet another argument for focusing on policy reform in agriculture as the centerpiece of Egyptian development strategy. They believe that even if agricultural development was not likely to directly trigger growth in other sectors of the Egyptian economy, the example of policy reform and growth in agriculture would serve as a powerful demonstration for other sectors of the benefits of change. Of all the various branches of the Egyptian economy, they argue, agriculture is the one where change would be easiest to start and would yield the quickest results.

This argument derives as much from an understanding of Egyptian politics as it does economics. Policy reform is always a politically sensitive issue, since the prevailing pattern of subsidies, price controls, and operating licenses clearly protects certain sections of the population. For example, Egyptian consumers may oppose the reform of agricultural policy since it is likely to result (at least initially) in higher food prices. Yet some Egyptian officials think an even broader constituency exists that would support agricultural policy reform. Millions of peasants favor altering the current pattern of state intervention and their concerns have found a voice in Parliament and national politics, through an agrarian elite of rich peasants and gentleman farmers. The government might then rely on the support of this constituency as it alters agricultural policy, balancing their enthusiasm against the complaints of consumers about higher prices.[143]

Officials admit that such a constituency for reform does not yet exist in other sectors of the economy. When the government debates questions of industrial policy, or tariff reform, or appropriate interest rates, it often finds the proponents of reform are an isolated minority, while the opponents of reform represent a well-entrenched body of vested interests. Agricultural policy reform, thus, should prove easier to initiate than changes in other sectors.

This argument deserves critical examination. The lobby for agricultural reform seems less coherent than some officials have claimed. One World Bank study suggests that under policy reform "fodder surplus farms and vegetable producers would lose because they use subsidized inputs and have protected outputs. Food deficit cotton producers, who are mostly the smallest farmers, would stand to gain most."[144] Would the agrarian elite in the Egyptian Parliament really press for reform if it became clear that its primary beneficiaries would be poorer peasants? In many cases the distinction between groups that would benefit and those that would lose under reform are elusive. The small peasant who would gain from rising prices may also own a buffalo whose value would drop. A much more detailed understanding of who supports and who opposes reform is needed before any decision can be made about how easy it will be—or what measures are necessary to make it easier.

The same officials at the Ministry of Agriculture who claim there is widespread support for policy reform also make specific assumptions about the role of the state in the reform process. They tend to think that the Egyptian state is overextended and overtasked. While none claims that Egypt can be turned into a Smithian "enterprise economy," where the state confines itself to the maintenance of an army and a postal service, they do think that the Egyptian government's mounting budget deficits and ossifying bureaucratic paralysis demonstrate its need to shed many of its current responsibilities. They think that policy reform will reduce demands on the state, freeing resources currently employed in agriculture for use in other tasks.

In practice, however, effective agricultural policy reform may not shrink the scope of state action, just redefine it. The state may behave in a more "market-conforming" manner, but the demand for state action may not diminish. The state may cease enforcing mandatory crop procurements, but become more energetic in assessing and collecting agricultural taxes. It may stop supervising prices, but become more active in promoting honesty and competition in agricultural markets and credit agencies. It seems unlikely that reform will curtail the demand for state involvement in agriculture. Here again, more detailed studies are needed of what roles the state may play after policy reform.

In the 1980s economists painted a fairly detailed picture of how resources and prices combine to shape agricultural output in Egypt. Their studies made a persuasive case for the necessity of policy reform. But the scope and pace of reform to date have been limited, and there are reasons to believe the chief obstacles to change have been political, not economic. A new generation of studies must focus on the politics of policy reform, with the aim of defining who supports and who opposes reform, and why. They must clarify what the role of the state has been—and might be—in the reform process. The following chapters sketch some highly tentative answers to the questions about reform; the answers reflect the limitations of the information currently available. Other scholars, by criticizing and superseding the answers suggested here, can move the debate along and provide a more reliable picture of the political forces that shape agricultural policy reform.

CHAPTER 3

State Power and
Agricultural Policy

IN MAY 1982 THE EGYPTIAN GOVERNMENT BEGAN TO STAGE PRE-DAWN raids on villages in the Nile Delta. Police troops, helmeted and heavily armed, roused villagers from their homes. Masked informants identified suspects from the resulting lineups. In Daqhiliyya Province alone fourteen thousand peasants were dragged before the courts. When the police could not find the suspects they were hunting for, they sometimes took members of their families hostage—a standard technique used to intimidate the political opposition.

But the villagers arrested in these raids were not members of the political opposition. They were merely peasants who had failed to grow the government-mandated quota of rice. In specific provinces the government obliged farmers to grow a ton and a half of rice for each feddan cropped, regardless of the size of their plot. After delivering the mandated quotas, the cultivators were reimbursed at a rate of £E 85 per ton—barely half the black market price of rice (£E 160-£E 190). This was scarcely enough to cover the cost of the expensive fertilizer and seed needed to produce the crop. Not surprisingly, many peasants tried to avoid planting rice, preferring other, more profitable crops. Rice production in Egypt dropped from 2.6 million tons in 1970 to 2.3 million tons in 1980.[1]

The Daqhiliyya raid was unusual. Normally, local representatives of the Ministry of Agriculture were responsible for imposing the rice quota. These agents worked without police support, relying on economic sanctions (such as the threat to withhold government credit) and small fines to put pressure on the peasants. But local officials did not apply the sanctions with much enthusiasm and peasant evasion had become increasingly widespread. After years of frustration, some

51

police officers concluded that a major demonstration of force might command more respect.

Instead, the Daqhiliyya raid focused public attention on the short-comings of government quotas and price controls. The conditions that provoked the raid scandalized most Egyptians. They thought that the prices the government offered farmers were patently unfair. They believed that to ram such prices down peasants' throats by coercion was an injustice. The raid rekindled a wide-ranging debate about government agricultural policy. Many Egyptians asked how the state had come to adopt an agricultural policy that required it to exploit and abuse its poorest and most humble citizens.

The way that Egyptians answered this question depended on whether their hero was Nasser or Sadat. Most debates about agricultural policy (or foreign policy or any policy) in Egypt are framed in terms of the legacy of these two men. Both were larger-than-life figures, with very distinctive personalities and styles of dress and rhetoric. Both seemed to embody the Egyptian government, its virtues and flaws. Yet they presented two very different visions of what Egypt should be, and an Egyptian who thinks one is a hero usually thinks the other was a demon.

Egyptian conservatives, whether aligned with the Muslim Brothers, the Wafd party, or some other grouping, despise Nasser. They believe that he, and the other officers who helped him seize power in 1952, understood nothing of economics. They think that his experiment in Arab socialism, which confiscated the land and factories of the old elites, was a political power grab with disastrous economic consequences. They blame him for the Daqhiliyya raid, because the quotas and price regulations governing the rice crop were imposed during his administration.

Egyptian radicals, whether Marxist or Nasserist, view Sadat with contempt. They view him as a tool of the Americans and the Saudis who sought to liberalize the Egyptian economy in order to open it to foreign exploitation. Nasser may have created the rice crop regulations, but he was always the champion of the poor Egyptian; he had given the peasants land reform and massive investment in agriculture. Sadat had reversed these policies. Leftists blame excesses like the Daqhiliyya raid on right-wing elements, promoted by Sadat, who were unwilling to temper government policy with sympathy for the common man.

These contending visions shape the debate over agricultural policy in Egypt. Both sides believe the key to devising an effective agricultural policy lies in appointing ideologically correct (that is, Nasserist or Sadatist) individuals to high public office. Both think that the character of the man at the helm is of decisive importance to the development of Egyptian agriculture.

During the 1980s, the conservatives enjoyed a clear advantage. Foreign development agencies, such as the U.S. Agency for International Development (AID) and the World Bank, generally shared their revulsion for Nasser. An American scholar, summarizing the common wisdom in Washington, wrote: "Cairo's economic difficulties are to a large degree a legacy of Gamal Abdul Nasser, who headed Egypt from 1952 to 1970. His socialist policies bred overcentralization, inefficiency, waste, and corruption. The nationalization of foreign-owned enterprises in 1956 deprived Egypt of foreign investment, while nationalization of domestic enterprises after 1960 spurred capital flight and an exodus of talented managers and other professionals. A cumbersome bureaucracy grew to oversee a swollen public sector plagued by obsolescent equipment, low productivity, and lack of competition. For political reasons, Nasser directed trade to favor the Soviet bloc and erected tariff barriers and other import restrictions on Western trade."[2] The development agencies that shared this vision had great clout in Egypt because of the billions of dollars in aid at their disposal. They did their best to promote the careers of conservatives and liberalizers while sidelining or harassing those they suspected of Nasserism.

The left and the right, Egyptian and foreign, share a mythological view of economic policy as an arena in which the forces of good and evil struggle over the soul of the nation. This vision substitutes a comforting simplicity for complex and painful realities. Although Nasser and Sadat were very different men who pursued distinct policies, their policies had many common features that their partisans overlook. For that matter, neither of them had nearly as much control over policy, for good or for evil, as is now imagined.

Price controls and crop regulations antedate Nasser; and they were continued under Sadat. The trend toward liberalization actually began during Nasser's administration, although it was accelerated under Sadat. Nasser was never a rigid, doctrinaire socialist, and Sadat's support of the private sector was always tempered by his ongoing enthusiasm for state intervention in the economy. Neither man had a deep understanding of economic issues, both relied heavily on the advice of technocrats and experts, and both pursued economic policies that zig-zagged alternately to the left and the right. Both tried to be pragmatic, adjusting their policies constantly to changing political currents.

Most important, Nasser and Sadat, for all their autocratic appearances or pretensions, ruled a divided and intractable polity. They discovered that state power in Egypt, even the ostensibly absolute power of the presidential office, was highly circumscribed. They understood that regulations drafted in Cairo, by whichever party, would be transformed into something completely different when they were implemented in the Egyptian countryside. Both adjusted to this situation and tried to devise policies that reflected what was possible rather than pursuing objectives that were desirable but impracticable.

Political weakness, and an understanding of the limits of what the state could and could not accomplish, did far more to shape the character of Egyptian agricultural policy than any ideological predilection. This chapter documents this weakness and tries to map some of its persistent forms.[3] Neither Egyptian conservatives nor radicals are likely to be pleased with the picture. Nasserists and Sadatists will both object to the portrait of their heroes that emerges. They should be disturbed by the evidence that a successful reform of Egyptian agricultural policy implies much more than just changing a few laws in Cairo. For reform may require revolutionary changes in the whole structure of public administration.

Agrarian Reform

In 1952 Nasser's newly installed military regime launched a mammoth land reform program that remains both the foundation of the agrarian regime and the touchstone for debate about agricultural policy in Egypt today. Rightists view the reform as the beginning of an assault on private property that would—had it not been aborted by Sadat— eventually have culminated in complete collectivization. Leftists see the same reform as the keystone of a humane regime that eased the misery of millions of poor Egyptians. Each of them interprets the significance of the reform in the light of subsequent developments which they either favor or abhor.

In reality, land reform was neither an assault on capitalism nor an exercise in state humanitarianism. The real motives behind land reform were quite different and have been largely forgotten. For that matter, the most important consequences of land reform have often passed unrecognized.

When Nasser and the Free Officers took over on July 23, 1952, they did not share a common vision of how to turn Egypt into a modern society. They were an unusually diverse and cacophonous group, which included Marxists and Muslim fundamentalists, partisans of existing civilian parties and advocates of military rule, socialists and free traders, admirers of the West and violent anti-imperialists. Beyond their operational plans for the coup itself, the only thing they had found time to agree on was the need to free Egypt from the deadening monarchy of Farouq and the landowning elite that supported him.

The Free Officers' economic policy reflected their inability to agree on anything but the lowest common denominator. In general, they left things as they were. They were interested in encouraging development through major public works (most famously, the High Dam) and promoting Egyptianization (much of the economy had been dominated by an enclave of foreigners, a legacy of the colonial era), but for their first five years in power, they did not tinker much in economics. Their only serious intervention in the economy was agrarian reform—a program whose logic appealed to Free Officers of all backgrounds.

The idea of land reform had been discussed in Egypt for several years. It had been raised in the 1940s in articles by intellectuals like Mirrit Ghali, in books by foreign advisers like Doreen Warriner, and in Parliament by Muhammad Khattab.[4] The trigger for this discussion was the growth of acute rural poverty. Although a handful of large landholders prospered, millions of peasants lacked enough land to support their families. Fully 44 percent of rural families were totally landless and had to work either on large estates or as migrant laborers. Landless peasants faced three brutal options: to join the sharecroppers on a large plantation, to join the casual laborers who maintained the canals and irrigation works, or starvation. For each member of the elite who owned fifty feddans or more, there were literally a hundred families who were completely landless.[5]

Population growth on a fixed area made the burden of landlessness steadily worse. Landless families grew from 24 percent of the rural population in 1929 to 44 percent by 1950.[6] Moreover, another 26 percent of rural families owned less than two feddans—the minimum land area necessary to sustain an average family.[7] As the size of plots available to farmers shrank, so did their incomes. Slowly and painfully, land hunger translated into food hunger. The problem grew markedly worse during World War II, when military requisitions created shortages of grain. While a handful of farmers made fortunes from profiteering, peasants in Qina and Asyut literally starved. This triggered the first *jacqueries* in a generation. Members of the landowning elite began to worry that a revolution was brewing.[8]

After the war, the problem of rural poverty clawed its way to the top of Egypt's political agenda. The issue appealed to a new generation of ideological, internally disciplined parties like the Muslim Brothers, Young Egypt, and the Communists, all of whom stressed the importance of social questions.[9] By 1950 these parties had included proposals for land reform in their programs. They focused attention on social issues by their participation in a growing wave of strikes, insurrections, and demonstrations. This unrest, a harbinger of the unraveling of the ancien régime, was largely urban, but it had its rural analogues. Discontented peasants, who in the past had been content to harass and murder local officials, began in 1951 to riot and demonstrate on a growing scale.[10]

The Free Officers were genuinely sensitive to the problems of the rural poor. Most of them had relatives in the villages and some spent their summers there.[11] But land reform appealed to them primarily as a means to restore social stability. The officers lived in mortal fear that the British might use Egypt's domestic instability as a pretext to intervene and reverse the military's coup—as they had done after General Urabi's coup in 1882. They intended to show that they could maintain order. After taking power they quickly moved forcefully against all demonstrators, even hanging leftist union leaders at Kafr al-Dawwar.[12]

Yet if land reform was essential as an instrument of social stability, the Free Officers also found it desirable as a political tool. The backbone of the ancien régime against which the officers had staged their coup was the class of large landowners. In 1952 the number of Egyptians owning plots larger than fifty feddans was very small, constituting only 0.4 percent of all landowners. Yet this tiny elite controlled fully 34 percent of all agricultural land. The two thousand largest landowners controlled almost a fifth of all agricultural land.[13] Buttressed by huge profits from the cotton trade, large landholders had dominated all of the older generation political parties (the Wafd, the Sa'dists, and so forth). Many of these magnates were descended from (or had intermarried with) the elite of Turco-Circassian mercenaries who had established the Egyptian monarchy and remained its staunchest defenders.[14]

The Free Officers uniformly hated the landed elite, viewing it as not only a privileged class but a foreign minority. They were united in their desire to "terminate feudalism" (*al-qada 'ala al-iqta'iyya*). While no officer proposed sending this aristocracy to the guillotine, they all saw land reform as a means both to strip the old elite of its power base and to punish it for generations of tyranny.

Although the Free Officers quickly agreed on the desirability of land reform, they were not confident that they could put it into effect. None of the officers had studied economics, and they worried that hasty or ill-conceived legislation might disrupt agriculture and create long-term obstacles to the development of the economy. So the officers assembled a committee of civilian experts to assist them in drafting and implementing land reform legislation.[15] This committee inaugurated a pattern of policymaking that persists in Egypt to this day, a process of consultation in which the officer in the executive office listens to advice from a wide range of civilian interests. In the 1950s and 1960s these consultations focused on an elite of civilian technocrats and experts. By the 1970s and 1980s they had expanded to include a large array of business and farmer lobbies.

The intellectuals and bureaucrats whom the Officers charged with drafting a land reform law tried to devise a program that would disrupt agricultural production as little as possible. They understood that a certain amount of dislocation was inevitable. Confiscated lands would be out of production while awaiting redistribution. Large landowners would immediately stop investing in land improvement. Marketed output would probably drop in the short term as some peasants insisted on eating a larger share of their produce themselves. But the experts focused on the potential for long-term losses of production. Their chief fear was that redistributing the land in smaller plots would sacrifice economies of scale, since the small peasant benefiting from reform lacked the wherewithal to risk planting a single specialty crop or to invest in tractors and other capital-intensive inputs.

Egypt already suffered from serious problems of land fragmentation. Population pressure and inheritance patterns (there is no primogeniture under Islamic law) left many peasants with plots too small to work

Table 3-1. Structure of Landownership, 1952 and 1965

Number of feddans per plot	1952			1965		
	Thousands of owners	*Thousands of feddans*	*Feddans per owner*	*Thousands of owners*	*Thousands of feddans*	*Feddans per owner*
Less than 5	2,642	2,122	0.8	3,033	3,693	1.2
5 to less than 10	79	526	6.6	78	614	7.9
10 to less than 20	47	638	13.6	41[a]	527	12.8
20 to less than 50	22	654	29.7	29	815	28.1
50 to less than 100	6	430	71.7	6	392	65.3
100 to less than 200	3	437	145.7	4	421	100.0[b]
200 and over	2	1,177	588.5	. . .	. . .	. . .
Total	2,801	5,984	. . .	3,191	6,462	. . .

Source: Robert Mabro, *The Egyptian Economy, 1952–1972* (Oxford: Clarendon Press, 1974), p. 73.
a. Adjusted figure.
b. Maximum holding allowed.

effectively. Dwarf plots, smaller than two feddans, could not produce enough to feed a family, much less to support investment in productivity.[16] The dangers of fragmentation became the centerpiece of debates about the nature of land reform. To promote social stability and the popularity of the regime, some experts argued that land should be redistributed to the poorest or landless peasants. Others argued that not enough land was available to give each poor peasant a viable plot and that any attempt to do so would parcel the soil out to people who could not make efficient use of it.[17] They argued that it would be better to redistribute the land to farmers who already owned at least three feddans and thus had the experience and resources to make profitable use of additional acreage.

The latter interpretation prevailed and land reform legislation was carefully constructed to minimize dislocations and fragmentation. Individuals could own no more than two hundred feddans of agricultural land, plus one hundred feddans for each dependent (see table 3-1). Holdings exceeding this limit were to be confiscated (with compensation) and resold in units of five feddans or less to peasants who already owned less than ten feddans. The way in which the law was implemented ensured that it did not aggravate fragmentation. Within a few weeks, the government had taken over the properties of the country's one hundred twelve largest landowners.[18] Title to these lands was redistributed to the peasants who were already working on these estates. As a condition for receiving title, peasants were required to join a (government) "supervised" agricultural cooperative. The government created such cooperatives by appropriating the existing farm administration of the large estates. Often the former magnate's farm supervisor was simply reappointed as the cooperative's chief.[19] Peasants thus continued to cultivate their old plots, under what amounted to the same system of labor organization.

This arrangement often increased the productivity of the land. Peasants worked harder since they now owned their plots and could profit from a larger share of its product. The supervised cooperatives continued to supply the capital and large-scale coordination once provided by estate owners. They distributed seed, fertilizers, and pesticides. With assistance from the state agricultural bank, the cooperatives replaced Greek moneylenders as the major source of rural credit. They owned tractors, pumps, threshers, and other expensive machinery and marketed the chief cash crop, cotton, for the peasantry.

The manner in which supervised cooperatives were created illustrates another enduring feature of Egyptian agricultural policy—it follows the line of least resistance. The regime rarely creates new institutions where old ones can be renamed and redirected. The government, always overextended and on a tight budget, prefers ad hoc solutions to radical reorganizations. Nasser once said, "I do not act, I react."[20] Although he was speaking about foreign affairs, his words apply to Egyptian economic policy as well.

The supervised cooperatives were not the only force working to minimize the disruptive potential of land reform; another feature of the new land law exploited certain features of the real estate market. When it was issued, the law permitted owners to sell off lands in excess of the 200-feddan maximum privately as an alternative to confiscation. By the time this loophole was closed in October 1952, magnates had dumped more than 145,000 feddans in distress sales. This amounted to one-third of all lands transferred during the reform.[21] Often, the beneficiaries of such sales were rich peasants, those with enough cash tucked away to take advantage of the opportunity. As a result, "the number of *medium-sized ownerships*, namely *ownerships* of 20 to 50 feddans, increased in *absolute* terms from 22,000 to 30,000 after the enactment of the first agrarian reform law, with an area rising from 650,000 to 800,000 feddans (an increase of 23% in acreage)."[22] The agrarian reform left the number of smallholders nearly unchanged in absolute and relative terms. Even after the reform 93.9 percent of landowners held 49.7 percent of the land while a mere 5.4 percent owned the remaining 50.2 percent.[23] In those cases where a transfer of title resulted in a change in who cultivated the land, the farmers were usually prosperous peasants who could keep the land productive.

Agrarian reform enhanced the power of rich peasants in several ways. Not only were they the primary beneficiaries of distress sales, but they were able to climb into the economic and political niches vacated by the elimination of the landed magnates. They now occupied the top rungs of the social ladder in rural areas, becoming an elite whom the government tended to respect and with whom it wanted to cooperate. This may not have been a conscious objective of the land law, but it was not an undesirable consequence for the regime. Rich peasants were economically productive and politically reliable. In Egypt, as in many other countries, land redistribution has helped "to [create] a conservative agrarian petty bourgeoisie and thus reduces the threat of social instability in the countryside."[24]

Land reform altered the government's relationship to agriculture, giving the state a direct and important role in rural production. To sustain the cooperatives, the state gradually became the dominant supplier of seed, fertilizers, pesticides, and rural credit, as well as a major cotton marketer. One ambitious official, Sayyid Mar'i (ironically himself a former large landowner) gradually consolidated and integrated the various agencies that supervised agriculture into a personal fief. Mar'i's Higher Committee of Agrarian Reform took control of the previously independent Agricultural Credit and Cooperative Bank in November 1955. In 1957 he took charge of the Ministry of Agriculture, which was reorganized to incorporate not only his earlier fiefs but also the largest land reclamation projects in the country. Finally in 1960 the agricultural cooperatives, which had been under the Ministry of Social Affairs, were transferred to his authority. The Ministry of Agriculture became a kind of superministry, with broad powers, and Mar'i emerged as Egypt's premier technocrat.[25]

But the growth of state authority in this area did not lead directly to bureaucratic control of agriculture, much less to collectivization. Sayyid Mar'i and his protégés were themselves large farmers and were dedicated to the independence and prosperity of landed property. In addition, the great majority of Free Officers endorsed the rights of private farmers. They might toy with property rights to ease the burden on small peasants, and some favored a leading role for the state in the economy, but none ever whispered a word about collectivization.[26]

Socialists formed a small but vocal minority among the Free Officers.

But as in so many Third World countries, Egyptian socialists were moved less by a desire to hold property in common than by the progressivist élan of industry. They wanted Egypt to have large-scale, mechanized, modern factories, and they thought that the government was best positioned to build these. In the 1960s, when Nasser adopted the idea of building an industrial public sector, these men gained an important voice in policy. They never, however, showed much interest in land reform or agriculture generally but only in land reclamation.

Land reclamation was the kind of large-scale project embodying the latest advances in science and social engineering that appealed to left-leaning officers. When Magdi Hasanayn, one of the most pro-Soviet officers, was given command of a large land reclamation scheme near Alexandria dubbed Tahrir (Liberation) Province, he tried to turn it into a socialist showcase.[27] Hasanayn proposed that reclaimed lands be farmed using peasants who would be resettled as work teams in model villages. Newsreels and pamphlets portrayed Tahrir as a utopian synthesis of collectivism, economies of scale, and modern technology. But in practice Hasanayn paid little attention to agriculture in Tahrir and focused most of his energy on his three highest priorities—"industry, industry, and industry."[28] Of the twenty-five thousand people the government settled in Tahrir, only two thousand engaged in farming; the rest worked in construction and manufacturing.[29] Conservative officers complained that Hasanayn was spending so much on factories and perquisites that the Tahrir project failed to meet its targets in land reclamation. In 1957 they engineered Hasanayn's downfall. The Tahrir project was absorbed by the Ministry of Agriculture and Sayyid Mar'i began redistributing its lands as private plots to small peasants. There had never been any danger that Tahrir would turn into a model for the collectivization of Egyptian agriculture generally.

Land reform accomplished all of the objectives the officers had set for it. It had dissipated the specter of revolution by easing rural poverty. Wages rose, landholding became more egalitarian, and between 1958 and 1965 the number of rural poor declined in both absolute and relative terms, dropping from 35 percent to 26.8 percent of rural families.[30] It had liquidated the bases for counterrevolution by eliminating large landholdings. And it had accomplished these ends without any sacrifice of agricultural productivity.

When the Free Officers took power they were enthusiastic about industry, the great symbol of modernization and the primary index of modern military power. But their high expectations were dashed by the conservatism of Egyptian businessmen, who preferred safer investments in commerce and real estate. As the officers grew impatient, they began to think of using the state directly as an instrument of industrialization. The government inaugurated its first experiment in comprehensive economic planning in 1958; both officers and technocrats were impressed by the results (despite heavy additions to the public debt). In 1960, the regime unveiled its ambitious First Five-Year Plan (1961–65), which aspired to raise the national income by 40 percent.[31]

The new plan focused on the development of industry, making steel mills and aluminum plants its key projects. Yet the planners acknowledged that progress in industry was impossible without parallel advances in agriculture. They thought that the agricultural sector would have to become the primary source of savings and industrial raw materials as well as of foodstuffs. To stimulate agriculture the planners called for major public investment in three "dream schemes": the Aswan High Dam, extended irrigation, and land reclamation. Together these projects constituted the biggest investment in rural areas in generations. On paper, the plan called for a perfect balance of agricultural and industrial development.

Implementing the plan, however, triggered many more radical changes than the planners had anticipated. Nasser and some of the other Free Officers increasingly saw economic planning as a means to dispense with Egypt's private sector elite. They suspected (and often knew) that former members of the landed aristocracy had simply transferred their assets out of agriculture and into industry. (For example, Fu'ad Sirag al-Din, Egypt's largest landowner in 1952, was its wealthiest industrialist in 1957.) So in July 1961, concurrent with the inauguration of the Five-Year Plan, Nasser struck what he hoped would be a death blow to the old elite. He ordered the nationalization of the three hundred largest private firms in the country.[32] This was quickly followed by several other nationalization decrees, including one that gave the state complete control over cotton marketing.

These nationalized firms turned public sector industry in Egypt from an experiment into a pillar of the economy overnight. Many Free Officers opposed this development, arguing that the private sector should remain the foundation of the Egyptian economy.[33] But Nasser overrode their objections and pressed for the construction of a new economic order based on Arab socialism. Nasser's socialism had no Marxist roots; it was a populist-nationalist ideology that sought to attain both equity and growth. After 1967, when it became clear that the Five-Year Plan had disrupted the economy and left Egypt heavily in debt, Nasser's own enthusiasm for socialism began to diminish. He began to back-pedal and call for greater reliance on market mechanisms.[34] But by this time much of the new economic order had already led to important changes in many sectors of the economy, including agriculture.

Nasser's socialist decrees both demanded more of agriculture (since it would have to finance the suddenly inflated public sector) and offered more to the peasantry (since they too were supposed to share the benefits of the new equality). Sayyid Mar'i resisted some of the rapid, radical changes the decrees required, so he was replaced as minister of agriculture by Abd al-Muhsin Abu al-Nur, a left-leaning military intelligence officer.[35] Under new and less conservative management, the Ministry of Agriculture expanded the already ambitious targets of the Five-Year Plan with three new programs.

First, within weeks of the industrial nationalizations a new land reform directive was issued reducing the maximum legal holding to one hundred feddans. This was intended to eliminate large landowners who had evaded application of the first agrarian reform by registering part of their holdings under the names of relatives. Implementation of the law was phased in over several years, again giving proprietors time to sell off their excess holdings, benefiting the rich peasants, and leaving landless peasants untouched.

Second, the government accelerated a series of programs designed to enhance production on peasant farms. The agrarian reform cooperatives were directed to encourage cultivators to use new seeds and more machinery by supplying them with more credit, fertilizer, and insecticides. With more modern inputs, peasants could begin to employ techniques pioneered by the Ministry of Agriculture that raised yields for some crops, particularly cotton, by as much as 45 percent.[36] On lands redistributed during the land reform, the Ministry of Agriculture required peasants to shift to a three-year crop rotation. Though this resulted in a decrease in short-term revenues, it also reduced the soil exhaustion that had resulted from the prevailing two-year rotation.[37]

Perhaps the most impressive such program was the scheme to promote "consolidated cropping." Experiments at Nawag in 1955 proved that major production increases were possible if peasants on adjacent plots planted the same crops in a common rotation cycle. Consolidated cropping increased efficiency by allowing irrigators, tractors, or cropdusters to work on large areas all at once. It also reduced losses that were common when different crops were planted in adjacent fields; pests that were common and harmless in clover plots were a serious problem in neighboring cotton fields and the heavy waterings required by rice could damage adjacent wheat crops.[38]

The third program, ultimately the most consequential, was the effort to extend the system of government "supervised" cooperatives from redistributed lands to the remainder of the agricultural sector. This program was essentially an extension of the other two since supervised cooperatives had already proven themselves the most effective mechanism for land redistribution and the extension of new production techniques.

In 1952 there were already 1,727 "voluntary" cooperatives in existence in rural Egypt.[39] Since 1910, villagers had banded together in these private cooperatives to make bulk purchases or to float low-interest loans that were not available from banks or moneylenders. In the 1950s the voluntary cooperatives had eagerly turned to the state Agricultural Credit Bank for additional credit, and their finances had increasingly become open to inspection—and manipulation—by the Ministry of Agriculture. The government now hoped to turn these associations into "supervised" cooperatives, appropriating an existing institution much as they had earlier assimilated the large landed estates.

At the government's request, the official press launched a campaign in autumn 1960 criticizing financial irregularities in the voluntary cooperatives. In December the government announced it was planning a comprehensive reorganization of these bodies. All four thousand private cooperatives that had participated in the supervised agricultural credit system were brought under tighter financial control. Central control over the assimilated cooperatives was to be exercised by a government-appointed agronomist.[40]

To encourage and sustain the participation of peasants in the new system, the government greatly expanded the volume and range of goods available through the cooperatives. The 1961 nationalizations made the government the sole source of fertilizer and pesticides. Credit extended through the cooperatives more than doubled during the 1960s and all of their loans became interest free. In fact, after 1962 the

Agricultural Credit Bank would no longer lend to individuals; to get credit, a farmer had to be a member of a cooperative.[41] Membership in a cooperative was also a precondition for receiving any land redistributed in the 1961 reform wave. New campaigns to enforce the rent control laws were launched, leading many peasants to seek the services of the arbitration committees that were authorized to resolve tenancy disputes. Cooperative membership expanded phenomenally.

Despite the increased flow of agricultural inputs, voluntary cooperatives did not immediately develop services comparable to those of supervised cooperatives. The latter commonly began with a pool of farm machinery and facilities inherited from the *'izba* (large estate), and they were likely to have one or more staffers appointed directly by the Ministry of Agriculture. Experiments begun in Bani Suwayf and Kafr al-Shaykh to see how voluntary cooperatives could be strengthened languished, and the converted voluntary cooperatives never developed the agricultural extension facilities or the degree of administrative discipline that characterized the supervised cooperatives.[42]

The new cooperative system did have a beneficial effect on agriculture, but it took time to develop. The productivity of major crops increased 40–75 percent between 1952 and 1972. But the most visible increases in productivity were in the late 1950s and 1960s: there was a five-year lag between government reform initiatives and tangible results.[43] This lag in tangible results proved important because it meant that the fruits of government investment in agriculture did not appear in time to aid in financing the industrial projects launched under the Five-Year Plan. (The failure of the cotton crop in 1961 only made things worse.) Nasser had to float short-term loans abroad to keep these projects going. Worse, the sudden increase in employment and salaries that attended his industrial drive stimulated demand for food. Agricultural production did not keep pace, so that by 1963 Egypt faced serious food shortages.[44]

By 1965, when the Five-Year Plan was scheduled to end, the government confronted a general economic crisis. Under extreme fiscal pressure, officials began to view agriculture simply as a source of revenue. Of course, agriculture had always been a major element of the state's tax base. (Cotton, after all, supplied 80 percent of export revenue until the 1950s.) But landed magnates had traditionally managed to keep agricultural taxes relatively low. Industrialists had long complained of the unfairness of this system, but it was not until Nasser assumed control over industry that he saw the need to increase agricultural taxation.[45]

The economic constriction of 1965 provided the regime with an incentive to raise taxes and the newly integrated system of rural cooperatives supplied it with the means to do so. The Egyptian state began to do what agricultural marketing boards in other African countries had been doing for generations: it paid peasants less for their crops than the government earned by reselling their produce in local or international markets. To prevent peasants from simply switching to other, untaxed, crops, the government required that all cooperative members plant certain volumes of taxable crops. The cooperatives shifted from being instruments of agricultural development into tools for revenue extraction.

In 1965 this system of compulsory deliveries was extended to all major cereals, and in 1966 to rice. Soon corn, lentils, onions, potatoes, and several smaller crops were subjected to the same regimen. At the time, officials and peasants thought that these were emergency measures, necessary to raise revenue to deal with a specific economic crisis or to finance the confrontation with Israel. But, as Aleksandr Solzhenitsyn noted, there is nothing more permanent than a temporary structure. Compulsory cropping remained a centerpiece of Egyptian agricultural policy for another twenty years.

Some scholars have described the resulting system as one of "state-controlled agriculture."[46] This is a reasonable description of the effects of land reform and compulsory deliveries, but is unfortunately broad. It permits critics of the regime to lump the Egyptian system together with the Soviet and Chinese systems. Yet even in its heyday, Egypt's Arab socialism bore less resemblance to Leninism and Maoism than it did to old Ottoman patterns of rule. The Ottomans, lacking reliable property registers or a modern bureaucracy, collected taxes from their citizens by posting assayers at strategic locations—bridges, passes, and ports. By the 1960s the Egyptian government had similarly asserted control over the strategic interstices of agriculture; it took over the cotton exporting companies, the fertilizer and pesticide factories, the major gins and mills. This gave the government enough power to tax, but not much more.

Despite its role in the cooperatives, Nasser's regime did not exercise much control at the level of the farm. Many peasants worked outside cooperatives, and those who worked within them often evaded government exactions. The effects of state policy were thus often quite different from their intended objectives. Nasser understood this problem well. As he once said, "You imagine that we simply give orders and the country is run accordingly. You are greatly mistaken."[47]

Urban Bias or Class Bias?

Throughout this century Egyptians have been debating whether their government levies a fair share of taxes on the agricultural sector. Before the 1952 coup, large landowners had rigged government policy to shelter their own estates and shift the burden of taxes onto commercial and industrial enterprises.[48] By the early 1970s some Egyptians were beginning to claim that the Free Officers had not merely redressed but reversed this imbalance, squeezing the countryside dry to finance their industrial ambitions. This criticism was made in a loud and belligerent fashion by Uthman Ahmad Uthman, who was (among other things) President Sadat's special adviser on food security. Uthman claimed that Nasser had crippled Egypt's development through his neglect of agriculture.[49] Uthman's outspokenness was unusual, but it reflected a widespread conviction among Egyptians—even among Nasserists—that government taxation had grown to the point that it left farmers with few incentives to expand production.

Foreign experts leveled even more scathing criticisms.[50] In the 1970s development experts became increasingly convinced that agricultural development was a necessary condition for successful industrialization. They worried that countries like Egypt that seemed to slight agricultural investment in favor of industry were actually crippling themselves. A World Bank study of Egypt suggested that the annual rate of taxation on cotton alone was so high that it exceeded government investment in the entire agricultural sector (see table 3-2). Heavy taxation of the peasantry, the poorest element of the population, seemed to make a mockery of Nasser's claim to champion the common man. Some foreign aid officials began to describe Nasser's agricultural policy as a thinly veiled variant of Stalinism, bleeding agriculture to finance industry.

There is a core of truth in these accusations. Many Egyptian peasants were being taxed in a manner that diminished their incentive to invest

Table 3-2. Net Effect of Agricultural Price Transfers, 1973–76
Millions of Egyptian pounds

Item	1973	1974	1975	1976
Transfers out of agriculture	178.8	313.8	183.0	192.4
Transfers to treasury of cotton organization	64.8	136.8	54.0	92.4
Exchange rate gains	114.0	177.0	129.0	100.0
Transfers into agriculture	101.6	106.4	232.8	160.6
Direct subsidies	15.8	12.7	101.5	56.8
Public sector investments in agriculture	51.0	54.0	84.0	49.0
Current expenditure of Ministry of Agriculture	16.4	19.8	21.3	26.0
Current expenditure of Ministry of Irrigation	18.4	19.9	26.0	28.8
Net flow to agriculture	−77.2	−207.4	49.8	−31.8

Source: Khalid Ikram, *Egypt: Economic Management in a Period of Transition* (Johns Hopkins University Press, 1980), p. 212.

in additional production. However, the charge that Nasser was a kind of petty African Stalin, who in the rush to industrialize the regime was bleeding agriculture dry, is misleading. It is important to understand just who lost and who benefited from Egyptian agricultural policy. A detailed examination of that policy will give a better picture of whose voice, and which ideas, influenced its formation in the past—and today.

For Egyptian peasants, compulsory deliveries seem like confiscations. They are not concerned about who the specific beneficiary of their produce is, when they themselves do not share in the benefits. But to officials responsible for agricultural policy, the question of distribution matters. A study of the distribution of agricultural revenues in Egypt reveals several surprises; industry and the state benefited far less than many observers have alleged.

A large share of the revenues appropriated through compulsory deliveries and other government regulations did not enhance state revenues. The state consistently paid peasants higher prices for wheat and corn than those prevailing in international markets. (But these inflated prices failed to stimulate domestic production because they were still less than the relative price of what farmers could earn cultivating alternative crops, particularly fodder, fruits, and vegetables.) Price controls on onions, groundnuts, and sugarcane did not benefit the state, but urban consumers. Official controls only generated government revenue from two crops—cotton and rice.[51]

Even on these two crops, the state's income was less than many have alleged. The Egyptian government has long overvalued its exchange rate—often fantastically so. In this way it lowers the cost of imports, in effect subsidizing factories that import machinery or individual consumers who import food. The cost of this subsidy is paid by exporters, who receive less for their products than they would at more realistic exchange rates. The chief exporter injured by the policy was the state, which sacrificed part of its revenue from agricultural exports. Overvalued exchange rates consistently understated the actual value of the receipts from cotton exports by half.[52] In this way a quarter of the potential revenue from cotton exports was indirectly transferred to consumers of imported goods, including farmers themselves.[53]

Besides overvaluing trade, the government also tried to protect the man in the street from sharp increases in the cost of living by charging less for cotton in domestic trade, thereby lowering the cost of textiles, an important wage good.[54] By the mid-1970s controls on cotton had reduced producer incomes by around £E 1.2 billion. Of this transfer, 85 percent went to consumers; only 15 percent accrued to the treasury.[55] This was a consistent pattern in Egyptian policies of the period; they were less successful at extracting revenue for the government than in transferring income from one section of the population to another. For example, customs policies had the effect of promoting investment in industry and trade while discouraging it in agriculture (nontradable) and housing.[56]

These policies do not resemble those of Stalinist primitive accumulation as much as they do what scholars have dubbed "urban bias." In many Third World countries, government policies tend to reflect the interests of urbanites, even at the expense of the larger rural population. "The actions of the powerful, in almost all developing countries, have shifted income-per-person—inefficiencies and inequities notwithstanding—from rural to urban areas. Agriculture, with 70 percent of workers and 40–45 percent of GNP, has in most poor countries received barely 20 percent of investment—but has, directly and indirectly, been induced or forced to contribute considerably more to saving. Public action renders farm products cheaper and farm purchases dearer, in domestic markets, than they would have been if such action were neutral. Education, while geared towards urban needs, transfers bright rural children to urban areas."[57] Egyptian policies include many familiar instruments of urban bias. Overvalued exchange rates promote living standards in the cities, where imports are far more important than in the countryside. Protective tariffs shield urban industries from having to compete with the surge of imports; agriculture enjoys no such protection. Government food subsidies also work to the advantage of city dwellers since rural people produce much of their food themselves and buy less from the market.

The idea of urban bias has gained currency among Egyptian intellectuals. Some think the problem has deep, cultural roots (they invoke the arguments of the French geographer Xavier de Planhol, who argued that Islam is fundamentally a religion of the cities and that Islamic societies have always fostered the dominance of the city over the countryside).[58] Egyptian studies suggest that in the 1960s and 1970s, not only did economic growth in rural areas lag behind the cities, but a growing share of the rural population lived near the poverty line.[59]

No doubt the hypothesis of urban bias sharpens understanding of political economy in Egypt, focusing on a terrible problem. But it is only a hypothesis, a tool for measuring reality, not a pigeonhole to cram it in. Too many observers have seized on it as the definitive explanation of what is happening in Egypt. Closer analysis suggests that the urban bias hypothesis supplies only a rough guide to tendencies in Egypt and needs to be qualified—or even revised—in important ways.

The hypothesis that there is an urban bias should be tempered by an appreciation of the level of Egyptian public investment in agriculture, for in reality the state endowed as well as taxed. The oft-repeated claim that Nasser deliberately and consistently neglected agriculture is simply false. The Big Push Five-Year Plan of 1961 embodied a strategy of balanced growth in which industry and agriculture were supposed to stimulate each other by growing at the same rate, so they were allotted commensurate levels of investment.[60] In the 1960s public investment in land reclamation, irrigation and drainage, and other aspects of agriculture was the highest it had ever been. Of course, some fraction of the cost of the High Dam, which was a water storage as well as a hydroelectric project, should be added to this tally. Essam Muntasser calculated that government investment in agriculture between 1960 and 1971 totaled £E 893.3 million; taxes on agriculture and profits from cotton and rice exports in the same period amounted to £E 912.1 million.[61] In Nasser's day, the government put almost as much into agriculture as it took out of that sector.

At the village level, government investment was even more evident in its commitment to distribute modern agricultural inputs (fertilizers, pesticides, upgraded seeds). Under Nasser these inputs were distributed at cost, but later, particularly after the rise in petroleum prices in 1973, the government fixed their prices and subsidized them. The government inaugurated these subsidies partly in an attempt to create a large market for the domestic fertilizer and pesticide industries. The regime's interest in developing local industry often spun off tangible benefits for many peasants.[62]

As early as 1962 the government began to offer subsidized credit to farmers through the agricultural cooperatives. Where previously tight collateral requirements and stiff terms limited access to bank credit to the rural elite, now most peasants qualified for a loan to cover the cost of seed and inputs. They were also eligible to apply for larger loans to finance purchases of livestock or agricultural machinery. In their first year these public programs generated loans worth £E 38 million. By 1978 they had expanded to £E 133 million.[63]

The state's investment in agriculture was not constant or uniform. The 1967 defeat by Israel forced a diversion of funds to the war effort. In the next couple of years construction of the Aswan High Dam was completed and funds for the construction of public works were cut back. Real investment in irrigation and drainage declined by half between 1969 and 1971. When Anwar Sadat succeeded Nasser in 1971, he reduced investment in agriculture even further. Agriculture's share of national investment dropped from 20 percent in 1965 to about 6 percent in 1975.[64]

Sadat did not glibly decide to restrict investment in agriculture; the decision was forced on him. He was at least as much interested in agriculture as his predecessor and suspected that it might be the key to Egypt's future development. But when he came to power in 1970 the Egyptian economy was already strapped and would deteriorate further with the onset of the world food crisis in 1972. Sadat himself claimed Egypt's desperate economic circumstances were part of what provoked him to launch the October 1973 war: "Our economic situation, six days before the battle, was so critical that I called a meeting of the National Security Council and told them we had reached zero. The army cost £E 100 million a month, and all our tax receipts in one year were £E 200 million, just two months' expense for the armed forces. There was nothing left for us but to enter the battle, whatever happened."[65] A few months after the war, in 1974, Sadat actually announced his intention to launch a green revolution, to encourage adoption of new agricultural technologies and accelerate land reclama-

Figure 3-1. Effect of Government Intervention on Agriculture, 1960–85

Millions of Egyptian pounds

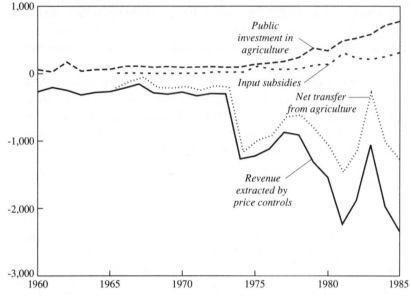

Source: Jean-Jacques Dethier, *Trade, Exchange Rate and Agricultural Pricing Policies in Egypt,* vol. 1 (Washington: World Bank, 1989), pp. 212 and 219.

tion. But this intention was not matched by any increase of appropriations; the money just was not there.

Stagnant public investment (actually declining in real terms) had a direct effect on production. In the 1960s and 1970s Egyptian agricultural output mirrored changes in public investment even more clearly than it reflected changes in market prices.[66] But in the early 1970s, Egyptian farmers were being squeezed from both sides. Not only was the government investing less, it was extracting more in real terms. The primary commodities boom of the 1970s drove up the value of many crops, but the Egyptian government did not pass this increase along to farmers. Desperate for revenue, it set price controls to maximize its own income. The effective rate of taxation on agriculture increased sharply (see figure 3-1). In response, Egyptian peasants worked even harder at evading government controls. Between 1970 and 1975 cotton production declined from 2.3 million bales to 1.7 million.[67]

The consequences in the countryside were not merely a downturn of agricultural statistics but acute human hardship. During the early years of land reform, and even during the radicalization of agricultural policy in the early 1960s, the standard of living in the countryside continuously improved. Between 1958 and 1964 (years for which full statistics are available) the number of rural poor declined in both absolute and relative terms, from 35 percent to 26.8 percent of the rural population. But after 1966 this trend reversed. By 1974 the number of rural poor—those who could not afford minimum nutritional requirements—had grown to nearly 6 million people, or 44 percent of the rural population.[68]

Thus, the real crisis of Egyptian agriculture developed not under Nasser but under Sadat. Sadat, understandably, blamed this on problems inherited from his predecessor, and Western observers who favored Sadat's foreign policies have been eager to agree.

The economics of public investment moderate the degree of urban bias that can be ascribed to Egypt. The politics of the village do the same. At the heart of the hypothesis of an urban bias is a political proposition that city dwellers find it easier to put pressure on the state than on rural folks. While this may seem true of the urban and rural populations when they are viewed as aggregate lumps, it is not valid when they are examined in detail. Unlike the French peasants who Marx once claimed were an undifferentiated mass, "much as potatoes in a sack form a sack of potatoes," Egyptian villagers differ sharply in their economic activities and political orientation.[69] While the majority may be passive victims of government policy, a subsection has become politically influential and has had a decisive impact on both the formulation and execution of agricultural policy.

One quick way to identify differences among Egyptian villagers is to look at the mix of crops they grow. Naturally, all villagers want to grow the most profitable crop mix imaginable. This means that they have to calculate the combined effects of the relative prices of crops in the market on the one hand and of government intervention and taxation on the other. In the 1970s it was easy to make this calculation for cotton, which was both highly taxed and relatively unprofitable. Wheat was also unattractive because although it was not taxed it was relatively unprofitable. Rice also presented a mixed picture, since it was moderately priced but heavily taxed. Three types of crops, however, were lightly taxed and highly profitable—*birsim* (clover fodder), fruits, and vegetables.[70] These were the crops that most peasants aspired to cultivate.

Yet not all villagers were equally capable of planting these three ideal crops. For some, geographic and technological considerations restrained their selection. Farmers in Giza and Minufiyya, within what agronomists call the Cairo vegetable zone, cultivated a high share of Egypt's fruits and vegetables because their districts enjoyed proximity to markets and long traditions of skill in these crops. There were also social and economic restraints that compelled people to grow less than ideal crop mixtures. Fruit trees, for example, can take years to mature; no poor peasant could afford to plant his plot with oranges and then wait five years for the first harvest.

Poor peasants were also vulnerable to government pressure about what to plant. They were attracted to agricultural cooperatives since membership assured them of access to fertilizer, pesticides, credit, and farming machinery. Most important, they had to become members of a cooperative in order to be eligible to receive land under the agrarian reform program. Yet part of the price of membership was accepting the government-defined schedule of crop rotation, which typically kept the land tied up in wheat and cotton for long periods. For poorer peasants, who needed state support and lacked the capital to thrust themselves into horticulture, the benefits of membership just outweighed (if barely) the burdens.

For richer peasants, however, the calculus was quite different. Since they had their own capital, the incentives for joining cooperatives were much weaker, and they tended to remain aloof from the cooperatives in order to retain the freedom to plant as they saw fit. They thereby avoided low-return crops like cotton and focused their energies on cultivating high-value vegetables or raising livestock. Typically, rich peasants prefer to grow fruit, vegetables, and other high-value crops, or to raise cattle and poultry.[71] For example, half of all citrus fruit is grown on farms of twenty feddans or larger.[72]

In interviews, Egyptian farmers are brutally eloquent about their reasons for evading the official cropping system. One explained to a newspaper that if he planted cotton he could actually count on losing £E 53 per feddan. He chose to plant high-value flowers and medicinal plants instead, asking "Why tire yourself out?"[73]

Yet, though rich peasants generally stayed outside the cooperatives, they often managed to enjoy most of the benefits that were supposed to be contingent on membership. For example, the strongest incentive for joining a cooperative was to gain access to land from the agrarian reform program. But in practice, rich peasants were the major beneficiaries of the land reform. The leading authority on Egypt's agrarian reform, Mahmoud Abdel-Fadil, has established that "the most notable trend over the period 1952–65 has been the steady improvement in the relative position (increase in *numbers* and *acreage*) of the medium-sized properties, and in particular owners of 20 to 50 feddans. As a matter of fact these medium landowners owned almost *one-third* of Egypt's cultivated land in 1965, while they made up only 5.2 % of the total number of landowners."[74] Some rich peasants did join cooperatives in order to claim land, but more often they bought plots from large landholders in distress sales held to avoid confiscation.[75]

In an even more disturbing manner, the rich peasants contrived to gain access to the subsidized inputs—fertilizer, pesticides, and fuel—that the state distributed through the cooperatives. Cooperative members were told how many acres to plant in cotton, on which dates, and just how much fertilizer to apply. The state delivered these inputs in specific amounts with instructions to apply them to the crops on specific dates. Yet, because cotton and other major crops were heavily taxed, many peasants did not bother following instructions but diverted these fertilizers and pesticides for use on alternative, higher-profit crops or sold them on the black market. A large share of the farm chemicals traded on the black market wound up being sold to rich peasants, who were technically not entitled to subsidized inputs but who could put them to profitable use on their own fields. Reliable studies of this diversion are rare, but one estimate is that 10–20 percent of the total value of fertilizer distributed through the cooperatives wound up being sold on the black market at markups of 150 percent (in Lower Egypt) to 300 percent (Upper Egypt) over the subsidized price.[76]

Similar diversions afflicted government-subsidized credit programs as well. The state-controlled Agricultural Bank had supplied commercial loans to farmers since the 1930s. But such credit had always been channeled primarily to wealthier farmers because they were able to offer more solid collateral and (it was thought) presented less of a credit risk. Moreover, the costs of administering loans are relatively fixed, so bankers generally prefer to make a few large loans rather than many small ones. When the government began to offer subsidized loans through the cooperatives in 1961, there was a real break with this practice. The great majority of peasants now had access to interest-free, short-term crop loans.

But most peasants did not gain access to medium- and long-term investment credits, because for these loans the cooperatives employed the same kind of criteria formerly used by the Agricultural Bank. The really critical investment credits, for livestock and agricultural machinery, were predicated on property guarantees. The less land a farmer owned, the less money he could borrow.[77] In the case of loans for machinery purchases, only farmers who owned a minimum of ten feddans could even apply. As a result, "small peasants, who represent the majority of debtors (83–85 per cent) and the most needy, get half the credit advanced by the cooperative system, while medium and large landowners get the other half. . . . When the government tried to check this trend by imposing a rate of interest of 4 per cent on loans advanced to holders of ten feddans and more, many large landowners reacted by dividing their holdings into plots of less than ten feddans to benefit from the exemption from interest."[78] As of 1978, 2.6 million peasants owning less than five feddans were receiving £E 71 million in government loans, 56 percent of the total available credits. But 195,000 farmers who owned five feddans or more collected £E 55 million, or 44 percent of the total.[79]

Some experts argue that these inequities are desirable, since the larger share of inputs flows to farmers of proven productivity. It is true that rich peasants, who owned five to ten feddans, were the most productive in Egypt. They had enough land to enjoy economies of scale and to justify the use of mechanized harvesting; they had enough capital to afford more water, fertilizer, and improved seeds.[80] By the late 1970s there were 128,000 such rich peasants, forming 4 percent of the farming population but cultivating 13 percent of arable land.

But rich peasants were not the only beneficiaries of the inequitable distribution of input and credit. Corruption in the cooperatives and black market resale of state-subsidized inputs augmented the fortunes of village notables, the rural gentry, and agrarian capitalists. (Table 3-3 defines these elements of the rural population.) These groups, consisting of farmers who owned more than ten feddans, had to hire laborers to work their estates. Compared to the family members who worked the lands of rich peasants, contract laborers were less industrious and productive. As a group, these wealthy strata controlled more than twice as much land as rich peasants and probably consumed a proportional share of agricultural resources. Thus, inequitable distri-

Table 3-3. Rural Class Structure, 1961

Class	*Definition*
Peasants	Cultivators who own less than ten feddans and primarily employ family labor
Landless peasants	Own no land; earn a living through a combination of sharecropping, employment on public works projects (canal digging), and casual farm labor (in 1961, comprised 37 percent of farming families)
Poor peasants	Own less than one feddan, too little to support a family (comprised 16 percent of farming families in 1961 and owned 3.4 percent of total cultivated area)
Small peasants	Own one to three feddans, just enough to support a family, and supplement their holdings by renting additional land (comprised 25.8 percent of farming families in 1961 and owned 18.5 percent of cultivated area)
Middle peasants	Own three to five feddans (comprised 10.5 percent of farming families in 1961 and owned 15.9 percent of cultivated area)
Rich peasants	Own five to ten feddans, producing sufficient capital for reinvestment and requiring some hiring of non-family labor (comprised 6.6 percent of farming families in 1961 and owned 17.7 percent of cultivated area)
Agrarian elite	Farmers who own more than ten feddans and hire laborers to do most cultivation; dominate the politics of rural areas (in 1961 comprised 3.5 percent of farming families and owned 44.5 percent of cultivated area)
Village notables	Generally own less than fifty feddans and reside in villages (formed the overwhelming majority within the agrarian elite in 1961)
Rural gentry	Generally own more than fifty feddans and reside on their estates or in provincial capitals; include members of the clans that traditionally dominate rural politics
Agrarian capitalists	Absentee landlords who reside in major cities

Source: Mahmoud Abdel-Fadil, *Development, Income Distribution, and Social Change in Rural Egypt (1952–1970)* (Cambridge University Press, 1975), pp. 14 and 44.

bution of farm inputs benefited the productive rich peasants, but it also squandered resources on their richer but less efficient neighbors.[81]

The seventy thousand farmers who owned more than ten feddans formed an agrarian elite that played an important role in local and national politics. (Indeed, it was their political influence, rather than their economic accomplishments, that permitted them to tap into the benefits the state distributed in rural areas.) This had been the pattern in the countryside for centuries.[82] In fact, many members of the agrarian elite were descended from three hundred prominent clans that have dominated politics in Egypt's villages throughout the twentieth century.[83] These clans controlled all the major political offices outside the major cities. Their members controlled 71 percent of the seats on provincial councils and 55 percent of district offices.[84] They supplied the bulk of the *'umad*, the village mayors. As Nasser built his new order in the countryside, they learned to dominate the cooperative councils as well.

They often exercised their power indirectly. For example, when the state took over the cooperative system in the early 1960s, it stipulated that a majority of cooperative board members had to own less than five feddans. However, the prominent clans were able to circumvent this restriction by working through poorer members of the family or land-poor clients who were eligible for board membership. Although a professional civil servant (typically an agronomist) was assigned by the Ministry of Agriculture to supervise the cooperatives, these bureaucratic appointees rarely managed to exert much authority. Real control over the cooperatives lay with the village elites who tended to dole out government resources in keeping with their own ideas about patronage.[85]

The power of the agrarian elite not only influenced the operation of the cooperatives, it reshaped and recast all government policies into a locally palatable form. Although the government determined how much water flowed through the irrigation canals into each province, the agrarian elite decided how much was actually directed to each village and farm.[86] Perhaps most important, this elite softened—and sometimes frustrated—the application of the land reform.

The first land reform of 1952 targeted only landed magnates, but the reform of 1961 (which dropped the maximum limit for landholding to 100 feddans) threatened to cut into the holdings of the agrarian elite. Many evaded this limit by redistributing the land title to other members of their clan. One notable who owned 477 feddans managed to keep his holdings intact as a productive unit by parceling out titles among his five grandsons and eight female relatives. He had not violated the law in any way, but he made a laughingstock of the maximum property limits.[87] In some areas notables were strong enough to compel local bureaucrats to overlook even more undisguised violations of the agrarian reform. The land reform in effect since 1969, which limits the maximum landholding to 50 feddans, has never been applied in even the most cursory manner.

Just how haphazardly land reform had been prosecuted was brought home to the Egyptian public in 1966 by an incident in the village of Kamshish. A local notable family, which had maintained hundreds of feddans in violation of the agrarian reform law, ordered the murder of a village activist who had tried to initiate an investigation of the family's power. Cairo magazines that investigated the story documented the extensive violations of the land law that had provoked the incident. These revelations stung the regime into action and in May the government formed a special tribunal, the Higher Committee for the Liquidation of Feudalism (HCLF), to move against those who violated the land reform.

The HCLF quickly determined that these violations were not confined to Kamshish but were common nationally. Ali Sabri, one of the officers on the committee, estimated that "on the average, each province had twenty to thirty families whose members either evaded the agrarian reforms, controlled the village administration and party organs, or exercised oppressive influence."[88] He guessed there were four hundred to five hundred such families nationwide. In some of the cases it uncovered, the committee ordered the confiscation of lands owned in excess of legal limits or even the arrest of their owners. But committee members were themselves divided over how far to push this campaign. Abd al-Hakim Amir, the chairman of the HCLF, himself the son of a rural notable, insisted the committee should not investigate anyone who owned less than one hundred feddans. He argued that unless the assault was confined to the very largest families, the regime would be left with only "the leftist solution" of abolishing private property. Kamal Rif'at and some other radicals on the committee countered that to limit the investigation in this way would ensure the continued nonapplication of land reform, since many of the worst offenders did not appear to own more than one hundred feddans.[89]

The debate between Amir and his opponents was never resolved. Deadlocked, the committee suspended its activities in September, four months after its formation. By the spring of 1967, as Egypt drifted toward war with Israel, all interest in reopening an antagonistic social wound had evaporated.

The regime had good reason for avoiding a breach with the agrarian elite. A serious move against them probably would have required the deployment of troops in the countryside and the complete reconstruction of rural administration. It also would have cost the regime much political support. The rural notables did not oppose the regime on any national issue except agricultural policy and had generally been happy to collaborate with the government. They played an invaluable role in maintaining order in rural areas, using their powers of patronage to prevent peasant poverty from being translated into demands for political change. Some scholars have gone as far as to claim that the agrarian elite formed a type of second stratum, a mediating group that bridged the gap between the political class and the masses.[90]

The initial activities of the HCLF were very much an exception to the general pattern of relations between the government and the agrarian elite. At the very least, the regime tended to tolerate the power of the village notables. But over time, the trend was for officials in Cairo increasingly to solicit advice and support from the agrarian elite.

After the 1967 War with Israel, Nasser saw that the state lacked the resources to pioneer economic development alone and encouraged increasing participation by the private sector. He took several steps to reassure the agrarian elite and promote their role in the economy. Immediately after the war he reappointed Sayyid Mar'i as minister of agriculture. The organization of agricultural cooperative boards was revised in a manner that secured the position of the rich peasants. (From that time on, board members had to be literate and four-fifths could own up to ten feddans.)[91] Certain lands that had been sequestered without due process were returned to their owners. By the time of Nasser's death in September 1970, all but three thousand of the sixty thousand feddans confiscated by the HCLF had been restored to their owners.[92]

Nasser's regime had never really abandoned its hopes for agricultural development. But during the late 1960s and early 1970s, the general economic crisis in society forced a net exploitation of the sector. This exploitation resembled urban bias but it was always combined with an element of class bias. Rich peasants and the agrarian elite worked the system so that they escaped its exactions and tapped its benefits. This trend would accelerate in the 1970s, as the power of the agrarian elite grew.

Rural Growth with Agricultural Stagnation

In September 1970 Nasser died and was succeeded by his vice-president, Anwar Sadat, who encouraged a major extension of the power of the agrarian elite. Few Egyptians thought that Sadat was a serious politician, so he began to search for constituencies that would support his personal power. He began to recruit a following among conservative elites, many of them outside the traditional centers of power in the officer corps and the Cairo bureaucracy. Sadat took office convinced that the only way to solve Egypt's fiscal crisis was to stimulate private-sector initiative. He continued, and greatly expanded, Nasser's policy of returning certain sequestered properties in an attempt to restore the confidence of investors. He hoped to encourage Gulf oil princes and Western businessmen to bring their capital and technology into Egypt. In 1973 he declared a new policy of economic opening (*infitah*) that removed many barriers to private investment.[93] He quickly built up a loyal following among businessmen, farmers, and Western governments.

One of the constituencies that embraced Sadat was the agrarian elite. Sadat had himself been born into a rich peasant family from Minufiyya and he shared many of the attitudes toward property, religion, and authority characteristic of this group. He issued a series of decrees that consolidated the power of the agrarian elite in rural administration. For example, minimum property requirements were instituted for candidates seeking election as village mayors. As a result, the number of peasants owning fewer than five feddans who served on the boards of cooperatives or in provincial assembles declined steadily during the 1970s.[94]

Sadat also greatly expanded the voice of the agrarian elite in Cairo. Since 1952 it had been government policy to assure peasants and workers 50 percent of the seats in Parliament. However, for electoral purposes anyone who owned less than twenty-five feddans was considered a peasant or worker, so most of these seats had gone to rural notables. Sadat diluted peasant representation further in 1974 by declaring that anyone owning fewer than fifty feddans was a peasant.[95] Members of the agrarian elite soon formed one of the largest and most important blocs in Parliament.

This agriculturalists' lobby in Cairo began to influence the character of government legislation. In 1973 when the government proposed exempting small peasants (originally, owners of three feddans or less) from a series of taxes and customs duties, they succeeded in having these benefits extended to all farmers regardless of the size of their holdings.[96] In 1975 they submitted new legislation that enhanced the power of landowners at the expense of sharecroppers and tenants. It passed after only six hours of debate.[97]

The agrarian elite's influence grew so rapidly, it began to worry Sadat. The primary spokesman for this elite was Ahmad Yunis, the head of the Federation of Agricultural Cooperatives. Using the federation's funds, Yunis had built a vast network of patronage that included many members of the national political elite and a third of the deputies in Parliament. Sadat's executives wanted to put this network at the disposal of the president's own Misr party, but Yunis insisted on remaining autonomous and toyed with the idea of throwing his support behind the formation of an opposition Wafd party. Officials in the intelligence services suspected Yunis was grooming himself for a bid for the presidency.[98]

In 1976 Sadat dissolved the Federation of Cooperatives while his staff engineered press campaigns and court proceedings that, together, ruined Yunis. Within a year Sadat had transferred the credit, fertilizer, and pesticide supplying mechanisms of the cooperatives to a new network of village banks under the central control of the Principal Bank for Development and Agricultural Credit (PBDAC) in Cairo. These measures curbed the independence of the agrarian elite, without reducing any of their privileges. On the contrary, the new village banks, which were instructed to insist on solid collateral before issuing loans, catered even more narrowly to the needs of rural notables.[99] This enabled Sadat to expand his following among the agrarian elite and to pack them into the backbenches of his own party.

One of the places where the growing influence of the rural elite made itself felt was in the government's crop pricing policy. From 1974, the government began to raise its procurement prices. In 1975 it raised the price it paid farmers for cotton substantially. These measures dropped the rate of implicit taxation on agriculture to about 17 percent by 1980.[100] However, crop prices were not really central to the agenda of the agrarian elite, many of whom grew unregulated crops. Much more of their energy was spent on the question of government investment in agriculture.

Figure 3-2. Public Investment in Agriculture, 1965–80

Millions of Egyptian pounds

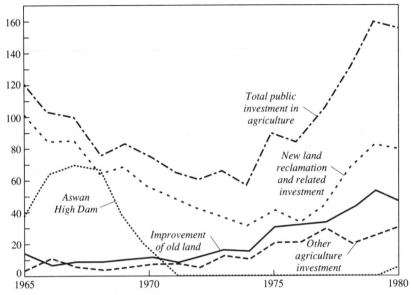

Source: Joachim von Braun and Hartwig de Haen, *The Effects of Food Price and Subsidy Policies on Egyptian Agriculture* (Washington: International Food Policy Research Institute, 1983), p. 41.

After 1975 the Egyptian government raised its budget for agricultural development sharply. This was made possible partly by a dramatic increase in Egypt's hard currency receipts. After the 1973 War with Israel, Egypt enjoyed an increasing flow of aid from the United States and the oil-rich Arab monarchs of the Gulf states. By 1975 its negotiations with Israel permitted the restoration of revenues from the reopening of the Suez Canal and its Sinai oil fields (both had been lost in the 1967 War). This boom eased—at least temporarily—the fiscal crisis. The government could afford to finance food imports out of general revenues rather than from agricultural taxation.[101] The state was also able to designate a relatively larger share of its investment budget for agriculture. (Figure 3-2 illustrates the absolute rise of government investment in agriculture.)

Very little of this new investment found its way into major projects (like the High Dam) of the kind that had been popular in the 1960s. In fact, much of it went into increasingly lavish government subsidies for rural districts. All the traditionally subsidized goods—agricultural machinery, fertilizers, pesticides, and fuel—were made even cheaper.

New subsidies were created to support poultry and livestock farming. An array of consumer subsidies that had once been restricted to urban areas was made available in the villages. For example, after 1977 imported flour, once supplied exclusively to city bakeries, was widely distributed in the countryside. By 1980 government-owned country stores accounted for over half of all wheat sales.[102] Although the government's food pricing policy showed a moderate urban bias, the combined effects of controlled food prices and subsidies actually showed a rural bias.[103]

Sadat's economic liberalization policies and the increasing availability of petroleum revenues combined to benefit the village in ways no one had anticipated. This was particularly evident in the case of workers' remittances.

Before 1967 the government, fearing that higher salaries available in the oil-rich Gulf countries and Libya would lure away Egypt's best-educated professionals and trigger a brain drain, maintained a series of travel and exchange restrictions that made it difficult for Egyptians to work abroad. However, officials eventually realized that restricting the movement of talented Egyptians both fueled employment problems at home and cut off a potential source of hard currency revenue. Slowly under Nasser, and rapidly under Sadat, the government removed its barriers and began to encourage Egyptians to seek work in the oil states.[104]

The first wave of emigrant workers consisted of urban professionals—teachers, doctors, and administrators. But after the 1973 revolution in oil prices, Egyptian construction workers and craftsmen (plumbers, electricians, and artisans) began to move to the Gulf states to exploit rapidly rising wages and greatly increased demand for employment in massive public works projects. In 1980 the outbreak of the Iran-Iraq War triggered a third wave of migration as Baghdad recruited hundreds of thousands of unskilled Egyptians to work in agriculture and as simple manual laborers to replace Iraqis conscripted into the military. (Jordan, Iraq's ally, also began to import Egyptian laborers at this time.)[105]

Workers leaving Egypt not only eased domestic unemployment, they earned far more than they could at home. In 1976 the value of officially recorded remittances from Egyptian expatriates had already reached $755 million. By 1983 the value had soared to $3.3 billion, the

Table 3-4. Officially Recorded Remittances, 1973–84

Year	Millions of U.S. dollars	Percent of gross domestic product	Percent of exports	Percent of imports
1973	123	1.33	11.00	16.54
1974	310	2.89	20.45	13.18
1975	455	3.64	32.45	11.57
1976	842	5.25	55.33	22.12
1977	988	4.71	57.83	20.52
1978	1,824	7.30	104.99	27.12
1979	2,269	12.73	123.33	59.13
1980	2,791	12.63	91.60	57.43
1981	2,230	9.29	68.98	25.39
1982	2,116	7.26	67.82	23.31
1983	3,315	10.44	103.13	32.26
1984	3,611	n.a.	114.90	33.50

Source: Nazli Choucri, "The Hidden Economy: A New View of Remittances in the Arab World," *World Development,* vol. 14 (1986), pp. 700–03.
   n.a. Not available.

equivalent of 9 percent of the gross national product and as much as the combined contribution of oil ($2.4 billion) and the Suez Canal ($974 million).[106] The government grew increasingly anxious to capture a share of this, to tap into the funds that were being saved abroad or that workers brought home in the form of commodities purchased overseas.

The first and most important step in this direction was the "own exchange" law issued in 1974. This law encouraged Egyptians to send their salaries home, permitting them to bring large volumes of foreign currency into the country, to open foreign currency accounts at Egyptian banks, and to pay for imports directly in hard currency without having to change money through official channels. This law had the intended effect; billions of dollars in hard currency began to flow back into Egypt (see table 3-4). The value of officially recorded remittances rocketed and the value of unrecorded remittances, cash brought back to Egypt and exchanged on the black market or spent directly in the nascent dollar economy, may have been even larger.[107]

In general this movement of labor (out) and money (in) was a great boon. More than any other development during the years of *infitah*, it was responsible for the rise in wages, the expansion of construction, and the availability of new imports. But its consequences were more extensive than many had anticipated. It affected politics by giving

Egypt a means of tapping into the wealth of the Gulf states without requiring it to maintain a foreign policy acceptable to the Gulf rulers, leading to a Middle Eastern version of "bonanza politics."[108] It affected social life by drawing male wage earners away from households and leaving their wives in charge of the family. It raised the social standing of anyone whose skills or connections made him a candidate for migration.[109]

The effects of migration took some time to percolate into rural areas, but when they did they were revolutionary. The moment laborers (especially construction workers) began to leave Cairo, country boys began to move into the city to take up the jobs they had relinquished. Villagers from middle Egypt, who had long-standing ties to cousins in Libya, began to leave to take advantage of the oil boom there. Eventually, rural labor bosses found ways to ship their clients directly to the Gulf states. Between 1972 and 1979 perhaps a half million agricultural workers left Egypt.[110] Even greater numbers left in response to the demand in Iraq for unskilled labor.

The first to leave were the landless peasants. But by 1980 many rural families had started to send one son, sometimes two if the household could spare the labor. Few of these planned to resettle permanently abroad; the work was arduous and living conditions harsh. Rather, they wanted to work for a few years, save up a nest egg, and return to Egypt. When they returned to Egypt, many spent their savings on real estate, pickup trucks, tractors, or other investments that could serve as the foundation of a small business. They showed a strong tendency to leave farming for other businesses upon their return home.[111]

Rich peasant families also might send one or more spare sons to work in the oil countries. Their remittances were often invested in agriculture. Many bought pumps or tractors (both for use on the farm and as a source of rental income) or acquired additional land. A construction boom swept the countryside as thousands of villagers sought to move from their old mud homes to new brick residences. The price of nonagricultural land increased by a factor of five in the late 1970s.[112] The demand for housing materials led to a major problem of land loss (*tajrif*) as fertile topsoil was scooped up, transported to kilns, and baked into bricks. By the early 1980s seventy thousand feddans of fertile land were being sacrificed annually in this way. The government outlawed the practice and began to use helicopters to detect infringements.[113]

Not everyone benefited equally from these changes. Although landless laborers were quick to migrate, studies show that poor peasants—those who owned less than the two feddans necessary to feed a family and yet enough to still tie them to the soil—were the least mobile element of the rural population. They often lacked the funds necessary to obtain visas and passage. They were trapped on their farms and remained miserable.[114]

But even those who could not leave Egypt themselves benefited from the way migration drained surplus labor from the village and forced a restructuring of employment patterns and wages. The landless peasants who supplied the mass of labor necessary during rice planting or the cotton harvest, and who spent the rest of the year cleaning canals and irrigation ditches, left the village for better-paying jobs elsewhere. The smaller work force that remained had to be paid more, either to draw them away from their own farms or to hold them in the country against the lure of jobs abroad. In the twenty-five years before 1973–74, real wages in agriculture had increased by only around 1 percent annually. During the six years between 1967 and 1973 they actually declined. Then they turned around; between 1973–74 and 1984, wages of adult males rose two and a half times.[115] This increase did not eliminate the attraction of migration; even domestic construction workers still earned three to five times as much as agricultural laborers. Yet real wages increased faster in agriculture than in any other sector of the economy except petroleum.[116]

As increasing numbers of peasants began to work abroad, send sons to the city, or supplement their farm income with small business profits, the character of the whole village changed. By 1977 only 50 percent of total rural household income came from agriculture; nearly one-third came from off-farm wages.[117] "Egyptian agriculture [had] become an economy of part-timers. Male, female, and child workers [took] off time from their principal activities in government employment, home animal husbandry, or school attendance to perform farm tasks. By 1988, what had been one job slot fifteen years earlier now employed numerous moonlighters, and increasingly they worked on a cash basis."[118]

From the late 1970s onward, the rural population enjoyed higher prices for their crops and higher wages for their labor, and they tapped into the lavish stream of hard currency remitted from abroad. Taken together, these changes greatly diminished the problem of rural poverty. The landless were precisely the people who first took advantage of the opportunity to migrate for work. In 1973, 60 percent of the rural population had lived below the poverty line; by 1982 only 18 percent still languished at this level.[119]

The new wave of rural prosperity was not always received with applause. Pundits in Cairo worried that it was undermining the foundations of productivity in agriculture. They warned that workers were leaving farming, land was being abandoned or degraded, and the hard-working peasants of old were being replaced by a new generation interested primarily in consumption.[120] Some raised an alarm that the old productive village was being replaced by a new consuming village characterized by "the flight of agricultural labor abroad. . .the sharp rise in labor wages, the invasion of consumer commodities. . .the change to urban styles of building including multiple-story residences, the growth of non-agricultural economic activities, the growth of the private sector in the provision of health services. . .the growth of new values, particularly individualism, and the decline of the spirit of solidarity and cooperation."[121]

Some of these concerns were misplaced. No study has ever shown evidence of an erosion in village work values; quite the contrary, workers returning from the Gulf used their savings to finance a boom in the growth of small industries.[122] The loss of farmland to construction and the rise of subsidized consumption were real problems, but ones villagers shared with urbanites. Indeed, during the 1970s the entire division between urban and rural life seemed to have eroded in Egypt. The cities had long been undergoing "villagization" as countrymen flocked into towns, settled in slums, and searched for jobs. By the 1980s a reverse trend had occurred, and growing numbers of refugees from Egypt's overcrowded cities were building weekend homes in villages. Many even made the village their primary residence and began to commute to their old jobs. In town and country alike the population shared a common passion for new multistoried villas, television, and washing machines. The flow of people and ideas and commodities trammeled the traditional distinctions between city and country. One exceptionally acute analyst described the process as "a dual phenomenon: the urbanization of the countryside and the ruralization of the city."[123]

Under these conditions, old worries about rural poverty and urban bias seemed increasingly irrelevant. Rural Egyptians could claim with pride that their economy was performing if anything better than the national economy.

Yet worries about the consuming village captured, albeit in a distorted form, a nagging anxiety about the structure of the rural economy. Money was flowing into the countryside, and much of it was being invested in productive enterprise. But agriculture was not receiving the portion of these funds it might have. Government subsidies partly compensated farmers for taxes on their crops, but not enough to make farming a high-return investment. Procurement quotas and price controls continued to make farming relatively unattractive. The wash of new revenues did not correct the worst flaw of Egypt's agrarian regime, its failure to supply adequate incentives for farming.

The flow of money into the villages masked these problems, but it did not diminish them. If anything, it reduced the prospects for any improvement. As anxiety about rural poverty receded, those who sought to reform agricultural policy lost some of their leverage. The rural population might be comparatively well off, but the agricultural sector was still not realizing its potential contribution to resolving the problems of food security and economic development.

Conclusion

Both Nasserists and Sadatists cling to an unrealistic and mechanistic vision of how agricultural policy is made. They believe that policymakers take decisions that are dutifully executed by bureaucrats and local government agents who, for good or ill, alter life at the village level. In fact, agricultural policy in Egypt is more like a sewer. Policymakers start the flow but lower officials and peasants all make their own contributions, so that what comes out at the terminus often bears little resemblance to what originally went in.

The process begins with the president and his elite advisers, who reach a compromise among themselves and then relay it to the minister of agriculture for execution. The minister may revise the policy to conform with his own inclinations, and his assistants will alter the policy still further to reflect their contending agendas. Then orders from Cairo descend to the local level, to the cooperatives, agronomists, and village banks. These agencies vary widely in their capacities and their responsiveness to central control. Some will have trouble interpreting their orders, others will lack the resources to execute them, and some—perhaps because their ties to the village are stronger than their bonds to Cairo—will simply neglect to act. Finally the new directives will be revealed to the peasants themselves. Their natural inclination will be to evade or undermine any policy that smacks of government intrusion in their lives.

This transformation of policy in the process of execution is typical in any organization. But in Egypt the scope of the transformation is extreme. Too often people assume that because a country has a flag and an army, it must have an effective state. They infer that, because a government is not restrained by a democratic constitution or a representative assembly, state power must be autocratic and unlimited. Westerners in particular tend to see Middle Eastern dictatorships like those of Nasser and Sadat as modernized versions of "Oriental despotism."[124] They presume that in Egypt the state is strong and society is weak.

The reality is almost exactly the opposite. Egypt has a very real state, but its powers are still circumscribed. Its institutions tend to be new and underfunded, and their staffs inexperienced and overworked. The state has grown up over a legacy of colonial administration that (reflecting the maxim of *divide et impera*) divided power between a handful of autocratic ministries in Cairo and diverse local elites in the provinces. The tendency of both Nasser and Sadat to use the civil service as a massive public employment program, guaranteeing jobs to all university graduates and making it difficult to fire inadequate workers or officials, did nothing to strengthen the quality of adminis-tration.

Egypt today possesses what Gunnar Myrdal called a "soft state": "The term 'soft state' is understood to comprise all the various types of social indiscipline which manifest themselves by: deficiencies in legislation and in particular law observance and enforcement, a wide-spread disobedience by public officials on various levels to rules and directives handed down to them, and often their collusion with powerful persons and groups of persons whose conduct they should regulate.

Within the concept of the soft state belongs also corruption. . . . These several patterns of behavior are interrelated in the sense that they permit or even provoke each other in circular causation having cumulative effects."[125] Neither Nasser nor Sadat invented Egypt's soft state (although both did things that made it softer). The softness of political institutions developed over several generations and is now relatively impervious to the ideological orientation of the ruler or even to the specific form of government (authoritarian or democratic).

The problem of the soft state is compounded by the fact that Egypt possesses a relatively hard society. Villagers, businessmen, and local elites all tend to be suspicious of the state. They enjoy a high degree of autonomy, evade government controls, and jealously defend their traditional privileges. They have prevailed in their struggle with the government by generally avoiding direct confrontation (like the Daqhiliyya raids). Instead they have mastered "the weapons of the weak"—"the ordinary weapons of relatively powerless groups: foot dragging, dissimulation, false compliance, pilfering, feigned ignorance, slander, arson, sabotage, and so forth. These Brechtian forms of class struggle have certain features in common. They require little or no coordination or planning; they often represent a form of individual self-help; and they typically avoid any direct symbolic confrontation with authority or with elite norms."[126] Even if Egypt's state was not so soft, these forms of resistance would greatly inhibit the effectiveness of government policy in rural areas.

Caught between its own flabby agencies and pervasive rural evasion, the Egyptian government has only the crudest idea of what life is like in the villages—much less how to change it. Even the most elementary facts are in doubt. In 1989 a debate broke out between two agencies over whether Egypt's population was 51 million or 54 million.[127] In 1988 the Ministry of Agriculture announced that the country's cultivated area, which was generally agreed to be about 6 million feddans, was actually 7.2 million according to an analysis of satellite photographs.[128] Getting information about how much people earn or how many hours they spend working at different activities is much more difficult, since citizens routinely lie about these facts to avoid taxation.

The state's weakness in rural areas is reflected in its choice of crude policy instruments. When the state sought to cheapen food for urban workers, it found it easier to do this by cross-subsidization (imposing price controls that reduced food prices for all classes) than by raising taxes and developing a graduated food rationing system. When it did have to collect taxes, it found it easier to seize control of a few crops than to erect a nationally administered system of value-added taxes. Even the land reform program reflected the dictates of expediency— dividing title among peasants who already worked on large estates and reappointing their former overseers as heads of the new agricultural cooperatives.

The limits to state power pose some serious problems for those who hope to stimulate Egyptian agriculture through a process of policy reform. Just because policies are changed in Cairo does not mean that life changes in the village. For that matter, even altering the policy in Cairo may require consultations and compromises among a bewildering host of interest groups. In a soft state (as the following chapters show) policy reform is fraught with special perils.

CHAPTER 4

Crony Capitalism and Agricultural Policy

MOST ANALYSES OF THE AGRICULTURAL REGIME IN EGYPT FOCUS ON TWO actors, bureaucrats and peasants. The former define policy, the latter suffer (or reshape) its application. The relationship between these two groups remains central to understanding the prospects for agricultural development. But by the late 1970s, a third actor had pressed its way onto the stage—businessmen. By the 1980s, businessmen had become generally more influential than peasants in determining the character of the agrarian regime and had begun to rival bureaucrats in their influence on policy.

Some Egyptian businessmen wear the traditional *galabiyya*, others dress in Western-style suits. Some inherited their fortunes, others are self-made men. In either case, they are distinguished by their possession of large sums of capital. Businessmen are not bound to a single enterprise by poverty or tradition. They choose ventures that promise profits, and if sufficient profits do not materialize or if there are higher profits available elsewhere, they will move their capital accordingly. They enjoy a flexibility and degree of influence that sets them apart from the mass of Egyptians.

The 1970s were a period of enormous growth for the Egyptian business community generally, thanks to Anwar Sadat's policy of economic liberalization and the oil boom throughout the Middle East. Businessmen (and a handful of businesswomen) became increasingly prominent in industry and commerce and particularly in agriculture. Lured by the much vaunted potential of the agricultural sector, businessmen began to invest in land and livestock, forming a new generation of agrarian capitalists. They pioneered more modern techniques in raising poultry and farming fruits and vegetables. They began to create new links between markets, tying the growth of oranges to the production of soft drinks, or producing high-value crops for export.

Their influence over agriculture, however, was not confined to their role in production. In the countryside they also took on the role of commercial agents, land brokers, machinery importers, and pesticide merchants. They had long controlled the marketing of fruits and vegetables, and gradually they won the right (monopolized by the state under Nasser) to trade in cereals and export crops. In the capital, they acquired a growing voice in the formulation of economic policy. Not only did they directly influence agricultural policy, but even businessmen with no direct interest in agriculture affected this sector by swaying government decisions on trade policy, budget allocations, and interest rates.

This reappearance of the Egyptian bourgeoisie occurred at a moment when pundits were heralding a new capitalist revolution in many Third World countries. Many development experts hoped that Egypt would soon enjoy the economic growth and political liberalism historically associated with entrepreneurship. They believed that businessmen would put pressure on the state to drop policies that obstructed development.

This faith in the healing powers of businessmen has been hotly debated by experts on Egypt. A number of excellent studies have dampened the optimism that prevailed in the 1970s. They suggest that the business community that has grown up in Cairo and Alexandria does not much resemble that which developed in London and Amsterdam three centuries ago. It has its own specific logic, its own modus operandi. It is not the heroic bourgeoisie made famous in textbooks about Western civilization.[1]

This chapter draws on some of the critical studies of Egyptian business and tries to tease out their implications for the agricultural sector. It spells out some of the ways in which Cairene businessmen have shaped agricultural policy. Culturally, they are not radically different from businessmen anywhere else. They are genuine entrepreneurs, who know how to count profits and understand the workings of supply and demand. But in the conditions under which they operate, the pursuit of profit does not always augment production or promote development.

The Evolution of Egyptian *Dirigisme*

Most Egyptian businessmen are *dirigistes*. They believe that the private sector cannot produce development on its own but must be guided and strengthened by an activist state. When they talk about their convictions, Cairene intellectuals may employ the vocabulary of Marx, Liszt, Keynes, Nasser, or Ibn Taymiyya, but the idea of state intervention is older and more pervasive than reference to these luminaries would suggest. Egyptians did not adopt *dirigisme* because of any narrow ideological influence, but rather as the result of a long stream of historical experiences which, they believe, demonstrated its validity.

Historical forces play a critical, often unrecognized, role in shaping economic thinking in all societies. In the United States, for example, citizens tend to discount the state's economic contribution. They know that the state plays an important role in the economy, that it supplies law and order, defines property rights and enforces contracts, invests in roads and education, organizes waterworks and postal services, and—through the defense budget—supplies the capital for a major section of industry. But in the United States, the business community had become both powerful and prosperous by the early nineteenth century, before the country developed an influential central state. American political culture therefore treats the state as an ancillary and derivative institution.[2] This is almost exactly the opposite of the Egyptian experience.

The origins of modern enterprise in Egypt date back to the days of Muhammad Ali Pasha, who ruled in Cairo from 1805 until 1849. Like some of his Prussian and Japanese contemporaries, Muhammad Ali was a traditional autocrat who dreamed of expanding his powers by appropriating modern technologies. He raised a huge army and built modern foundries and gunpowder plants to keep it equipped. He recruited European experts to advise him on these programs. To enhance his revenues, he constructed a network of modern spinning and weaving factories. He advanced agriculture by clearing old irrigation works and building new canals. His experts introduced and promoted the crop that made many Egyptians rich in the nineteenth century—long-staple cotton.[3]

At the beginning of this century, Egypt was one of the most advanced economies in the Third World. The rising demand for cotton in the nineteenth century had spurred Egyptian farmers to plant new lands, raise yields, and invest in new irrigation systems. The country had a highly developed system of telegraphs, railroads, and ports. Statistically, the per capita income of the average Egyptian in 1913 was higher than that of his counterparts in India or Japan.[4]

Yet Egyptians felt (and still feel) that they had been cheated of the full benefit of this growth. In 1882 the country had been occupied by the British, who remained in the country to ensure that Egypt repaid its foreign debts. It did not matter that these debts had often been fraudulently exaggerated by Western creditors and been contracted to build public works, like the Suez Canal, that benefited the West far more than Egypt.[5] The British drastically cut funds for education, the military, and public health, so that every year they could assemble £E 4 billion to keep up payments on Egypt's foreign debt.[6]

Under British administration the bulk of Egyptian cotton was exported to Manchester, England, and then reimported to Egypt as finished textile goods. Businessmen in Egypt drew an obvious lesson from this: by developing a local textile industry they could eliminate transportation costs, draw on cheap local labor, and tap into the advantageous terms of trade for manufactured products. But the British actively discouraged such plans by a variety of devices, including an 8 percent excise levied against all goods manufactured locally, and treaties that prevented Egypt from raising tariffs against foreign manufactures.[7]

When Egyptians look back over this experience, they extract the crude but powerful lesson that economic development in Egypt required the exercise of political power. The world was full of countries and groups eager to exploit Egypt's resources, without sharing their fruits with Egyptians. Foreigners had the advantage of being economically more advanced and enjoyed the support of powerful, modern states. Their industries would suck profits out of Egypt's farms. Their well-established corporations could swamp the efforts of Egypt's fledgling family firms. Only with the full support of their own state could Egyptians hope to compete in such an environment.[8]

A few visionaries argued that the creation of national economic institutions was essential for Egypt to industrialize in the face of this opposition. In 1910 Tal'at Harb, a young lawyer, began writing a series of articles that called on Egyptians to pool their economic resources for a national economic struggle against the British. His campaign led, in 1920, to the formation of Bank Misr, which was supposed to break the monopoly of the large foreign banks and supply funds for indigenous Egyptian enterprises. Bank Misr sponsored the development of an impressive array of enterprises, including firms in textiles, marketing, insurance, and air and maritime transport. Unfortunately, many of these firms ran into trouble during the Great Depression of the 1930s. Bank Misr had to both cut back its operations and rely increasingly on foreign capital. Although it remained an important force in Egyptian business, it failed as an experiment in asserting economic independence.[9]

An alternative avenue for promoting Egyptian industry appeared in 1922, however, when the Egyptian state was granted titular independence from Britain. Businessmen could now turn to their own government as a counterbalance against the power of foreign states and economic rivals.

> The various economic visions put forward in the years after World War I all accorded an important role to the state. The proponents of a private enterprise system in Egypt—whether they were large landowners or members of the domestic bourgeoisie—expected the state to continue to discharge its traditional responsibilities for education, public health, hydraulics and state railways. . . . But these groups also realized that private enterprise could not prosper in Egypt unless state power was used to loosen the international bonds that tied Egypt to Europe as an open, agricultural, export economy. The main elements of the Egyptian domestic elite were eager to see Egypt capture more of the profits of its export trade and supply more of its internal market with local manufactures. What stood in the way of these advances was a variety of European controls over the economy, including the marketing of cotton, tariffs fixed at 8 percent ad valorem by international treaties, and the Capitulations.[10]

To press the new state in this direction, in the 1920s businessmen in Egypt banded together into a carnival of federations and associations that lobbied for a wide array of protectionist or supportive policies.[11]

The first triumph of these lobbies came during 1930–35, when the autocrat and industrialist Isma'il Sidqi served as prime minister. Sidqi was supported by a coalition of cloth and cotton interests which had been forged by I. G. Levi, the secretary of the Egyptian Federation of Industries, in deliberate emulation of Germany's famous alliance of iron and rye. Together these groups devised a package of new tariffs that increased the profits of local industry and agriculture. Heavy duties were levied on imports of textiles, wheat, and sugar, while tariffs were lowered for fertilizers, agricultural machinery, and fuel. As a result, foreign manufactures lost their privileged status and the foundations for autonomous Egyptian industrialization were laid.[12]

After World War II, when the popular nationalist Wafd party took power, the array of state concessions to local business was expanded even further. To promote the textile industry, the government introduced an export tax on cotton in 1948 (which had the effect of making high-quality cotton cheaper for local firms). It granted special state subsidies to export-oriented firms selling to hard currency markets. A preferential exchange rate allowed manufacturers of export goods to trade their hard currency earnings for larger volumes of Egyptian pounds.[13]

Contrary to the textbook versions of Egyptian history, the period before 1952 was not one of laissez-faire. Instead, businessmen sought and received active state intervention corresponding to their interests. By the time Nasser took power from the Wafd in 1952 the pattern of state support for local industry was well established. During the 1950s the measures he employed to promote local firms, or to nationalize foreign assets, did not represent any sharp turn to socialism; they were very much an extension of the existing program of economic nationalism.

For the first few years after the military coup of 1952, many businessmen were cheered by the stance of the new regime. The Free Officers moved swiftly to suppress strikes and dismantled the growing, leftist-led union movement. They inaugurated a major program of public works. They seemed well disposed to the interests of local businessmen and their economic program reflected antipathy toward only two groups. First, they loathed the landed magnates who had been the backbone of the ancien régime. They adopted land reform as a means of liquidating this elite. Second, their nationalist sentiments made them hostile toward foreign enterprises and the cosmopolitan minority that dominated the trade of Alexandria. The British-French-Israeli invasion of 1956 gave the Free Officers a pretext for acting on this antipathy, and they confiscated the properties of many resident foreigners and Jews. Local businessmen were not distressed by these nationalizations, even though they would form the core of a growing public sector. After all, local businesses benefited from reduced foreign competition and the distress sale of foreign assets.

However, there were clouds on the horizon. The "feudalists" and foreigners that Nasser hoped to eliminate had been linked to the local business community. This link grew even stronger after the land reform, with magnates often taking the proceeds from the sale of their estates and reinvesting them in industrial or commercial ventures. One case that particularly irked Nasser was that of Fu'ad Sirag al-Din. This pillar of the Wafd party and symbol of the old order had been the largest landowner in the country. After land reform he became one of the largest industrialists. The military coup of 1952 had not employed the guillotine; the old aristocracy survived, albeit in a new form. Nasser feared that men like Sirag al-Din were waiting in the wings, not only conspiring against him but still deriving political influence from their economic prosperity.

In 1961 Nasser felt this threat especially strongly. He was dueling with Saudi Arabia for influence in the region, and faced a residue of organized Muslim Brothers opposition at home and a rising tide of dissent in Syria about his management of the United Arab Republic. He decided to strike first to weaken the network of enemies he feared was closing in around him. He personally drafted the list of companies to be targeted by the nationalization decrees of 1961. These decrees authorized state control of all financial institutions, especially industrial firms.[14] They also nationalized virtually all aspects of the cotton trade. From 1961 onward the state owned all the large textile plants, all the ginning facilities, the depots, and the distribution networks. It alone was authorized to export cotton, and it set the price that farmers received for this crop.

In 1962 and 1963 Nasser implemented a series of measures designed to eliminate the possibility that private capital would ever serve as a base around which his enemies might organize. First, he launched an effort to build a mass political party, the Arab Socialist Union (ASU), which was supposed to consolidate the popular forces of workers and peasants into an effective political bloc defending his regime. Second, he announced the Big Push of the first Five-Year Plan. The switch to comprehensive planning was not designed to regulate the private sector out of existence; it actually called for nearly half of all investment to come from the private sector. But it was designed to create and consolidate a massive public sector which would forever eclipse private enterprise and neutralize it politically.

The ASU never developed into the disciplined mass party Nasser hoped for. Only its command units ever really developed, and mass support remained very passive. The Five-Year Plan had more substantive accomplishments. Many factories were built and the public sector was established as an important element of the economy. There was enormous investment in infrastructure. Yet a high price had been paid for these modest attainments. The new factories failed to show the kind of profits necessary to make the plan self-financing. The private sector, antagonized or newly regulated, failed to contribute the expected investment. The state soon ran out of funds. By 1965 the government was not only unable to meet the final round of investment targets, it was increasingly forced to borrow abroad just to meet short-term expenditures. Egypt entered the period called *inkimash*, or constriction.

There had always been a group of men around Nasser who cautioned him against excesses of populism or socialism. Some of the more conservative technocrats, like Sayyid Mar'i, had been sidelined during the early 1960s. But Nasser could not shut out the complaints of the more conservative Free Officers, many of whom continued to exercise real influence. Men like Husayn Shafa'i, Abd al-Latif Baghdadi, Zakariyya Muhyi al-Din, and Anwar Sadat occupied important positions and formed an influential network. As the failure of the Five-Year Plan became evident, their voices grew louder than those of the surviving left-wing officers.

These conservative officers were increasingly supported by new groups that felt that private enterprise had been slighted at the expense of national development. A growing share of these officers had some personal experience of the dynamism of the private sector. Some had learned something of the complexity of the economy by acting as administrators of sequestered properties. Others had, as part of seeking a social status commensurate with their newfound influence in society, married into the business community. Some were just men who could not resist using their public power for personal profit, men who used their inside knowledge to profit from the sale of state lands or to anticipate changes in the market. Many had entered into partnerships with private businessmen, offering their political support and knowledge in exchange for a share of the profits. These officers and their partners became the nexus of a peculiarly Egyptian military-industrial complex, one that did not produce weapons (yet) but that exhibited the same combination of political and economic power that made its American counterpart so awesome.[15]

Businessmen themselves were highly receptive to the overtures of these officers. The business community had not been demolished by the nationalizations; even after 1961, the old elites continued to live handsomely off money smuggled abroad or investments in real estate, retailing, and small industry (enterprises that proved more resistant to state control than large factories and overseas trade). Small-scale businesses had never been nationalized. The severity of state intervention had been enough to cow them (they were never actually much of a political threat), and the survivors were prepared to cooperate.

But fear was not the only incentive for cooperation. Those businesses that had not been destroyed by populist measures found that the new economy could be quite lucrative. They enjoyed heavy protection against foreign competition. Government licensing requirements reduced the number of competing firms and allowed those that remained to enjoy monopoly profits. Exchange controls encouraged imports of machinery and consumer goods. Government subsidies made capital and industrial inputs cheap.

Those businessmen active in the 1960s remember it as a decade-long "golden age" of prosperity. During these years a "parasitic symbiosis" developed between the public and private sectors. The state took responsibility "for capital formation and investment, much of which are directed towards infrastructure projects—roads, ports, dams, schools, hospitals, housing—which in turn are contracted out to builders, fitters, electricians, plumbers, suppliers, etc. During the Egyptian first Five Year Plan (1960–65) 40% of total public investment outlays went to private contractors, and this at a time when the regime was going through its most self-consciously socialist phase. Contracts can be, and frequently are awarded on a non-competitive basis with kickbacks, side deals and a whole series of quasi-legal commissions and handling fees that may raise the value of a project by 30 or 40%. . . . The important point is that the private sector comes to depend upon the vast flow of publicly-disbursed funds for its survival, while public sector officials jockey for positions where they can control, and benefit from, the disbursement of these funds."[16]

The existence of these profits was no accident. Despite the hostility dividing Nasser from the business community, both shared in the *dirigiste* ideology common to Egyptians. Both believed that the state should intervene in the economy to dampen foreign competition and to promote productive enterprises. Many of Nasser's interventions and regulations greatly boosted the profits of businessmen. Subsidies and price controls lowered the costs of key inputs (energy, wages, raw materials) for many enterprises. State-regulated interest rates effectively subsidized the cost of capital. Overvaluing the currency depressed the cost of imported foodstuffs and machinery. Import licenses, tariffs, and customs quotas produced monopoly profits, allowing Egyptian firms to conduct trade without fear of competition.

The purpose of such interventions was to alter the pattern of rents. Markets create rents, "that part of the payment to an owner of resources over and above that which those resources could command in any alternative use."[17] These areas of high profit attract investment, raise production, and thereby eventually drive down prices. But Egyptian officials and businessmen were not happy with the pattern of rents created by the foreign competition, and political insecurity combined to suppress market rents in areas where many Egyptians wanted to see development. In many areas where Egyptians hoped for development, start-up costs were high and the prospects for profit distant.

Political intervention, Egyptians hoped, could attract investment into sectors where the allure of market incentives was weak. Subsidies could raise the short-term profits accruing on investments in industry. Regulated interest rates could be used to discourage borrowing for short-term commercial ventures and encourage longer-term investments in agriculture, mining, and other more apparently productive ventures. Tariffs could lower the pressure of foreign competition and shift opportunities to Egyptian businessmen. These forms of political or state-created rent could, at least in theory, raise the incentives and lower the risks of investment in sectors that market forces neglected.

Egyptian businessmen thus welcomed some of the interventions of the Nasser era. Using the state to create rents for business was, after all, already a well-established practice before 1952. Businessmen learned to accommodate the opportunities that the state-directed economy created.

Yet, generally, businessmen bristled under Nasser. After 1952 they lost much of the control they had formerly enjoyed over where rents were created. In the 1960s officers and technocrats made the key economic decisions (the system was no longer just *dirigiste* but etatist). Some state interventions (such as minimum wage and labor laws) created rents not for businessmen but for workers. Other interventions (such as cotton price controls) were disguised forms of taxation. Nationalization had not only undermined the rights of private property but created a large public sector that competed with private enterprise. Businessmen responded to the new regime with caution and petulance. They took the profits made available to them but were slow to invest or innovate.

The atmosphere began to improve after the June 1967 War with Israel. Already disappointed by the results of the Big Push, Nasser now had to shoulder the costs of a major military buildup. He grew eager to attract foreign economic support and sought to repair relations with the domestic business community. He quietly began to liberalize key trade policies. Conservative officers grew more influential (such as Anwar Sadat, who was appointed vice-president), and right-wing technocrats (like Sayyid Mar'i) were rehabilitated. By the time Nasser died in 1970, his government had already turned to the right and had taken the first steps toward economic liberalization.[18]

Sadat, Nasser's successor, greatly accelerated and expanded this trend. His accession was opposed by a group of left-wing officers led by Ali Sabri. To overcome their opposition, Sadat formed a countercoalition of his right-wing supporters. He won support within the military by loosening ties to the USSR and turning to Saudi Arabia (and eventually the United States) for assistance. He earned immediate support from the business community by proclaiming his intention to denationalize certain enterprises and expand the opportunities for the private sector.

From the moment he had consolidated power, Sadat began to criticize the excesses of the Nasser era. He encouraged a public campaign of de-Nasserization which stimulated public criticism of old economic priorities like self-sufficiency, comprehensive planning, and etatism. He authorized desequestration of some lands and enterprises (movie theaters, department stores), thus relegitimating private economic activity.[19]

Finally, in 1974 Sadat's office issued the October Paper, which declared a comprehensive reorientation of the economy. The new policy, called *infitah* or "opening," was designed to attract investment in Egypt from the oil-rich Arab states of the Gulf and from Western commercial banks. *Infitah* created a host of tax breaks, subsidies, and exemptions from labor laws designed to stimulate foreign investment. Egyptian businessmen quickly learned to profit from these facilities by taking on foreign partners. The new orientation also removed many of the regulations restricting trade and currency exchange, permitting an explosion of new imports. It encouraged the formation of private banks and made it easier to launch new firms. It provided a massive stimulus to private enterprise.[20]

The effect of the new policies was compounded by regional economic conditions. The Arab oil embargo and price rises of 1973 turned the Middle East into a major center of capital. Gulf sheikhs had huge sums available for investment and their governments were generous in their aid to Egypt. Western businessmen flooded the capitals of the region— including Cairo—trying to tap into these funds by peddling goods and development schemes. Egyptian businessmen prospered by acting as local intermediaries and agents. Wealthy Egyptians who had fled to the Gulf under Nasser, particularly those affiliated with the suppressed Muslim Brothers, returned to Cairo.

In 1974 and 1975 the position of business in Egypt was revolutionized. The casino at the Nile Hilton was once again full of entrepreneurs. New four-star hotels sprouted in Cairo like Nile weeds. Telephones and teletypes sprawled like jungle vines. The number of banks multiplied and the free-trade zone in Port Said was overrun by the warehouses of importers. Growing numbers of Egyptians concluded that the private sector was the true key to the country's prosperity.

Infitah has often been misrepresented, by its advocates and its opponents, as marking a change from a state-directed to a free-market economy in Egypt. It unquestionably led to important changes in economic structure, but fostered only limited liberalization. It legalized a wide range of imports, but kept tariff barriers high. It promoted private banking, but kept interest rate regulations intact. It left most price controls in place and expanded consumer subsidies (such as the food subsidies discussed in chapter 3). It created a more liberal economy, but one whose basic features were still clearly *dirigiste*.[21]

Sadat and his advisers remained convinced that state intervention was necessary to keep the economy healthy. They worried that decontrolling prices would lead to inflation. They wanted to encourage foreign investment, but not in a way that would allow foreign businesses to compete with established Egyptian enterprises. (Foreign firms found that it could take years of wrangling and concessions to win approval from Sadat's Investment Authority to begin operations.) The influx of foreign aid meant that the government felt it could afford to expand subsidies to both consumers and businesses.

Businessmen, too, advocated preserving the *dirigiste* foundation of the economy. They favored liberalization in certain areas, where the reduction of taxes or bureaucratic impediments helped to make new enterprises profitable. They urged Sadat to continue his slow program of denationalization; by 1978 stock in public sector enterprises was being sold to private buyers. But they were staunch supporters of those rents that bolstered the profits of their own firms. They did not favor a reduction of subsidies on energy or industrial raw materials. They opposed opening the economy to serious foreign competition.

The liberalization associated with *infitah*, then, had a specific, limited character. It reduced the antagonism between the government and the business community. It restrained the control of technocrats over economic policy and opened new areas for private initiative. But it preserved or expanded the vast array of state subsidies and in no way reduced the price of the state contribution to the economy. It did not abolish the state's role in creating economic rents, but redefined it in a manner more consistent with the interests of the business community.

Uthman Uthman and Land Reclamation

Egyptian loyalty to *dirigisme* is a logical, modern response to deficiencies in the economy and not some atavistic cultural holdover. Educated Egyptians, whether they work for the private or the public sector, are able to present persuasive arguments for why the state must act to stimulate and coordinate the development of the market economy. In coffee-house discussions, the arguments advanced for *dirigisme* seem compelling.

Unfortunately, in practice *dirigisme* has proven much more expensive and less effective than these arguments imply. State efforts to encourage private investment by creating economic rents entail certain obvious costs. When the government tries to reduce operating costs by subsidizing energy or food (the latter makes it possible to lower wages), the subsidy is reflected in the state budget. When it attempts to bolster infant industries by raising tariffs or regulating import licenses, the cost is evident in higher prices for consumers. But in addition to these obvious expenses, state creation of economic rents often imposes a host of hidden costs.

For example, the state does not always make wise decisions about what activities to sponsor. Bureaucrats may lack the training necessary to determine which activities are really likely to become profitable enterprises, or they may be swayed by political considerations, or they may just lack the information necessary to make accurate projections. If any of these conditions prevail, the rents they create may not stimulate profitable, productive activities. Equally important, for the same reasons bureaucrats may not know when to reduce or terminate the rents they have created, either because the rents have proved a failure or because they are no longer necessary.

Another hidden cost of rent creation lies in the unanticipated and often undesirable market distortions that intervention inevitably creates. Government incentives, mandated by law and administered by bureaucrats, are notoriously slower than market mechanisms at responding to changes in supply and demand. When the government creates investment incentives for a particular activity, it intends to lure capital from other sectors; but the incentives are often so lavish or left in place so long that they saturate the targeted sector while starving others. Similarly, a government subsidy on one good (say, food) may meet a specific need but stimulate demand for a host of others—creating new shortages and inflation and unpredictably shifting the whole pattern of investment.

A third hidden cost of *dirigisme* is the waste that results from rent seeking. Private firms that enjoy state-created rents show an increase in profits that is just as real (and probably less risky) than any they might earn from investments in technology, resources, or skill. In a *dirigiste* society businessmen will face strong temptations to influence the creation and allocation of such rents in a manner that benefits their own firms. They will devote part of their time, energy, and capital to wooing the government officials who administer rent-creating policies. The resources devoted to this pursuit of influence must be diverted from other, more productive activities, such as investments in technology, plants, or training. Rent seeking may be highly profitable for a firm, but it results in waste, since the resources diverted to it improve the performance of neither the economy nor the government.[22]

Rent seeking compounds the other problems of *dirigisme*. If officials are swayed by blandishments from businessmen, they become even less likely to make prudent decisions about which government investments best serve the national interest. And if businessmen successfully master the art of rent seeking, the number and impact of market-distorting state interventions will multiply.[23] This, sad to say, seems to be exactly what has happened in Egypt.

The problem of land reclamation offers a concrete example of how these hidden costs manifest themselves. On the one hand, land reclamation is exactly the kind of project where *dirigisme* seems essential; it has traditionally been such expensive work that the private sector could rarely finance it on its own. On the other hand, the state creation of rents to encourage reclamation has opened the door to all sorts of abuses, such as highly unproductive transfers of income from public coffers to an influential minority.

The most obvious constraint on the development of Egyptian agriculture is the relative shortage of land. The overwhelming majority of the 6.5 million cultivated acres is in the Nile Valley and Delta. The rest of the country is desert. Desert means more than just the absence of water; there is no soil, no scrub to shelter from wind. The vast majority of this land cannot be cultivated with any available technology.

There are, however, a number of marginal areas which, after expensive preparation, are potentially suitable for cultivation. Most of these lie at the edges of the Nile Delta, on lands that may contain some alluvial soil (and that may have been cultivated in the distant past) or that are at least near water. Others lie along the Mediterranean shoreline, either in northern Sinai or west of Alexandria. Finally, there are a series of oases in the deserts west of the Nile Valley that sit atop ancient aquifers. The government hoped that by preparing all these "new lands" for cultivation, the area of Egypt's farmlands might be doubled.

Officials of the U.S. Agency for International Development (AID) and other foreign advisers have questioned the economic viability of new lands projects. In the 1950s the Americans had been actively involved in Egyptian land reclamation, but they withdrew when relations with Nasser deteriorated in the 1960s. When AID resumed its operations after 1974, its officials were no longer enthusiastic. The agency commissioned two massive studies of Egypt's land reclamation potential.[24] Both suggested that reclamation was so expensive that even with government subsidies it would never be profitable. They recommended that the government invest its funds elsewhere. As a result, AID declined to support any additional work in reclamation.

This did not stop the Egyptians. After all, other development agencies were much less critical of the dream to turn the desert green. The World Bank saw greater potential in reclamation and invested in an important new lands project at Nubariyya. Even inside AID there were dissidents who argued that reclamation's potential was being underestimated; the agency's project managers were notorious for underestimating the future benefits of current investment.

Inside Egypt there has been no debate. Almost without exception, Egyptians believe passionately that reclaiming the desert is essential to their country's development. They have clung to this dream for over a century. In fact, some of today's "old lands" were themselves reclaimed during the nineteenth century. As population pressure has increased, so has the allure of the new lands. The arable area available per person in Egypt peaked in the 1930s. The public expects the government to do something about land reclamation, and Nasser, Sadat, and Husni Mubarak have all complied.

But the expense involved in claiming a plot back from the desert is staggering. Before reclamation can even begin, roads have to be built to the target fields, trees planted as windbreaks, power lines laid to fuel both farm machinery and farmers' houses. Then water has to be brought to the fields, which requires some combination of trucks or canals, pumps, fuel, sprinklers or pivot irrigators, much of which have to be imported and all of which are costly. Finally, the soil has to be improved by applying trucked dirt, fertilizer, and irrigation-borne nutrients, and cropping under barley or other soil-replenishing plants.

It may take years, even decades, before these measures result in economic crop yields. And there is a high risk that farms on reclaimed lands will never be profitable. "Comparatively slight differences in lift distances, water use, yields, prices or crop mix can easily tip a new lands project over into the red."[25] Unexpected changes in the price of the energy required to raise the water pressure that sprinklers need on sandy soils have ruined many projects. And, because of soil deficiencies, yields on new lands have averaged only half those attained on old lands. Of the 1.1 million acres reclaimed by the early 1980s, only 34 percent were producing a surplus above the variable costs of production.[26]

Not surprisingly, this combination of long-term investment, low profits, and high risks has made businessmen reluctant to absorb the costs of reclamation by themselves. Private corporations initiated the first land reclamation projects just before World War I. As their costs rose, these firms lobbied hard for public guarantees and subsidies. By the 1920s the government had already become their main sponsor. After the 1952 coup, the military government itself took over the leading role in reclamation. The new regime, which had already decided to redistribute agrarian reform lands only to successful peasant farmers, hoped that newly reclaimed plots would ease the hunger of less successful landless peasants.

In the 1950s the government launched three major reclamation schemes: Abis, Tahrir, and the New Valley.[27] But the real push of reclamation projects occurred between 1961 and 1965, during the first Five-Year Plan. In this area, the achievements of the plan almost matched its ambitions—452,800 feddans were actually reclaimed, 87 percent of the area targeted. But the cost of this drive was even higher than projected; reclamation consumed about £E 178 million, 85 percent of all investment in agriculture.[28]

In the economic crisis that followed the Five-Year Plan, there was little additional money for reclamation. Indeed, after its 1967 defeat by Israel, the government even lacked the money to properly maintain the lands it had already reclaimed. Some reclaimed lands had been administered as "agro-industrial units," large-scale state farms, which had proven predictably unprofitable. Others had been redistributed to peasant cooperatives, but these too required heavy subsidies to stay in production. By the early 1970s the officials at the Ministry of Land Reclamation were desperately trying to cut their costs by privatizing the lands under their administration.

The ministry began to experiment with a series of privatization programs. One popular program granted plots of twenty to thirty feddans to the graduates of agricultural projects while reserving smaller adjacent plots for peasants. It was hoped that the graduates would pioneer technological innovation while the peasants would supply labor. This led to a few shining successes and many dark disappointments. Other lands were simply auctioned off to the highest bidder.

But most buyers did not actually cultivate the land; they held it instead as a future investment.[29] By 1980 Sadat had decided to privatize all reclaimed lands. Peasant settlers and college graduates would get 40 percent; the remainder would be auctioned or sold to large private firms.[30]

The transfer of ownership, however, did not mean an end to the state role in reclamation. The new private owners relied heavily on state subsidies to ensure the profitability of their plots. While some of these subsidies were also offered to farmers on the old lands, they were especially important in the reclaimed new lands. For example, water, the key ingredient in any reclamation project, was supplied free. The cost of lifting the water to reclaimed lands was reduced by an array of subsidies. Pumps, sprinklers, and other imported technologies benefited from the customs exemptions that had been erected to encourage mechanization. Cement, plastic pipes, and other materials used for irrigation could be bought from the public sector below cost. Of course, the diesel fuel or electricity used to pump the water was heavily subsidized.

Unlike farmers on the old lands, those working in reclaimed areas were likely to get the land itself at less than cost. During the privatization experiments of the 1970s, large blocks of reclaimed land were distributed free to agricultural engineers and university graduates. After the 1973 War, veterans and the families of military casualties also received free plots.[31] By the 1980s land was no longer given away; rather, its price was strictly controlled. While prime Delta land was selling for $22,000 an acre, reclaimed lands could be bought at auction for more like $3,500 an acre.[32] Plots transferred to "graduates and youth" were even more of a bargain: in 1988 the minister of agriculture, Yusuf Wali, affirmed that the Ministry of Agriculture would not allow the price of such lands to rise above £E 400 a feddan.[33]

As if subsidies on inputs and land were not enough, capital and investment in reclaimed areas were also proffered on soft terms. Law 143 of 1981, which institutionalized the privatization of reclaimed lands, also created loans to pay for improvements to reclaimed lands. The Principal Bank for Development and Agricultural Credit was ordered to issue loans for 80 percent of the costs of reclamation and farming at interest rates of only 3 percent. The government extended loans worth £E 1.6 million in 1981–82 and £E 588,000 in 1982–83. A program introduced in 1983 led to even more abundant credit, with £E

698,000 loaned in November of that year and £E 753,000 in December.[34] Moreover, investments in reclaimed lands were granted a tax exemption for five years. In 1984 this moratorium was extended to ten years.[35]

The government had intended to calibrate these subsidies according to the needs of the recipients. Poor peasants were supposed to benefit from them all, from free land to subsidized machinery. Firms farming more than five hundred feddans, on the other hand, were not supposed to enjoy the tax moratorium and many other perquisites. But the potential availability of such rents elicited the fiercest entrepreneurial instincts of private firms. If they could figure out a way to enjoy the benefits of double dipping, a way to get all the possible (not just all the legal) rents, they would.

In practice, the level of state support a farmer received tended to be a function of his political influence rather than his economic need. Small peasants who lacked political clout had to wait years for the bureaucracy to deliver the inputs to which they were entitled. The rich and the influential, on the other hand, were able to command rapid attention. The distribution of subsidies tended to be an inverse image of official policies.

Just how lucrative these facilities could be is apparent in the way they were milked by the most masterful manipulator of state-created rents in Egypt today, Uthman Ahmad Uthman. The story of his participation in land reclamation is convoluted, but illuminating.

Uthman is the richest man in Egypt, with an estimated wealth of $1.5 billion.[36] In 1949 he founded a small office for engineering consulting which later grew into the famous Arab Contractors Company. Arab Contractors is not only the largest engineering firm in the Arab world, it is the hub of an empire through which Uthman controls dozens of corporations with assets over $2 billion.[37] Uthman rightly boasts about his humble origins, because he can claim to be one of Egypt's few genuinely self-made men. But he also brags, far less honestly, that his career testifies to the virtue of free enterprise: "Experience taught me. . .to trust in free competition as the road to manufacturing progress, and the path to prosperity. I believe free competition is a sphere in which men can innovate and create together, giving their best, finding themselves, whatever their position was in the functioning economy: worker or owner. Experience taught me that the comprehensive economy which depends upon the ownership of the state of the means of production sows jealousy among men and kills their disposition to create and give, and turns them into cogwheels in the machine of production, completely plundering their desire."[38] Despite these businesslike pieties, the truth is that most of Uthman's wealth derives from his skill at using public facilities to the best private advantage.

In 1961 Nasser nationalized Arab Contractors but allowed Uthman to remain at the helm and retain title to Arab Contractors' foreign operations. Uthman quickly learned to turn this arrangement to his advantage, by transferring some of the profits from his Egyptian operations to foreign subsidiaries while shifting expenses, such as fully depreciated machinery, to the public parent at home. He soon learned that there were many advantages to being part of the public sector, including guaranteed markets, subsidized inputs, and the like. But Uthman's real wealth dates to the 1970s, when his close friend Anwar Sadat (their children intermarried) became president of Egypt. In 1973 Uthman was made minister of reconstruction. He promptly sold off five state construction firms which he claimed were no longer profitable. This meant that his own firm, Arab Contractors, had a virtual monopoly on the work of rebuilding the Suez Canal zone. This involved billions of dollars in U.S.- and Arab-funded contracts.[39] State-sponsored projects remain the foundation of Uthman's wealth. In 1984 the Arab Contractors group secured construction projects worth $684 million, one-third of all those awarded in Egypt.[40]

Using profits from his Suez coup, Uthman built up an extensive business empire centered on the Canal zone. His holdings were quite diversified, ranging from a truck fleet to one of the most influential private banks, Bank of Suez Canal. Fourteen of these holdings were concentrated in the area of food and agriculture. He set up a network of farms, a livestock operation, a fish farm, a major food retailing organization, and one of the largest poultry ranches in the country (Sharikat al-Isma'iliyya li-Dawajin).[41] All of these operations benefited from abundant soft loans and input subsidies which the state provided to promote food security projects (see the discussion of poultry in chapter 5).

One of Uthman's more interesting investments in food security netted him a major share of the Egyptian soft drink market. First he assumed control over the nationalized carbonated water works; then he entered into joint ventures with Seven-Up and Canada Dry, and became the local representative of Schweppes.[42] These deals were especially profitable for both parties because the government offered a variety of special incentives for foreign investment. While this coup did not actually enhance Egypt's food security, it inaugurated a whole new strategy of investment for Uthman.

These deals had also been attractive to Uthman because, under the terms of Law 43 of 1974, any public sector firm that participated in a joint venture was legally treated as a private sector firm. As joint ventures his activities continued to enjoy full state support but were exempted from price controls, given independent budgeting authority, and able to retain profits instead of contributing them to the treasury.

While the first of these deals had been passed fairly easily, subsequent ones drew public protest. Many Egyptians seemed to feel that these projects benefited foreign firms and a few rich Egyptians rather than the general public. People were no longer convinced, as they seemed to be at first, that soft drinks were a direct contribution to the Egyptian food supply. They wanted more tangible evidence. So by 1979, when Uthman was negotiating a deal with Pepsico, he had to worry about selling the project to the National Assembly.

For Uthman, the ideal solution was to persuade Pepsico to expand its operations beyond bottling and into agriculture. Back in the United States, Pepsico had extensive agricultural operations, in milk, livestock, and so forth. Through a subsidiary, Arizona Farmers Corporation, it had even developed expertise in dryland cultivation. And at one time Pepsico and Coca-Cola had looked at Egyptian oranges as a possible source of syrup for their European bottling operations. If Pepsico were willing to invest in dryland cultivation in Egypt, it would both help to lower objections to its bottling operations and make a direct contribution to Uthman's farming operations.[43]

Uthman asked Pepsico to invest in a massive land reclamation scheme that his engineers had been surveying in the drylands west of Ismailiyya. He had built pilot farms there using water from the Ismailiyya Canal in 1978, near the new community of 10 Ramadan City. His plan called for reclaiming 150,000 feddans, developing 50,000 feddans for farming in each of three phrases, to be launched in 1980, 1986, and 1991. The total project would cost £E 293 million. By January 1982 infrastructure had already been laid on 56,000 feddans, half in Salihiyya and the other half in the neighboring Youth Province.[44] This would be the largest land reclamation project ever attempted in Egypt.

Salihiyya became a showcase for work on sandy soil. Uthman's greatest problem was irrigation. Instead of traditional flood irrigation, which required huge volumes of water, he planned to install new systems of sprinklers and pivot irrigators. These used water much more efficiently and, by simultaneously applying fertilizer and chemicals, could even produce crops using water with a high salt content.[45]

In 1979 Uthman won Pepsico's participation in this project. He formed the Middle East Company for Land Reclamation in which Pepsico originally held 15 percent directly and another 5 percent through its agricultural subsidiary, Arizona Farmers, while Arab Contractors controlled 60 percent. Gifford Hill, which manufactures irrigation equipment, took another 10 percent and SAPA, a group that handles international agricultural marketing, took 10 percent.[46] Uthman also won support from the Egyptian government. On paper this looked like exactly the kind of project that *infitah* had been launched to encourage—a joint venture that married foreign expertise with Egyptian resources to mutual benefit. Uthman bragged that the success of the Salihiyya project would show that the private sector could completely replace the government as the engine of land reclamation.

The Egyptian government—which in those days meant Sadat personally—was grateful, and eager to support this project. In 1978 Sadat toured the western desert to announce the beginning of the Green Revolution. The plan was to convert 1.25 million hectares of desert into farmland; this would mean a 44 percent extension of agricultural land.[47] Uthman presented his project as the embodiment of these ambitions. As a result, he was given blocks of land as free grants from the state. As if that were not enough, his farms tended to encroach on lands that did not belong to him. (These encroachments were retroactively legitimized as transfers from the provincial governor.)[48]

Despite the ostensibly private character of the project, the state paid the lion's share of development costs. (It put up £E 1,400 per feddan for basic infrastructure like roads and electricity).[49] It also paid for the main water pipes and pumping stations. The contracts for installing these facilities were routinely awarded to Arab Contractors itself. Thus, years before Salihiyya ever produced a profitable crop, Uthman was making money on it.[50]

These state supports were essential to the prospects of the project. Despite the much-heralded application of "modern American technologies," Salihiyya's economic prospects remained marginal. The project is 120 meters above the Ismailiyya sweet-water canal, so lifting water to it consumes expensive energy. Under the 1979–84 Five-Year Plan, the state had allotted £E 895 per feddan toward reclamation in the project; by 1983 more than £E 2,000 per feddan had been spent.[51] The experts at AID had begun to criticize Salihiyya as an expensive white elephant. They estimated its real cost at $4,150 per hectare.[52] After a big push in the first couple of years, the pace of reclamation slowed. By 1984 Uthman claimed to have planted 50,000 feddans. Outside observers put the total closer to 17,000 and they estimated that the cost of reclamation had risen to nearly $9,000 per feddan.[53]

By this time, Pepsico had bailed out of the project. It had developed worries early on, when Uthman purchased lots of expensive equipment but failed to hire a single qualified agronomist. But the real trigger for Pepsico's withdrawal was a government decision in 1981 that joint-venture companies working in land reclamation should pay international prices for oil and fertilizer. Uthman urged Pepsico to release its share in Salihiyya so that Arab Contractors' Agricultural Projects Division could once again claim to be a public sector company and enjoy access to subsidized loans, fuel, and fertilizers. Pepsico, which had always seen its farm operations as a goodwill token, dropped out of the project; but it retained its lucrative soft drink factory.[54] One American official angrily (but accurately) described the key to Uthman's success: "We give Arab Contractors low marks. They want to be a private company when it's good for them and a public company when it's good for them."[55]

The first of Salihiyya's three reclamation phases was officially completed on January 29, 1982. Uthman had to fight hard to win any additional funding. Investigations revealed that Uthman was employing, on the government budget, three thousand workers whose monthly wages totaled £E 600,000. But most of the food production plants on the project were still incomplete. Only a handful of the twenty chicken hatcheries were operating and a £E 3 million imported peanut-processing plant worked only twenty-five days a year. So, two thousand of Uthman's workers were not really working.[56]

For his part, Uthman complained that the government was solely responsible for any failing at Salihiyya. He now claimed that if his life had taught him anything, it was the need for quick decisions. Instead, Salihiyya had increasingly been hobbled by parliamentary investigations, cost-benefit analyses, and assorted bureaucratic complications.[57]

In one sense, the state campaign to promote land reclamation by creating rents was working. Uthman and hundreds of other businessmen were investing in this area, and the sands at the edge of the Nile Valley were slowing giving way to green. There were 56,000 feddans of producing (but unprofitable) farmland near Ismailiyya that would not have been there without state support. But projects like Salihiyya were certainly not cheaper or noticeably more productive than the state-managed reclamation projects of the 1950s and 1960s. The large private land companies seemed as eager to exploit state-supplied rents as their public sector predecessors. They had not shown that land reclamation projects could ever be profitable if state subsidies were withdrawn.

The wisdom of state-sponsored, large-scale reclamation projects remains open to question. It is quite possible that the funds siphoned into this program might have been spent more productively elsewhere. The lands reclaimed since 1952 have only offset the area lost to *tajrif*—that is, the loss of farmland to urban sprawl, brickmaking, and erosion. If the government had diverted part of the funds it invested in land reclamation into enforcing building codes, encouraging the construction of towns outside the Nile Valley, or development of a cheap concrete industry, Egypt might have spent less and still had the same arable area today. An effective program to combat *tajrif* might have been more cost effective than land reclamation, while achieving much the same goal.

By the late 1980s an alternative to large-scale land reclamation projects was emerging. The development of "plasticulture" technology (cheap polyvinylchloride greenhouses or *subat zira'iyya*) meant that private entrepreneurs could afford to reclaim certain lands on their own initiative. After investing a few thousand pounds in plastic tents, drip-irrigation tubes, and trucked water, a businessman could begin planting on reclaimable land almost immediately. Plasticulture, however, could not abolish the need for state investment. The *subat zira'iyya* required capital investment which was beyond the reach of most peasants, and the greenhouses were profitable only when planted in high-value crops like fruits and vegetables. (The limited market for such horticulture is discussed in chapter 7.) Plasticulture may ameliorate the demand for large-scale land reclamation projects, but it will not eliminate it.[58]

So Uthman's farm and other large-scale reclamation projects seem likely to be a drain on the public treasury for years to come. They will not only suck up funds targeted for reclamation but impose a host of hidden costs as well. In an effort to help Salihiyya show a profit, the state subsidizes Uthman's poultry operations as well. In an attempt to encourage foreign investment in such projects, it extends subsidized, public sector inputs to private sector firms. In order to stimulate the interest of domestic businessmen in reclamation, it permits them to form large estates on the new lands, undermining the land reform law. And by easing the flow of capital into this sector, it diverts funds from other, potentially more profitable, activities.

Most Egyptians, like people everywhere, find it difficult to conceptualize these problems in terms of the complex interactions between economic entrepreneurship and state power. They prefer to personalize the issue, to assume that Uthman is the problem. In the same way that many Americans think Charles Keating was the cause of the savings and loan crisis, Egyptians tend to see the avarice, incompetence, and criminal behavior of individuals as the forces that have sapped the benefits from land reclamation. Most think Uthman shows little sense of patriotism, that he places personal profits before national welfare. They view him as a member of a small but prominent subsection of the business community, a parasitic bourgeoisie that does not promote production in Egypt but profits by purveying foreign commodities.

The perception that such parasites were the primary beneficiaries of *infitah* has fostered ambivalent feelings about economic liberalization. Those feelings fueled public demand that the government curb the parasites and devote its rents to promoting the productive national bourgeoisie. Some Egyptian academics have tried to assist the government in this task by mapping out the differences between the parasites and the patriots; the former supposedly engage in commerce rather than industry, in imports rather than exports, in consumer goods rather than capital goods.[59] This perspective is now common to most political parties in Egypt. They all claim hearty admiration of the private sector and say they want to promote the fortunes of honest businessmen. Even Egyptian Marxists claim that they are opposed only to *compradors* while fully supporting the "national bourgeoisie."[60]

But the evidence suggests that this distinction has little basis in reality. Industrialists take state subsidies as happily, and fight as hard to preserve them, as importers who fight for favorable exchange rate and customs policies. The sheer size of the Salihiyya project combined with Uthman's reputation for wheeling and dealing to form an ideal target for muckraking journalists and opposition politicians. But there are a dozen other large companies working in the area of reclaimed lands. Reputedly, most of them have engaged in similar practices (although perhaps on a smaller scale.)[61]

The abuse of state-created rents is not a product of Uthman's personality or lack of patriotism. The most patriotic businessman will take advantage of rents so long as he profits from doing so—just as the most patriotic citizens consume subsidized bread, even though they burden the state in the process. Businessmen are supposed to be entrepreneurs; they are supposed to seek out opportunities to profit. If Egyptian businessmen did not exploit the existence of rents, something would be deeply wrong with them.

Corruption, the Political Price of Rent Seeking

By 1980, state-created rents were so pervasive that they touched the operations of nearly every business in Egypt. Even the tiniest firms lit their offices with subsidized electricity, paid their employees less because of subsidized foods which lowered the cost of labor, worked with imported goods—from ball-point pens to facsimile machines—made cheaper by overvalued currency. Of course, for most firms these economic rents only offset the costs of government regulation, which also influenced wages, prices, working hours, and many aspects of business. State-created rents did not assure either success or failure for most Egyptian businessmen.

Those businesses that prospered did not always owe their success to the system of state-created rents; but those that stayed successful had to accommodate. Sooner or later their managers had to learn the art of rent seeking. They learned how to bolster their profits by securing access to state supports and how to lower their costs by sidestepping noxious regulations. The wealthiest and most prominent businessmen built up the kind of political influence necessary to make the system work for them.

The techniques by which businessmen turn the system of rents to their advantage are numerous and diverse. An academic who opens a consulting firm may rely on old school chums in the bureaucracy to help him win government contracts. An importer may bribe officials at the Alexandria Customs Authority to gain an edge over his competitors by being exempted from certain quotas and restrictions. A clever tractor manufacturer may build up a network of friends and allies within both the AID mission and the state agricultural bank with an eye to winning a monopoly over distribution of farm machinery. The number of variant roads to political advantage is constantly being increased by the combination of human imagination, ambition, and greed.

Still, certain patterns are evident. The key to successful rent seeking is to build some form of political influence that can be translated into economic privilege. As the political system evolves, the easiest means to this end also changes. Before 1952, businessmen could influence the state in a fairly public and transparent manner. They banded together into associations like the General Agricultural Syndicate and the Federation of Industries to devise common programs. These lobbies commanded the kind of wealth and power necessary to win allies among the competing political parties. When a particular party took power, it worked to reward its business constituency. Parties often came to power by monarchical fiat or as a result of British intervention, but otherwise the pattern of lobbying was similar to that found in many Western democracies.[62]

Under Nasser, parties were banned and business associations were placed under tight state control. Technocrats and officers acquired final say over where and how the state would intervene. This did not mean that businessmen were powerless, but they had to exercise their influence in more covert and individualistic ways. One ancient, but still effective, technique was to intermarry with the ruling elite. Many businessmen formed working alliances with the Free Officers by marrying their daughters off to the latter. The legacy of this approach was during Sadat's reign: one prominent businessman, Ashraf Marwan, was Nasser's son-in-law while two others, Uthman Uthman and Sayyid Mar'i, had intermarried their own clans with Sadat's.[63]

Another favorite approach was to form old-boy networks. Businessmen and officers who shared some bond often found they could collaborate to make each other both rich and powerful. For example, many prominent Egyptians respected the claims of *dufu'at* which link together former schoolmates. A businessman and a bureaucrat who attended the Officers Academy or university during the same years probably felt they owed each other a few favors. Or they might have developed ties to each other through membership in the same *shilla*, a group of friends or acquaintances who have worked to promote each other's careers over the years.[64] These kinds of reciprocal bonds were not, of course, uniquely Egyptian—they could be found in Stalin's Georgia, Carter's Georgia, or almost anywhere.

When Sadat took power, these techniques remained important. The new regime showed greater favor to businessmen but still barred them from organizing publicly. By the mid-1970s, however, a new factor began to reshape the prevailing mode of rent seeking—the growth of revenues from abroad and of discretionary state resources.

Sadat's alliance with Saudi Arabia, his leadership in the 1973 War against Israel, and the subsequent boom of oil revenues led to a cash windfall for the Egyptian government. Between 1974 and 1981 the value of official aid from Gulf governments to neighboring Arab states amounted to $54 billion, not including grants by individual princes.[65] Even though Arab aid began to decline after 1977 because of Egypt's leading role in the peace process with Israel, the flood of cash continued. But by this time foreign aid from the United States and commercial loans had pretty much replaced the missing Arab funds. And Egypt's own oil revenues leapfrogged ahead after Israel evacuated its Sinai oil fields in 1976.

This cash windfall positioned the Egyptian state to offer greater largesse and more lucrative rents than ever before. Sadat seized on this opportunity to consolidate his authority. He had never managed to emulate Nasser's personal popularity among the mass of the population, nor had he been able to create a disciplined power base for himself. The new cash assets of the Egyptian government gave him a chance to build a constituency for himself by reviving one of the oldest tools of political influence, patronage.[66]

Sadat kept the army loyal by raising salaries, building special military housing complexes, and opening special stores where soldiers could buy subsidized imports, thereby exposing officers to a lifestyle that had previously been restricted to the wealthiest elites. He consolidated his following among businessmen by doling out lucrative state contracts (like the Suez Canal reconstruction program that made Uthman Uthman wealthy), import licenses, and other privileges. He worked to keep consumers happy by vastly expanding the state subsidy programs. Even his closest associates admitted that he sometimes carried this approach to extremes; on occasion he wooed foreign diplomats by giving them pharaonic antiquities removed from the Egyptian Museum.[67]

Sadat's use of patronage was highly personalistic. He decided what to give to whom, and the political loyalty of his clients was directed toward him personally rather than toward the Egyptian state. The Arab Socialist Union, the mass party he had inherited from Nasser, was an amorphous affair ill suited to use as a political machine. Egypt lacked the tribal structures that permitted states like Saudi Arabia to construct comprehensive national patronage systems. This absence of the kind of political infrastructure that buoyed other Arab rulers did not inhibit Sadat's exercise of patronage, but it did lead to problems. He was never able to fully institutionalize his power or to control the use of patronage.[68]

Sadat was not the only Egyptian official who tried to use state assets to cultivate a political clientele. His example encouraged other members of the government to foster their own. Cabinet ministers, party hacks, and district governors all applied patronage with a new enthusiasm. Soon there were dozens of increasingly potent patron-client networks, operating at all levels of government. Cabals of officers, salons of businessmen, and old-boy networks of every variety were reinvigorated by a newfound ability to tap into state resources. Many of the patronage networks that grew up were unrecognized by, let alone subordinate to, the office of the president. They became cysts in the body politic, small preserves of independent power.

In the Egyptian soft state, the president had never been able to fully control the lower echelons of government. But as a result of the oil boom and the proliferation of patronage, the soft state became even softer.

Most of the officials who exercised independent patronage had no intention of challenging Sadat's authority. They had no ideological grievance against the regime and their political ambitions were limited. They traded on the power of their office to make themselves rich and influential. When they awarded a state contract or overlooked a regulation at the behest of a client, they often expected to be repaid in cash. An official at the Ministry of Agriculture might expect to be paid for ignoring the responsibilities of his office and permitting a client to build housing on land reserved for farming. Another official at the Post and Telephone Bureau would extract a personal payment before he would exercise his powers and authorize installation of a phone for a client who had already paid the legally mandated fees.

Graft became increasingly commonplace in Egypt. A growing

number of officials left their desk drawers open, indicating that they were amenable to *bakshish* or *rashwa* (a bribe). Citizens learned, through a complex chain of underground communication, what scale of graft was appropriate for which official. A bribe of $1 to a local functionary could get a person's identity card renewed without trouble. A firm offering bribes worth $5 million could secure a $200 million contract for construction of a paper mill despite a lower bid by a competing firm.[69] Egyptian businessmen learned to count these subventions as part of their overhead costs, agreeing with the Iraqi merchant who noted that officials are like "dogs and one best deals with dogs by tossing bones to them."[70]

To facilitate his personal patronage and profits, Sadat had deliberately crippled the public watchdog agencies that Nasser had created to restrict corruption.[71] Government employees quickly discovered that not only were the risks of corruption less than ever before but the potential economic benefits much greater. The salaries of civil servants had not kept up with inflation, much less expanded to accommodate the consumer binge that accompanied *infitah*. In 1980 the average wage for a government employee was £E 50 a month; doctors in government clinics earned only £E 60.[72] Even the most cursory comparison of these salaries with the cost of living in Cairo suggests that civil servants lived under horrifying economic strains. A kilogram of bananas or a box of tissues cost £E 1, a dress shirt £E 19, a visit to a private medical clinic £E 20, a locally manufactured refrigerator £E 398, and a locally assembled small car £E 10,000.[73] To survive, much less to prosper, most civil servants had to either work a second job, transfer to the higher-paying private sector, or take bribes.

Patronage, legal or not, is an important instrument of authority in most societies. But when patronage is not supervised and controlled by a party, political machine, or some other organization, it tends to degenerate, with public resources diverted for purely personal purposes.[74] In any soft state, where officials are underpaid, poorly trained, and loosely supervised, corruption tends to be a problem. In Nasser's Egypt corruption had already been evident. But during the 1970s, as the state's discretionary income rose and as Sadat's personalistic style of rule eroded the discipline of the administration, corruption increasingly tainted all aspects of government.

Graft accompanied patronage even at the highest levels of state, and not just among financially strapped provincial bureaucrats. Sadat's wife Gihan was reputed to have invoked her husband's influence to make millions developing land in the Muqattam district on Cairo's fringes. His son Gamal engineered the dismissal of a university professor who caught him cheating on exams. And his brother Ismat, who had been a humble truck driver in 1970, made himself wealthy by organizing protection rackets, smuggling hashish, and slipping contraband through customs.[75]

Under Sadat, patronage and corruption became invaluable tools for rent seekers. With the softening of the state, businessmen found it easier to manipulate the allocation of rents, with the result that rent seeking became both more common and more lucrative. Another dimension of the career of Uthman Uthman suggests how this affected the economy. Land reclamation was only one of several areas where Uthman Uthman skimmed from the government. Another of his notorious schemes for bilking the treasury involved his control over the government's Popular Development Program (PDP). Of course, he enjoyed privileged access to Sadat, and his use of rent seeking was both extreme in scope and unusually well documented. But what Uthman did on a grand scale and in public view, other businessmen often did more subtly and quietly.

In 1976, to much public applause, Anwar Sadat announced the creation of his Popular Development Program. The program consisted of a fund, a bank, and a number of public agencies charged with sponsoring private sector projects in the food security sector—poultry farms, fish farms, private markets, and so forth. The PDP was one of Sadat's "brainwaves." The initial rationale for this program had been genuinely economic; there was hope that the private sector could increase food production and manage food imports with greater efficiency than the stagnant public sector. But the PDP also figured in Sadat's political dreams. Through the PDP he hoped to prove to Egyptians that private enterprise was the hope for Egypt's future; if he could do this, it would lay the groundwork for a massive reduction of the recalcitrant powers of the state bureaucracy.[76] Even in the short term, the PDP could pay off politically by breeding a loyal constituency among the business community.

Sadat was also Egypt's modern master of clientage politics. He understood that any and every state program, even those created for purely economic purposes, could be bent to the service of political largesse. He never created an agency commanding discretionary funds without seeing in it a potential pork barrel. He expected that capital contributed by the PDP might be repaid in political loyalty rather than cash.

Sadat attached the PDP to the National Democratic party (NDP), his own institutional power base. He hoped that the PDP would augment the party's power, since businessmen who became clients of the PDP could be pressed into a role as backbenchers for the NDP. The PDP's primary goal was the creation of a chain of patronage that descended from Sadat through the party to the business community. Not surprisingly, he put the PDP under the direction of the man who knew most about how to turn political power into private wealth, his close friend Uthman Ahmad Uthman.

By 1980, the PDP had grown into an array of committees, party funds, and banks supporting hundreds of private ventures. Projects were set up to undertake certain activities the NDP Committee for Popular Development designated as eligible for Popular Development support. These projects were encouraged to apply for low-interest loans through the National Development Bank or one of its twenty-one semi-independent branches. This bank had been created specifically to support the PDP with £E 100 million in capital—70 percent of it contributed by public sector corporations.[77] By 1983 the PDP had assembled £E 606 million in capital distributed among 159 individual projects representing investments of £E 1.5 billion.[78]

Initially the government made great claims for the PDP. It credited the program with providing for food security, relieving the burden on the public sector, and bringing Egypt the fruits of private enterprise.[79] Then, in October 1981, a former member of the PDP board named Rashad Uthman was put on trial in Cairo. Rashad, a former cigarette smuggler turned big-time profiteer, faced a battery of charges ranging from bribery to theft of state lands. In his defense, he alleged that the charges against him had been placed by influential figures who opposed his efforts to clean up the PDP. He claimed that the chairman of the PDP had put pressure on him to do business with a company called Eric, but that when he discovered that Eric was swindling the public rather than providing for food security, he had refused.

Eric Company had been founded and directed by Tawfiq Abd al-Hayy, a one-time student radical who had become an ardent capitalist and a protégé of Uthman Uthman. The PDP had supplied much of the original capital for the firm. Eric had begun as an advertising agency, but soon branched out into retail distribution and wound up specializing in meat imports. Shortly after Rashad Uthman brought Abd al-Hayy's name to public attention, customs officials noted that rats nibbling on Eric consignments often dropped dead. On closer inspection they discovered that the meat of the consignment in question had been frozen in 1973 and was no longer edible. When Abd al-Hayy heard that he now faced criminal charges and that an investigation of Eric had been opened, he marched straight to his bank, where he borrowed another £E 14 million, including £E 500,000 of PDP funds,[80] and then caught a plane for Panama.

In the wake of this scandal, the press and opposition parliamentarians pressed for an investigation of the PDP. They discovered that most of the food security projects the program had funded were importing or distribution ventures which added little to the country's production. They learned that some of these private sector projects had drawn 65–90 percent of their capital from the state, not including various grants of land, access to public facilities, and other subsidies.[81] They became aware that although the government had loaned more than £E 500 million for food security projects by the first quarter of 1982, only £E 298 million had actually been invested in this area. The outstanding £E 200 million in low-interest loans had sometimes been invested in nonfood projects and sometimes just been deposited in private bank accounts.[82]

Of course, the prime beneficiary of these activities had been Uthman Uthman. His Arab Contractors Company was awarded construction contracts for twenty-nine PDP projects which represented 85 percent of PDP companies that reached the production stage.[83] One of the largest single investments by PDP was £E 100 million for Uthman's land reclamation company working at Salihiyya.[84] The PDP projects added many names to the roster of Uthman's clients, both men loyal to him and those with whom he simply did business. This was important, since Uthman's political ambitions were large and he was not content to rest his power on his personal relationship with Sadat alone. In addition to his original power base in Arab Contractors, he now controlled an array of important food security and land reclamation companies. He had a voice in the financial community through his interest in the Suez Canal Bank. He controlled the influential Engineers' Syndicate, which owned a conglomeration of thirteen companies.[85] And he also curried influence within the cabinet by building ties to a series of ministers, including Anwar Abu Sahli (minister of justice), Abd al-Razzaq Abd al-Magid (minister of economy), and Yusuf Wali (minister of agriculture).[86] Uthman had built a power base that he thought (correctly) would assure him of a voice in Egyptian government policy for years to come.

Sadat had tolerated or encouraged the extension of Uthman's patronage because Uthman was part of Sadat's clientele. But while patronage may promote the power of a ruler, it does not always do so. For the government to derive political benefit from a bribe, a series of conditions must be met. The official taking the bribe must be bound to a national political purpose, either by personal conviction or by careful supervision by his superiors. The bribe giver must be dependent on the government in some way; the bribe should not be a simple service fee or cash-and-carry transaction, but part of a network of favors and exchanges that leaves the giver in debt, so that the government may invoke reciprocal services at some later point. A middle-echelon functionary of the NDP who assists some businessman may be helping to extend the authority of his party and president, or he may just be a venal parasite who is trading public assets for his personal profit. When businessmen and bureaucrats swap favors, it is not always clear who is buying whom.[87]

To keep control of such a system, the state must be strong enough to demand good terms, and centralized enough to prevent lower-echelon bureaucrats from going into business on their own. Egypt lacked the kind of political structures that would make such a system of centrally coordinated exchanges possible. Personal networks typically worked more often to insulate lower echelons from above, rather than to exert control. A handful of successful political machines existed on the local level; none ever developed at the national level. Political parties were far too ephemeral to take on the coordinating tasks.[88]

Lacking such controls, corruption in Egypt served private purposes more often than public. Very few of the corrupted customs officials, black-market moneychangers, or businessmen who took loans for nonexistent investments did anything that enhanced the government's power. It may be that, on balance, many businessmen got rich through the PDP, but only a few were transformed into dependable clients for the government.

The PDP also had very few economic accomplishments to brag

about. It was supposed to stimulate activity in the private sector, but most of PDP investments were financed by the public sector. It was intended to encourage small businessmen, but the bulk of projects were actually controlled by a few magnates like Uthman. The projects received the usual host of public subsidies—free land, industrial inputs at controlled prices, and so forth.[89] Yet very few of the projects planned and funded ever reached fruition. In four years the program authorized 159 projects, but only 43, with a combined capital of £E 158 million, reached the stage of production. And only 24 of these were food security projects; 12 worked in housing and 7 in services.[90]

The failings of the PDP illustrate a painful truth. As the stain of corruption spread, it represented not only a lost opportunity for the regime but a major drain on resources. The expansion of smuggling cheated the government of millions of dollars in lost tariffs. Managers of state-run fish farms and poultry plants sold their produce on the black market instead of through official channels. Pilfering from public stocks at hospitals, schools, and factories led to major losses. The greater part of the cement produced at public sector factories was diverted in this way. Managers of the *gam'iyyat*, consumer cooperatives directed by the Ministry of Supply to distribute subsidized consumer goods, routinely diverted much of their stock to the black market.[91]

The state suffered major losses through corruption in the theft of land. In 1972 the government reclaimed 29,000 feddans in Lake Manzala. Battles between the reclamation agency and Parliament over how to distribute the land delayed the formal allocation of title for more than five years. By the time formal titles were awarded, most of the land was already under cultivation by an assortment of opportunists and squatters.[92] In many areas, organized cliques turned land theft into an important enterprise, farming or building on public lands and concealing the loss from the authorities in Cairo. A major survey by the Central Accounting Agency uncovered the theft of 27,000 feddans, worth £E 33 million, in 1983 alone.[93]

Egyptians had no way of knowing how pervasive corruption had become. Officials did not respond to questionnaires asking how much of their salary was earned illegally and ministries were not candid about the extent of their losses to theft. But anecdotal evidence suggested that corruption was widespread. The newspapers were full of rumors about scandal in high places. Anyone who visited a *gam'iyya* or applied for a license from a government office could see some evidence first hand. Egyptians were surrounded by smoke, and they suspected the fire must be fairly extensive.

Egypt was not, it should be emphasized, a kleptocracy. Sadat was not the kind of Third World dictator who expected his tenure in office to be short and was primarily interested in plumping his Swiss bank account while he had an opportunity to do so. Sadat inaugurated his campaign of patronage for strictly political purposes, to bolster his influence and authority. But he lacked the organizational means to ensure either his own monopoly over patronage or its full repayment in political fealty.

To some degree, Sadat understood this weakness. He saw that patronage could win him momentary favor with a group, but not long-term loyalty. So he contented himself with a more limited objective. Patronage gave him just enough influence among competing cliques and cabals so that he could hope to orchestrate contending forces in a manner that preserved the balance of power. He systematically played the left against the right, the Islamist movements against the socialists, and businessmen against labor. He hoped that by playing paired groups off against each other, he could preserve his own paramountcy.

During most of the 1970s, this strategy had served Sadat well. But by 1981 the Egyptian left and right had begun to make very similar criticisms of Sadat, and he found that instead of neutralizing each other there was a potential for them to ally against him. Sadat's peace treaty with Israel, his decision to offer refuge to the shah of Iran, and the growing taint of corruption surrounding his regime united his enemies. Sadat then reversed strategy and opened a massive campaign of repression. In September he tried to decapitate the opposition by arresting fifteen hundred opponents from every color in the political spectrum. On October 6, the brother of one of the Islamist radicals netted during this sweep turned his submachine gun on Sadat during a military parade.

By the time Sadat died, it was already clear to millions of Egyptians that corruption was sucking resources and revenue away from the state while generating only a modest return in political loyalty. The man in the street tended to see corruption as either just another burden the government imposed on citizens, or as a system of favors linking political to economic elites. The spectacle of Sadat promoting his relatives and cronies cost him much of the popularity he had won during the 1973 War. Resentment over these practices festered and the new Islamic movements grew especially adept at using Qur'anic language to denounce Sadat as a "new Pharaoh" who "was of those who make corruption."[94] Corruption had become—and remains—one of the most important and sensitive issues in Egyptian politics.

Parties and Lobbies, New Instruments of Rent Seeking

Sadat's successor, Husni Mubarak, promised to preserve the main lines of his predecessor's policies, even controversial ones like peace with Israel and *infitah*. But he assured the public that these would now be conducted fairly and impartially, without corruption. In Mubarak's very first speech as president, he asserted that "there should be no contradiction between words and deeds, and there should be no hypocrisy, corruption or trading with the livelihood of the people."[95] This remark elicited thunderous applause.

Mubarak fired most of Sadat's ministers and purged many at the upper echelons of the political elite. He dismissed Sadat's ministers for supply, industry, and telecommunications, all of whom were implicated in corrupt activities.[96] He appointed a new cabinet drafted from younger, reform-minded technocrats. He gave an energetic new prime minister, Fu'ad Muhyi al-Din, unprecedented powers to reinvigorate government.

At first, the main thrust of Mubarak's anticorruption campaign was a series of show trials staged at the Court of Ethics, an extraordinary tribunal that Sadat had created to muzzle his opponents. He hoped that by humiliating the heads of the largest patronage networks he could intimidate lower-echelon bribe takers. Things did not work out as he wished.[97]

The most important of these show trials revolved around Ismat Sadat, an unpopular figure who may have amassed as much as $150 million by abusing his brother's influence.[98] Ismat was convicted, but when he emerged from his trial, he threatened: "There has been a truce between me and those concerned. Now that the ruling has been pronounced, the truce is over; I am going to disclose what I have to the people."[99] This dampened the enthusiasm of witnesses at many subsequent trials. The trial of Rashad Uthman had already shown how quickly a chain of corruption could be traced from him through Tawfiq Abd al-Hayy to Uthman Uthman and many other prominent figures in the regime. Very few members of the national elite were free of the taint of corruption. Ismat Sadat's practices differed from the commonplace dealings of the elite only in degree, not in kind. No one was eager to denounce his neighbor when he understood that he might be next.

The trial of Ismat Sadat showed that successfully prosecuting corrupt officials was going to be difficult and risky. It threatened to alienate much of the political elite from Mubarak. This took the wind out of the government's plan to discipline the burgeoning patronage cliques by making an example of a few kingpins. Mubarak and his advisers cast about for a new means to reassert control. Slowly they evolved a strategy that was in keeping with their powers and Mubarak's own leadership style.

The government pioneered its new strategy in its treatment of the Islamist movements. As with so many of the cliques that Mubarak found troublesome, Sadat had encouraged the growth of the Islamist movements as a balance against his left-wing opponents. Only after 1979 had he begun to recognize that the growing mass appeal of the Islamists posed a threat to his authority. A ruthless government campaign of arrests, torture, and assassination, both before and after Sadat's death, had failed to eliminate the Islamists or dent their appeal.[100] Containing the Islamist challenge was the highest priority of the Mubarak government and it was eager to try a new approach.

The keystone of Mubarak's strategy was the old colonial device of dividing the opposition. Some of the Islamists were genuine revolutionaries, dedicated to the overthrow of the government by any means and uninterested in any power-sharing arrangements. Mubarak continued the campaign of repression against them. But many of the Islamists, particularly those affiliated with the Muslim Brothers, were more tractable. Mubarak sought to temper the demands of these Islamist "legalists" by offering them a measure of power in exchange for their renunciation of revolutionary tactics. His government permitted them to publish, to organize in the open, and even to run for public office. In the 1984 elections, the Muslim Brothers won an important voice in the People's Assembly.[101]

This approach proved far more successful than oppression alone. The Islamist legalists, having decided to campaign in elections and share in the responsibilities of government, moderated their demands. They now had a stake in the system and opportunities to promote their influence by legal means. Several Islamist groups, like Tanzim al-Gihad, split into legalist and radical factions. Citizens who inclined toward Islamism now had a choice of voices, and a majority turned toward the legalist alternative. The Islamist radicals survived and continued to organize underground, but their power became marginal.

The Islamists were just one of many political cysts whose development Sadat had encouraged and that now threatened state authority. A few of these were bound, like the Islamists, by ideological ties, but most were just interest groups, patronage networks, and other secular cliques. Yet in many ways they all presented the state with the same problems and options. So long as they operated underground, the government had trouble identifying them or supervising their actions. If they could be encouraged to redirect their activities into legally recognized, institutionalized channels, they might be forced to moderate their claims and the government might gain a measure of control over them. Mubarak and his advisers began to deal with these groups as they had dealt with the Islamists, to offer them a chance to act publicly in exchange for some self-restraint. Mubarak's basic strategy would have been appreciated by Lyndon Johnson, who said that he would rather have his enemies "inside my tent pissing out than outside my tent pissing in."

One way by which Mubarak hoped to temper the activities of these cliques and cabals was by inducing them to affiliate with political parties.[102] Sadat had authorized the existence of competing parties but had carefully kept their powers insignificant. He regularly suspended publication of party-sponsored newspapers and ordered heavy censorship of all public media. He denied the People's Assembly any real influence over policy, so that even when the opposition was represented, it had minimal influence. Mubarak reversed all of these stances.

Mubarak's government gave the press unprecedented freedom, so that opposition newspapers developed into vigorous sources of criticism. He began to respect the autonomy of the judicial system, so that critics might hope to challenge government action in court. He permitted the People's Assembly greater say on policy questions and gave opposition parties a greater chance of winning office. He did not, of course, convert Egypt into a genuine liberal democracy. The police did not have to be concerned about civil liberties while prosecuting their campaign against Islamist radicals. Biased election laws and poll rigging guaranteed Mubarak's own party a comfortable majority in the assembly. But he liberalized the political system just enough so that many citizens felt they had more to gain by participating in it than by subverting it.[103]

Businessmen were particularly eager to take advantage of this opening. By the 1980s many had grown confident that they no longer needed to conceal the influence they exercised through backroom cabals. The private sector no longer stood in the shadow of the public sector. "By 1985, one-third of industrial output, 60 percent of the gross domestic product (when the agricultural and service sectors are included), and 55–70 percent of industrial jobs were generated by private activity."[104] The business elite in Cairo and Alexandria was no longer content to merely adjust to government policy decrees; it expected to be consulted and began to speak assertively about the changes it wanted.

The political parties, for their part, were eager to recruit supporters from the business community. With one exception, all Egyptian parties strove to represent the business community in economic debates. And, as Mubarak sought to strengthen his power base by including opposition parties in a national policy dialogue, the interests of businessmen were increasingly reflected in the laws issued by the Parliament.

The oldest (and smallest) of the opposition parties is the Liberal (*Ahrar*) party led by Mustafa Kamil Murad. During the 1970s Murad was the head of the Federation of Chambers of Commerce where he built a career defending the interests of small businessmen. In 1977 he put together one of the first probusiness coalitions in the Parliament to lobby against Law 119, which would have limited the maximum profit on imports to 30 percent. (Sadat, shocked by the energy this coalition displayed in opposing his legislation, retaliated by issuing regulations in 1978 that curtailed the power of the chambers of commerce.) The Liberals have never been able to win a following at the polls. Murad is a classical liberal who preaches the virtues of economic competition. Adherents of the mainstream, rent-seeking business community think he is a bit out of step with the times, although they admire his dedication to his principles and speak fondly of the years he has spent battling the state bureaucracy.[105]

A far more effective voice for the business community is the New Wafd party. The party is headed by the same men who led the old Wafd party until Nasser's 1952 coup drove them from power. They are, not surprisingly, stridently critical of Nasser and his socialist policies and favor repealing rent controls, dismantling much of the public sector, and returning many sequestered properties. Yet the New Wafd is, if anything, less liberal in its economic stance than its progenitor.[106] It accepts the need for the state to maintain a safety net of price controls and subsidies that protect the livelihood of the poorest elements of the population. It now gives the concept of social justice a central place in its platforms.[107] This revision of their ideology has permitted the party leaders to retain not only their old power base among the commercial bourgeoisie (particularly in Alexandria) but to win a new following among small entrepreneurs and conservatives.

The most passionate defense of business interests in Egypt today may come from the Islamic parties. The oldest and largest of these, the Muslim Brothers, is directed by men with strong business ties. Many of them made personal fortunes in Saudi Arabia after Nasser expelled them from Egypt in the 1960s. They have spoken out in defense of the Islamic money management companies and have led the campaign against rent controls in Parliament. They advocate replacing Egyptian civilian codes with Islamic law, which they feel offers greater security and latitude to owners of private property. They note with pride that the Prophet Muhammad was himself a merchant. Yet they, too, are not economic liberals in the Western sense. They emphasize the moral bonds that constrain relations between employers and employees; they believe that the state should regulate markets to ensure that prices are fair; and, of course, they condemn all forms of interest as usury.

Still, these are restrictions with which many Egyptians, including businessmen, are comfortable. As Egyptians sought an alternative to the government and the official economy in the 1980s, the Islamic movement gained momentum. The Muslim Brothers proved the most effective magnet for luring votes to the opposition. In the 1984 elections it formed an alliance with the New Wafd party, which won 13 percent of the popular vote and all fifty-eight opposition seats in Parliament. In the 1987 elections it switched and formed an alliance with the Liberals and the Socialist Labor party which took 17 percent of the popular vote and fifty-six seats. (After breaking with the Muslim Brothers, the Wafd's share in the Parliament dropped to thirty-six seats.)[108]

Only one party in Egypt has been immune to the growing influence of Islam and capital. The National Progressive Unionist party (Tagammu'), an alliance of Marxists and unreconstructed Nasserists, still insists that the state must play a leading role in the economy and is highly critical of both *infitah* and the business elite it fostered. The Tagammu' has a strong following among intellectuals, including some of the brightest social analysts in Egypt today, and its newspaper, *al-Ahali*, is widely respected. But it remains a tiny party, commanding only three seats in the People's Assembly. Its program has gradually been moderating, and many of its members now speak like moderate social democrats. Tagammu' no longer favors rent control; instead it supports an active private sector and even countenances privatization of some parts of the public sector. Its leftist heritage remains most evident in its protests against the inequalities bred by *infitah*, its defense of consumer subsidies, and its criticism of Egypt's reliance on foreign loans and aid.[109]

By mustering its intellectual capital, the Tagammu' has been influential in setting the terms of debate on major issues before the People's Assembly. But even on the rare occasions when they have won support from other opposition parties, such coalitions have been dwarfed by the absolute majority commanded by the government's party, the National Democratic party (NDP).

Mubarak himself has attempted to woo support within the business community. He sought to attract businessmen into the ranks of his own organ, the NDP. In his case, however, this was just one facet of a much wider effort to build a popular constituency for the party. Sadat, who had created the NDP, ensured its majority in Parliament by fairly blatantly rigging elections. On election day the Ministry of the Interior simply packed the ballot boxes; any plebiscites Sadat supported were always approved by at least 98 percent of the votes. Mubarak had to curb such electioneering in order to win wider participation in legal political processes. Yet he could not afford to allow his party, the NDP, to lose its majority. He tempered, although he did not eliminate, voter fraud. And he charged his intimates with devising a way to widen the NDP's appeal with the electorate.

Ironically, this ultimately opened the door for the persistence of the patronage politics that had eroded public authority under Sadat. The NDP lacked an ideology, program, or symbols that might have endeared it to the public. Under Sadat the party had been little more than a supporting chorus for the president, whose membership consisted entirely of people who were trying to promote careers in government. Many Egyptians believed that NDP membership was a condition for holding public office. The party had no real cadres, just employees; to a large extent, the party and the state were coterminous.[110] Lacking an ideology or a record of public service, the NDP's leadership had only patronage as a tool for winning a constituency; it traded material benefits for the votes of the electorate.

A natural target of this patronage was the business community. Many of Sadat's rent-seeking cronies, like Uthman Uthman and Mustafa Khalil, were already members of the party. Other businessmen joined and turned the party's Economic Committee into a powerful lobby for influencing legislation. Under Mubarak, "the National Democratic party has tried to operate as the principal steering committee of Egypt's private sector, aggregating its demands, arbitrating its internal conflicts, and serving as its conduit for state largesse."[111] The NDP cannot claim to be the sole or even the primary spokesman for business interests. But its control over government largesse has won a large enough constituency among businessmen to draw away support from the Wafd and smaller parties that articulated a clearer program of economic liberalization.

Businessmen with agricultural interests form an especially potent wing inside the NDP. In the 1984 elections, the party leadership had noted that voter turnout in rural districts was dramatically higher than in urban areas.[112] Villagers tended to vote in blocs, with each individual casting his ballot for the party his entire clan had agreed to support. Clans, in turn, tended to negotiate their votes with local notables; they would throw their ballots to the candidate who offered the most generous patronage. Often the way an entire village was going to vote could be decided by a handful of local clan chiefs, the village mayor, and a few local notables.[113] This provided an ideal environment for the NDP to employ its powers of patronage. The party began to play up the policy changes it had made that would benefit the peasantry. Through its influence over the Interior Ministry and the Ministry of Local Government, the NDP could offer village elites tangible and tailored perquisites.[114]

From 1985 onward the NDP made capturing the rural vote a major priority.[115] At its November 1985 congress, the NDP retired some of its older, ex officio functionaries and elected a younger, more energetic leadership council.[116] The party's new secretary general was Yusuf Wali, the minister of agriculture. Politically astute, Minister Wali was also the man who happened to control the best instruments for winning the rural vote. Wali consistently urged the party and the government to terminate government crop procurements, partly as a means to secure the support of rural voters.

Some of the agricultural interest groups that associated themselves with the NDP during Wali's tenure—poultry breeders, fruit exporters, rich peasants, and others—were formally affiliated with the party. Even those that were not sought to influence the deliberations of the NDP's Agricultural Committee and Economic Committee. Many of these groups, in fact, developed into institutionalized, independent lobbies, which solicited favors from the NDP, other parties, and the cabinet itself.

The development of such lobbies was an important trend in the 1980s, encouraged partly by Mubarak's strategy of luring private cliques into public life. Under Nasser and Sadat the only organs through which businessmen were permitted to organize and voice their interests were the Federation of Chambers of Commerce and the Federation of Industries. Both of these organizations included firms from the public sector and were effectively controlled by the state. But in 1981 local businessmen (with support from the U.S. Embassy) formed the American Chamber of Commerce in Cairo, which was independent of government control. It became the model for a new generation of autonomous business organizations. A competing group of Cairenes formed the Egyptian-American Businessmen's Association. The most influential importers and exporters at Egypt's major port banded together to create the Economic Committee of Alexandria, which had successfully garnered a role in trade policy. None of these groups had more than three hundred members; their influence reflects their wealth and connections rather than their numbers.[117]

The most important of these new lobbies is the Society of Egyptian Businessmen (established in 1982). Its membership is generally restricted to the private sector, although a few government economists and officials have been permitted to join. In May 1984 it had around two hundred fifty members, the cream of Egypt's business elite, each of whom paid £E 1,000 in annual dues. Of its members, 28 percent owned firms specializing in commerce and 17 percent in food or textiles; the rest were scattered between construction, consulting, advertising, tourism, and transportation. More than a dozen members were former government ministers, including two of its founders, Sultan Abu Ali (Ministry of Economy) and Fu'ad Sultan (Ministry of Tourism).[118]

The power of these lobbies grew steadily in the early 1980s and attained a critical mass in 1985. In that year the prime minister convened a Joint Committee for Government and Business which created a formal institutional channel for contact between the two communities. It included two delegates from the prime minister's office and five from the line ministries and fourteen businessmen.[119] Representatives from the business community began to work through direct meetings with the ministers and their advisers, often preparing position papers for them. When the government announced an important series of revisions to customs and tariff policy in August 1986, the business lobbies convened a formal meeting with the ministers of economy, trade, and foreign affairs to sort out the application of the new laws.[120]

At the beginning of 1987 the government unveiled the draft of its new five-year economic plan. Kamal Ganzuri, the minister of planning, asked the Society of Egyptian Businessmen to make suggestions on how to execute the objectives of the plan. The society prepared a detailed critique, questioning the plan's assumptions and suggesting that its growth projections be revised downward. It also noted that since the private sector was expected to undertake half the projects, it should be considered a half partner—with all the benefits and obligations that would entail.[121]

Formally or informally, business lobbies had emerged as a major force in economic policy. This development might be considered a victory for Mubarak's battle against corruption. Such lobbies were public organizations that operated through recognized legal channels. The government could negotiate with them and temper their demands. Yet the growing popularity of lobbies did not restrain rent seeking much. Rent seeking was increasingly conducted in parliamentary committees rather than at secret soirees, but its popularity and scope remained unchanged.

The development of lobbies and parties reduced corruption but certainly did not eliminate it. This was evident to any Egyptian who picked up the newspapers and read headlines like "£E 250 Million Leak from the Insurance Funds," "The Ministry of Economy Suggests a Revision of the Exchange Law in the Interests of al-Mahjub, Chief of the Mafia, and His Assistant al-Bashir," and "New Scandal in the Ministry of Economy."[122] Government officials were still interested in graft, leaving corruption as an alternative for those who either could not afford to join a lobby or had failed to attain their ends through lobbying.

In 1986 alone the Ministry of the Interior made 98 arrests for embezzlement, 454 for tax evasion, 101,000 for pilfering state assets, and 385 for theft of state lands. It estimated—very conservatively— that Egyptians spent £E 666 million on bribes and influence peddling that year.[123] Mubarak tried to put the best face on these facts, but there was always a hint of resignation in his voice. In an interview in 1989 he admitted: "Corruption will continue to exist as long as there are human beings. . . . The concept is to fight this scourge and limit the resulting damage."[124]

On an even more pessimistic note, Egypt's leading sociologist, Dr. Sa'd al-Din Ibrahim, contends that in Egypt today "corruption has become a science and an art. It has become a craft and a practice, to the point that we can now say that it has crystallized in the last few years into a ruling organization. We no longer face miscellaneous incidents of corruption in a given regime, rather we face 'a comprehensive system of corruption,' which has its own encompassing principles, mechanisms, symbols, language, and practice."[125]

Conclusion

Egyptian businessmen share with their counterparts in other countries an earnest desire to make money. They differ from the economists' image of capitalists, and perhaps from some businessmen in other countries, in one respect. Their historical experience has convinced them that an active state role in the economy is necessary to coordinate their individual investments, shelter them from unfair foreign competition, and underwrite the risks and costs they absorb when pioneering new activities. Theirs is an attitude toward the state that is characteristic of businessmen in much of the Third World.[126]

Egyptian bureaucrats are also *dirigistes* and have been happy to intervene in the economy whenever they suspected that there was a constituency for doing so. This does not mean that their relations with businessmen have always been affable. They have often favored one group of businessmen (industry, small firms) at the expense of others (trade, large firms). They have assessed the value of intervention not only in terms of its impact on economic development but in terms of its political effects on their enemies and clients. In the early 1960s, under Nasser's leadership, they staked out for themselves primary and autonomous responsibility for managing the economy.

Despite these quarrels, Egyptian bureaucrats and businessmen have never contemplated a divorce. Even Egyptian Marxists doubt that the state has enough power to liquidate the business community, or that the economy could be developed without the energy that entrepreneurs provide. Although the dusty, dimly lit offices of Cairo bureaucrats with their sheaves of disorganized files may remind visitors of Warsaw or Sofia, no significant group of Egyptian officials ever contemplated turning their country into a centrally planned economy on the Eastern European model. Over the long run, the private sector and the public have worked to accommodate each other.[127]

Over the past twenty years, in fact, Egyptian businessmen have won back much of the influence and autonomy they formerly enjoyed. First through patronage networks and later through parties and lobbies, they have regained some control over the pattern of state intervention. They have learned to cultivate political influence and to translate it back into economic privilege. Today Egyptian officials, from the head of state down to the lowest provincial functionary, must take heed of the interests of the business community.

Many Western analysts think that this kind of cooperation between businessman and bureaucrat must be beneficial. They blame the economic problems of Nasser's Egypt on his alienation of the business community, suggesting that his hostility frightened entrepreneurs away from local investments and encouraged capital flight. They suggest that he would have been more successful if, like the military regime in Brazil (1964–85), he had cultivated an alliance with local and foreign businessmen.[128] There is some truth in this.

But the pattern of collaboration between businessmen and bureaucrats under Sadat and Mubarak illustrates some of the perils of such a course. As businessmen gained greater control over the scale and location of state intervention, the allocation of state-created rents did not become markedly more rational. The cash and energy squandered in rent seeking grew steadily. So did the scope and seriousness of political corruption.

The political-economic system that emerged in Egypt can aptly be called "crony capitalism."[129] In such a system businessmen and bureaucrats ally in cabals to seek mutual benefit by influencing the pattern of state intervention in the economy. They do not peg the allocation of state-created rents to the performance or productivity of recipient enterprises, so the system augments personal profits and private power without promoting national economic development.

Forms of crony capitalism are commonplace throughout the Third World. In some countries, like Pakistan or the Philippines, a few hundred old families have learned to control a newly independent state and to turn its resources to personal benefit. In others, like Egypt and Indonesia, a "new class" of state officials has gradually interwoven its fortunes with those of the business community.[130] In all of these societies some enterprises, with or without state support, do turn into profitable and productive ventures. But the economic burdens of rent seeking and the imposition of a political calculus on business decisions make such successes a statistical rarity. Crony capitalist societies develop slowly, if at all.

The form of crony capitalism constructed in Egypt includes some virtues missing in others. The Egyptian state has intervened not just to protect elite interests but to shelter lower-class consumers from price rises and to redistribute land to relatively powerless peasants. But a price has been paid for this generosity. As the number of groups with access to state-created rents or entitlements has expanded, so has the burden on the national treasury. Similarly, as the scope of rents has widened, so the disincentives to real productivity, whether by businessmen or factory laborers, have become more pervasive.

By the late 1980s the costs of crony capitalism threatened to overwhelm Egypt. The state could no longer absorb the costs of guaranteeing incomes for all the different groups it had courted. Political authority was being undermined by corruption and by the constant struggle to appease contending interest groups in conditions of growing economic austerity. Most Egyptians agreed upon the need for comprehensive economic reform. Few, however, concurred about where, when, and how to initiate such reform.

CHAPTER 5

Price Liberalization in a Rent-Seeking Economy

WHEN HUSNI MUBARAK SUCCEEDED ANWAR SADAT IN OCTOBER 1981, he promised an immediate review of his predecessor's economic policies.[1] He assured investors that he would preserve the broad outlines of Sadat's reforms, including the opening of the Egyptian economy to the outside world and the expansion of opportunities for the private sector. Yet he also admitted that *infitah* had a dark side. It had produced very little concrete foreign investment, had been abused by importers and profiteers, and had bred social inequality, corruption, and unrest. Mubarak suggested that its central flaw was that it had liberalized consumption, and he claimed that his administration would focus on liberalizing production. He wanted the Egyptian economy to become leaner and stronger, more competitive, and he pledged to follow the economic path pioneered by Japan and South Korea.

Mubarak's first cabinet choices gave hope that he might deliver on these promises. For prime minister he selected Fu'ad Muhyi al-Din, a physician, a man of integrity with a zealous interest in setting the country's finances in order. Muhyi al-Din organized a series of national economic conferences that gave businessmen, experts, and lay citizens a chance to air their complaints, offer alternatives, and participate in the redefinition of policy.[2] He purged Sadat's cronies and anyone suspected of corruption from the cabinet, replacing them with a new generation of technocrats who had proven their dedication to reform.

The new cabinet's mandate for reform extended to agricultural policy. The new minister of agriculture, Yusuf Wali, came as close to subscribing to the ideology of economic liberalism as any Egyptian can. He very clearly understood how tampering with the market creates disincentives for production. He often argued that the gap between individual behavior and social good in Egypt was largely a product of state interference. He suggested that the state should shepherd private forces but do no more than that.[3]

Wali was unusually blunt in his willingness to affix blame for the problems of the agricultural sector. He linked them squarely to the industrialization drive of the 1960s, and the Nasserists' willingness "to depend on financing from the agricultural sector, the sector most advanced and developed at that time. To achieve this, the government executed several price and marketing policies to transfer the greatest possible share of the surplus of the agricultural sector to other sectors. Then it defined prices for the chief crops and monopolized markets in order to benefit from their surplus revenue during the industrial development plan."[4] This discouraged farmers, encouraged migration to the cities, and in turn left the country vulnerable to the effects of the world food crisis in 1972.

Yet Wali was also happy to blame Sadat. He had some unkind words for the food subsidy program, which he felt was responsible for the dramatic increase in consumption. (Wali was one of the earliest proponents of the reduced-consumption strategy.) In the 1970s the government should have admitted that there was a problem and sought to encourage farmers to produce more. Instead it had sought to bridge the food gap by increasing imports, thereby mortgaging the entire economy.[5] (See figure 5-1.)

Dr. Wali's agricultural price reforms finally took root—in 1988, seven years after he began pushing his program. Even then, several key crops—cotton, rice, sugar, and to a lesser degree, wheat—were still subject to government control. This price reform is an achievement that should not be dismissed, but its contribution should not be exaggerated either. It was implemented very slowly, and during the interim Egypt's economic problems got much worse. When Dr. Wali took office, Egypt's population was under 44 million. By the time his reforms took effect, farmers—with essentially the same land area available—had to feed an additional 6-8 million people. In the same period the ability of the Egyptian government to raise investment for agriculture had deteriorated. In 1982 the Egyptian government had enjoyed revenue from oil prices as high as $34 a barrel and a steady flow of foreign loans. By 1987 oil prices had dropped to $16 a barrel, foreign loans had dried up, and Egypt was desperately trying to

Figure 5-1. Egypt's Race against Time, 1971-81

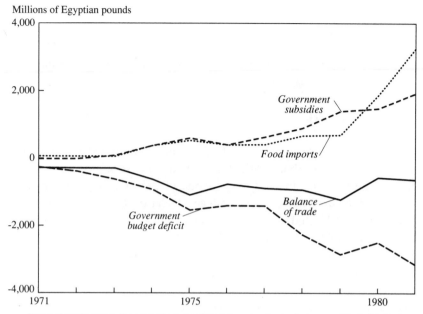

Millions of Egyptian pounds

Source: Grant M. Scobie, *Food Subsidies in Egypt: Their Impact on Foreign Exchange and Trade* (Washington: International Food Policy Research Institute, 1983), pp. 56 and 59.

assemble $2.7 billion to make the following year's payments on its outstanding foreign debt.[6]

Dr. Wali was aware of the price Egypt had paid for delay. His personal hopes for the development of Egyptian agriculture centered on a plan to increase agricultural exports, particularly to the lucrative European market. When he took office several members of the European Community were offering to waive the restrictions created by its common agricultural policy (CAP) and permit low-tariff imports of Egyptian fruits and vegetables. Egypt did not take full advantage of this offer; domestic constraints on production meant that it shipped less produce than European quotas would have allowed. By 1987, when Wali's policy reforms finally began to take effect, the opportunity to plead for an expansion of these quotas had passed. Other countries, like Morocco and Jordan, had increased their horticultural exports to Europe at Egypt's expense. And the European states, hurrying to complete arrangements for their economic union in 1992, were no longer receptive to making special arrangements for Cairo.[7] In economic development, as in seduction, timing is everything.

Why did the Egyptian government take so long to accomplish so little? This chapter surveys some of the complex forces that have slowed, obstructed, or distorted efforts to reform economic policy.

Yusuf Wali, Reformer

Dr. Wali was born in 1930 in the Fayyum, a valley west of the Nile long famous for its high agricultural yields and specialty crops (like flowers and sugar). In 1951 he was one of the first graduates of the newly established agricultural college at Cairo University. He later traveled to the United States, where he earned a doctorate in agronomy at the University of Arizona in 1958. After returning to Egypt, he obtained a professorship at another new institution, Ayn Shams University just outside Cairo. Here he built a career as one of the country's leading experts in horticulture, especially fruit production, and eventually was voted a special chair.[8]

In 1981 he was a genuine unknown in Egyptian national politics. To most, he appeared to be a simple technocrat. But in fact he had a lifelong interest in politics. Between 1954 and 1957 he had served as national director of President Nasser's youth organization. He had gained hands-on experience in how to manage power and cliques.[9] At Ayn Shams he was still thought of as a politico, as someone who kept a line open to the regime, and even perhaps as a police spy. In the early 1970s he began to work as a consultant to the Ministry of Agriculture. In this capacity he became a close friend of Mahmud Dawud, Sadat's last minister of agriculture. Dawud may have been the man who proposed Wali as his replacement to Mubarak.

In 1982 when Wali moved into his new office at the Ministry of Agriculture complex in Duqqi, he surprisingly showed only moderate interest in establishing his personal authority within the ministry. Instead, he delegated administrative responsibility to a coterie of close friends and advisers whom he appointed as undersecretaries to various divisions. Some of his followers were power brokers, men who knew how to turn money, favors, and family contacts into sources of influence. For many years he employed Muhammad Abbas, a politico with family connections to President Mubarak, as his deputy secretary.

But the majority of Wali's devotees were intellectuals, men like Ahmad Guwayli and Uthman al-Khuli who shared his interest in reforming agricultural policy. They wrote most of *Agricultural Strategy for the 1980s*, which Wali adopted as his policy blueprint. Over the years they were joined by a new generation of Young Turk agronomists like Hasan Khidr and Adil Biltagi who spoke English and had attended American universities—skills that assisted Wali in dealing with his counterparts and sponsors at the U.S. Agency for International Development (AID).

Wali himself displayed much more enthusiasm for dealing with national and international politics than he did for bureaucratic infighting. It was his success in these arenas that made him stand out within Mubarak's cabinet. Over the years Mubarak appointed many reform-oriented technocrats to ministerial positions. Most of them were disasters.[10] Either their mastery of politics was too weak to allow them any real impact on policy, or their enthusiasm for wheeling and dealing sucked them into promoting their personal careers at the expense of their reform programs. Wali was different. His personal power increased steadily, and he became the single most influential technocrat in the cabinet. In the late 1980s he was frequently rumored to be one of Mubarak's favorite choices for the prime minister's office or the vice-presidency. Yet his commitment to reform never waned.

Dr. Wali's political skills were both evident and necessary in the first few months after he took office. Eager to avoid Sadat's mistakes, Mubarak called for—and got—a wide-ranging public debate over national economic policy. He authorized a series of conferences at which ministerial staff, businessmen, and intellectuals reassessed the strengths and weaknesses of *infitah*. He encouraged Parliament to review its economic legislation. Arguments about mechanization, rent controls, price controls, and other aspects of agriculture figured prominently in all these debates. In this atmosphere, Dr. Wali faced two dangers. One was that some faction in Parliament or the polity—perhaps one opposed to reform—would win the debate and impose its views on the Ministry of Agriculture, turning it into a simple executor of policies defined elsewhere. The other was that debate would just muddy the waters, leaving people confused and skeptical, making it difficult for the ministry to win the public support it needed to implement reform.

Dr. Wali moved quickly to lend his own voice to these debates and helped to define their terms. He devoted long hours to addressing the various production conferences held in 1982. At the seventh conference of Egyptian economists he presented a controversial paper outlining his argument that price and marketing controls were the chief cause of the food gap. He did not convert all of his opponents, but he did persuade them that he was thoughtful and sincere. More than that, the attendance of officials like Wali sent a signal to conference participants that the government was looking for their input and encouraged their cooperation.[11]

His performance before Parliament was even more impressive. The Agricultural Policy Committee of the Consultative Assembly held a lengthy series of hearings about agriculture and charged Sa'd Hagras (a former deputy to Sayyid Mar'i) to draft a detailed report on recommended policy changes. This report called for decisive action in three areas: combining fragmented plots into large, integrated farming areas; revising price policy to give real production incentives to the peasantry; and lifting rental controls to encourage the most efficient use of land. Parliament appeared determined to seize the initiative and take control over the direction of agricultural policy. The committee summoned the new ministers for agriculture, supply, and irrigation to answer its complaints.

When Yusuf Wali testified before the committee he was not defensive; rather, he seized the opportunity to reassure the parliamentarians of his own intentions. He outlined his own plan for reforming agricultural policy and stressed its congruence with the committee's concerns.[12] He urged the assembly to focus its attention on the immediate problem of price reform and to delay changes in the more complicated issue of land rents. He told the delegates of his belief that the key to success lay in raising prices for farmers. He said, "It is well known that the secret to getting farmers to accept cultivation of crops like *ful* [broad beans] is for the state to buy the harvest from them at international prices."[13] He stressed that the effects were especially crippling in cotton production. His repeated appearances won him a permanent coterie of allies and assured his personal control over agricultural policy.

During this period of public debate, Dr. Wali showed a knack for public relations that would continue to serve him well through the years to come. The reforms he urged were not substantially different from those advocated by his predecessor, Mahmud Dawud.[14] But

Dawud tended to be reticent, had little contact with the press, and spoke very cautiously about Egypt's agricultural potential. Wali, in contrast, cultivated the friendship of the press, gave reporters long interviews in which he outlined his plans, and tried to seem continuously (perhaps excessively) optimistic. In his first press conference he painted an elaborate picture of the problems of land loss (*tajrif*), the protein shortage, the need to export vegetables. He also raised a theme that would remain central to his public relations strategy for years to come—the importance of food security.[15]

Wali was not, of course, the first minister of agriculture to invoke the problem of food security, but he harnessed it in a new and more effective manner. He continued the traditional practice of raising the specter of hunger to scare other officials into granting him greater funding and authority. He let no press conference pass without quoting President Mubarak's remark that "he who doesn't own his food doesn't own his freedom."[16] But he also tried to highlight Egypt's progress in meeting its own food needs, arguing that past attainments justified future investment. He asserted that with a bit more effort, Egypt could attain complete self-sufficiency in seven years.[17] This approach enabled him to keep the food security issue alive in the early 1980s, when international wheat prices were down and hard currency revenues were up.

As part of this public relations strategy, Dr. Wali took to bragging about his ministry's accomplishments sooner than anyone could reasonably have expected results. He rightfully boasted that, with American assistance, he had unified the agricultural research and extension systems.[18] But he misrepresented things a bit when he took credit for sudden increases in the production of lentils and broad beans—the harvest of the former had declined sharply just before he took office and was only returning to normal levels.[19] The truth was that there was no dramatic increase in the production of any crop but corn before 1985. Statistics compiled by the United Nations' Food and Agriculture Organization suggested that total annual growth of agricultural production in Egypt actually declined from 3.5 percent in the period 1970–80 to 2.6 percent in 1980–83 and 0.2 percent in 1984. The drop was largest for major crops like cotton, rice, and sugar. Dr. Wali's reform program had not yet progressed far enough for its effects to show.[20]

Production of the decisive crop for Egypt's food security calculus, wheat, only began to improve in 1987.[21] This slow response reflected three factors. First, it took Dr. Wali more than four years in office before he could implement major changes in crop price policy. Second, the iron logic of cropping cycles meant that it took several years before these changes in state policy percolated down into farmers' field practices. And third, despite his many claims, it seems that Wali never actually believed Egypt was capable of attaining self-sufficiency in wheat.

Wali understood that the only way for Egypt to meet its wheat demand purely from domestic resources would be to rip out all other crops and plant every inch of arable soil in grain. The projections and documents prepared by his ministry reflected this awareness. The 1982–87 Five-Year Plan, for example, noted that in 1982 Egypt imported more than 5.4 million tons of wheat and flour and forecast that by 1987 it would be importing more than 6.4 million tons. For Egypt to be self-sufficient it would have to triple domestic wheat production from 2.5 million to 7.5 million tons. Assuming that it could get a high average yield, like 1.5 tons a feddan, this would require devoting 6 million feddans to wheat. But Egypt's total cultivable land area is only 5.8 million feddans, so that even if it gave up cultivating every other winter crop it would still be short by 200,000 feddans.[22] Wali thought there was no economic justification for such a radical approach.

Privately, Wali did not believe that Egypt could attain self-sufficiency, but he did have some thoughts on what an appropriate food security strategy might be. He was one of the most outspoken officials on the need to curb consumption of wheat. He often noted that consumption had increased from 80 kilograms a person in 1950 to 200 kilograms in 1985 and charged that most of this increase was actually being fed to animals. To discourage such waste, he supported efforts to increase the price of bread to 2 piasters.[23]

But he did not believe that consumption could be reduced enough to eliminate Egypt's dependence on imported wheat. Rather, he argued that Egypt should increase its agricultural exports to ensure that the country earned enough hard currency to cover the cost of necessary cereal imports. He wanted Egypt to cultivate its comparative advantage. Although Egypt's wheat yields were high, they could not quite match those attained in countries like the United States and Australia, where large, flat grasslands were ideal for growing cereals. On the other hand, Egypt's abundant sunshine, regular and cheap water supply, and proximity to European markets gave it an edge in growing fruits and vegetables. Even when wheat was very expensive on global markets, the most efficient use of Egyptian land and capital lay in horticulture, not cereals. (Egyptians often called this approach "the California strategy" since Wali and other officials often cited studies prepared by experts at the agricultural school of the University of California at Davis.)[24]

Wali urged farmers to grow more high-value crops that could be marketed abroad, like tropical fruits, cloves, and jasmine. He personally launched a campaign to encourage Egyptian farmers to plant strawberries, a crop that fetched outrageous prices on the European winter market.[25] He advocated major reforms in the national export marketing system, including the creation of a Federation of Fruit and Vegetable Producers and Exporters that would serve as a private sector alternative to public sector firms like Nile Company and Wadi Company for agricultural exports.[26]

Eventually, long after his personal authority was firmly established, Wali began to share his doubts about self-sufficiency with the public. He began to admit that his ministry was only trying to promote wheat production up to the level of 50 percent of domestic consumption. Eventually he confessed that self-sufficiency in corn, the main fodder crop, was also impossible.[27] He tried to explain that as the population grew, the country would have to devote ever larger resources to maintaining its current sufficiency in the production of rice and other food crops.[28] By 1987 President Mubarak had publicly endorsed this change of policy.[29] Through a deft public relations campaign, Wali succeeded in redefining the central objective of Egyptian agricultural policy and substituting his own vision of food security.

Wali was adept not only at leading the press into highlighting his accomplishments but diverting them from his embarrassments. One of these was his personal relationship with the Israelis. As a horticulturalist, Wali had taken an early interest in Israeli-pioneered technologies for cultivating arid land, such as drip irrigation. Soon after Sadat opened relations with Israel, he began to cultivate friendships with Israeli experts in this area and organized a series of private seminars that brought them together with their Egyptian counterparts.[30] Israeli experts actually began to work on certain Egyptian agricultural experiments. Wali was not always able to keep these contacts quiet. In 1986 the Egyptian press went wild when they discovered he had assisted a group of Israeli investors who wanted to lease an island in the Nile for a tourist project.[31] Wali weathered these revelations, but he paid a price in prestige for violating the unwritten rule that (ten years after Camp David) still prevents most Egyptian intellectuals from making unofficial contact with Israelis.

This price was somewhat offset by the fact that Wali's Israeli connections helped to endear him to the Americans. The official justification for AID's mission in Egypt was to bolster the Camp David peace process, and Wali seemed to be a living embodiment of this goal. Moreover, Wali appealed to the Americans for other reasons. Unlike some other foreign agencies, AID had come to share the Egyptian conviction that agriculture was the key to the future. And, like Wali, the Americans thought that decontrolling prices was the key to agricultural development. From the moment he took office, Wali found the Americans eager allies in his reform campaign.[32]

American support bolstered Wali in a number of ways. In 1982 Wali worked closely with E.T. York and a team of American experts who came to Cairo to prepare a report, *Strategies for Accelerating Agricultural Development*. The York report generated a good deal of attention (and criticism) inside Egypt.[33] Since its recommendations were very similar to Wali's own, he was able to present the report to the cabinet as a vindication of his own policies by scientific experts from Cairo's strongest ally and most valuable source of aid. In particular, this American imprimatur helped to convince Mubarak that Wali was on the right track.

In other cases the value of American support was material rather than political. During the first decade of AID's activities in Egypt, its rural programs were project oriented, supporting development of a host of agricultural activities (see table 5-1). These projects were useful to Wali because they contributed not only expertise but funds. For example, AID budgeted $49 million for a Small Farmer Production Project (SFPP) designed to improve the supply of rural credit. American experts devised new packages of seeds and crop rotations and, to encourage their adoption among Egyptian farmers, AID offered loans worth £E 76 million.[34] Some of its Egyptian managers also used SFPP to augment the influence of the minister of agriculture. The Egyptian codirector of the project, Muhammad Nur, used to walk through the fields handing out rolls of dollar bills to cooperative farmers as a way of building rural clientage networks to support his old schoolfriend and patron, Yusuf Wali.

Table 5-1. U.S. Assistance to Rural Programs
Funding in millions of dollars

Program	Year started	Scheduled year of completion	Project funding Total	Average annual
Agricultural productivity projects				
Water Use and Management	1976	1985	13.00	1.44
Rice Research	1977	1987	20.90	2.09
Agricultural Mechanization	1979	1987	37.60	4.70
Canal Maintenance	1977	1984	30.00	4.29
Irrigation Pumping	1977	1985	18.90	2.36
Agricultural Development Systems	1977	1986	14.90	1.66
Poultry Improvement	1977	1984	5.40	0.77
Aquaculture Development	1978	1988	23.40	2.34
Major Cereals Improvement	1979	1987	52.40	6.55
Small Farmer Production	1979	1987	49.00	6.13
Agricultural Cooperative Marketing	1979	1983	4.70	1.18
Small Scale Agricultural Activities	1979	1984	1.60	0.32
Agricultural Management Development	1980	1986	4.10	0.68
Irrigation Management	1981	1991	340.00	34.00
Agricultural Data Collection	1980	1988	5.00	0.63
National Agricultural Research	1985	1993	130.00	16.25
Agricultural Production and Credit	1986	1993	123.00	17.57
Total			873.90	102.96
Local government and decentralization programs				
Local Development (LD II)	1985	1992	231.00	33.00
Development Decentralization I	1978	1987	26.20	2.91
Basic Village Services	1980	1988	225.00	28.13
Decentralization Support Fund	1980	1989	100.00	11.11
Total			582.20	75.15

Source: USAID Cairo, *Status Report: United States Economic Assistance to Egypt* (U.S. Agency for International Development, Cairo, September 1988).

After 1985 American interest in project aid began to wane. By 1987 the Americans had closed down all but three of their agricultural projects and shifted to a new approach, policy dialogue. Instead of tying up American dollars and talent in small, complex programs, the new strategy involved giving economic aid as straightforward cash grants that the Egyptian government could spend as it pleased. Release of these grants, however, was made conditional on Egyptian policy reforms; unless the government could produce evidence that it was decontrolling prices, cutting subsidies, or narrowing its budget deficit, aid would be withheld. This AID policy dialogue sought the same ends and used the same mechanisms as the structural adjustment loans offered by the International Monetary Fund (IMF). In fact, AID officials saw their agency, the IMF, and the World Bank as triumvirs executing a common campaign to force the Egyptians into reform.[35]

Many Egyptian officials were horrified by this new approach. It meant that in the midst of Egypt's own economic crisis the Americans were complicating and delaying the delivery of aid. Wali himself was not happy; the reduction of project aid meant the loss of discretionary funds that he used to tap from missions like the Small Farmer Production Project. But he quickly learned to turn the new situation to his advantage. The Americans were, after all, putting pressure on the Egyptian government to undertake precisely the reforms he was interested in promoting. And he, in turn, was one of the few Egyptian officials who could deliver what the Americans wanted. In October 1987 he won World Bank approval for a $200 million loan for agricultural projects and was able to claim that his ministry had done more than any other to redress donor skepticism about Egypt.[36] As a result, he gained even more influence in cabinet discussions of major issues like the budget and foreign affairs.

As a result of favorable press coverage, American support, and his own control over the ministry's influence over the lives of the rural population, Wali's power grew and he became an increasingly prominent figure in national politics. By 1984 he was serving as the government's principle conduit for discussions with the opposition. (He was well placed to do this, since he had toyed with the idea of joining the New Wafd party in 1977).[37] He had formed a working alliance with the minister of the interior, as a result of which he was able to parachute some of his protégés into influential positions in local government. Ahmad Guwayli became governor of Damietta, Yahya al-Hasan governor of Minufiyya, and Uthman al-Khuli president of Minufiyya University. In the 1986 elections to the upper house of Parliament, twenty-three of the thirty-one newly elected members owed some debt to Wali; many were drafted from the agricultural colleges and labor unions he controlled.[38]

Wali's ascent culminated in his appointment as secretary general of the National Democratic party in the fall of 1985. His elevation was partly grounded in the hope that he personally could help to deliver the rural vote for the party. But it was also an acknowledgment of the fact that, of all the reform-minded technocrats Mubarak had brought into power, Wali had shown by far the most skill at managing political affairs. He had built a formidable power center and had given the Ministry of Agriculture more authority than it had enjoyed since the days when Sayyid Mar'i implemented land reform in the 1950s.

Despite all of his triumphs, Yusuf Wali had greater success at mastering the system than he did at changing it. His personal influence flourished, but paradoxically his ability to implement his reform agenda did not grow apace. He suffered from the irony that afflicts reformers everywhere; he became enmeshed in the very system he hoped to reconstruct.

Wali's influence was rooted in his knowledge of the realities of power in Egypt. He sought to strike deals with those who already had some authority. His own power center drew strength from its collaboration with other power centers. Before he issued his *Agricultural Strategy for the 1980s* report, he discussed it privately with officials at the Ministry of Planning, the National Institute of Planning, the American experts of the York mission, the inner councils of the National Democratic party, and the Policies Committee of the cabinet.[39] In each of these consultations he won some support, but he also revised his language, compromised on certain changes, and lost a bit of his original energy and momentum.

A similar process of consultation and compromise surrounded each policy change Dr. Wali hoped to make. For example, whenever he sought to change a crop price, he had first to make a recommendation to the Higher Committee on Planning, which includes representatives from other concerned ministries (particularly Supply, Planning, and Industry). Once these officials had hashed out a common position, they forwarded their proposal to the cabinet, where a second round of debate might ensue. The cabinet then submitted the draft legislation to the Agriculture and Irrigation Committee of the People's Assembly for another round of debate. After the committee secured parliamentary ratification, the proposed changes would be finally issued as a presidential decree. During this multistep process, a host of interested agencies would have an opportunity to try to influence the decision, including the "Ministerial Production Committee, the Cotton Higher Board, the Cairo Chamber of Commerce, National Institute of Planning, Federation of Vegetable and Fruit Exporters, General Authority for Export and Import Controls, Green Revolution High Commission, Ministerial Economic Commission, National Development Bank, Agricultural Orientation Agency, Agriculture and Irrigation Committee of the People's Assembly, Plan and Budget Committee of the People's Assembly, National Democratic Party, National Food Security Company, Ministerial Committee for the Development of Animal Wealth, and the Ministries of Agriculture, Supply, Economy and Finance, Trade, and Planning."[40]

Some of these voices lent support to Wali's proposals, but many opposed them. The minister of supply constantly dueled with the minister of agriculture over who was ultimately responsible for the country's food security; they clashed frequently over the issue of whether to reduce consumption by increasing bread prices. The minister of industry also resisted raising crop prices since this would raise the cost of industrial inputs (especially cotton) and of wage goods, creating pressure for an increase of salaries.[41] For many years the minister of planning led the opposition to decontrolling agricultural prices, reflecting his belief—shared by many government officials—that subsidies were "a means of moderating pressure to raise wages of public-sector employees in addition to promoting social equity and price stabilization."[42] Even within the Ministry of Agriculture there were pockets of institutional opposition to reform. The Principal Bank for Development and Agricultural Credit drew half of its revenue from its monopoly of fertilizer sales, and its three thousand employees uniformly opposed reducing subsidies or permitting private marketing of this input.[43]

As Wali's power grew, he was increasingly successful at overcoming some of these objections. But he was never able to make changes as rapidly as he had hoped. Among most Egyptian officials, there was a consensus that reforms had to be implemented slowly. Even among those members of the cabinet who shared an interest in decontrolling prices there was a general belief that changes had to be made gradually, with careful attention to public relations, and that the burden on consumers could be raised only incrementally or it would provoke public protest—perhaps even revolution.

Riots and Subsidies

When justifying their commitment to gradualism, Egyptian officials uniformly begin by reciting an admonition about the riots of 1977. They charge that pressure for rapid economic reform by well-meaning but uninformed foreign agencies (particularly the IMF) was the real cause of these demonstrations. Changes that seemed economically advisable were politically disastrous, since the austerity they imposed was harsher than the Egyptian public could tolerate. The widespread and violent protests they ignited came perilously close to toppling the government. The specter of the 1977 insurrection has haunted discussion of economic reform ever since.

Western aid officials have heard this litany so many times that they have grown tired and skeptical. Many suspect that the Egyptians have exaggerated the violence and danger actually posed by the 1977 riots. Some, seeing how Egyptian officials today use the memory of the riots to forestall foreign pleas for reform, suspect that the demonstrations themselves may have been a political ploy. They allege that in 1977 Sadat deliberately delayed controlling the riots in the hope that the fiasco would chastise the IMF and give him greater room to maneuver in negotiations with foreign creditors. A few even charge that Sadat actually sought to provoke demonstrations by promulgating reforms in a rushed and callous manner.

Neither the fears of Egyptian officials nor the suspicions of their Western counterparts accurately convey the impact of the 1977 events. The immediate background to the riots were the negotiations conducted between the Sadat government and the International Monetary Fund.[44] In 1976 Egypt, desperate for hard currency, sought support from the IMF in its quest for aid from the Americans and loans from private Western banks. The IMF, in turn, urged its conventional package of reforms on Cairo—a sharp devaluation of the Egyptian pound and programs to balance the budget, including a drastic reduction of subsidies for consumer goods. In particular, the Fund wanted a sharp reduction in the subsidies on bread and flour, which cost Cairo £E 250 million a year. Eventually the two sides reached a compromise accord and on January 17, 1977, the deputy prime minister, Abd al-Mun'im al-Qaysuni, informed Parliament that the government intended to reduce the annual appropriation for all consumer subsidies by 50 percent, from £E 553.7 million to £E 276.4 million.[45]

Even though this proposal was more modest than those the Fund had originally urged, it was a lot for Egyptian consumers to swallow. The cut in subsidies would raise prices 50 percent for bread, 25 percent for sugar and rice, and 35 percent for tea and *butagaz*.[46] In 1977 many Egyptian families lived on the margin of poverty, not yet enjoying the income from workers' remittances or the 1979 oil boom. The average per capita income was just £E 100, and half of all urban families relied on subsidies to fund 22–48 percent of all their annual purchases.[47]

At 8:30 on the morning of January 18, demonstrations against the proposed price increases broke out among workers at the mills of the public sector Misr Textile Company in Hulwan. They began a march on downtown Cairo and were joined by workers from neighboring factories. By the time the march arrived at the Parliament building, its numbers were swollen by thousands of local university and high school students. Police attempts to disperse the crowd with tear gas only shifted the protesters into adjacent neighborhoods where they attracted a large following of poorer Cairenes. By evening the demonstrations had metastasized throughout the entire city and turned violent. Protesters smashed shop windows, overturned trolleys, and attacked police stations.

Similar demonstrations had broken out in Alexandria on the same day. By the 19th they had spread to seventeen smaller cities. In the provinces government offices, administration buildings, and governors' residences were attacked and burned. The police had long since lost any semblance of control and began firing directly into the crowd. For the first time since 1952, regular army troops had to be called in to restore order.

Even military intervention did not halt the violence. The demonstrations only subsided after 2:30 P.M. on January 20, when the radio broadcast the government's decision to reinstate subsidies and rescind all price increases. The government estimated that the protests had left seventy-seven dead, two hundred fourteen wounded, and thousands under arrest, but many Egyptians insist that the toll was several times larger. But a simple tally of dollars and death would not, in any case, indicate just how breathtaking the confrontation had been for the majority of Egyptians. Violence on this scale signaled a revolutionary loss of faith in the government. Anwar Sadat seems to have appreciated this. According to Egypt's premier journalist, throughout this period Sadat had a plane standing by to whisk his family to safe exile in Iran if need be.[48]

Foreigners like to stereotype Egyptians as a placid, happy-go-lucky people, and this may partly explain why they failed to appreciate the full menace of the 1977 events. It is true, after all, that individual Egyptians do not share in the cult of firepower, or the romance of violence, found in other parts of the Middle East. But collectively Egyptians have always been prepared to turn to violence when they feel oppressed or exploited. Since the Middle Ages Egyptians have rioted whenever their grain supply was threatened.[49] In 1919, economic hardship triggered a series of rural insurrections that turned into a full-scale revolution against British rule. In January 1952, rioters attacked symbols of Western influence in Cairo, discredited the Wafdist government, and paved the way for Nasser's military coup. Every decade has witnessed a major *jacquerie*. A student rebellion stunned Nasser in 1968 and simmered for the following six years.[50] Violent strikes have periodically paralyzed the country's major industrial complexes, including al-Mahalla al-Kubra (1975), Kafr al-Dawwar (1976 and 1984), and Hulwan (1989).[51] When Egyptians mention the memory of 1977 they are not referring just to an event, but invoking a symbol of a powerful and ancient tradition of revolt.

Outsiders who doubt the potency of this tradition were somewhat chastened by the riots of Central Security Force (CSF) draftees in February 1986. The CSF, a hundred-thousand-strong paramilitary force under the control of the Ministry of Interior, had been created by Sadat after the 1977 riots so that he could deal with demonstrations without summoning the army. When CSF troops, mostly poor and illiterate village boys, heard that their term of conscription might be extended from two to three years, they went on a rampage and began burning casinos and tourist hotels. The army had to be sent in to restore order with helicopters and antitank missiles. This rioting "refreshed the leadership's memory of how little is needed—in this case nothing but a rumor—to provoke violence."[52]

Sadat called the 1977 riots "an uprising of thieves" and tried to portray them as a communist-inspired conspiracy against his regime. This was obviously false, but so was the leftist picture of the riots as the last desperate reaction of the starving masses in the face of growing repression. The groups that initiated the riots were relatively privileged—industrial workers, students, and *muwazzafin* (public sector employees). By Egyptian standards they were almost middle class; they had regular jobs, decent wages, and a guaranteed future. They demonstrated not because they were in imminent danger of hunger; for them the IMF's austerity program meant constriction, not strangulation. Rather, they were moved into the streets by a feeling of injustice, by a violation of their standards of fairness.[53]

Table 5-2. Annual Budget for Food Subsidies, 1973–82
Millions of Egyptian pounds

Product	1973	1974	1975	1976	1977	1978–79	1980–81	1981–82
Wheat	70.8	194.1	135.1	152.3	117.5	481.8	358.2	587.2
Flour	8.2	27.0	27.6	25.8	31.6	106.4	152.8	202.4
Yellow corn	4.4	16.5	29.2	23.1	40.6	38.4	63.7	125.4
Lentils	0.6	2.2	6.3	9.0	9.4	14.1	24.5	31.8
Broad beans	0.3	0.7	5.2	6.0	2.0	12.7	13.0	30.0
Sesame	0.4	0.3	2.7	0.4	0.3	n.a.	5.6	6.6
Cooking oil	16.8	45.2	72.1	41.0	48.4	133.7	114.2	123.7
Fats	2.9	13.6	19.1	16.4	36.4	66.4	80.3	63.9
Mineral oil	1.0	0.2	n.a.	n.a.	n.a.	n.a.	n.a.	n.a.
Butter	n.a.	0.4	n.a.	n.a.	n.a.	n.a.	n.a.	n.a.
Frozen meat	n.a.	n.a.	n.a.	20.4	n.a.	41.4	67.3	98.3
Frozen chicken	n.a.	n.a.	0.5	n.a.	n.a.	n.a.	7.6	26.3
Fresh meat	n.a.	0.6	0.3	n.a.	n.a.	n.a.	n.a.	2.0
Frozen fish	0.5	n.a.	3.0	0.2	0.4	2.9	18.5	18.6
Sugar	n.a.	16.2	19.5	n.a.	n.a.	n.a.	97.8	131.4
Coffee	n.a.	0.5	0.3	3.3	5.6	n.a.	n.a.	n.a.
Tea	n.a.	n.a.	n.a.	n.a.	18.3	54.6	27.4	24.4
Local rice	n.a.	n.a.	n.a.	n.a.	n.a.	43.0	43.7	52.5
Other	2.1	10.00	5.2	n.a.	n.a.	n.a.	n.a.	24.9
Total	108.0	327.5	326.1	297.9	310.5	995.4	1,074.6	1,549.4
Total direct subsidies	108.0	418.9	621.9	427.3	464.6	1,856.9	1,563.0	2,000.0

Source: "al-Bada'il al-Matruha li-Muwajahat Mushkilat al-Di'am," *al-Ahram al-Iqtisadi*, October 8, 1984, pp. 49–50.
n.a. Not available.

On January 18 the crowds had chanted rhymed slogans like "You who live in palaces: where's our breakfast?" or "He wears the latest fashion, while we live ten to a room!"[54] Their anger focused not so much on the harshness of the austerity program as on its injustice—it did not touch the privileges of the rich. They had watched anxiously as Egypt's wealthy elite recovered its social confidence and political influence. They had listened sulkily to the growing noise from lavish weddings at the Hilton, discos at the Pyramids, and bars in Zamalik. They had seen Sadat's friends and cronies get rich without ever doing an honest day's work.[55] They grumbled: Why should the workers, and not the parasites, be the ones to pay the price of economic reform? Equity had long been a central issue in Egyptian politics.[56] Nasser had captured and held the adoration of the common Egyptian by striking at privilege. He had earned applause by confronting foreign plutocrats, by assaulting Egypt's landed notables. Sadat, in contrast, had shown a personal affection for large palaces, gaudy uniforms, and the company of foreign potentates. Occasionally he switched into a *galabiyya* and visited his ancestral village, but most Egyptians were unimpressed. In 1977 he was still searching for an instrument that might persuade his subjects that he cared about the misfortunes of the common man. After 1977 he was convinced that consumer subsidies could supply that instrument.

Until the 1970s, consumer subsidies had played a relatively modest role in the government's arsenal of appeasement. They had been created in 1941, when wartime economic dislocations meant a real brush with famine for many Egyptians. Like so many temporary measures, they had never been repealed. Yet under Nasser spending on subsidies remained a trivial element in the state budget. In 1961 the total cost of subsidies was still only £E 9 million and even in 1967, after the declaration of Arab socialism, spending on subsidies only increased to £E 46 million. In fact, after the 1967 War, when the Egyptian government was especially hard pressed for funds, Nasser actually cut real per capita spending on subsidies by 30 percent.[57] During these years the Ministry of Supply acted not as a pork barrel but as a real rationing system, ensuring the equitable supply of scarce essentials. In 1970, when Sadat took power, the state budget for subsidies had dropped back to £E 24 million.[58]

The transformation of this rationing system into a national dole occurred under Sadat (see table 5-2). This change resulted partly from factors beyond his control. In the 1960s grains had been relatively cheap, but after the world food crisis of 1972 the price of a ton of wheat soared from £E 30 to £E 103.[59] Between 1972 and 1974 Egypt's budget for food imports exploded from £E 112 million (equal to 3 percent of the gross national product) to £E 409 million (10 percent of GNP).[60] By 1975 the government bill for subsidies was about £E 600 million (16 percent of GDP); food subsidies cost £E 463 million, or 77 percent of the total bill.[61]

But changes in international prices were not the only reason for the rising cost of subventions. After the 1977 riots Sadat not only reinstated the subsidies that had been cut, he expanded subsidies to cover a whole new array of goods. He confiscated $2 billion from the coffers of an Arab aid agency (the Gulf Organization for the Development of Egypt) and used it to finance massive imports of frozen beef and chicken. He raised the value of existing subsidies until they ranged from 72.6 percent for cooking oil to 761 percent for buffalo meat.[62] He created a new system of bonuses that were doled out to public sector employees on national holidays. He greatly increased the cost of food imports by ordering the Ministry of Supply to begin distributing subsidized flour in rural areas (it had been a strictly urban program), where it quickly became a staple.[63]

Sadat's flair for the politics of patronage fostered a whole new pattern of public consumption. According to the 1978–82 Five-Year Plan which he promulgated, the five main tasks of the government were "a) to guarantee a job and an income to all, b) to provide social services (housing, health, education) to all, c) to protect the consumer from price increases, d) to manage public services and the main production units, and e) to make available to the public necessary food items."[64]

Sadat embraced and popularized the idea that consumer subsidies were not just a safety net protecting the poor, but an expression of equity granted to the mass of society as a counterbalance to the privileges enjoyed by the rich. He rewrote the social contract, substituting the words "cheap meat" for "social justice." Sadat's use of the old "bread and circuses" ploy and his reconstruction of Egypt as a Third World welfare state did not win him much respect. But it did buy him some time. From 1978 onward the mass of Egyptians began to share in the buoyant feeling of prosperity that rich Egyptians already enjoyed.

This illusion of prosperity, however, came at a great price. Direct government subsidies that had been only £E 434 million in 1976 rocketed to £E 1.4 billion by 1979. Put another way, they rose from 30 percent of the value of government revenues to 48 percent.[65] When Sadat died in 1981, Egyptian economists and their foreign advisers were already wailing that the country could not sustain this burden for long. After Mubarak took power and government revenues began to decline, the difficulty of financing subsidies grew increasingly acute.

In 1982 Mubarak convened a national economic conference to solicit the advice of the country's most prominent officials, businessmen, and intellectuals. The conference's final report charged that the taproot of Egypt's economic problem was the persistence of budget deficits, which fueled inflation and foreign borrowing without providing adequate funds for development. The majority of delegates blamed the rising cost of subsidies for the government budget deficit.[66] Following up on this report, the Financial and Economic Affairs Committee of the upper house of Parliament prepared a detailed proposal for cutting subsidies.[67] In the short term (one to three years) it proposed to freeze budget outlays for subsidies at current levels, raise the prices of subsidized foods until they matched costs, and limit the ration of subsidized foodstuffs available.[68]

The members of Mubarak's cabinet generally shared his interest in cutting subsidies, but they felt they lacked the political security to do so. Mubarak had not yet established his legitimacy and his authority was being contested by a burgeoning Islamic movement. The 1977 riots had been followed by a series of smaller demonstrations that suggested the public was still touchy about the cost of basic goods. Mubarak's advisers searched for less painful, more politically palatable ways to reduce outlays for subsidies. Eventually, they devised three distinct programs.

The first program involved increasing controls on the distribution of subsidized goods or even a shift to outright rationing. Limited controls were already in force. Each citizen was allotted a fixed monthly quota of sugar, tea, cooking oil, and rice at subsidized prices through the *gam'iyyat*, the government-run consumer cooperatives. But these were available to all citizens, rich and poor alike, and quantities beyond the rationed quota could be purchased for a higher (but still less than free market) price. Moreover, wheat, whether in the form of bread or flour, was available on demand in unlimited quantities.[69]

A shift to more rationing appealed to many Egyptians. Surveys showed that most Egyptians felt that government subsidies were generally unsuccessful precisely because subsidized goods did not reach those who deserved them most.[70] Better distribution controls might confine access to subsidized goods to the truly needy and also encourage restraint in consumption.

Mubarak's cabinet entertained a number of different rationing schemes. One proposal, modeled on the American food stamp system, would have subjected citizens to a means test and awarded currency-equivalent coupons to those who proved needy.[71] This idea was rejected because the government lacked the resources to administer it. Instead it was decided to reconstruct the existing networks of *gam'iyyat* around a more elaborate system of quotas. Most of the public received green ration cards, which entitled them to specific quantities of sugar, tea, oil, and cheap fabrics.[72] Citizens known to have higher incomes were given red ration cards, which required them to pay higher prices or receive smaller rations. The *gam'iyyat* were divided into three groups, with those in wealthier neighborhoods carrying a wider array of higher quality goods and charging higher prices. By 1984, most of these changes had been put into practice.[73]

The new system slowed the growth of subsidies but was less revolutionary than its proponents had hoped. In large measure this was because the *gam'iyyat* did not function at the local level the way that the government expected them to. There are only two thousand *gam'iyyat* in the greater Cairo area, about one for every six thousand people. The ratio of patrons is much higher in the poorer, denser neighborhoods, so the lines can be terrifying, particularly on days when especially scarce goods, such as soap, arrive.[74] To avoid the nightmare of customers having to wait in line all day, the cooperatives long ago developed informal arrangements for allocating goods. Managers, who can barely balance their books by selling at official prices, routinely divert a portion of their stocks for sale under the counter. Patrons willing to pay a premium price simply cut to the head of the queue. The manager may also advance goods to *dallalat*, women who sit in front of the *gam'iyya* hawking the same goods sold inside to anyone who would rather pay a bit more and spend less time in line.[75] These mechanisms meant that the volume and price of goods sold often bore little resemblance to the rations specified by the government.

Moreover, as could be expected in a country where corruption is commonplace, there were major problems with fraud. Hardly anyone used the new red ration card because it was very easy to buy a counterfeit or "previously owned" copy of the preferred green card. By 1985 10 million Egyptians were using green cards.[76]

The second strategy that Mubarak's advisers experimented with was called "cash compensation." This was an old idea (it had first been raised by the National Council on Production and Economic Affairs in 1975),[77] but it was resurrected and presented to Mubarak by Ali Lutfi, director of the Economics Committee of the ruling National Democratic party. The basic principle was to eliminate all commodity subsidies while replacing them with cash emoluments paid directly to the poorest Egyptians. Lutfi proposed to do this by adding an annual bonus to public sector payrolls in urban areas and offering special grants through the village banks in rural districts. He argued that this would save money by eliminating government subventions to prosperous professionals, artisans, factory owners, and shopkeepers; owners of more than ten feddans; expatriates; and any family that earned more than £E 3,000 annually, which—he calculated—formed around 23 percent of the total population.[78]

Mubarak named Lutfi as prime minister in 1985, but he proved far too ineffective to put his own proposal into practice. (Many claim he spent more time ensuring himself a lucrative retirement than attending to the national economy.) But the idea lived on and was finally implemented, in a revised form, by Atif Sidqi, who replaced Lutfi as prime minister in 1986. Sidqi took office at a moment when Egypt desperately needed an agreement with the IMF to strengthen its hand in negotiations with the Paris Club to reschedule the nation's debt.[79] To win the approval of the IMF, Sidqi needed to cut subsidies sharply. He dramatically increased energy prices and began a phased series of increases in the prices of cigarettes, sugar, and many other consumer goods. He seized on the idea of cash compensation as a means to soften the impact of this inflation on the average Cairene.

The price hikes went into effect in the spring of 1987 and paved the way for an agreement with the IMF in May. Then, in July, Sidqi approved an across-the-board 20 percent increase in public sector wages. This did not totally insulate the *muwazzafin* from the wave of price increases, but it made the burden tolerable. It also, of course, undercut the reduction of demand that the IMF had expected the cutting of subsidies to achieve. The IMF refused to release the second tranche of the loan it had offered to Egypt, but it did not interfere with Egypt's debt-rescheduling agreement with the Paris Club.

Of course, Egypt paid a price for this subterfuge—but in the unpredictable long term rather than in the desperate short term. Cash compensation, as applied by Sidqi, had not done much to balance the state budget. Nor had it advanced the government's contribution to equity. The beneficiaries were all urban, public sector employees, while rural Egyptians and poor urbanites had no insulation against rising prices. Raising wages without increasing productivity led, inevitably, to simple inflation.[80]

Mubarak also authorized a third subsidy-reduction program which was discussed only in closed sessions of the highest echelons of the cabinet. This strategy was a camouflaged slow reduction of subsidies. Atif Ubayd, one of Mubarak's closest advisers, argued that the real obstacle to eliminating subsidies was perceptions. If people thought they were being subjected to a major assault on their standard of living, they rioted. But if the government moved quietly, tinkering a bit with a single subsidy, there would be no protest. Thus by acting gradually, unannounced, perhaps even surreptitiously, the government could transform the whole system. Some have called this "reform by stealth."

Privately, one Egyptian official explained this strategy using an analogy of boiling frogs. If a frog is put in a pot above a strong flame, it will feel the heat and quickly jump out. But if it is put in the pot above a weak flame, the frog's metabolism will adjust and he stays put. So long as the temperature is raised in tiny increments, the frog will adjust—it will stay in the pot right up to the moment when it finally boils to death. In a similar manner, if consumer subsidies are reduced gradually, the public will find it easier to adjust and will be unlikely to jump into the streets in protest.

The classic example of this camouflage approach has been Mubarak's slow reduction of the bread subsidy. The increase of bread prices, as much as anything else, triggered the 1977 riots. Yet cheap bread formed the most onerous element of the subsidy budget—£E 850 million in 1983. At 1 piaster a loaf, Egyptian bread was not only the cheapest in the world, it had actually (thanks to inflation) been growing steadily cheaper since the 1960s. Yet when parliamentarians called on the government to raise the price of bread to 2 piasters in May 1983, public outcry was so intense that the suggestion was soon stifled. The press complained that the proposed price increase amounted to a policy of *man la yajid khubzan ya'kul baqlawa*—those who can't find bread should eat baklava (or "let them eat cake").[81]

The camouflage strategy allowed the government to circumvent these objections. In 1981, the government introduced a new bread loaf that cost 2 piasters, made from higher-quality wheat. The old 1 piaster loaves gradually grew harder to find and their quality deteriorated. The public steadily bought fewer 1 piaster loaves and more of the kind that cost 2 piasters. By 1984 the 1 piaster loaves were not only rare but also dirty and full of sawdust. In 1985, when the 1 piaster loaf was finally phased out, most consumers had already switched to the 2 piaster loaf voluntarily.[82]

This strategy continued to operate throughout the 1980s. In 1986, the size of the 2 piaster loaf began to shrink; loaves that had formerly weighed 169 grams were reduced to 135 grams.[83] The loaf continued to shrivel. In 1988 the government again cut the wheat content of 2 piaster bread by 20 percent, ostensibly to improve its quality. (The government admitted that this would allow it to import one million fewer tons of wheat, at a saving of £E 350 million.)[84]

This was precisely the strategy the government employed to resolve the bread crisis of 1989 (described in chapter 2), when bakers began to divert flour for use in baking *tabaqi* loaves, which were not price controlled. Initially the government responded by raising the price farmers were paid to grow wheat from £E 45 to £E 60 per ardeb. Officials projected, with unusual confidence, that the domestic harvest would reach a record high of 3.2 million tons.[85] Privately, however, they acknowledged that most of the new wheat planted would wind up as livestock feed rather than bread. The bread shortages could not be ended by just pumping more wheat into the system because they resulted more from the way flour was distributed than from any absolute shortfall.

But Yusuf Wali proposed a way to use the "reform by stealth" strategy to end the bread crisis. He authorized the creation of two official *tabaqi* loaves, one 18 centimeters and the other 20 centimeters in diameter. Consumers liked these loaves because they contained less bran than the old *'aysh baladi* and cost significantly less than their free market counterparts. (The 20-centimeter official loaf sold for 5 piasters, compared to 10 piasters for its private counterpart.) Yet these loaves also saved the government money; they were priced by diameter rather than weight and actually contained 20 percent less flour than traditional loaves.[86] Consumers switched to these new loaves, reducing demand for the unofficial *tabaqi* bread and thereby curtailing the diversion of flour. By May 1989 the bread crisis was over, and the government had not had to resort, as some had proposed, to increased police supervision of bakeries.[87]

The same approach was applied to a host of subsidized goods. The cheaper brands of cigarettes were gradually phased out and replaced by more expensive versions that resembled foreign brands. The cheaper grades of gasoline became increasingly scarce and it was rumored some had actually been adulterated with alcohol or water.

Combining these three strategies (rationing, cash compensation, and camouflage) gave the government the ability to deal with subsidy costs on a class-by-class basis. Rationing was supposed to curtail consumption by the rich; compensation was designed to permit a cutback of subsidies to the middle class; camouflage was applied to the most elementary staples, the goods most important to the poor. None of these programs worked quite as it was supposed to. Still, it was a clever idea, which might have permitted more finely tuned reductions and greater sensitivity to the political volatility of various groups.

The government moved as expeditiously as it could; it was certainly better prepared than Sadat's government had ever been. Yet it still occasionally pushed things past the limits. There is no magical formula that permits a government to predict a specific group's limits of tolerance. In September 1984 the government announced increases in basic prices, including the price of bread. Thousands of workers at the textile plant in Kafr al-Dawwar rioted and police shot three dead.[88] Hauntingly similar demonstrations broke out in September 1988 when Mubarak announced that workers would not be receiving their annual schooling grants (one of the cash subventions Sadat had instituted). Troops had to arrest more than one hundred fifty workers.[89]

Repeated incidents of this kind began to change the public dialogue on the question of subsidies. Experts still agreed that they were a burden and had to be reduced. But they began to admit that the monster that Sadat had created was here to stay. Mubarak himself began to say it was not possible to eliminate at least the basic subsidies for the poor.[90]

The net effect of all three subsidy reduction strategies, then, was relatively moderate. The subsidy bill continued to grow every year, but its rate of growth was cut. The subsidy budget slowly shrank in comparison with the growth of government revenues and national income. Even the IMF, traditionally skeptical of Egypt's reform programs, admitted: "In 1986/87, the Egyptian authorities introduced a more forward looking set of economic policies. In the real sector, a number of administered prices were adjusted, while liberalization measures were introduced in agriculture. . . . In the financial area, the overall fiscal deficit/GDP ratio was reduced to about 17 percent (from 23 percent in the previous year) largely through a general compression of expenditures, including investment outlays. Moreover, subsidy costs declined, reflecting mainly falling international commodity prices, although prices of certain commodities were also increased for amounts supplied above the basic ration."[91] Any cut in the subsidy burden had effects that multiplied throughout the economy. Some economists suggest that if the cost of subsidies could be cut by just 10 percent (without increasing the overall budget deficit) it would have the effect of strengthening the value of the Egyptian pound by 3 percent as well as reducing the inflation rate by 5 percent.[92]

Price Controls and Wholesale Marketing Monopolies

Dr. Wali was eager to decontrol agricultural prices as a way of making investing in production more attractive for farmers. But he recognized that a rise in crop prices would increase the cost of food and textiles. In cabinet deliberations, his colleagues urged him to slow the growth of agricultural prices so that consumers, already feeling the pinch of steady subsidy reductions, would not confront any intolerable jump in the cost of living. During his first four years in office, these pressures prevented Wali from making any radical changes in the agricultural price control and crop procurement system.

The cabinet allowed Wali to raise the procurement price for major crops incrementally each year. In the case of wheat and rice, he was actually able to raise prices fast enough to start narrowing the gap between domestic and international prices. But this was relatively painless, since both crops were largely consumed inside Egypt. Wali had much less success at pressing for a reform of cotton prices, since any increase in the price paid to farmers would have to be deducted from the revenue the government earned when it exported the crop.

Wali thought that price reform was not advancing rapidly enough and he was unhappy with the restraints that the cabinet imposed on changes in official policy. So he found ways to liberalize prices unofficially by relaxing the enforcement of government controls. In 1982 he instructed his subordinates to stop levying fines against farmers owning one feddan or less who violated price controls. While continuing to define an official price for wheat, he made the delivery of this crop voluntary rather than compulsory. He urged ministry inspectors to assign a lower priority to identifying control violations and made an annual practice of forgiving fines that had been levied against farmers who got caught. In 1984 the Ministry of Supply complained about the Ministry of Agriculture's lax execution of its duties, and wheat deliveries were again made compulsory. But Wali kept the fines assessed for price infractions low enough so that the more prosperous farmers could continue to ignore official controls.[93]

Wali's relaxation of official supervision—his personal version of reform by stealth—did not have the same effect as a complete liberalization. The Ministry of Industry still monopolized all cotton sales and was effectively able to control domestic pricing. The Ministry of Supply also maintained price inspectors in all urban markets, greatly dampening the pressure for real changes in farmgate prices. Farmers could take advantage of Wali's informal decontrol only to the extent that they found ways to avoid the controls imposed by other ministries, so the overall effect of his reforms remained modest.

Wali's first opportunity to experiment with more radical changes came in 1985—a watershed year for economic reform in Egypt. By 1984 the government had foreseen that the country was about to enter a profound economic crisis. Oil and other revenues had been declining (see chapter 2). Repayment of Egypt's foreign debt was ballooning—American military loans contracted after 1979 came with a five-year grace period, so repayments began to come due after 1984. Egypt was going to require aid, advice, and forbearance from the Americans, the IMF, the World Bank, and other friends to weather this crisis. And unless it gave evidence of a more earnest, more rapid approach to economic reform, Egypt could not count on additional support from these friends. Suddenly reform proposals that had once seemed outlandish schemes became more plausible. Egyptian officials saw that they had to do something even if it was painful and risky.

In the fall of 1985 Mubarak put his full prestige behind a new wave of economic reforms. He gave a major speech calling on Egyptians to curb their consumption; he appointed Ali Lutfi (who was expected to reform the subsidy system) as prime minister; and he promoted Yusuf Wali to the position of secretary general of the NDP (National Democratic party). Earlier in the year he had sanctioned an ambitious (and unsuccessful) campaign by Mustafa al-Sa'id, the minister of finance, to reform the exchange system, devalue the currency, and thereby restrict imports. But one of the most important products of this reform fever actually occurred with little public notice. Early in the year, three ministers had formed a quiet working alliance to collaborate on a series of critical reforms. They were Yusuf Wali at Agriculture, Nagi Shatla at the Ministry of Supply, and Muhammad Abd al-Wahhab at the Ministry of Industry.

All three ministers wanted a reform of customs policies to facilitate international trade. Wali and Abd al-Wahhab were both interested in promoting Egyptian exports; they hoped that Egypt might follow the lead of South Korea and other newly industrializing countries that had enjoyed rapid growth after adopting a strategy of export-led development.[94] With Shatla they also shared an interest in simplifying the import of machinery, meat, and other key commodities. Together they led a drive to abolish the import rationalization committees which complicated the import process. Yusuf Wali went even farther, sponsoring legislation that created many new opportunities for private traders to import staple foodstuffs.

These three ministers also cooperated in a second series of reforms. Shatla, newly appointed as minister of supply, felt that his agency was badly overextended and needed to narrow its focus of operations.[95] He encouraged the Ministry of Industry to take responsibility for the import of tallow and vegetable oil. Dr. Wali volunteered to relieve the Ministry of Supply of responsibility for importing corn—the second most heavily subsidized agricultural product. Reforms within the Ministry of Supply also gave Yusuf Wali a chance to influence one of the major instruments affecting agricultural production, retail price controls.

Since the 1960s the Ministry of Supply had subjected fruit and vegetable trade to mandatory price ceilings. It calculated the costs of production, transportation, and handling and likely storage time and then imposed a price ceiling that covered those costs and included a profit of about 5 percent. It enforced different price levels for producers, wholesalers, and retailers. The ministry was never able to completely suppress black market trade in agricultural goods, but its supervision limited price vacillations even in the black market.[96] By the early 1980s, however, this system appeared increasingly untenable. As trade grew, ministry inspectors found themselves swamped. Black market violations became increasingly common and the growing interest in economic reform made the mission of price control itself seem increasingly less justifiable. In 1983 the ministry abolished most controls on grapes, citrus fruits, bananas, and watermelons, although temporary controls were periodically reimposed when prices surged.[97]

Yusuf Wali, who still could not win support for decontrolling the prices of major crops (wheat, cotton, rice), had more success persuading his colleagues to decontrol the prices of minor crops administered by the Ministry of Supply. He argued that the supply of these crops had actually been growing, so there was a good chance market prices would not rise too rapidly. Indeed, he hoped that if trade in the crops were liberalized, competition among traders would actually reduce the portion of their price taken as profit.[98] With support from the minister of supply, his argument prevailed. On May 11, 1985, the Ministry of Supply issued a decree announcing it would no longer control the prices of fruits and vegetables.

This news was received with joy at Rawd al-Farag, the vegetable market serving greater Cairo. The wholesaler warehouses of Rawd al-Farag cover three square blocks near Shubra, Cairo's sprawling northern suburb. Beside them stand three hundred fifty stalls rented by five hundred merchants (some rent only half of a shop). But there are also thirty-five hundred merchants who operate without official license working as agents for larger traders; they make up a kind of black market.[99] Here a few hundred merchants, supported by a thousand brokers, trade their goods with the forty thousand retailers in the city. Officially, they shared the government's confidence that free trade would ensure a larger supply of goods at lower prices.

The government expected prices to rise only moderately after decontrol. After all, except for the watermelon crop, which had been reduced by bad weather, supplies of fruits and vegetables were up. Yet from the day that the free-trade regime was inaugurated, prices at Rawd al-Farag skyrocketed. A kilogram of tomatoes, which had cost 23 piasters, rose to 75 piasters; okra rose from £E 0.70 to £E 3.50; cantaloupes from 25 piasters to 110 piasters; apricots from £E 2.00 to

£E 2.50.[100] Initially the cabinet hoped this inflation was driven by a bubble of speculation that would soon burst and allow prices to stabilize. But prices continued to climb and by June many Cairenes could no longer afford vegetables.

The daily papers ran interviews with shocked consumers, parliamentarians gave long speeches on the problem, and the government ordered an investigation. The first indications, summarized in a report by the Cairo Chamber of Commerce, were that most of the price rise was due to gouging by retail merchants. In some neighborhoods, retail prices were marked up 200–300 percent over wholesale costs.[101] The Ministry of Supply then devised a plan that would seek to control retail prices while allowing wholesale prices to float. Under the new system, known as "friendly pricing," fair retail prices were supposed to be defined at weekly meetings of a special committee that would include officials from the Ministry of Supply and representatives from the wholesalers at Rawd al-Farag, the Chamber of Commerce, and the state-owned *gam'iyyat*.[102] The prices set by this committee were to be enforced by the merchants themselves, not by the Supply Police (the field inspectors of the Ministry of Supply). The ministry hoped to stabilize prices without going back into the business of regulating them.

Friendly pricing had mixed results. The rise of prices slowed—but prices did not decline. By the time this new system was operating, new questions about the marketing structure for fruits and vegetables had arisen. Farmers began to complain that while retail and wholesale prices had climbed, farmgate prices had remained stagnant. For example, under the system of compulsory price controls, producers got 18 piasters for a kilogram of bananas (£E 180 a ton) which were then sold for 35 piasters officially or 50–60 piasters on the black market. But after controls were removed, and consumer prices for bananas soared to 100–150 piasters, the farmer got only 25 piasters for a kilogram. Generally, while retail prices jumped 200–300 percent, producer prices rose only 30 percent. Economists noted that wholesalers were passing only 10–20 percent of the profits from price increases back to farmers.[103] This undermined the entire rationale of decontrolling prices, which had been to stimulate production.

Similar complaints were also being heard from retailers, who insisted that wholesalers were the motor behind inflation. They insisted that they had to accept the prices that the wholesalers of Rawd al-Farag dictated.[104] They argued that retail prices had remained around 50 percent above wholesale, where they had been before controls were removed. The Ministry of Supply discovered that wholesalers were deliberately withholding some crops, like watermelons and potatoes, that could be stored, in order to raise prices.[105] The wholesalers were making windfall profits.

In retrospect, it is surprising that the government had not anticipated this. Five hundred different wholesalers operated at Rawd al-Farag, but this did not mean there was any real competition among them. All but 10 percent of them came originally from the same three villages in Suhag (Upper Egypt).[106] Over forty years, kinship, clientage, and common business interests had forged the wholesalers into a few small cliques headed by five families that the press had dubbed "the Lords of Rawd al-Farag." Each of these families specialized in the trade of specific crops. They controlled networks of agents in the countryside who telephoned them about the changing fortunes of the crops and negotiated sales from local farmers. They controlled the fleets of trucks and depots necessary to bring the crops from the markets to Cairo. In some areas the wholesalers actually leased orchards from farmers and assumed direct control over production.[107] Under normal circumstances they controlled 70 percent of Cairo's fruit and vegetable trade. And the May 1985 decontrol had, perhaps inadvertently, augmented the power of their oligopoly. Karam Zaydan, Ahmad al-Usayli, Muhammad Ibrahim, and Rashad Ibrahim—the men the government chose to negotiate for the wholesalers under the friendly pricing system—were the representatives of the five families.[108]

The government had never been able to control these wholesalers. "It is hard to observe wholesale markets," the chief of the Supply Police explained, "because the wholesale merchants deal only with a limited number of people known to them personally and in advance. Therefore, it is hard to uncover their transgressions, particularly since those who deal with them fear to inform on them or be witnesses against them. But retail merchants deal with the masses and therefore it is easy to arrest them!"[109] The wholesalers had used their oligopoly to fix prices in the past; the decontrol and withdrawal of the Supply Police had simply allowed them to do so on a larger scale with more dramatic results.[110]

Officials at the Ministry of Supply knew all about the operations of the five families at Rawd al-Farag. For decades they had worked hand in glove with these men to regulate prices. But this information about the sociology of wholesale marketing was never incorporated into government studies of agricultural economics or into plans for policy change. The agronomists and economists who prepared such studies and plans had few contacts with the Supply Police. Instead, they sought advice from foreign development experts. Their studies tended to mirror, and sometimes mimic, analyses of the marketing system commissioned by AID which neglected or dismissed sociological problems.

Officials of AID took an early interest in the agricultural marketing system. In 1981 they had sponsored a conference on the subject which had produced a long-term research agenda. Studies commissioned under this program demonstrated major problems in the marketing system. Produce was infrequently and inconsistently graded; it was roughly handled and packed in low-quality cartons. Shipping was uncoordinated, leading to uncertain delivery dates and frequent delays.[111] One American authority summarized Egyptian conditions: "Cairo now has one principal wholesale vegetable market (at Rod al-Farrag). Built in the late 1940s, when the population of the city was some 2.5 million, it is surrounded by a high wall and has two main entrances, each just wide enough to let two trucks in abreast. Packing and handling are *entirely* unmechanized; as a result, considerable damage is done to the produce, especially to the fresh vegetables which come in on donkey carts packed in handicrafted palm or bamboo crates. Such woeful inadequacies are repeated at every level, from the overcrowded road network to the jammed ports."[112] The very high rates of bruising and spoilage meant that for delicate produce like tomatoes, often half the crop was lost before it reached market. One detailed study of three fruits and vegetables concluded that on average 16 percent of the crop was lost before it reached retail markets.[113]

Experts worried that the bottleneck at Rawd al-Farag would interfere with AID's plan to foster export agriculture in Egypt (discussed in chapter 7). They emphasized the need for technological changes that would reduce marketing costs and crop losses and promote more timely deliveries. They hoped to reduce spoilage by promoting such advances as new plastic wraps, mechanized fruit-handling machinery, better roads, more refrigerated trucks, and computerized inventory procedures. Some of these improvements were funded directly through AID projects aimed at modernizing Egypt's transportation system. But for the most part, technology transfer in marketing was thought to be best left to the private sector. The AID experts suggested that Egyptian entrepreneurs, perhaps in joint ventures with American firms, were best placed to make decisions about which technologies would be most cost effective.

American economists, and many Egyptian reformers, had full confidence in the Egyptian business community's capacity to pioneer development. They shared a conviction that Egyptian businessmen were like their counterparts "everywhere," that once policy restraints were removed they would rush to develop a lucrative market. They believed that the government was the only force restricting competition. They would not have been surprised to learn about the five families and their oligopoly; they would have replied that state intervention was precisely what made such monopolies possible.

Historically this was correct. During the 1960s the Ministry of Supply had encouraged the concentration of fruit and vegetable wholesaling; it lacked the manpower to police hundreds of scattered markets and preferred to focus its supervision at Rawd al-Farag (and at Nuha, Alexandria's main food market). The five families had erected their oligopoly in this period. They cooperated with the Ministry of Supply and acquiesced in the imposition of price ceilings; in exchange the state unofficially sanctioned their monopoly. For years this system had been very profitable for them. Many reformers assumed that once state supervision of these markets was repealed, the underpinnings of monopoly would vanish.

But the five families of Rawd al-Farag had not only created a monopoly during the decades of price control, they had acquired the means to defend it.[114] They were entrenched. Not only had they accumulated huge fleets of trucks and networks of agents, they had forged long-term bonds with thousands of peasants, offering them credit to carry them through lean years. They had curried influence among local officials, who could be relied on to discourage potential competitors. Their oligopoly was no longer dependent on official collaboration; it was independent and vigorous. In 1985, when the Supply Police withdrew from Rawd al-Farag, the monopoly of the five families persisted. New entrepreneurs were unable or unwilling to break into fruit and vegetable wholesaling.

The summer of 1985 represented a disaster for reformers in the Egyptian government. Cairene consumers, facing sharp rises in the price of their diet, became very touchy about government talk of any further austerity measures. Farmers, the group the government had expected to benefit immediately from price reform, had been left in the cold. The spectacle of five families at Rawd al-Farag getting rich at the expense of the rest of the public was exactly the kind of story that infuriated the equity-sensitive Egyptian public. For many Egyptians the affair confirmed their belief that price controls protected the people and liberalization benefited only wealthy elites. Even the most ardent champions of liberalization were forced to moderate their claims. The Wafd party, for example, had championed price reform for years. When fruit and vegetable prices began to climb, it initially blamed gouging retailers for the problem. But most of its information on the problem came from Karam Zaydan, a Wafdist deputy in Parliament and also the leading wholesaler at Rawd al-Farag. When Zaydan's own opportunism came to public attention, the Wafd was humiliated. Clearly the fiasco in fruit and vegetable marketing had a chilling effect on calls for rapid reform in many different sectors of the economy.[115]

Once officials realized that wholesalers were the nub of the problem, they scrambled to devise remedial measures. The Ministry of Agriculture tried to relax the stranglehold of Rawd al-Farag by halting its own sales to the wholesalers. At American prompting, the minister of supply tried negotiating directly with the five families. He said that the government would be compelled to break their monopoly if Rawd al-Farag did not stabilize prices and pass more of its profits back to the farmers by August 15. Nagi Shatla, the minister of supply, consulted with the ministers of construction and interior on a plan to build a new, competing wholesale fruit and vegetable market for Cairo. A French consulting firm, which had helped to set up the wholesale market for Paris, was awarded a contract to draft plans for the new market.[116]

These threats, however, did not carry much weight. The government lacked the expertise and resources to provide an alternative to Rawd al-Farag's provincial marketing system. Only two public sector corporations worked in this area—the Egyptian Company for Fruit and Vegetable Marketing and the Public Company for Meat and Food Procurements—and both were plagued by management problems. They handled less than 1 percent of fruit and vegetable marketing.[117] Moreover, officials knew from experience that trying to set up new marketing systems could be very expensive. In the early 1980s, Uthman

Ahmad Uthman had decided to try to raise the profitability of his land reclamation scheme at Salihiyya by bypassing the wholesalers at Rawd al-Farag. He discovered that to do this he had to buy his own fleet of trucks and planes and build his own network of retail stores. His refusal to deal with Rawd al-Farag wound up costing him much more than he would have spent if he had let them handle his produce. For smaller, private farmers, who lacked Uthman's access to government subsidies, this approach was unthinkable.

The crisis in vegetable prices stretched through the summer. The first meeting of the new, reform cabinet headed by Ali Lutfi, which took office in September, was largely devoted to this problem. Dr. Lutfi sponsored a series of remedial measures such as transferring surplus vegetables from the Ministry of Agriculture to the Ministry of Supply for marketing at reduced prices. He also ordered increased surveillance over distribution centers and the creation of special *gam'iyyat* for the distribution of fruits and vegetables.[118] Yusuf Wali also worked out a plan with the Ministry of Supply to build up a reserve of critical commodities to be released whenever shortages appeared.[119]

None of these measures, however, had any immediate effect on prices. So when the five families did not cave in, the government had to resort to the one power it still possessed, a return to price controls. The Supply Ministry was not happy about this. It had already begun to reassign its personnel from market inspection to desk jobs.[120] But on September 17, the minister of supply emerged from a meeting with his counterparts in agriculture, interior, and local government to announce a series of new decisions.[121] The government invoked its emergency powers to reduce the prices of tomatoes, squash, and potatoes. It defined a new set of official prices for onions, potatoes, and two varieties of eggplant.[122] Finally, it announced its intention to restrict the margin of profit for wholesalers to 7 percent and 25–30 percent for retailers. To enforce these regulations, the Supply Police were ordered back into the souks. Price controls were reinstated, and runaway inflation came to an end.

The 1985 crisis was an important setback, but it did not force Yusuf Wali to reconsider or abandon his commitment to price reform. Instead he learned from the crisis that any attempt to decontrol fruit and vegetable prices would have to be carefully planned and the groundwork laid in advance. The moment the crisis broke he began to consult with horticulture experts about tactics that might surmount the monopoly of the five families. Together they discussed proposals to build new markets for producers outside the control of the wholesalers, to improve transportation systems, to establish a public sector corporation for collecting crops, and to promote federations of producers and exporters.[123]

In one way the crisis at Rawd al-Farag played into Wali's hands. It alarmed officials in many different agencies and disposed them to support Wali's plans for modernizing the national marketing system.[124] The Ministry of Supply was obviously eager to cooperate. President Mubarak himself became concerned with the problem and selected it as a key theme for his second inaugural address in October 1987.[125] At his behest, a national conference of experts was convened in April 1988 to discuss reform of the marketing system. Even the World Bank lent its support, entertaining a proposal to extend $120–$160 million for the improvement of marketing.[126]

The Ministry of Supply made a tangible contribution to this campaign. It sponsored the development of a number of small, independent wholesale markets for fruits and vegetables scattered across the Cairo area.[127] In late 1987 it announced plans to construct modern wholesale markets in three of the new communities in the Greater Cairo area— al-'Ubur to the northeast, 6 October City in the west, and 15 May City in the south.[128]

These actions did not abolish the monopoly of the five families, but they exerted enough pressure to force wholesalers to moderate their behavior. The big traders at Rawd al-Farag began to worry about consumer resentment and about the threat to their ties to farmers. To defend their position they began to pass a larger share of their profits back to producers. Farmgate prices slowly began to rise.

By 1987, these changes had gone far enough to encourage Wali to give price reform a second try. In January 1987 he proclaimed the government's intention to eliminate price and acreage controls for all crops except cotton, rice, and sugarcane. He timed the announcement early in the year to give farmers a chance to alter their spring plantings. By July, the new policy was in operation.[129] Wholesale prices rose for all major crops and surveys suggested that, this time, farmgate prices were rising proportionately.

The effects of this price reform were immediately evident in the way farmers allocated their land between crops. The area planted in

Table 5-3. The Agricultural Price Revolution of 1988

Crop	Government procurement price (Egyptian pounds per metric ton)			Area planted (thousands of feddans)			Yield (metric tons per feddan)			Change over two years (percent)		
	1987	1988	1989	1987	1988	1989	1987	1988	1989	Price	Area	Yield
Wheat	200.0	266.0	400.0	1,373.0	1,421.7	1,532.5	1.98	1.99	2.08	100	12	5
Barley	197.0	233.0	n.a.	130.0	88.7	118.2	1.17	1.23	1.06	n.a.	-9	-9
Lentils	875.0	1,000.0	972.0	20.9	19.0	17.0	0.67	0.79	0.80	11	-19	19
Corn	178.5	321.0	393.0	1,352.7	1,959.9	2,007.5	2.16	2.12	2.30	120	48	6
Rice	175.0	200.0	275.0	981.0	837.0	982.4	2.45	2.54	2.72	57	0	11
Sugarcane	30.5	43.0	50.0	204.7	267.6	267.6	36.00	40.00	40.00	64	31	11
Cotton	n.a.	927.0	1,213.0	979.7	1,013.9	1,055.0	0.36	0.35	0.27	n.a.	8	-25

Source: U.S. Department of Agriculture, *Annual Situation Report: Egypt* (1988, 1989, and 1990).
n.a. Not available.

corn and sugarcane grew impressively (see table 5-3). Even wheat production, stimulated by speculation about an impending food security crisis, expanded. By 1989 the government believed that it could get farmers to increase the acreage planted in wheat by almost 50 percent to 2 million feddans (compared with 1.4 million in 1987). In this way the Ministry of Agriculture hoped to increase domestic wheat production to 5 million tons from 3 million in the preceding years. Egypt's total consumption of wheat in 1988 was 8.5 million tons; if it could manage to grow 5 million tons, it would achieve and exceed Yusuf Wali's goal of 50 percent self-sufficiency.[130]

Some foreign advisers expressed skepticism about the impact of this price reform, noting that the three crops still under control (cotton, sugarcane, and rice) traditionally took up a quarter of the cropped area.[131] But even before price reform, only 50 percent of the rice crop had been subject to control. The area planted in sugarcane (a strategic crop whose production is carefully regulated, even in the United States) remained subject to controls primarily because it is a very thirsty crop and allowing an unregulated expansion could draw down Egypt's limited water reserves. Yet the government encouraged a steady expansion of production by setting its fixed price for sugar higher than the international market price. Already in 1985, when the international price was £E 14, Cairenes were paying £E 20–£E 24 for a ton of sugar.[132] And in 1988 the domestic procurement price was raised to £E 38–£E 50.[133]

The government did maintain the full battery of controls on cotton. Proposals to decontrol prices on this crop ran into stiff opposition from the Ministry of Industry, which counted on cheap deliveries to feed its textile mills, and the Ministry of Finance, which saw export sales as an invaluable source of hard currency.[134] But the decontrol of prices on other crops gave farmers a growing number of lucrative alternatives to cotton. Egyptian cotton production slumped from 406,000 tons in 1986 to 352,000 in 1987 and 347,000 in 1988. In 1989 the government hoped that farmers would grow 300,000 tons and export 60,000 tons to earn $300 million. But with the new opportunities opened up by decontrol, even larger numbers of farmers defected from cotton planting. Actual production was only 5.9 million *qantars* (295,000 tons), a record low.[135]

A year after this reform was implemented, only modest changes in yields were evident. This is not surprising; it may take several seasons before farmers feel secure enough about the new system, or have assembled enough capital from their profits, to contemplate major changes in their pattern of cultivation. But just how much change farmers will make depends in part on other variables. In the late 1980s credit became very tight. Imported seed, pesticides, and machinery became more expensive.

American and Egyptian experts alike hoped that price reform in Egypt would stimulate the same kind of agricultural revolution it had produced in China. Beginning in 1979 the Chinese government abolished mandatory crop deliveries, disbanded many rural communes, and decontrolled many produce prices. Chinese farmers, no longer imprisoned by confiscatory controls, immediately began to raise their output. As trade increased and grew profitable, entrepreneurs spontaneously crystallized out of both the urban and rural populations to develop marketing networks.[136] The ensuing growth was spectacular. Per capita farm income more than doubled between 1978 and 1984. China had been a net importer of agricultural products in 1980; by 1984 its agricultural trade showed a $4 billion surplus.[137]

Parts of the Chinese experience (particularly the importance of raising farmgate prices) were relevant to Egypt; others were not. In China the state had completely suppressed private agricultural marketing at the national level for thirty years. In Egypt the state had not abolished private markets but incorporated or enmeshed them in a rent-seeking economy. These two marketing systems responded to liberalization in very different ways. In China, once the state relinquished its monopoly over trade there were no insurmountable obstacles confronting private citizens who wished to enter this business. In Egypt, even after the state stopped policing markets the oligopoly of the five families remained intact.

The Egyptian government discussed several proposals that might produce more competition in wholesale marketing over the long term. The minister of supply, Nagi Shatla, wanted to encourage new entrepreneurs to enter vegetable marketing at the provincial level.[138] If merchants were able to wrest control from the five families at the local level, their enterprises might eventually grow large enough to challenge the control of the five families in Cairo. This approach, however, would probably have entailed an expansion of the very subsidies that the government was trying to curtail. To loosen the bonds between the five families and farmers, the government would probably have been forced to make a larger volume of cheap credit available to fruit and vegetable growers. And to sustain provincial marketing firms past their infant-industry phase, the government would probably have had to help subsidize the purchase of trucks, grant state lands for the construction of storage depots, expand low-interest loan programs, and so forth. In 1985 Cairo simply lacked the resources for such programs.

Lee Feller, an American expert on agricultural marketing, has suggested attacking the problem from the other end, by strengthening Cairo's retail markets. He argued that, historically, more efficient marketing systems had developed "by the *integration* of the wholesale and retail function in the form of a *chain*, be it corporate, voluntary, retailer co-op, or consumer co-op."[139] He noted that if Cairo retailers banded together in some type of federation, they would enjoy economies of scale that would allow them to begin modernizing the whole marketing process. A large-scale combination would also have been able to break into wholesale trade, competing with the five families and forcing them to offer more competitive farmgate prices.[140]

Egyptian officials who expressed some interest in Feller's proposal were discouraged by the cold reception he got from AID officials. The U.S. Agency for International Development had been pressing the Egyptians to dismantle its existing urban *gam'iyyat* and the village cooperatives. They thought that any form of cooperative in Egypt carried the taint of socialism and would aggravate Egypt's problem. But Feller's ideas were quintessentially capitalist. In Europe some of the largest supermarkets, such as those of the Swiss firm Makro, have grown out of consumer cooperatives. Even in America, cooperatives play a much more important role in agricultural marketing than AID officials seem to appreciate. In 1975, farmers' cooperatives supplied 32 percent of the fertilizer, 29 percent of the petroleum, 20 percent of the chemicals, 20 percent of the seeds, and 18 percent of the feed used on American farms.[141]

Discussion of long-term strategies for introjecting competition into an economy long accustomed to monopoly continues in Egypt. The price reforms of 1985 and 1987 chastised the Lords of Rawd al-Farag but did not eliminate their influence. In the summer of 1988 they were still able to manipulate a shortage of tomatoes to their profit.[142]

Moreover, the wholesale vegetable trade is only one of many subdivisions of agriculture where businessmen have erected lucrative oligopolies.

In the late 1980s AID was putting pressure on the Principal Bank for Development and Agricultural Credit to privatize the distribution of fertilizers, pesticides, and agricultural machinery. But the distribution of pesticides was monopolized by six large firms that controlled sales in even the smallest provincial towns.[143] Only three or four well-connected dealers had controlled the private import of tractors and agricultural machinery. There was concern that turning supply of these goods over to the private sector would trigger the same surge of profit-taking that characterized the Rawd al-Farag affair.

Lifting Subsidies and the Poultry Lobby

The conflict with the five families at Rawd al-Farag reminded Egyptian officials that businessmen could complicate economic reform at least as much as lower-class protests. Yet the wholesalers at Rawd al-Farag had not actually opposed price reform; they just behaved in a manner that made reform more painful and less attractive to the general public. But Yusuf Wali also stumbled into a conflict with poultry producers in which he discovered that businessmen could directly and deliberately oppose reform itself.

During the spring of 1985, concurrent with his effort to liberalize horticulture prices, Dr. Wali was trying to reduce government spending on corn imports. Since 1970 corn had developed into Egypt's second most costly food import (after wheat) and the volume imported was growing alarmingly fast.[144] Wali was irritated that his country, which used to be self-sufficient, was now importing 700,000 tons annually.[145] In 1984 Cairo had paid $222 million for U.S. corn—even more than the $212 million it spent on U.S. wheat that year.[146] Most of this crop was not used for human consumption but as animal fodder, especially chicken feed. So poultry breeders, not surprisingly, proved to be the major opponents of Dr. Wali's attempt to reduce the corn subsidy.

Traditionally, Egyptian poultry farmers were primarily peasants who raised a few chickens in a coop behind their homes. Women tended the birds, feeding them scraps and seed in order to add a few eggs to the family diet. In the 1970s, however, these family operations became increasingly professional, and a new generation of capitalist entrepreneurs grew up who invested in breeding farms. This transformation mirrored a change in the Egyptian diet. As higher oil revenues and worker remittances flowed into Egypt, consumers who had traditionally gorged on cereals began to develop a taste for meat and other high-protein foods. Between 1960 and 1980 total production of red meats, poultry, and fish in Egypt grew 50 percent from 415,000 tons to 622,000 tons annually. During the same period consumption of these proteins rose by 116 percent.[147] By 1980, chicken and eggs were staples in the diet of the Egyptian middle class. Thousands of peasants and businessmen rushed to meet the demands of the burgeoning poultry industry.

The government encouraged this trend. In the 1960s it had started to encourage poultry production for the national market as part of its campaign to promote cultivation of higher-value product lines. Sadat whetted the public appetite for meat when, as part of his response to the 1977 riots, he inaugurated a massive program to import frozen chickens.[148] Imports of frozen poultry soared from 9,000 tons in 1978 to 27,000 tons in 1979, then to 76,000 tons by 1980.[149] The state-controlled General Poultry Company, which had pioneered commercial chicken and egg production in Egypt, worked to encourage the growth of private farms. It imported eggs of high-quality breeder stock and advanced them to peasants to be raised. The public sector banks made hard currency available for the import of medicines, waterworks, feeder stands, and other key inputs.[150] The Ministry of Agriculture offered a wide array of extension services, including technical advice, special medicines, and subsidized feed.

Of course, the value of these public incentives was partly offset by the usual network of government controls. The Ministry of Agriculture set a maximum legal price for table eggs.[151] And, unlike fruits and vegetables, the government possessed the infrastructure to enforce domestic poultry prices. The General Poultry Company operated the largest chicken farms in Egypt, sold its produce directly to the Ministry of Supply's *gam'iyyat*, and produced half of all the broilers raised in Egypt.[152]

Most farmers felt that, on balance, government intervention made poultry production attractive. The key to their profits was cheap feed. As early as 1975–76, when corn sold for the equivalent of £E 80–£E 90 a ton in international markets, the Egyptian government's

Figure 5-2. Price of Corn, 1974–85

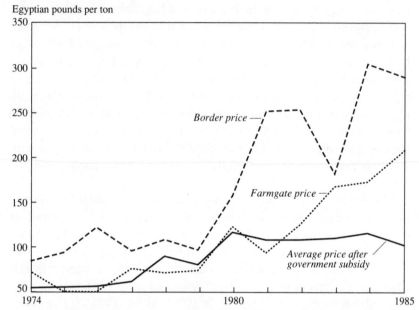

Egyptian pounds per ton

Source: Jean-Jacques Dethier, *Trade, Exchange Rate, and Agricultural Pricing Policies in Egypt,* vol. 2 (Washington: World Bank, 1989), pp. 53, 62, and 76.

subsidy kept the domestic price of this subsidy at around £E 50.[153] The importance of this subsidy became clear to farmers in 1977, when a sharp increase in international grain prices pressed the government to eliminate the corn subsidy (see figure 5-2). Deprived of cheap feed, thousands of peasants went bankrupt in 1978–79 and national production shriveled.[154]

The government was soon forced to respond to this crisis—not by small peasant farmers but by a new generation of modern poultry farmers who had recently entered the business. The high rate of profit in poultry had attracted investments by some of Egypt's most influential businessmen (including Uthman Ahmad Uthman) and many upper-echelon bureaucrats. For example, Muhammad al-Khishn, director of the General Poultry Company, left the public sector in 1977 to form Ismailia Misr Poultry Company, a private firm. He took much of General Poultry's best managerial and scientific talent into the private sector with him.[155] These men knew the most effective ways to lobby their former colleagues in government. They typically had established their farms on cheap desert plots and had petitioned the government to install roads, water, and electricity under the terms of the land reclamation program. When the government cut corn subsidies, they knew where to apply for their restoration.

In 1978 the government not only restored the corn subsidy, but raised it to unprecedented levels. American exports of corn to Egypt climbed from 180,000 tons in 1973 to 1,586,000 tons by 1983.[156] Local demand for chicken, and the profits of breeders, continued to rise. Consumers grumbled that, despite their rising incomes, they could not obtain enough meat. The press took up a discussion of "the protein crisis."

Yusuf Wali took command of the Ministry of Agriculture during the height of the protein debate, and he made increasing meat supply one of the three highest priorities in his report *Strategy of Agricultural Development in the Eighties*. The report outlined a plan to increase production of white meats like poultry and fish, since producing a kilogram of red meat (beef, lamb, or camel) consumed 7 kilograms of feed while an equal weight of white meat took only 2 kilograms.[157] To support investors wishing to start poultry farms or chickenfeed plants, the Ministry of Agriculture thus sponsored £E 750 million worth of soft loans, bearing 7 percent interest and repayable over five years (not including a two-year grace period).[158] Wali also helped to inaugurate a parallel program of loans extended by the ruling National Democratic party as part of its Popular Development Program (PDP).

The result was an explosion of poultry production. In 1975 only 300 Egyptian farms had specialized in fattening broilers; by 1984 there were 18,623. The Five-Year Economic Plan for 1981–82 through 1985–86 called for production of 2.7 billion eggs annually by 1986–87; in fact, production in 1985 had already reached 7.5 billion eggs, a volume the plan had not anticipated until the year 2000.[159]

This boom, however, had been built on a very weak foundation. Rapid growth had exposed a number of bottlenecks. There were not enough mechanized slaughterhouses or old-fashioned butchers to convert all this chicken into meat. There were not enough refrigerators available in Cairo (much less elsewhere) to keep the meat fresh until sale. Most important, it had proven impossible to provide enough chickenfeed, particularly at subsidized prices, to keep up with the expansion of consumption.

There were actually two problems with the supply of chickenfeed. First, the growth in the poultry industry surpassed the government's ability to expand the supply of subsidized corn. The government supplied corn for £E 60 a ton, even though it paid £E 280 a ton for it on international markets. By 1985 this subsidy alone cost the government £E 300 million a year.[160] In addition, the government had to invest in new fodder factories and depots. When the foreign exchange crisis of 1985 broke, it was obvious that supplies would have to be curtailed.

Just as important, however, were problems in the distribution of the corn that was available. Since the government could never supply enough corn at the subsidized price of £E 60 a ton to meet the demand, a parallel free market emerged in which corn traded at closer to the international price, usually around £E 200 a ton. The vast gap between official and private prices naturally encouraged pilfering from government stock for resale on the black market. Sometimes this transfer occurred through outright theft of government stocks, but more often it occurred when farmers drew more fodder from the Ministry of Agriculture than their own coops required and sold the surplus on the parallel market.

The government tried to take steps to curtail this practice. Technically each farm received an allotment of feed in strict ratio to the number of chicks and broilers it had.[161] However, these limits were widely abused. The larger, more influential agribusinesses were well positioned to draw more than their allotted quota, either by misrepresenting the size of their flocks or by bribing officials at the feed factories. Feed factory managers often found it convenient to collaborate in this, since the quick drawdown of their stocks gave them a case for appealing to the ministry for expanded input supplies and newer equipment.

The government's declining ability to finance corn imports and the highly uneven distribution of feed within the private sector combined with disastrous effect in the spring of 1985. In June 1984 the government's warehouses held a strategic reserve of 226,000 tons of corn. In November the government, strapped for cash, began to reduce its corn imports; reserves shrank to 69,000 tons by January 1985 and to 14,000 tons by March. This was enough to cover the needs of chicken growers for only three days. Despite the reduction of imports, the General Poultry Company and private agribusinesses were permitted to buy subsidized corn in volumes that equaled or exceeded their 1984 allotments. In fact, disbursals of subsidized corn in the first half of 1985 were larger than they had been in the last half of 1984.[162]

By late March 1985 the government corn reserve was virtually exhausted, and small farmers were forced to turn entirely to the black market for their feed supplies. This ignited a panic, and the free market price quickly spiralled to over £E 250 a ton. A lot of farmers simply could not find or afford enough feed to stay in business. They stopped taking deliveries of chicks from the General Poultry Company. The company then discovered it had imported millions of chicks for which a local market no longer existed. Short on feed itself, it could not afford to raise them into broilers on its own. The company's director gave orders to eliminate the chick surplus. Four million chicks were then killed by bulldozers.[163]

The public was dumbfounded. For a majority of Egyptians, an egg a week was still something of a delicacy, a savory. The spectacle of food being wasted—in a society where bread rinds are left on walls for use by the needy—was shocking. The government responded by importing massive quantities of corn. Yusuf Wali told a special meeting of the NDP elite that he planned to double the productivity of yellow corn to 24 ardebs per feddan and to produce 10,000 feddans of corn during the coming year.[164]

In the wake of the crisis, there were outraged demands for a public inquiry. Wali, who had recently taken over responsibility for the provisioning of corn from the Ministry of Supply, was in the hot seat. His answers to queries about how the crisis had developed did little to clarify matters, and his primary concern was clearly to minimize damage to his own authority rather than to advance the public reckoning of the affair. For months he had insisted that there was no shortage of corn and that stocks were ample. He stood by this claim for two months after the killings, until his own ministry's report on the crisis confirmed the failing of the supply system.[165] He immediately sacked the director of the General Poultry Company, blaming him for thoughtlessly executing millions of chicks. When the director protested that the executions had been ordered by the minister of agriculture himself, Wali denied this and insisted that his own preference would have been to distribute the doomed chicks to local government enterprises.[166] Had Wali deliberately allowed government corn stocks to fall, hoping that shortages would supply evidence that subsidies were too expensive? Or had he simply miscalculated the demand for corn and not understood how perilous the situation was becoming? It is hard to say.

During the months after the crisis broke, Wali and other officials blamed the poultry producers for triggering the crisis. The breeders' refusal to accept chicks had forced their destruction. The press alleged that the producers may have done this deliberately to underscore their demand for an expanded supply of subsidized corn. The public, which had just witnessed masterful manipulation of the market by the Lords of Rawd al-Farag, tended to believe this. But the government never produced evidence of a conspiracy and breeder behavior was understandable as a simple reaction to market forces.

But the crisis changed the way that breeders behaved. The public uproar it provoked gave breeders a new sense of their potential power in national affairs. During the 1980s the large poultry firms had grown in both number and influence. The successful examples of men like Uthman Ahmad Uthman and Muhammad al-Khishn lured many groups to invest in modern poultry farms. Government officials, particularly officers in the police and army, saw poultry as a high-profit, capital-intensive sideline that might provide attractive income for retirement. As the national alliance of businessmen and public sector officials grew tighter, breeders found it easier to influence national policy.

That was true, for example, of the largest private poultry hatchery in Egypt, a two-hundred-feddan chicken and egg farm at Kafr Faqr. The primary owner was Muhsin al-Tunsi, an ambitious businessman who had made his fortune as a middleman in Egyptian-Israeli trade and owned extensive interests in food distribution. His subordinate partner was Asaf Yaguri, a retired general (who had commanded an armored brigade during the October 1973 War) whose army connections helped the firm secure cheap equipment and lucrative contracts from the powerful Ministry of Defense. (Yaguri had also done contract work for Uthman Uthman on the latter's Salihiyya land reclamation project.)[167] Between them, these men had access to the highest officials in the country. When the poultry crisis erupted, Mubarak himself traveled to al-Tunsi's farm to hear the breeders' side of the story.

In 1981, the year Mubarak took power, poultry farmers were already strong enough to ensure that corn subsidies would be exempted from the upper house of Parliament's report that recommended reducing all subsidies.[168] In the following years their influence grew even more extensive, particularly at the provincial level. In 1983 breeders in Giza formed a producers' association which recruited a well-connected government minister as its director. In Gharbiyya three millionaire breeders who monopolized the marketing of chickens became major forces in local politics.[169] During the 1985 crisis the provincial councils of Sharqiyya and Qalyubiyya provinces acted as conduits for the poultry farmers, passing on to the central government their demands for increased supplies of cheap feed and credit subsidies.[170]

The breeders had long complained that government price regulations were depriving them of a legitimate part of their profits.[171] Even before the poultry crisis of 1985 they had been lobbying the cabinet for redress. They wanted the government to raise the purchase price of eggs, to reduce competition by halting credit or support for the construction of new poultry farms, and to reduce imports of foreign table eggs and chicken meat. Finally, they hoped to extend the grace period for repayment of their low-interest government loans.[172] However, they had done their lobbying as uncoordinated agribusinesses and had had no major successes.

Ironically, Yusuf Wali played a major role in the formation of a more effective national poultry lobby.[173] To drum up support in his effort to persuade the government to lift price controls, Wali encouraged the formation of a series of producers' associations. In 1984 he led the fight to authorize formation of an Association of Agricultural Producers and Exporters, which originally recruited members from farmers licensed to export potatoes and peas.[174] Similar associations combining exporters of fruits and vegetables soon followed. By 1985 Wali had come under pressure from poultry farmers to give them similar rights to organize nationally. He won approval of their proposal from the cabinet's Policy Committee, and the Poultry Producers Association was born.[175] Within months of its formation, the new association would clash with Wali over the critical question of whether to preserve corn subsidies, the key to their profits.

Despite his ties to the poultry association, Wali remained eager to take his ministry out of the subsidized corn business. Even with reduced imports, the subsidy cost the Ministry of Agriculture £E 200 million annually. Chastised by the experiences of 1985, Wali had devised a highly subtle strategy for reducing this burden. First he allowed feed stocks to dwindle again. Chickenfeed factories stopped working because of the shortage of yellow corn. Chicken growers, faced by a shortage of feed, were forced to fill their feeding troughs with bread and even macaroni bought on the black market. (The government was selling wheat for £E 25 per ardeb, but on the black market it fetched £E 40 as feed.) The free market price of corn peaked at £E 450 a ton.[176]

Then in June, when demand was at its highest, Wali suddenly doubled the official price to £E 120 and flooded the market. Made desperate by massive shortages, producers paid the new price happily. It was, after all, still only a fraction of the $120 import price.

Wali followed this change with an interesting offer. In July 1987 the Policy Committee proposed that the government drop the subsidy on corn and eliminate that appropriation from the state budget. As compensation it offered to shoulder the burden of debt interest for poultry producers for the next three years (about £E 50 million).[177] Wali hoped that the poultry producers would accept this offer and that he could get out of the subsidized corn business. To keep the pressure on breeders, he let it leak that in November corn prices would be increased again to £E 180.

Wali's new approach was not painless. Three times there were mass slaughters and shutdowns in the broiler industry.[178] (Unlike the year before, several of these crises did seem to be deliberately engineered by breeders to provoke government action.)[179] But these incidents were on a far smaller scale than the year before, and the public remained confident that the government was in control of the situation. Most important, Wali's strategy led to direct negotiations with the Breeders Association.

The negotiations dragged on for almost a year. The second increase in corn prices slated for November 1986 was postponed until December and then rescheduled for June 1987.[180] This in itself was a victory for the Breeders Association, insulating its members through another year and a critical period of adjustment. Corn prices were finally raised from £E 120 to £E 180 in June 1987. They were raised again to £E 220 in January 1988. At that price, the Ministry of Agriculture paid about £E 80 a ton for corn subsidies.[181] This weighed most heavily on small producers, many of whom were driven out of business. Half of the egg-producing farms declared bankruptcy and 80 percent of the poultry-fattening farms stopped paying their bank loans.[182] The larger producers did not complain about this restriction of competition, which left them with a larger market share.[183]

Indeed, in their negotiations they won a series of government measures that made it more difficult to import chicken meat. In 1984 Egypt imported 100,000 tons of chicken meat, a volume equal to total domestic production. In 1985 imports declined to 73,000 tons, and in 1986 they declined even further.[184] In 1987 the government banned the importation of eggs (except hatching eggs) altogether.[185]

The Breeders Association also secured Wali's commitment to expand local feed production. In 1988 a high-priority plan was announced to produce three million tons of fodder each year using nontraditional agricultural byproducts.[186] By 1989 a pattern had been established, with the government letting prices rise but working energetically to prevent shortages.

The Poultry Breeders Association, with Wali's blessing, fought for additional government support. Sharif Sami, its president, launched a public appeal for policies to facilitate the import of necessities like mechanical slaughter equipment, to reduce interest rates on existing breeder loans to 6 percent, to raise retail chicken and egg prices, to slow future increases in corn prices, and to treat poultry as an industrial rather than an agricultural project (so that it could qualify for long-term, rather than medium-term, loans).[187] The association eventually won a number of these battles. On December 5, 1985, the cabinet's Policy Committee proposed rescheduling poultry farm debts in order to postpone payment for one to three years. (In practice, few banks cooperated with these guidelines.) Wali himself consistently recommended removing all price controls from eggs and chicken and rescheduling debts. In 1987 the new minister of supply, Galal Abu Dhahab, finally agreed to a gradual rise in prices.[188]

In a national address on Farmers Day in September 1988 President Mubarak endorsed a new round of protectionist measures for poultry breeders. He said: "I have instructed the prime minister to calculate the real cost of poultry and egg production at these prices and add a considerable profit margin, and to grant suppliers a degree of freedom. I want all the farms which have stopped production to work again. Egypt used to produce 4 billion eggs. This has dropped to 2 billion. Egg- and poultry-producing countries, like America and others, will be pleased with this fall in egg production. They will want to export eggs to us at low prices, but they want hard currency."[189]

It would be fair to say that businessmen were gradually moving away from their historic support of pure subsidies (figure 5-3). But this should not be confused with the notion that they were moving toward

Figure 5-3. Progress in Reducing Subsidies, 1976–87

Ratio of subsidies to GDP and government income

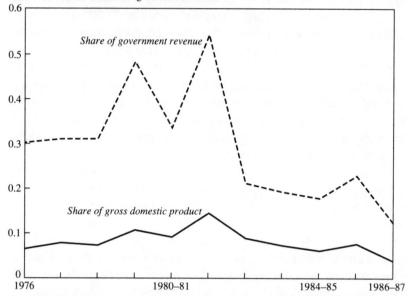

Sources: World Bank, *Arab Republic of Egypt: Current Economic Situation and Economic Reform Program* (Washington, October 1986), pp. 88, 98, and 102, and *Egypt: Country Economic Memorandum* (Washington, January 1989), pp. 4, 24, and 28.

laissez-faire. Government supports now took the form of import controls (including the denial of hard currency to chicken importers) and investment in industrialized, high-cost means of providing fodder. Market forces were permitted to work in some areas—where they reinforced the profits of those who commanded political influence. They were not allowed to work in other areas (like international trade).

Businessmen had learned to play a kind of shell game. They worked with the government to help eliminate the specific subsidies to which AID and the World Bank objected. In exchange for this cooperation, they sought new types of subsidies and rents in areas that foreign development agencies were not supervising. This eased the political pressure for reform. But it did not markedly reduce the drain on the state budget or contribute to the liberalization of the Egyptian economy.

Conclusion

Egyptian bureaucrats are no longer staunch opponents of economic liberalization. Years of dialogue with representatives of AID and the

World Bank have persuaded many of the virtues of reform. Some have discovered opportunities for personal profit in privatization programs and, employing the revolving-door approach, have used their government positions to prepare for more lucrative careers in business. Almost all have seen ample evidence that the current system condemns Egypt to negligible growth and a future of debt, dearth, and dependence. While such officials continue to complicate the reform process by engaging in the turf battles and nest-feathering that plague bureaucracies everywhere, few actively oppose or raise principled objections to liberalization.

Egyptian consumers also present a less serious obstacle to reform than they once did. Some understand that their country confronts a grave and massive economic crisis, and that sacrifices today are necessary to rescue any hope of growth in the future. Others suffer and complain about their tightening circumstances but are unlikely to riot so long as they are uncertain as to who is responsible for their pain. The strategy of reform by stealth has given the government a viable means for implementing changes without provoking a massive threat to the social order.

Ironically, businessmen raise increasingly serious challenges to economic liberalization. In principle, most Egyptian businessmen sincerely favor a more market-oriented economy. They would be happy working in an enterprise society that minimized their contact with the government and held the opportunity for greatly expanding their profits. But in practice, Egyptian businessmen have been enmeshed in the prevailing pattern of rent seeking. When they are led to the edge of the precipice and asked to leap—to shed the tariff protections, subsidies, and oligopolies that ensure their current profits—many balk. They know that the development of a more genuine market economy is possible only in the long term, and they worry that in the short term they will not survive the surrender of their perquisites. They are trapped in a variant of the prisoner's dilemma.[190]

Businessmen, of course, are not the only Egyptians who have doubts about the short-term costs of liberalization. But unlike the traditional opponents of reform, they are increasingly well placed to translate those doubts into political influence. During the 1980s many of the members of the proliferating businessmen's lobbies in Cairo had interests in agriculture. In addition to these catholic organizations, like food importers, textile manufacturers, and farm machinery dealers, a number of more narrowly focused interest groups, like the Breeders Association, developed to articulate the concerns of agriculturalists. The select group of farmers (often actually urban entrepreneurs) who were involved in the export of fruits and vegetables formed their own producers' association which enjoyed close ties to the Ministry of Agriculture. Under Mubarak, rich peasants found a new avenue for pressing their demands through the revival of the national Federation of Agricultural Cooperatives, which Sadat had disbanded in 1976. Agronomists and other graduates of agricultural colleges who, as a result of government patronage, owned a large share of Egypt's reclaimed lands found a voice through the Syndicate of Agriculturalists. The syndicate was headed by Sa'd Hagras, who was also the chair of the National Democratic party's influential Agriculture Committee.[191]

Some agricultural interests acquired a say in the formation of government policy through representation by political parties. The Lords of Rawd al-Farag had close ties to the Wafd party, which also sought to represent absentee landowners with an interest in reforming the rent law. The Tagammu' party attempted to develop its own peasant federation to represent the interests of smallholders, although its influence remained limited to a handful of provinces. The most successful vehicle for the representation of farm interests may have been the National Democratic party itself. Its backbenchers were drafted from the ranks of rich peasants and rural notables. But the party also included influential representatives of the rising class of agrarian capitalists, a small group (perhaps fifteen thousand strong) of highly educated and well-financed entrepreneurs who are pioneering a more technically advanced style of farming in Egypt. This group, with interests in citrus, vegetables, exotic plants, and red-meat production, is well positioned to translate its urban links and official university connections into political influence.[192]

This profusion of business lobbies was abetted by AID and other extensions of the U.S. government as part of their campaign to promote economic growth in Egypt. In the mid-1970s the U.S. government brokered the creation of the Egyptian-American Business Council, a forum for combining the energies of businessmen in both countries to promote the role of the private sector in Egypt. And in the early 1980s, the U.S. Embassy worked hard to create the American Chamber of Commerce in Cairo to advance the same purpose.[193] Even the Egyptian Businessmen's Association, the most powerful of the various local lobbies, had been formed in 1982 as a byproduct of meetings between the Egyptian government and the Egyptian-American Businessmen's Association.[194]

American advisers commonly believed that the source of Egypt's economic woes was state intervention, pure and simple. They hoped to correct this problem by promoting the power of the private sector. Yet this approach often misfired. The friendly pricing system, the stopgap measure by which the Egyptian government hoped to get the Lords of Rawd al-Farag to voluntarily restrain horticultural prices, was devised by a senior economist of AID in Cairo. The Cairo representative of the U.S. Department of Agriculture worked as a consultant to the Breeders Association, helping it draft reports and devise graphic presentations to win concessions from the government.

These Americans thought that by shifting the balance of power between bureaucrat and businessman in Egypt they could end the distortions in the economy. They could not. Pouring water from one bucket into another does not transform it into wine. Giving businessmen more power simply enhanced their ability to defend their existing perquisites. What was needed was some way to change the way they used power, to redirect their energies to more productive and efficient pursuits.

The cases of Rawd al-Farag and the Poultry Breeders Association shed light on conditions that might make liberalization a bit easier. For example, the problem of raising corn prices suggests that those development economists who have insisted that reforms should be both rapid and comprehensive do have a point. By phasing in price increases, Yusuf Wali gave the Poultry Breeders an opportunity to organize and develop a counterstrategy. If the government had raised prices to their maximum target in one firm move, the change would have been more painful but political opposition to it would probably have been less effective.

This does not mean that rapid change is always the key to successful reform. Reforms that affect the business community must contend with the organized opposition of a small group. Reforms that affect large and amorphous constituencies, like consumers of subsidized bread, have a very different political logic. Urban consumers (much less rural) are too large and disparate a body to organize themselves under the umbrella of one political institution. Their response to painful reforms is likely to be spontaneous, even violent. There is thus no political advantage lost—and much to be gained—by implementing reforms that affect them gradually.

Egyptian officials learned this lesson in 1977; officials in other Arab states have learned it since. In 1984 both Morocco and Tunisia embraced IMF standby packages. In both countries, the action prompted riots that were severe and protracted. In 1988 and 1989 Algeria and Jordan accepted similar programs and experienced even more violent riots. In the latter two instances the government, in an effort to restore some semblance of legitimacy, called democratic elections. And in both elections, a plurality of voters, moved partly by a sense that their government was corrupt and was mismanaging the economy in the interest of a few *qitat samik* (fat cats), cast their ballots for Islamist candidates. The rise of militant Islamist opposition in both countries weakened the existing regime and made additional reforms even more difficult.[195]

Speedy change is inappropriate in applying some reforms, and insufficient in executing others. For example, speed had little to do with the problems experienced at Rawd al-Farag. Here too the problem was that businessmen had organized to secure the advantages they enjoyed under the system of crony capitalism; their organization was directed not to influence government policy but to inhibit the workings of the market. Slow or fast, the removal of government controls only revealed the private monopoly underneath.

Private sector monopolies are a common product of crony capitalism. Even after government policy changes, they persist. The resources and connections they have built up during years of government protection give them an edge against potential competitors. They obstruct the growth and efficiency that price reform is supposed to produce. To "get the prices right," a developing country must find some way of dealing with them.

One approach, partly manifest in the Egyptian government's reaction to the Rawd al-Farag affair, is for the government to act to induce competition by offering incentives for new businesses to enter a sector. By building infrastructure—new roads on which farmers might more cheaply move their goods, new markets in which entrepreneurial wholesalers might get a start—the government can lower the costs of competing with established monopolies. Unfortunately, most government incentives just create new distortions and undermine the very purpose of market-oriented reform. For example, the Egyptian government entertained a proposal to subsidize the purchase of trucks in the hope that new merchants might build up transport fleets to compete with the Lords of Rawd al-Farag. But the progress envisioned by this new subsidy would have been at least partly discounted by the costs of intervening in the market, of redirecting capital and credit into truck purchases instead of other uses, not to mention the burden added to the government's deficit.

Another strategy is antitrust legislation. The Egyptian government might have charged the Lords of Rawd al-Farag with price rigging and mandated a restructuring of their operations into a number of smaller, more competitive units. But governments in developing countries often lack the administrative resources to pursue this option. Egypt has no body of antitrust or bankruptcy law that would have provided a basis for acting in this manner or a practical set of guidelines for implementing restructuring. A reorganization of Rawd al-Farag would have to have been engineered by the government ad hoc, and its success would have depended heavily on finding private partners who were willing to supply the expertise and assume the risk of entering this sector.

And such private partners are hard to find. Egypt does not suffer from a lack of entrepreneurs—the extent of rent seeking testifies to the craft and energy with which Egyptian businessmen pursue profits. But the rules of rent seeking in Egypt are well understood and its costs are often surprisingly low. In contrast, many businessmen lack both the information and the capital necessary to be confident about entering a new sphere of competitive enterprise.

There is, encouragingly, one strategy on the horizon that might stiffen the competitive capacities of Egyptian business, making it easier to circumscribe or circumvent the monopolies that have grown up under crony capitalism. This is a change in the availability of credit and financial services, which would make it easier for businessmen to invest in new activities. Some experts think that reform in Egypt's financial sector could trigger a wash of new investment for agriculture and other activities. The following chapter discusses proposals for such a financial revolution.

CHAPTER 6

Agricultural Credit and Financial Reform

WHAT KEPT NEW ENTREPRENEURS FROM COMPETING AGAINST MONOPOLIES like Rawd al-Farag after the removal of price controls restored their incentives to do so? The groundwork of the monopoly in fruit and vegetable wholesaling was laid in the 1940s, when four families from neighboring villages, bound by clan ties that superseded market temptations, agreed to form a business alliance. By the 1960s a fairly modern oligopoly had grown up over this archaic foundation. At the village level, the families had deployed networks of skilled agents who had telephone access to information about changes in demand and had the capital to contract to buy crops in bulk. At the provincial level, the families owned the fleets of trucks and the aisles of storage bins necessary to transport and process large quantities of produce. In Cairo itself, they controlled the one major market and had tied thousands of wholesalers to them through various credit networks. They had achieved a kind of vertical integration in which they could swamp potential competitors entering at any one level by denying them access to the facilities at the next.

The kind of barriers raised did not make competition impossible. Anyone with a truck could drag produce from Giza into Cairo, and many did. Yet even after Rawd al-Farag lost its government protection, the high entry costs served to discourage competition. Anyone hoping to rival the four families needed the capital to match Rawd al-Farag's accumulated facilities. And they needed to be able to take risks, to spend years developing their own networks before showing major profits, or even to fail and then pick themselves up again.

Unfortunately, neither capital nor a risk-taking mentality abounds among Egyptian businessmen. A Cairene entrepreneur, even one who faces no serious competition, still has to cope with unpredictable changes in inflation, vacillating exchange rates, and capricious government policies. The country lacks genuine capital markets, so the odds are that the entrepreneur's capital represents the sum of his family resources, either saved over long years or inherited from some glorious ancestor. One of the reasons that rent seeking is such a popular technique among businessmen is that it holds risk to a minimum. It is a way of getting the government to guarantee against the risks of certain ventures. As a result, Egyptian businessmen are not unimaginative, but they are justifiably cautious.

The same forces of scarce capital and high vulnerability to risk that dampen competition against Rawd al-Farag affect the entire agricultural sector. They discourage new firms from competing with established enterprises in the import of pesticides and agricultural machinery or the development and distribution of seeds. Even farmers are not well positioned to take advantage of the new price incentives to improve production. If they saved most of their profits they would, over the long term, be able to afford new technologies. But, in the short term, the addition to their income is not enough to enable them to buy new pumps, machinery, and greenhouses. Shortage of capital, not "the innate conservatism of the peasant" that officials in Cairo sometimes complain about, is the primary obstacle to innovation in farming practices.

Much of the apparent caution of businessmen and farmers could be reduced if Egypt had a more developed financial system. A more elaborate system of banks, bonds, and equity markets would help entrepreneurs to raise the money necessary to compete with established monopolies or to pioneer whole new enterprises. Such a system could also provide the information and hedging systems permitting reduced risks, thereby making bolder energetic ventures less dangerous.

Many economists thought that the cases of South Korea and Taiwan (and, to a lesser extent, Indonesia and Chile) showed how important the contribution of financial institutions to development could be. Taiwan liberalized its financial system in the 1950s and South Korea in the 1960s. In both cases the result seemed to be a rapid rise in savings, an inflow of foreign capital, and the growth of an array of financial services that made businesses easier to establish and more likely to be successful. Other Asian economies followed suit, and observers soon began to speak of a financial revolution in Asia.[1] Reflecting on this experience, an influential school of economists

formed which argued that financial reform should actually take precedence over other policy changes in developing countries. They concluded that the financial sector "is unique in the degree to which its
markets, prices, institutions, and policies impinge upon all others.
Money is the only good that trades against all other goods. Interest
rates are the relative prices that have most pervasive relevance to
economic decisions."[2]

In the 1980s both the International Monetary Fund (IMF) and the
World Bank began to assign priority to financial liberalization among
the policy reforms they urged on developing countries. They made
careful studies of the development of financial systems in Asia and
urged similar courses on other developing states and on the liberalizing
economies of Eastern Europe.[3] They made financial reforms, particularly the decontrol of interest rates, a standard element in the package
of conditions they imposed on countries seeking to borrow from them.
Partly under the stimulus of this pressure, a legion of Third World
countries began to experiment with financial liberalization.[4]

Proponents of financial revolution thought that Egypt cried out
for reform. Although Cairo's financial sector had been somewhat
liberalized since 1973, by the mid-1980s it was still highly underdeveloped. There is no real market in bonds; private traders are not eager
to hold notes, most of which are low-yield instruments issued by the
government either in exchange for the reserve requirements it imposes
on banks or to compensate individuals whose lands or firms have been
confiscated. Price controls and manipulated exchange rates have stifled
the development of a futures market for commodities. The existing
stock exchange does a tiny volume of business. Because of inflation,
the real rate of return on most financial instruments is negative. And
although the country has plenty of banks, many are barely solvent and
even those that are liquid lend very cautiously—largely for short-term
commercial transactions. Rates of return on all financial instruments
(except for banking profits) are low or even negative.

Some idea of what this financial "shallowness" means for the wider
performance of the economy is evident in table 6-1. In 1987 Egyptians
saved only 8 percent of their gross domestic product. In comparison,
the average volume of savings for countries at comparable levels of
development, what the World Bank calls lower-middle-income countries (with GNP per capita of $481 to $2,000), was 21 percent of GDP.
For upper-middle-income countries (GNP per capita of $2,001 to

Table 6-1. Financial Activities in Egypt and Four Other Countries, 1987

	Percent of gross domestic product		Ratio of savings and investment to consumption (percent)
Country	Gross domestic savings	Gross domestic investment	
Egypt	8	19	30
India	22	24	58
Indonesia	29	26	77
South Korea	38	29	106
United States	13	16	33

Source: World Bank, *World Development Report, 1989* (Oxford University Press, 1989), pp. 180–81.

$6,000), a group that includes many of the newly industrializing countries like South Korea and Brazil, the volume of savings is even larger, averaging 27 percent of GDP.[5]

While this low rate of domestic savings did not prevent Egypt from raising investment funds abroad, it clearly imposed a heavy burden on the economy. The repayment of foreign loans soon turned into a life-sucking drain on the country's hard currency assets. The small volume of savings available to domestic banks provided little opportunity for them to evolve beyond being specialized, conservative institutions supplying little impetus for wider economic development.

Financial activities in rural areas are even more poorly developed than in the cities. Few private banks can afford to maintain branches outside the larger cities. Even the curb market of moneylenders and informal credit facilities is not very elaborate.[6] Partly this reflects concern about the riskiness of lending to farmers, whose fortunes vacillate with the vagaries of weather and pest infestations and who (quite undeservedly) have a reputation for poor repayment records. But the most important force suppressing private finance in the countryside is probably the Principal Bank for Development and Agricultural Credit (PBDAC), the state agricultural bank.

Reform of PBDAC

In 1985 officials in the Cairo offices of the U.S. Agency for International Development (AID) who hoped to trigger a financial revolution in the Egyptian countryside drafted a bold plan to reform the Principal Bank for Development and Agricultural Credit. This bank had developed out of the land reform of 1952. The peasants who received plots under the reform lacked the capital necessary to match the inputs of fertilizer and machinery that the old landed magnates had employed. Eager to avoid a drop in productivity, the government charged its General Organization for Agricultural and Cooperative Credit (itself a reconfigured extension of the older Agricultural Bank) to provide credit in kind—seeds, fertilizer, pesticides, and access to agricultural machinery—to all members of agrarian reform coopera- tives. Since the General Organization was also the body that collected the state's compulsory crop deliveries from peasants, it simply deducted the cost of the goods it advanced (plus a minor interest charge) from government payments to farmers.[7] In 1976 Anwar Sadat, as part of his campaign against Ahmad Yunis, declared the General Organization officially independent of the cooperatives and renamed it the Principal Bank for Development and Agricultural Credit.

The functions of PBDAC were the same as its predecessor's, but with an important difference—it acted a bit more like a commercial bank. After its local branches were made independent of the coopera- tives, they found it easier to insist on repayment of loans. While arrears and defaults had been a major problem in the 1970s, by 1984 the repayment rate had reached 98.8 percent.[8] Furthermore, the type of lending PBDAC engaged in had changed. Between 1960 and 1975 some 97.4 percent of the General Organization's lending had been in short- term loans. By 1984, however, only 71 percent of PBDAC's loans were short term.[9]

This shift was significant, because the social profile of short- and longer-term borrowers was very different. Short-term loans, which were granted as credit in kind with little or no interest charge, were available to any cooperative member. Although richer peasants took a disproportionate share of the credit thus extended, poor peasants made up the vast majority of borrowers (93 percent in 1978). Medium- and long-term loans, on the other hand, carried higher interest rates and had to be covered by collateral in land. They were monopolized almost entirely by richer farmers (those owning five feddans or more).[10]

The increasing tendency of PBDAC to favor larger, richer farmers drew criticism inside Egypt. Egyptian leftists chided the government that it had abandoned the original mission of state finance in rural areas to assure the flow of credit and raise the productivity of small peasants.[11] By the end of the 1980s, even mainstream parliamentarians had begun to echo this critique.[12] These complaints, however, had far less political impact than a very different set levied from outside Egypt by foreign development experts.

Experts at AID's Cairo office, in particular, drafted a long list of criticisms of PBDAC. They argued that by supplying credit at highly subsidized rates (3 percent a year on short-term loans), PBDAC stifled any interest that private banks might have in servicing the countryside.[13] Yet, they charged, PBDAC provided a very inadequate substitute for private finance. The village banks were highly bureaucratic and inflexible. They loaned money according to strict formulas (credit could not exceed more than 80 percent of the value of collateral for medium-term loans). They were not supposed to finance business ventures at all but confine themselves to lending to farmers. Their accounting procedures were crude and they supplied little real information to farmers.

Some cynics thought that the leaders of PBDAC were not particularly interested in banking at all. Interest and charges on the bank's loans supplied only 53 percent of its operating revenue in 1983–84; the remainder came from the distribution of agricultural inputs and crop marketing. The financial activities of PBDAC employed 7,000 people working in 17 provincial banks, 140 district banks, and 751 village banks. But another 11,700 worked in the bank's input distribution wing, which administered 4,300 *mandubiyyat*, or district warehouses.[14]

Officials at AID began to focus on these problems at PBDAC in 1984, as they evaluated the final results of their Small Farmer Production Project (SFPP). This program had had two components. In one, American and Egyptian researchers had collaborated to produce packages of high-yielding seeds, fertilizers, and planting schedules that would maximize agricultural yields. In the other, similar teams had worked to reorganize local branches of PBDAC to make more credit available for financing adoption of these packages. By 1986 SFPP had prompted PBDAC to extend 70,751 special loans worth $64 million. The production packages of SFPP led to astounding yield increases, and despite the unusually high interest rates that the loans for the program carried (14 percent), the delinquency rate was very low (0.5 percent).[15]

Outside auditors deemed SFPP a resounding success.[16] But it was only a pilot project, operating in a few dozen villages in three provinces (Asyut, Qalyubiyya, and Sharqiyya). As SFPP's eight-year mandate was drawing to a close, AID agents had begun to investigate how its benefits could be extended throughout Egypt. (As SFPP progressed, three additional provinces were added to its scope and two more successfully lobbied for inclusion.)[17] Although PBDAC remained the chief instrument of government control in the countryside and the only viable vehicle for administering an extended program, AID officials doubted very much whether it could successfully administer a national program. They commissioned three detailed studies of PBDAC which tended to confirm their doubts.[18]

All of these studies made criticisms of PBDAC's "supervised credit" approach. By supplying a fixed package of inputs, this approach stripped farmers of important choices. They could not tailor their inputs to local conditions or their personal crop preferences. Since they could only obtain inputs from PBDAC, their prices were probably higher than they would have been if competing, private suppliers had been available. Moreover, by obliging PBDAC to check on the use of the inputs it supplied—thus taking on the role of an agricultural extension service as well as a bank—supervised credit actually raised the costs of administering loans.

Lending costs were a serious problem for PBDAC. Its SFPP loans were made at an interest rate of 14 percent, which was very high compared to the subsidized rate charged on most of the bank's loans. But PBDAC paid 8.9 percent to raise funds for SFPP loans, 7 percent to administer them, and 1 percent to cover bad debts; so it actually lost 2.9 percent on an SFPP loan. It would have to have charged 17 percent just to cover its costs.[19] But PBDAC could not charge more without a special act of Parliament; Egypt had stiff usury laws which placed a ceiling on interest rates.

Taken together, the studies commissioned by AID sketched a picture of how these problems might be surmounted. First, they urged that PBDAC's input distribution functions be phased out and that the private sector be encouraged to take over these tasks. Second, they stressed the need for PBDAC to behave "more like a bank" and less like a government agency. They wanted to see it lending at commercial rates, employing commercial lending criteria, and training its staff in the skills that prevailed in private banks. Overall, privatization became the watchword for AID's plans to promote rural financial services.

In 1986 AID's Cairo office inaugurated its follow-on project to SFPP—the Agricultural Production and Credit (APC) program, which sought to lay the groundwork for the privatization of rural finance in the medium term. One of AID's studies had cautioned that rapid privatization of input supply would lead to the same kind of problems that prevailed at Rawd al-Farag. If PBDAC shed its supply management functions too quickly, the main beneficiaries would be a handful of merchants who already dominated the private trade in pesticides and other inputs.[20] But AID allocated the bulk of APC's funding ($100 million) for policy dialogue. The APC funds would be released to PBDAC in installments, each tranche conditional on the Egyptian government's adoption of some policy reform that AID deemed necessary for gradual privatization—decontrolling crop prices, raising rural interest rates, or stiffening input prices. (Outside of the APC framework, AID also began to promote the operations of certain private firms—Pioneer Seed Co., Tanta Machinery Co.—that it considered critical to the privatization of input supply.)

Another, smaller, component of APC was dedicated to reorganizing PBDAC. These funds ($23 million) would be spent retraining PBDAC personnel, installing computer equipment in the village banks, improving accounting techniques. Its general objectives were to push PBDAC into providing "full banking services, interest rates at near market levels, rapid and efficient loan approval, and increased extension services to the farmer."[21]

Officials at PBDAC and the Ministry of Agriculture were not happy with the reorganization required of them. But so long as the Americans insisted on it as the price for the extension of SFPP-type services at the national level, they had little choice. The average SFPP seasonal loan had been for £E 175 and PBDAC had 3 million potential clients. Covering this demand would require £E 525 million a year and could easily cost twice as much once loans for livestock and other ventures were factored in.[22] To cover this expansion, PBDAC desperately needed the $100 million of capital the Americans were offering.

As such things went, APC was one of the most thoughtful and ambitious AID programs for Egyptian agriculture. But it faced real problems. Although PBDAC formally endorsed the American recommendations, AID had its hands full trying to get it to comply with their spirit rather than just their letter. Egyptian officials, particularly the elite who had experience working with the Americans, had learned to take advantage of the gap between plans and implementation, agreeing with the Americans on the former, then incorporating their own interests into the latter. More important, APC's success hinged on changes in the wider financial sector.

If PBDAC was going to raise the funds for a national program of SFPP-type loans, it would have to leverage its capital by borrowing from other Egyptian banks. If APC's privatization dimension was going to work, private banks would have to develop an interest in working in the countryside. If PBDAC or any other bank was going to turn a profit on agricultural lending, state regulation of interest rates would have to be liberalized. While AID had some direct influence over the medium-term success of APC's objectives, the long-term mission of the project really depended on the progress of liberalization in the financial sector as a whole.

Financial Repression in Egypt

The battle to reform PBDAC could be viewed as the opening engagement in a wider war to liberalize the Egyptian financial system. If it succeeded, the success of PBDAC reform would encourage similar developments throughout the entire sector. Yet the likelihood of an AID victory hinged very much on the progress of the wider war for financial liberalization. How much PBDAC could be liberalized (much less privatized) depended on whether interest rates could be decontrolled, capital accumulation enhanced, accounting practices improved, and competition spurred throughout the whole financial sector. Would Parliament approve a general increase of interest rates? Would private banks be willing to lend funds to PBDAC? Would they begin to augment its services in rural areas?

Few of PBDAC's problems were the product of its rural focus or its management by the public sector; rather, they were common throughout the Egyptian banking system. The entire sector suffered from what economists call "financial repression," an array of government policies that had the effect of retarding financial development.[23] The most common symptoms of financial repression are disincentives to the provision of financial services, constraints on the accumulation of capital, and subtractions from the volume of capital that can cripple development by fostering sluggish credit markets, inflation, and capital flight. The two policies that are most commonly blamed for triggering financial repression are directed credit and the inflation tax.

Directed credit occurs where the government intervenes, either by law or through a system of subsidies, to reduce the interest rates on loans for economic sectors in which it hopes to promote growth. Since the 1960s Egypt has employed three different forms of directed credit. First, through sector-specific banks—like PBDAC in agriculture, the Industrial Development Bank in manufacturing, and the National Development Bank in food security programs—it pays a direct subsidy to hold down interest rates for targeted activities. Second, it regulates the legal maximum interest rate offered by all banks, public and private, in a way that biases lending in favor of certain activities. For example, in 1987 a bank extending a one-year loan could have charged no more than 13 percent interest if the project was in agriculture or industry, or 15 percent if the funds were for a project in the service sector. If the borrower was seeking to finance a commercial transaction, the bank could charge whatever interest the market would bear.[24]

Directed credit was supposed to make it easier for certain sectors (especially industry and agriculture) to obtain financing. It often had just the opposite effect. Many private banks preferred to avoid lending to targeted activities because they could earn more on loans to other sectors, thereby limiting the credit available to the former. Directed credit also had an effect on the level of savings accessible to banks. Conventionally, banks have to charge borrowers more than they pay depositors in order to make a profit. So caps on the rates that banks could charge borrowers limited the rates they could pay depositors to attract funds. The Egyptian government compounded this effect by regulating the maximum interest rates on deposits as well. In 1987 the most Egyptian banks could pay was 13 percent on five-year term accounts.[25] The low rate of savings evident in table 6-1 is at least partly a result of these government regulations which lower the interest rates Egyptian banks offer to attract funds.

Regulation of interest rates was attractive to the Egyptian government for a second reason. Many of the enterprises seeking directed credits for agricultural or industrial projects were public sector firms. For that matter, the state itself often borrowed directly from the banks to finance its purchases of wheat and other commodities, or to cover part of the fiscal deficit. The shortfall between what the Egyptian government collected and what it spent was substantial (see table 6-2),

Table 6-2. Government Budget, Various Years, 1975–88
Millions of Egyptian pounds unless otherwise specified

Item	1975	1979	1982–83	1983–84	1984–85	1985–86	1986–87	1987–88
Revenues	1,524	3,684	9,749	10,371	11,311	12,793	13,499	15,983
Suez Canal, petroleum	75	659	2,085	1,832	1,747	2,021	1,577	1,832
Investment self-financing	210	374	1,507	1,628	2,011	2,347	3,041	3,571
Customs and sales taxes	629	1,472	2,839	3,222	3,351	3,297	3,651	4,362
Expenditures	3,015	7,097	14,496	16,537	18,484	20,526	21,237	26,832
Defense	587	772	1,683	2,120	2,385	2,646	2,734	2,986
Civilian wages and salaries	n.a.	n.a.	2,202	2,620	3,158	3,446	3,691	4,570
Subsidies	622	1,352	2,342	2,609	2,749	2,766	2,270	2,737
Investment	863	2,547	5,020	5,518	6,556	7,761	8,024	11,022
Deficit	1,491	3,413	4,748	6,166	7,173	7,733	7,738	10,849
Gross domestic product	5,218	12,705	24,170	28,504	33,132	38,356	43,687	55,340
Deficit as percent of GDP	29	27	20	22	22	21	18	20
Gross foreign financing	310	1,135	1,354	1,441	2,042	2,098	2,793	3,706

Source: David W. Carr, "The Possibility of Rapid Adjustment to Severe Budget-Deficit and Other Economic Problems in Egypt," *Journal of the Developing Areas*, vol. 24 (January 1990), p. 231.

n.a. Not available.

so it imposed a variety of regulations on banks in an effort to keep its deficit manageable. For example, the government required all private sector banks to transfer 25 percent of their local currency deposits to the Central Bank as an interest-free reserve requirement.[26] This amounted to a massive loan to the government.

The Egyptian government was particularly concerned to ensure that it had priority access to the hard currency, especially dollars, that circulated through the banking system. After 1985, when its need for hard currency (to cover debt repayment and food imports) began to grow while its receipts of foreign exchange (from oil sales and Suez Canal revenues) began to contract, the government imposed a new series of credit regulations. These were designed to give the public sector an advantage in tapping the hard currency assets of the banking system. Private importers were forced to deposit cash to cover the full amount of letters of credit and could not request cover for more than 50 percent of the value of the goods they imported.[27] Banks were required to restrict the total value of their private sector loans to only 2.5 percent of the previous year's lending.[28] These measures were justified as an attempt to cope with Egypt's rising balance of payments deficit, but they were formulated in a manner that assured that the burden of adjustment would fall on businessmen rather than the state.

As a result of these and similar policies, the government became the largest borrower in the country—the total value of the government's domestic borrowing equaled 70 percent of the gross national product. This was high even by the standards of developing countries. The ratio of government domestic borrowing to GNP in Mexico was 40 percent, in Turkey 28 percent, and in Brazil only 7 percent.[29]

Neither reserve requirements nor credit restrictions ever came close to eliminating the Egyptian government's fiscal deficit. They were not supposed to; rather, they were only to aid in supplying critical operating capital. The Egyptian government was, in fact, largely resigned to the existence of fiscal deficits. Most government economists believed that in a developing country the demand on state services, particularly those that promoted development, would inevitably exceed the revenues available from taxation and fees. Indeed, at least some Egyptian officials understood that running a deficit could actually ease the burden of public finance.

Deficits can, in effect, actually increase government revenues because of the "inflation tax."[30] Governments (unlike private firms) always have the option of covering their deficits by just printing new money. The increase in the money supply triggers inflation. Since the Egyptian government pays no interest either on its issue of money or on the reserves it holds from the banking system, its decision to increase the money supply acts like a tax on banks and all currency holders. This rationale may partly explain the Egyptian government's tolerance of budget deficits that amount to 20 percent of GDP or more (see table 6-2).

It is very difficult to calculate the effects of the inflation tax in Egypt because there is little agreement about what the rate of inflation is. In a May 1990 interview, Prime Minister Atif Sidqi stated that his government had informed the International Monetary Fund that the rate of inflation in his country was 14–20 percent. But Dr. Sidqi had reasons to deliberately understate the rate he quoted to the Fund. Later in the same interview he admitted that his personal estimate of the rate of inflation was between 17 percent and 24 percent, and that other economists variously estimated it to be 20 percent, 26 percent, or even 30 percent.[31]

World Bank data suggest that the average rate of inflation in Egypt between 1980 and 1988 was 10.6 percent, but economists at the Bank admit this significantly understates the real rate.[32] The Economics Section of the U.S. Embassy in Cairo calculates that the real rate of inflation during the period 1984–88 was 20 percent or more, and that the rate tended to increase in the late 1980s as the Egyptian government began to eliminate consumer subsidies and devalue the currency.[33]

Assuming an inflation rate of 20 percent, the effective inflation tax (roughly, the decline in purchasing power of average reserve money) in Egypt amounted to 6.6 percent of GNP in 1987. This was quite high by international standards; in the same year the inflation tax equaled 4 percent of GNP in Argentina, 3.7 percent in Mexico, and 2.8 percent in Turkey. (Although Egypt's inflation rate was comparatively modest, its inflation tax was made heavier because of the relatively high level of reserve money.)[34]

Up to a point, the inflation tax can act as an effective fiscal policy.[35] Egypt, however, has almost certainly exceeded those limits. Although its rate of inflation is modest by the standards of some Third World countries (price controls checked any tendency toward hyperinflation), inflation has still wreaked havoc with the economy. Its effect on savings has hampered operation of the financial system. If, during the late

1980s, the rate of inflation in Egypt was around 20 percent and the maximum interest rate on savings deposits was 13 percent, then the highest real rate of interest that savers could expect on their accounts was −7 percent. Since money held with official banks actually lost value, Egyptians had little real incentive to save with them. Instead of promoting investment, this feature of the financial system encouraged consumption. Negative real interest rates are, sadly, a common result of financial repression in lesser developed countries. They discourage savings and investment alike. Many development experts charge that they are the worst single obstacle to financial development.[36]

It might seem that under these circumstances banks could not even function. In fact, between 1961 (when Nasser nationalized the banks) and 1974 (when Sadat authorized some liberalization of the banking system) there were only eight banks in Egypt—all managed by the public sector.[37] Yet with just the stimulus of Sadat's limited liberalization, the number of banks grew explosively. By 1984 there were ninety-seven licensed banks in Egypt with collective deposits of $20 billion.[38] How could these enterprises thrive in an environment of negative real interest rates for depositors, regulated interest rates for loans, and persistent inflation?

The four largest banks—the National Bank of Egypt, Banque du Caire, Bank of Alexandria, and Bank Misr—were still owned by the state. As agents of the government, the country's largest borrower, they enjoyed a huge volume of business. Together they controlled 70 percent of all banking assets in 1985.[39] Moreover, they were subjected to rather less trenchant regulation than private banks. For example, they made very little (8–16 percent) provision for bad loans despite a high number of potential defaults. Nevertheless, the ratio of their profits to their assets was very low—just over 0.2 percent in fiscal 1988–89.[40]

The myriad private banks that made up the rest of the financial sector found a variety of ways to make higher profits on a smaller volume of transactions. One popular technique was to specialize in lending for short-term commercial transactions. Given Egypt's burgeoning demand for imported goods, these were very low risk loans. More important, interest rates on loans to commercial ventures were not capped by the government, so banks could charge something like a market rate. Furthermore, in Egypt interest rates were a less important factor in a bank's balance sheets than elsewhere. The Central

Bank authorized a generous fee structure that permitted banks to charge a margin of 6 percent over their cost of funds. The combination of focus on commerce and high fees could make banking extremely profitable. By the early 1980s the highest average return on private investment, around 70 percent, was in banking.[41]

Sadly, the fact that banks were making money did not mean that they were contributing to financial development. The loopholes that permitted bankers to make money did not redress the constraints on savings and investment imposed by financial repression. Rather, they attested to the fact that bankers, like other Egyptian businessmen, had learned to play the rent-seeking game to their advantage. Many of the Egyptian state's interventions in the financial sector had the effect of stifling competition, thereby creating rents for the established banks. For example, by law banks were the only financial agencies permitted to offer any interest rate higher than 7 percent. This legislation effectively stifled efforts to create a private bond market in Egypt.[42] Despite the reopening of the Cairo stock exchange, no competing equity market ever developed.[43] Indeed, by 1984 the Egyptian government decided that the existing financial system was already overcrowded and imposed a ban on the opening of any new banks.[44]

Bankers also sought, and received, legislation that hampered competition from foreign banks. After the 1974 liberalization, twenty foreign concerns (including Bank of America, Citicorp, and Chase Manhattan) opened branch banks in Cairo.[45] But the banking law only permitted them to deal in foreign exchange; they could not make loans or take deposits in Egyptian currency. Government officials and Egyptian bankers collaborated closely on a variety of policies that ensured that foreign banks never became a threat to local institutions.

For example, in May 1987 (as part of a standby agreement with the IMF) Egypt restructured its currency exchange regulations. One of the regulations issued at the time specified that Egyptians could not apply for hard currency through official exchange facilities to repay loans or letters of credit opened before the reform. This regulation devastated the business of foreign branch banks. They could not accept repayment of loans in Egyptian currency and their clients could not buy foreign exchange to repay them. And because, under the new system, the exchange rate was liable to depreciate, few borrowers wanted to contract new loans from foreign branch banks because of the exchange risk involved.[46]

As a result of these pressures, many foreign branch banks closed their operations in Egypt. Midland Bank, Lloyd's, and Royal Bank of Canada pulled out. Chase Manhattan and Bank of America sold off their stakes in joint-venture banks. The foreign firms that remained survived only by specializing in specific foreign exchange operations.[47]

These official restrictions on competition were augmented by the banks' mode of operation. Each bank tended to cater to its own specialized clientele (particularly with respect to noncommercial loans). This was partly a response to the lack of reliable accounting procedures. Egyptian bankers understood that the balance sheets submitted by their clients were often useless as a gauge of the risk of a loan, since they were heavily doctored to evade taxes. To compensate, banks preferred short-term loans, required hefty collateral and guarantees, and relied heavily on the personal contacts and reputation of the borrower. They focused their credit on familiar clients who were well plugged into Cairo's old-boy networks. Banks tended to cater to established businesses and shy away from new ideas and blossoming entrepreneurs. Egyptian bankers were highly conservative, some bragging that they did not come close to lending the 60 percent of deposits that the government permitted them.[48]

By servicing cliques of familiar clients, each bank tended to become ever more specialized in its area of operation. The Egyptian-American Bank and the Misr-Iran Bank dominated lending in the tourist sector; the Faisal Islamic Bank built a following among Muslim entrepreneurs; the Export Development Bank specialized in funding export concerns; and the National Bank of Egypt had a virtual monopoly in the oil and gas sector.[49] This pattern had the beneficial effect of building up expertise about different sectors of the economy, but it also suppressed competition.

One technique that foreign and Egyptian banks alike used to bolster their profits was to attract funds in hard currency and then deposit them outside the country. In 1980, for example, foreign banks stored 27.3 percent of their funds abroad, and Egyptian banks 60.5 percent of their holdings.[50] Funds held in hard currency were relatively shielded from the effects of inflation and depreciation. Deposited abroad, they often earned a higher interest rate than they could inside Egypt. But most important, Egyptian interest rate regulations did not apply to deposits or loans in hard currency.[51] This was an arena in which banks could levy something like market rates.

This tendency to convert money into hard currency or to move it abroad was another common symptom of financial repression, called "demonetization." Since Egyptian currency had very limited financial utility, people tended not only to not save it but to abandon it altogether. People in the countryside converted their Egyptian pounds into tangible assets, buying jewelry or land or a cow which would hold their value better than currency. For urbanites, the simplest solution was to convert their currency into dollars, usually through the burgeoning currency black market. While they kept some of these dollars inside Egypt for their personal use—many businesses preferred to accept payment in dollars—they used official banks or informal mechanisms to deposit much of it abroad. By the late 1980s it was estimated that this capital flight from Egypt amounted to between $50 billion and $100 billion.[52]

The Egyptian trend toward dollarization was neither unique nor even extreme. (In Argentina, about $20 billion—40 percent of GNP—was in local circulation.)[53] Yet AID officials viewed dollarization as one of the worst obstacles to financial development in Egypt. (They worked very hard, incidentally, to make certain that the dollars they injected into Egypt as assistance did not aggravate this problem.) Two consequences of this trend concerned them. First, when Egyptians converted their earnings into dollars, the funds tended to flow out of the domestic economy rather quickly, constricting the domestic circulation of money and restricting the opportunity for financial intermediation. Second, and even more important, dollarization seemed to leave fewer savings inside the domestic economy in a form accessible to investors.[54]

Officials at AID feared that dollarization, like inflation and low savings rates, could strangle their efforts to use financial reform to stimulate Egypt's private sector. But AID did not have wide expertise in the area of financial reform; the agency had traditionally specialized in project aid, particularly construction of public works. Only a handful of its contractees had any familiarity with banking. So in their efforts to end financial repression in Egypt, AID officials tended to follow the lead of the institution that had developed specialized talents in this area, the International Monetary Fund.

The Fund had been one of the earliest partisans of the strategy of financial revolution. Its monographs and journals (*IMF Staff Papers* was recognized as the leading academic journal on questions of developing countries' financial systems) preached the importance of financial liberalization among academics and bureaucrats.[55] And it had a long-standing interest in Egypt. Between 1965 and 1987 it had negotiated four standby agreements and one extended fund facility with Cairo, including the famous 1977 reforms which provoked massive rioting.[56] The Fund urged Egypt, and any other country suffering from financial repression, to adopt three reforms.

First, the fiscal deficit should be reduced. This would both cut inflation and remove much of the pressure that promoted government imposition of credit restraints and stifling reserve requirements on banks. The deficit reduction techniques that the Fund urged differed according to the character of the target country. In some countries it urged changes in the taxation system, such as adoption of a value-added tax.[57] Since Egypt lacked a developed public administration, the Fund recommended that Cairo pursue a series of more straightforward budget cuts. It was particularly concerned that Egypt reduce its effective subsidies on oil, gas, and electricity, which not only drained away government revenues but distorted prices throughout the economy. Yet Egyptian government deficits were so high, and progress toward price reform was so slow, that the Fund did not expect rapid progress on this front.

Second, the Fund urged countries to seek more realistic exchange rates. In Egypt and other financially repressed countries this meant devaluation.[58] Devaluation had always occupied pride of place in the Fund's reform programs, because it addressed many different economic problems simultaneously. The Fund saw devaluation as a quick and effective solution to a host of problems; it could improve the balance of trade by reducing demand for imports, promote exports by making them cheaper, and limit distortions of domestic prices created by the artificial cheapness of imports.[59] Another reason the Fund favored devaluation was that it tended to redirect money from the hidden economy of black market moneychangers back into official banks. This would not actually halt dollarization or capital flight, but it would provide greater scope for financial intermediation. It would also prepare the economy to respond more rapidly to the third element of the Fund's program for financial reform—raising interest rates.

Officials at the Fund saw raising interest rates, so that they matched or exceeded the rate of inflation, as the essential foundation for any effort to liberalize Egypt's financial system.[60] They hoped that higher

Table 6-3. Status of Bank Loans, November 1988

Type of bank	Total loans		Nonperforming loans		Nonperforming percent of total loans	
	Number of clients	Millions of Egyptian pounds[a]	Number of clients	Millions of Egyptian pounds[a]	Number of clients	Millions of Egyptian pounds[a]
State-owned commercial	10,352	5,290.4	1,531	1,122.6	14.8	21.2
Joint-venture commercial	9,286	6,860.3	1,543	1,555.0	16.6	22.7
Investment and business (local and foreign currency)	3,105	2,158.1	396	420.3	12.8	19.5
Investment and business (foreign currency)	1,060	1,585.1	169	700.0	15.9	44.2
Specialized state-owned	1,317	1,474.3	543	318.2	41.2	21.6
Total	25,132	17,368.2	4,182	4,126.0	16.6	23.8

Source: David Butter, "Flushing Out the Bad Debts," Middle East Economic Digest, October 20, 1989, p. 8.
a. Exchange rate: $1 = 2.32 £E (November 1988).

interest rates would attract more savings and generate more capital for investment. They might also curb the government's temptation to run a large deficit (by making borrowing from commercial banks more expensive). This is why Atif Sidqi had tried to convince the Fund that inflation was only between 14 percent and 20 percent. The lower the inflation rate, the smaller the increase in interest rates the Fund would push for.

The Egyptian government was anxious to avoid a sharp increase in interest rates for a variety of reasons. Although higher rates might attract more savings in the long term, in the short term they would raise the cost of borrowing. Higher capital costs could easily trigger inflation and a recession in the fragile Egyptian economy.[61] For this very reason, in fact, many private Egyptian bankers were also ambivalent about raising interest rates. Cairo's bankers were in principle sympathetic to the idea of deregulating interest rates. Larger deposits and more profitable loans appealed to them. But they were also horrified by the prospect of a recession. They were not just worried that higher rates might mean fewer borrowers; the rates might be adjusted so that a higher profit margin offset a declining volume of loans. Rather they feared that many of their existing loans might suddenly turn bad because the firms that held them could not acquire the new capital they needed to stay in business.[62]

The old-boy networks through which many Egyptian banks attracted clients did not supply a reliable means for assessing the risks of loans. In the volatile economic conditions of the late 1980s, inflation, devaluation, and sharp vacillations in hard currency revenues all played havoc with business plans. Inevitably, Egyptian banks were stuck carrying a large number of bad loans on their books (see table 6-3). Virtually every type of bank showed a nonperforming balance amounting to 20 percent of its assets or more. While most banks remained liquid despite this burden, they could not afford to carry much more. A rise of interest rates might make it impossible for many firms that had so far scraped by to continue servicing their debts.[63]

The reluctance of the Egyptian government and bankers to raise interest rates, however, was not enough to enable them to ignore the IMF. The Fund would not sign a standby accord unless Cairo agreed to an economic reform program that included a rise in interest rates. (The IMF had pioneered the concept of conditional lending, which was later emulated by the World Bank and AID.)[64] And by 1989, Egypt desperately needed another standby agreement with the IMF. This was not so much because Cairo needed the IMF credits that accompanied such an accord; in 1989 the most the Fund would offer Egypt was $500 million. But during the global debt crisis of the 1980s, the Fund had emerged as a kind of auditor of national economic performance and an agreement with it was taken as an endorsement of a country's economic plans. After 1987 most of Egypt's creditors insisted that Cairo conclude a standby agreement with the Fund before they would consider extending additional support of their own.

By 1989 AID was withholding $230 million of cash assistance to show its disapproval of the slow rate of economic reform in Egypt. These monies would only be released once Egypt signed an agreement with the IMF. In the same year, the World Bank negotiated $300 million of new loans for Cairo, but release of the credits was made conditional on the signing of a new standby agreement. Most important, Egypt needed to cope with $8–10 billion in foreign debts that were either in arrears or would fall due by December 1990. Its best hope was to apply to the Club of Paris, the international forum for negotiations on sovereign debt, for a rescheduling. But an agreement with the Fund was a precondition for convening the club.[65]

A constant flow of offers and counteroffers were telexed between the Egyptian government and the IMF in 1988. By January 1989, Cairo began to feel the heat. Egypt needed new foreign finance by June if it were going to keep its payments on U.S. debt from falling more than 365 days in arrears. And if Egypt failed to meet this deadline, the Brooke Amendment would automatically terminate all American assistance. The Fund agreed to send a delegation to Cairo in May. Even before this mission arrived, the Egyptian government announced a series of reforms that it hoped would preempt some of the Fund's demands. It cut energy subsidies by 30 percent, passed a new investment law, and voted a new budget that should have cut the fiscal deficit to the equivalent of 10 percent of GDP.[66] (The last measure was not as impressive as it sounded; Egyptian state budgets routinely understate their likely deficit by a substantial margin.) In May Egypt also increased the ceiling for interest on deposit accounts by 3 percent (making the highest legal interest rate on savings 16 percent).[67]

The Fund's delegation arrived in June (they were delayed a month by wrangling within the Egyptian government). At first the Egyptians were optimistic that they could reach an accord quickly. But the Fund mission insisted that Egypt make further reforms in the exchange system and raise interest rates still higher. They wanted deposit rates of at least 20 percent, which was roughly what they estimated the rate of inflation to be.[68] Negotiations dragged on through the summer. The American government generally backed the tough line of the Fund, although it did help Egypt to avoid default under the Brooke Amendment through a legal subterfuge.[69]

By early 1990, Egypt was reported to have met the Fund's demands by agreeing to raise deposit rates to 20–21 percent.[70] But the Fund still held out, pending agreement on a timetable for cuts in subsidies and the devaluation of the exchange rate. Indeed, with respect to interest rates there were hints its position had hardened, and it was asking not just for an increase but for full deregulation.[71]

The Fund, however, waited too long to settle. Its leverage over Egypt began to evaporate when Iraq invaded Kuwait in August 1990. Washington, eager to keep Egypt tied to the coalition of Arab states opposing Iraq, reversed its position, dropped conditionality, and began to work to ease Cairo's economic burdens. In November it forgave all of Egypt's military debts to the United States and pressed other members of the Paris Club to do the same. It interceded on Egypt's behalf with the IMF, pressing the Fund to rescind its demand for radical increases in energy prices. By May 1991 it appeared likely that Cairo would soon sign a new IMF accord on very soft terms. Egyptian interest rates were slated to rise by 5 percent or less.[72]

Role of the Hidden Economy

Officials in Cairo and Washington generally agreed that an increase in interest rates was the key reform necessary to stimulate a financial revolution. They disagreed over how large an increase was necessary or possible. But not all economists agree with the IMF's contention that manipulating key prices like interest rates is a necessary or sufficient tactic for triggering a financial revolution. Critics often point to the wide gap between the formal rules and regulations that govern the financial sector, on the one hand, and the actual practice of financial institutions, on the other. While manipulating interest rates should be decisive in theory, its effects have been more complicated in practice.

Many of the studies that stress the importance of interest rates focus on the experience of South Korea and Taiwan in the 1960s. In both of these states, raising interest rates increased deposits at official banks. But did liberalization actually increase the aggregate rate of savings? Detailed studies by revisionist economists suggest that it did not.[73] Positive real interest rates at official banks had attracted funds that otherwise would have been deposited with the informal financial institutions of the curb market—with moneylenders, under household mattresses, or with rotating savings and credit associations (ROSCAs).[74]

Higher interest rates did not actually change the propensity of individuals to save; they just transferred savings from one set of institutions to another. In recent years, even officials at the Fund have begun to concede this. However, they still insist that a change in official interest rates is desirable. As Abdel-Shakour Shaalan, head of the Fund team responsibile for negotiations with Egypt, puts it: "There is evidence that the interest rate has a significant effect on the volume of *financial* savings. In countries experiencing prolonged bouts of financial repression (for example, negative real interest rates), a large proportion of savings are held as inflation hedges such as real estate, consumer durables, precious metals and gems, and foreign currency. Where such countries have significantly increased interest rates, a large positive effect on financial savings has been observed."[75]

The debate about interest rates did not end in spite of the Fund's conceding the point on savings. The Fund position implies that if savings are not deposited with official banks, they are primarily held as relatively unproductive tangible assets. Yet many of the savings held outside the official banks are deposited with informal financial institutions. And studies by neostructuralist economists—including researchers at the World Bank—suggest that these informal financial institutions may be nearly as effective at accumulating funds and making them available for investment as official banks, particularly where the latter are hamstrung by various forms of financial repression.[76]

Officials at the Fund rejected this contention. They believed that informal financial institutions were traditional bodies, inherently limited in the scale and speed of services they could provide. So they stood by their insistence on raising interest rates as a way of diverting deposits to the more modern bodies of the official banking sector.

While few Egyptians have ever heard of neostructuralist economics, many are quite aware—in a very practical way—of the debate over the relative efficacy of official versus informal financial institutions. In the 1980s Egypt developed one of the most elaborate informal financial systems to be found anywhere in the world. It included intricate networks of overseas accounts, a hidden dollarized economy, myriad black market money changers and traders, and a host of new "Islamic" financial institutions whose operations rivaled those of official banks. Many Egyptians wondered whether there was any reason to embrace the painful, inflationary effects of raising interest rates in the official sector if these informal institutions already supplied a viable avenue for encouraging savings and financing investment.

Egypt's hidden economy is uncommonly large and relatively sophisticated. All societies have hidden economies, spheres of economic activity that are not effectively regulated by the government and that pass unreflected in official statistics. In developing countries, where the reach of the state is limited and the majority of economic transactions are small scale, the hidden economy may account for a very large share of the gross domestic product. The hidden economy provides perhaps 33 percent of GDP in India, 38 percent in Mexico, and 40 percent in Brazil. Even in communist China, a private sector of 1 million enterprises employing 30 million workers in 1989 managed to largely evade state control and taxes.[77]

Hidden economies, however, are often poorly integrated and not of much importance as a force for development. In Egypt, for example, the hidden economy long included an illicit sector of enterprises that were likely to remain banned under any economic regime—drug smuggling ($2–$4 billion worth of hashish passes through Egypt every year), theft, and prostitution (see table 6-4).[78] If the theft of state stocks, bribery among public officials, and other forms of corruption are included, this sector is economically significant. But it consists of thousands of individual transactions, not integrated by institutionalized firms or even social networks. It is hard to imagine how it could foster economic growth.

Similar problems plague another dimension of the traditional hidden economy, the so-called informal sector. This comprises a grab bag of occupations that escape the official accounts—casual laborers, street vendors, domestic servants, porters. According to Egypt's leading authority on the hidden economy, Mahmoud Abdel-Fadil, 16 percent of the urban Egyptian population earn their living from one or more

Table 6-4. Components of the Hidden and the Official Economy

Economy	Components
Official	Activities whose product is reflected in the national accounts: public sector enterprises, official banks, large-scale industry and commerce, publicly registered enterprises
Hidden	
Illicit sector	Activities likely to remain illegal under any economic regime: bribery, theft of state land and stocks, tax evasion, drug smuggling, burglary
Informal sector	Activities where small-scale or absence of cash transactions effectively prevents inclusion in national statistics: peddlers, moonlighters, microenterprises, small-scale industry, rural barter transactions
Parallel sector	Highly organized activities, often denominated in dollars, that occur outside the legal economic framework: free trade zones, black market money changers, Islamic money management companies

of these trades.[79] In practice, the informal sector is much larger. Many of the workers in the informal sector are poor or unemployed, including the 250,000 Cairenes who supplement their incomes by begging.[80] Yet many public sector employees also augment their paltry salaries by moonlighting, taking on second jobs as hawkers, cab drivers, or consultants. Informal labor might properly be expanded to include housekeeping, cleaning, harvesting, and all the diverse forms of labor performed by women which, in Egypt as in the rest of the world, go unremitted, undocumented, and unappreciated.

For decades the International Labour Organisation (ILO) has tried to encourage governments not to neglect informal activities simply because they are small scale and unregulated.[81] Its experts have argued that informal activities make a critical contribution to employment and ease the hardships of the jobless. But they have never claimed that these occupations formed a motor for national economic growth.[82] The traditional hidden economy created employment and recycled money, but it was not characterized by the accumulation of capital, accelerator effects, or the linkage of markets necessary to sustain development.

Yet during the 1970s, the character of the hidden economy began to change. Certain sectors expanded and grew far more lucrative. They began to develop larger-scale firms which integrated diverse, heretofore segmented markets. New, sophisticated financial institutions began to grow outside of the system of official regulations. By the early 1980s

Egyptians had begun to speak of some of these sectors as forming a parallel economy which performed functions similar to—and showed at least as great a potential for development as—the official economy.[83]

This change resulted from two key factors. First, the flow of petrodollars from the Gulf states into Egypt fueled a startling expansion of the hidden economy in the 1970s. Workers' remittances played a critical role in this process because, unlike official assistance from the Gulf states, they accrued not to the government in Cairo but to hundreds of thousands of persons scattered around the country. Even official figures show that these remittances form an important part of the country's hard currency revenues, but most experts agree that official statistics drastically underestimate the value of these funds. Nazli Choucri has argued that in 1983, when the official figure was only $4 billion, remittances may actually have been on the order of $18 billion.[84] Other scholars dispute this specific figure, but agree with the thrust of Choucri's argument. Delwin Roy, for example, suggests that remittances are probably in the neighborhood of $12 billion—three times the official figure.[85] Even if the more conservative figure was correct, the capital available to the Egyptian hidden economy still amounts to one-third of the value of the officially recorded GDP.

Second, the legal framework of economic activity encouraged the growth of the hidden economy. If Egypt's economy had been completely financially repressed or fully liberalized, most of these petrodollar remittances would have flowed into the official economy, private or public. But *infitah* had led to only halfhearted liberalization. The banks and exchange system had not enjoyed enough deregulation to be able to compete successfully for private deposits. Yet the economy had been deregulated enough so that the government could no longer compel people to process their remittances through official channels. As a result, for most Egyptians the political and legal risks of using the hidden economy appeared less forceful than the economic lure of the services this sector rendered.

The first sector of the hidden economy to benefit from the combination of remittances and haphazard liberalization was contraband trade. Before the late 1970s many migrants remitted their earnings to Egypt by simply purchasing goods abroad and packing them in their trunks when they returned to Egypt. But local entrepreneurs soon learned to import the televisions, electric fans, coolers, and other goods the migrants demanded.

Much of the expansion of Egyptian import trade in the 1970s was perfectly legal and officially recorded. Yet, despite the much-touted deregulation of the *infitah* period, it was not always easy for importers to get goods through customs. The policy reforms of the 1970s had legalized the import of many goods, but they had not touched tariff rates—which remained prohibitive for imports that threatened any Egyptian manufactures.[86] In 1979 the government had complicated matters by giving the Customs Authority the right to block imports until their owners proved they had brought an equivalent value of foreign exchange into the country.[87]

The difficulties confronting importers increased in 1981 when the government established a series of import rationalization committees. These committees were supposed to lower the costs of imports by expediting customs procedures, but in practice they did quite the opposite. The committees soon became part of the rent-seeking circus. They banned the import of certain goods while in other cases traders lobbied them successfully for exemption from normal customs procedures. To make matters worse, they issued regulations requiring that importers sell their goods at prices no more than 30 percent higher than their declared customs value.[88]

In the political environment created by Sadat, where corruption was commonplace and state supervisory agencies hamstrung, many importers chose to circumvent these obstacles. It was often cheaper to bribe a customs inspector than to pay the mandated tariffs. A subvention to the right official could ensure that a shipper's goods were not checked against the list of proscribed imports. A great number of importers learned to take advantage of the free trade zones that Sadat had created, particularly the one at Port Said. These zones had been intended to attract foreign investment and serve as bases for export-oriented industries; in practice they were little more than lines of warehouses crammed full of duty-free goods. Individuals could drive to Port Said and return to Cairo with a trunk full of imports without worrying about inspection.[89]

There are no reliable estimates of the volume of goods imported to Egypt in this way. The U.S. Department of Agriculture estimates that the free zones handle $5 million worth of American chocolates, nuts, raisins, soft drinks, and canned food every year, but this is obviously a tiny fraction of total trade. Some informal estimates suggest contraband goods flowing through the free zones reached a value of $1 billion in

1983.[90] Cairene officials admit that smuggling of this kind is massive but decline to assign a value to it. This much is clear: Egyptians recognize that the importers of Port Said have enjoyed some of the highest and fastest-growing business profits in the country.[91]

The growth of trade (official or contraband) triggered the expansion of another sector of the hidden economy—black market money changing. Since the 1960s Egypt had overvalued its currency through a complex system of pegged exchange rates.[92] This benefited the government by making it easier to pay for imports of wheat and capital goods for the public sector. It might also have encouraged the man in the street to import consumer goods, but the elaborate system of import controls prevented this. These controls did not prevent the formation of a black market currency exchange in Egypt, but for many years they kept it small and made using it risky.

The overvalued exchange rate also made it less profitable for Egyptian firms to export their goods, preventing the country from pursuing an export-oriented development strategy of the kind that stimulated industrialization in South Korea and Taiwan.[93] Even more painful, once Egyptians began to acquire dollars from remittances, the exchange rate encouraged them to import recklessly, leading to steady growth in the balance of payments deficit. For this reason, the IMF, which favored both free trade and export-oriented development, considered the exchange rate to be a key price—like interest rates—and pressed the Egyptian government to devalue.[94]

By the late 1970s the Egyptian government had already begun to tinker with its exchange system in hopes of luring capital back to Egypt. It created the "own exchange" system (see chapter 3) and a special parallel exchange rate to facilitate the use of hard currency. These changes did lure money back, but they did not fully satisfy public needs. The "own exchange" system allowed people to hold dollars but did not ease converting them into local currency. The official parallel exchange rate was still so overvalued it did little to encourage expatriates and tourists to convert their dollars into pounds. Official banks remained painfully slow in processing applications for letters of credit and, since the government had first claim on the hard currency held by banks, there was never any guarantee that funds would be available.[95]

Egyptians sought to surmount these barriers by avoiding the official exchange system. They increasingly turned to black market currency traders. The relaxation of official regulations and the spread of corruption made this much safer than in the past. Egyptians who had dollars were happy to sell them on the black market, where they could earn much more than at the official rate. Those who needed dollars were willing to pay the premium, because the hard currency shortages and delays at the banks made it difficult for them to get the dollars they wanted.

By 1980 Egypt's black market exchange had grown to the point where it seemed one shop in four did a backdoor business in currency exchange, and currency traders had emerged among the richest businessmen in the country. The most successful such trader, Sami Ali Hasan, had become a national celebrity. Until 1985 the government tolerated this development, viewing it as a safety valve that lubricated the wheels of trade and encouraged the flow of dollars into Egypt. Even public sector enterprises routinely turned to the black market when they could not acquire the hard currency they needed from official banks. As these transactions grew more legitimate, officials stopped using the term black market and began to speak of the grey market or the parallel rate of exchange.[96]

It is no easier to estimate the size of this grey market than to guess the value of the remittances that supplied its operating funds. In 1984 the director of the Central Bank claimed that only 15 percent of imports were financed through the black market.[97] But most experts think this widely understates its role. One scholar estimated that the official banks exchanged about £E 3 billion a year and that the amount exchanged on the black market amounted to 30 percent of this, or £E 1 billion.[98] Even this figure may be conservative.

The most exciting consequence of the flow of remittances into the hidden economy, however, was the growth of a new generation of enterprises. Only a fraction of the remittances flowing into Egypt ebbed back out again to pay for imports; there was also a sharp increase of demand inside Egypt. A sizable share of remittances was spent on locally produced goods, particularly housing but also foodstuffs, clothes, and many other consumer goods. Egyptians with dollars found that not only were domestic goods and services a bargain, so were domestic investments.

At first much of the investment generated by remittances focused on high-profit activities such as speculation in real estate, food imports, or trade in precious metals.[99] But new patterns of consumption and foreign trade links had also created real opportunities for investment in manufacturing. Remittances spurred a surge of demand for shoes, clothing, furniture, housewares, and the like, all of which could be produced by small firms using small volumes of capital. As a result, the dollars flowing through the foreign exchange sector of the hidden economy triggered the growth of another variety of underground firms—microenterprises.

Small firms, employing nine persons or fewer (often members of a single extended family), have long been a critical element of Egyptian manufacturing. In 1967 such enterprises employed 284,000 people, one-third of the industrial work force.[100] The employees of small firms are often members of a single family, including children, so a significant part of the labor force never even receives cash wages. The government lacked the administrative capacity to collect taxes from such firms, and it never tried to impose the laws regulating labor practices and wages on them. Even though they enjoyed no economies of scale, small firms often showed a durability and flexibility that larger enterprises lacked.

In the 1980s the flood of petrodollars reinvigorated and expanded the operations of Egyptian small firms. Studies show that "one out of four owners" of small firms had worked abroad, and 35 percent of these "had used their remittances as the main source of capital to establish a new workshop of their own."[101] Most of this growth was felt in Cairo, where demand for the consumer goods such firms produced was highest. Indeed, artisans in provincial towns discovered that the new generation of microenterprises in the cities were drawing away many of their customers and part of their skilled work force.[102]

Microenterprises were sufficiently dynamic to attract the attention of foreign aid organizations. One of AID's subcontractors in Egypt, Agricultural Development Cooperatives, launched a project to link Egyptian artisans' production to the world market. This program not only sought to encourage entrepreneurs to export Egyptian craftworks but also to encourage artisans to tailor their production to international standards and tastes (too much of existing production tends toward such "tourist kitsch" as carved stone mummies and pharaonic ashtrays). Some of the crafts targeted for inclusion in the program include bedouin silverwork, hand embroideries, and furniture.

Not all of the small firms sustained by the flow of remittances were family enterprises producing handicrafts. An important minority were small-scale but technologically modern and highly capitalized businesses. The expansion of international trade, far from destroying local manufacturers, had affected local tastes and preferences, creating opportunities for domestic firms to meet new demands and "to produce substitutes for imported consumer goods." Competition even resulted "in established domestic producers becoming more efficient."[103] For example, the spread of greenhouse cultivation created a rush of demand for polyvinylchloride sheeting. While at first this material had to be imported, within a few years a number of smaller Egyptian firms were manufacturing it locally. Chemicals production has become one of the fastest growing new enterprises, particularly in the new communities being built in the deserts around Cairo where, in an effort to relieve population pressure, the government offers subsidies and tax holidays to businesses that are willing to relocate.[104]

Of course, most of these new high-technology firms were part of the official economy, in the sense that the government was aware of their operations and included their product in the national accounts. Yet many of them bore the stamp of their origins in the hidden economy. They used the free ports to circumvent import restrictions, relied on the black market for their supply of foreign exchange, and derived much of their capital from remittances. This last feature, the formation of capital within the hidden economy, is especially interesting.

The expansion of trade, exchange, and manufacturing fueled demand for development of the financial system. New businesses had a growing need for loans; migrant workers looked for outlets for their savings. The official economy did not meet the need for financial services. Negative real interest rates made the official banks unattractive for savers; and borrowers found that the focus on short-term commercial loans deafened the system to their requests for venture capital. In the late 1980s when the official economy stagnated, the banks ran short of hard currency and lacked the funds to cover even routine letters of credit.

Most Egyptians, confronted by banks that charged stiff fees for rudimentary services, had already begun to develop informal financial institutions. Many banded together into informal savings clubs, a type of ROSCA wherein friends or neighbors contribute a fixed sum every month to a common pool which members could then tap for credit.

These informal institutions were often the only source of finance for poorer Egyptians who lacked legal collateral.[105]

Another financial alternative grew out of the black market for foreign exchange. Black marketeers had plenty of cash on hand and they found themselves surrounded by petitioners who could not finance imports of nonessential goods through the official banks. By 1985, therefore, virtually all imports of "cement, steel, trucks and lorries . . . [were] financed through the black market."[106] But finance is an especially risky business to conduct on the black market (where contracts were not legally enforceable), so the interest charged on such loans was typically usurious. Black marketeers began to look for ways to reduce their risk and increase the volume of their financial transactions.

In the early 1980s they began to experiment with a new type of unofficial but large-scale financial institution. These alternative financial bodies were called "*sharikat tawzif al-amwal al-islamiyya*," which roughly translates as "Islamic money management companies" (IMMCs). As their name implies, they operated less like banks than like money management funds. They exploited two loopholes in Islamic commercial law that Muslims had long used to evade the general Qur'anic ban against charging or receiving interest. One of these devices, the principle of *musharaka* (partnership), permits Muslims to receive a regular dividend on money they have deposited with an institution so long as those dividends are understood as a form of profit sharing rather than interest.[107] The complementary mechanism of *mudaraba* permits an association to lend capital and receive payment in excess of principal, so long as this surplus is cloaked as profits on a fictitious commercial transaction.[108] What made these devices so alluring to the founders of the Islamic money management companies was that, since dividends paid under *musharaka* and *mudaraba* were not technically forms of interest, they were not subject to the government regulations controlling interest rates.

Moneymen rushed to exploit the legal loophole latent in these "Islamic" dividends. Since these institutions were not registered banks, they were not subject to the elaborate credit controls imposed by the government. They could invest with, or lend to, whomever they wished. And since they were not paying interest, their dividends could be as large or small as they liked. They attracted huge deposits from thousands of savers by offering dividends that averaged 25 percent—

in a period when official banks offered less than half as much. They quickly became the preferred channel for workers remitting money home to Egypt.

In the 1960s Abd al-Latif al-Sharif, who fled to Saudi Arabia to avoid Nasser's persecution of the Muslim Brothers, established the first Islamic money management company. His firm stood alone, however, until the 1980s when his idea was suddenly and widely emulated. By December 1986, one hundred ninety such companies had registered with the government. The vast majority of these were very small, but a handful blossomed into financial giants. In 1982 the Abd al-Fattah brothers established Rayyan, which grew into the largest IMMC. Five other firms developed into major financial institutions: Sa'd lil-Istithmar, Huda Misr, Badr lil-Istithmar, Hilal, and Hijaz.[109]

Not all of these money management companies were "Islamic"; some of the smaller ones maintained purely secular identities. But many, including all of the larger ones, claimed to uphold the principles of "Islamic economics."[110] Sometimes this reflected a sincere religious commitment. But even among firms whose directors' protestations of piety were less credible, embracing the mantle of Islam was a savvy business move. The rhetoric of Islam lent some legitimacy to their activities; they invoked it for the same reason that American financiers try to include terms like "trust," "home," or "security" when they name a bank. This ploy is not confined to the parallel economy. Many official banks, such as the Faisal Islamic Bank, also claimed to operate according to the principles of Islam.[111] The managers of the Islamic money management companies and many official bankers both claimed to be motivated by piety, but both seemed to mix religiosity with simple self-interest.

Higher (and more realistic) interest rates electrified Egyptian savers. By offering a 2 percent dividend every month, or 25 percent annually, the Islamic money management companies not only drew away deposits from the official banks, they increased the total volume of savings by creating a new way of hedging against inflation. And this was not the only reason they were attractive. Islamic money management companies also offered a much higher level of service and flexibility than the official banks.[112] Free from government regulation, they acted more quickly and with less paperwork. Competing with each other for customers, they developed a strong service orientation; to attract depositors several erected special stores that offered merchandise at a discount. Unlike the official banks, they had access to large amounts of hard currency. Indeed, after the government began its campaign to close down black market money changing after 1985, they became the primary channel of hard currency for the bulk of the population.

The money management companies were an especially attractive vehicle for channeling remittances back to Cairo. Egyptian workers in the Gulf sent checks denominated in Egyptian pounds to their families. If their families had submitted these checks to banks, they could not have cashed them immediately, since the banks waited for funds to be transferred to their accounts before honoring checks. They preferred to take their checks to Islamic money management companies which would cash them immediately, and remit the checks to the money changers who drafted them abroad and transferred funds to the companies' foreign accounts.[113]

Many of the IMMCs continued to make profits in the black market as well. Rayyan, for example, used its dollar deposits at the American Express Bank in Frankfurt to buy deutsche marks in January 1986 when a dollar was worth DM 2.44. Within a year the deutsche marks had appreciated 32 percent to DM 1.86. When earnings from this transaction were translated into Egyptian pounds (which had depreciated) they showed a 92 percent profit. For Rayyan, paying 24 percent returns in a country with 30 percent inflation was not much of a feat.[114] One estimate claims that some IMMCs held 80 percent of their deposits abroad for use in this manner.[115]

Some IMMC directors had well-honed skills in this sort of arbitrage. In July 1983 the ministry of the interior prepared a list of Egypt's fifty-five top black market money changers. Ahmad Tawfiq Abd al-Fattah and his brother Muhammad, the founders and managers of Rayyan, were ranked as numbers two and three. Number four on the list was Ashraf Ali al-Sayyid Sa'd, founder of Sa'd, another of the four largest IMMCs.[116] These men had been experts at attracting and managing hard currency remitted by Egyptian expatriates long before they discovered a way to make money on deposits. For them, the creation of Islamic money management companies was only an expansion of their services.

As a result, the IMMCs grew steadily larger. By the late 1980s Rayyan, Sharif, Sa'd, and Badr claimed at least $1.3 billion in deposits belonging to more than 254,000 investors.[117] This equaled 14 percent of all commercial credit. Among experts, estimates of the number of

**Table 6-5. Value and Distribution of the Deposits of the Major
Islamic Money Management Companies, 1988**
Values in millions of Egyptian pounds

Company	Number of depositors	Value of deposits
Rayyan	175,000	1,700
Sharif	115,000	823
Sa'd	61,000	394
Huda Misr	40,000	350[a]
Badr for Investment	[b]	125
Zahra	2,100	13
Sinfad	2,100	[b]
Hijaz	11,000	8
Total	406,000[c]	3,413

Source: Mahmud Abd al-Fadil, *al-Khadi'a al-Maliya al-Kubra* (Cairo: Dar al-Mustaqbal al-'Arabi, 1989), p. 17.
Figures are rounded.
   a. Also had deposits of £4.3 million in sterling and $300,000.
   b. Undeclared.
   c. Approximate.

depositors involved went as high as 500,000, with total deposits of £E 12 billion, in both Egyptian and foreign currency.[118] *Al-Ahram al-Iqtisadi* estimated real deposits to be even higher than the IMMCs claimed—$3.5 billion for Rayyan and $1.6 billion for Sa'd. Even the most conservative estimates placed the companies' held deposits at at least £E 8 billion (see table 6-5).[119] In comparison, the National Bank of Egypt, largest of the four main banks in the public sector, could claim deposits of only $3.2 billion. At the end of fiscal 1986–87 the deposits of the (official) commercial banks totaled £E 34.1 billion ($14.9 billion).[120]

The Islamic money management companies were the crowning flower of the hidden economy. Their formation marked a breakthrough in the level of financial services available to Egyptians, both by promoting capital accumulation and by facilitating payments. Their operations linked the manifold branches of the hidden economy in trade, exchange, and manufacturing, transforming it into an increasingly integrated whole. Indeed, following this transformation it seemed misleading to speak of a hidden economy at all; its operations had become both large-scale and highly public. Instead, it would have been more accurate to speak of a "parallel economy," working outside the legal framework of the official economy but no longer confined to small shops.

When economists contemplated the parallel economy in all its parts, roots, stem, and branch, it appeared quite impressive. In 1983 one scholar estimated that the hidden economy comprised 13 percent of national production. A review of the subject in 1985 argued it was closer to 20 percent. And the most comprehensive study of the subject, written in 1989 by an American expert with years of experience in Cairo, suggested it had reached 35 percent of GNP.[121]

The parallel economy not only loomed ever larger, its performance appeared to contrast favorably with that of the official economy. After oil prices began to decline in 1985, the official economy began to shrivel. The government reacted with an array of austerity measures that tightened bank credit, restricted imports, and raised domestic prices. Officials worried that these changes would trigger riots similar to those provoked by the adjustment program of 1977. Yet violence failed to materialize, and Egyptian economists believed that this was because the parallel economy had blunted the pain of official austerity measures. Egyptian workers in Iraq continued to send money home, their families in the Nile Valley continued to be able to afford refrigerators, and the parallel economy continued to process remittances, imports, payments, and all the other functions necessary to buoy the standard of living.

Even government officials began to pay backhanded tribute to the contributions of the parallel economy. The IMF (among other things) was trying to press Egypt to reduce its fiscal deficit, which Fund officials estimated was equal to 20 percent of GDP. Cairo responded with position papers that argued this overestimated the size of the deficit, since the Fund figure for GDP only included production in the official sector. They contended that if production in the hidden economy was included, the budget deficit was really only 15 percent of GDP.

Many Egyptians began to think that the parallel economy offered solutions to the country's economic problems that the official economy could not. They viewed the businessmen in this sector not as criminals or as barter-bound primitives, but as the best entrepreneurial talent in the country. They thought the parallel sector illustrated how successful the economy could be if the government deregulated and permitted Egyptian capitalists to work on their own.

In 1988 a Peruvian economist, Hernando de Soto, caught global attention by arguing that hidden economies were the most dynamic sector in many Third World countries and potentially the most powerful motor for their development. He viewed the hidden economy as a great reservoir of untapped economic energy, capital, and entrepreneurship: "Competitive business people, whether formal or informal, are in fact a new breed. They have rejected the dependence proposed by the politicians. They may be neither likeable nor polite—remember what people say about minibus drivers and street vendors—but they provide a sounder basis for development than skeptical bureaucracies and traffickers in privileges. They have demonstrated their initiative by migrating, breaking with the past without any prospect of a secure future, they have learned how to identify and satisfy others' needs, and their confidence in their abilities is greater than their fear of competition."[122] To unleash this pent-up entrepreneurial energy, de Soto called for a wide-ranging retreat from state intervention and major changes in the legal framework of economic activity that would make it easier for informal enterprises to register title to property, acquire operating licenses, and gain access to credit.

Many Egyptians endorsed this vision. They viewed the money management companies as the white knights of finance. Informal financial institutions had sustained trade and manufacturing in a period when the official economy offered only stagnation. They gave citizens a viable hedge against inflation and new incentives to save and invest. Egypt's parallel economy operated on an even grander scale and with greater technological sophistication than the informal economy of Peru that had inspired de Soto. Its expansion, while official economic institutions contracted, seemed almost miraculous, almost as if its Islamic allegiance had earned it God's favor.

Battle of the Banks

Not all Egyptians shared this sympathy for the hidden economy. Some economists questioned whether the IMMCs could really offer such high rates of return and still make necessary provisions for their financial risks.[123] Government officials worried both about the stability of the parallel economy and about the threat it posed to their own regime of financial repression. However, the most ardent and tenacious critics of the parallel economy were found in banks.

The decline of Egypt's hard currency revenues after 1985 had undermined the banks' comfortable arrangements with the state. To ensure that hard currency was available for its own expenses, the government restricted the volume of credit that banks could extend to the private sector. Until 1988 new lending by banks was curtailed to no more than 2.5 percent of the value of the preceding year's loans. The government also made it more difficult for borrowers to apply for finance; to obtain a letter of credit they generally had to deposit cash equal to 35 percent of its value with the lending bank.[124] Even after these restrictions were formally eased in 1988, official finance remained difficult to obtain. Unless a trader had hard currency in hand, it took three months or more to get a letter of credit approved by the Central Bank. Most found it cheaper to pay the 5–6 percent margin for black market hard currency that enabled them to secure letters of credit more promptly.[125]

In this environment, official bankers watched the rise of the parallel economy with all the enthusiasm that Slavic peasants used to feel when Mongol horsemen assembled on the plain next to their village. The official exchange rate made it difficult for the banks to lure customers away from black market money changers. By law, the banks could not offer anything like the interest rates the IMMCs offered. And their own internal practices compounded their lack of competitiveness. They were woefully ill prepared to compete with the money management companies for the business of thousands of small, unknown depositors and borrowers.

The banks did attempt to improve their competitive position economically, but their primary response to the rise of the parallel economy was political. In the late 1970s Egypt's official banks had combined to form their own lobby, the Association of Banks, whose membership roster read like a who's who of Egypt's wealth and power. It included Uthman Ahmad Uthman, the richest man in the country and founder of the Suez Canal Bank; Mustafa Khalil, one of the founders of the National Democratic party and former prime minister; Ali Nagm, former director of the Central Bank; and Fu'ad Sultan, long-time director of the Misr Iran Bank, later minister of tourism and architect of the government's privatization drive. The association included representatives from both the public and private sectors and worked largely behind the scenes. Its deliberations were not made public, except to the degree that they were reflected in the speeches of its unofficial spokesman, the minister of finance. (This office, formerly a mere functionary, grew in prestige partly as a result of its ties to the association and partly as a reflection of Egypt's growing concern over the international debt crisis.) According to some authorities, the association became the most effective lobby in Egypt.[126]

The association's main objective had always been to influence the government's financial regulations. In the 1980s, it became increasingly interested in official controls to restrain the growth of the parallel economy. The government was not always eager to cooperate. Some officials feared that too hard a blow to the parallel economy could produce a national depression or financial chaos. But the representatives of the banks hammered away at the threat that underground firms posed to the official financial order, in which both they and the government had a stake. The state, after all, had a material interest in promoting the official banks. As the government faced a hard currency squeeze, it relied increasingly heavily on credit from the banks. If it could divert funds from the parallel economy into the official sector, it would increase the stock of foreign exchange from which it could borrow.

In 1984 bankers persuaded the government to crack down on their rivals, the major black market money changers. This crackdown, which culminated in January 1985 with the arrest of dozens of money changers and a new, ham-handed battery of exchange controls, triggered a sharp drop in the value of the Egyptian pound. The Society of Businessmen, whose constituents counted on the black market for access to hard currency, challenged the government campaign in the press, the Parliament, and the courts. It succeeded in driving the minister of economy from office (by revealing that members of his immediate family were heavily involved in illegal currency trading) and the government campaign quickly collapsed.[127]

This duel, however, convinced the government that the money changers and their allies were a political as well as an economic threat. At the end of 1986 the Egyptian pound began to lose value, declining from £E 1.90 to the dollar to £E 2.25. Government officials were convinced that this was the result of a deliberate conspiracy by money changers against the pound. (Many economists thought it was a fairly natural reaction to the growing stagnation of the Egyptian economy.)[128]

The desire to strike at the money changers was very much on the minds of Egyptian officials in 1987 when they negotiated a new standby agreement with the IMF. Fund officials were pressing Egypt to devalue and unify its exchange rates, and Egyptian functionaries saw this as a means to undermine the black market. In May 1987 an accord was signed that consolidated Egypt's old tourist and commercial exchange rates into a single tier whose rate was adjusted daily by a committee of bankers. The value of the pound fell from £E 1.36 for a dollar to £E 2.17, a level very close to the black market rate.[129] Under the best of circumstances, this would have cut deeply into the profits of the money changers. But the government also gave the banks access to no less than $1 billion so that they could intervene in the market and assure the triumph of the official rate.[130] In August the government also ordered the arrest of fifty-two money traders and the impounding of their assets.[131]

These measures disrupted the business of the money changers. In its first year, the new system siphoned millions of dollars out of the hidden economy and into the official exchange system. Where the banks had previously processed only $200,000 each day, they now garnered $10 million.[132] This shift was a godsend for the government. There was a fourfold increase in letters of credit opened for the public sector by commercial banks after the reform.[133] The official banking system took in about $3.5 billion, including more than $1 billion from tourist receipts alone.

The difference between the official commercial rate and the black market's rate fell below 10 percent. Yet by the end of the year the money changers had made a modest comeback, albeit with greatly reduced profits. What kept them in business was an article of the May reform that required applicants for letters of credit to make a 35 percent cash deposit in hard currency. This forced cash-short businessmen to turn again to the hidden economy; even public sector companies resumed their practice of buying hard currency from money traders.[134] At least $1.5 billion still flowed into the black market, which continued to provide an array of services the banks could not match.[135]

The 1987 IMF accord provided only a temporary respite for the official banks. Despite access to a growing volume of dollars, they were still taxed by the government's growing appetite for hard currency. They found it increasingly difficult to meet commercial demand and by the beginning of 1989 they were clearly running short. In this context, news that the United States was going to be withholding $230 million of aid as a sign of displeasure at the slowness of economic reform in Egypt triggered another drop in the value of the pound. The black market rate for the dollar declined to £E 2.80 (16 percent below the official rate). The government tried to intervene by suspending hard currency trading at Port Said.[136] But while the police were able to arrest the most prominent money changers, they could not suppress the curb market, and the government's shortage of hard currency kept a profitable gap alive between official and black market rates.[137]

Gradually, the government found that its need for hard currency exceeded the supplies available to the official banks. Ministries and public sector firms were forced to turn to the hidden economy for assistance. Particularly after the food crisis of 1988, they began to borrow from the IMMCs to finance imports of sugar, cooking oil, timber, and steel when the public sector ran out of foreign exchange. (The Ministry of Agriculture used the money management companies to finance imports of broad beans and corn.)[138] But these loans were made at much stiffer terms than those that were formally available from the official banks, encouraging some government officials to contemplate a new campaign to redirect remittances from the former to the latter.

This campaign was also promoted by the Association of Banks, which feared competition from the IMMCs even more than from the money changers. Already in 1986 Ali Nagm, then director of the Central Bank and later a prominent figure in the association, had sworn to destroy the money management companies.[139] His stance was supported by other government officials, many of whom were unconcerned about the economic practices of the companies. Many in the ruling elite feared the political implications of the success of the Islamic money management companies.[140]

The IMMCs appealed to growing numbers of middle-class Egyptians who were attracted to the Islamist trend. There was speculation that the IMMCs had made a $6 million contribution to the Muslim Brothers' war chest during the 1987 parliamentary elections.[141] They were even alleged to have contacts with more radical, underground Islamist movements. One of the IMMCs won the support of Sheikh Umar Abd al-Rahman—chief theorist of Tanzim al-Gihad, the group that shot Sadat—by employing him as the middleman in a major business deal.[142] The regime feared that the companies formed the financial wing of an incipient Islamist revolution and that their prosperity encouraged the public to believe the slogan of the Muslim Brothers—*al-Islam huwa al-hall* ("Islam is the solution").

Not all those who felt threatened by the money management companies responded from economic or political self-interest. A number of legitimate economists did not believe that the companies could sustain their high dividend rates through secure or legitimate economic activities. They feared that the companies drew their profits from financial sleight-of-hand.[143] Spokesmen for the Association of Banks also harped on this theme. Ali Nagm insisted that "it is simply unreasonable for an individual to invest his monies and receive a profit which reaches 2 percent monthly or 25 percent annually."[144] He charged that the IMMCs drew most of their profits from pyramid schemes that paid dividends out of principal. If this was so, the companies could operate only so long as they expanded. Sooner or later they would saturate the market, have trouble attracting new depositors, and find themselves unable to pay their dividends. Then the whole edifice would come tumbling down.

Even when such allegations were tendentious, they had the effect of shaking public confidence in the Islamic companies. The companies reacted with a public relations campaign of their own. Late in 1986 they formed their own public relations committee, chaired by Tariq Abu Husayn (chairman of Huda Misr), to counter the charges against them.[145] They began to take full-page advertisements in Egyptian papers. The companies also began to woo allies within Egypt's political elite. Rayyan hired influential politicians like Nabawi Isma'il (formerly minister of the interior) and Abd al-Razzaq Abd al-Magid (formerly minister of commerce and dean of the Commercial Employees Syndicate) as consultants. Kamal Rida, undersecretary for finance at the Ministry of Agriculture, received a £E 60,000 commission for mediating a land purchase in Nubariyya. Rayyan also invested a great deal to win the support of local newspapers. Its regular, full-page advertisements became an important source of revenue, and it advanced millions of dollars to semiofficial publications like *al-Ahram* and *al-Musawwar*.[146]

Through these mouthpieces, the Islamic companies tried to explain how they could sustain high dividends without recourse to fraud. They argued that if hidebound official banks could make profits of 18 percent, any reasonably savvy investor should be able to do better. They claimed that most of their money was placed in solid investments. Rayyan claimed that 35 percent of its assets was invested in long-term projects, 25 percent was liquid, and 40 percent was in short-term investments.[146] The Islamic companies portrayed themselves as genuine venture capitalists.

In reality, the managers of the IMMCs were neither the noble entrepreneurs they claimed to be, nor the simple financial charlatans their opponents charged. Originally their profits had come primarily from foreign exchange speculation, but they gradually branched out into a variety of domestic activities. By 1984 they had invested £E 1.3 billion in various ventures—49 percent in tourist activities, 24 percent in housing, and 12.9 percent in industrial and agricultural projects.[148] By the later 1980s they had begun to focus their investments on projects that offered quick, high profits. They built supermarkets, restaurants, sweetshops. Many put money into trading lumber, steel, and agricultural commodities. The Sa'd company specialized in trading new and used cars, and it developed a branch that imported and assembled refrigerators.[149] Rayyan formed integrated trade monopolies in red meats, corn, and paper.[150] The only firm that actually put the bulk of its investment into industry—and thereby conformed to the public perception of a progressive capitalist—was Sharif.

For the most part, in other words, the money managers of the parallel economy invested in the same activities that attracted their counterparts in the official economy—real estate, trade, and commodity speculation. Businessmen in both the parallel and the official economies were entrepreneurs, in that they were motivated by the pursuit of profit, and both seemed drawn to the same type of investments. Even though Islamic money management companies did not enjoy government influence and official guarantees, their managers were neither free traders nor industrial pioneers. If anything, they regretted their lack of state-sponsored rents and sought to gain access to them. Several of the companies tried to attach their firms to the official banking sector. Sharif took over the board of the Islamic International Bank for Investment and Development, and Rayyan tried to buy out the local branch of Bank of America.[151] By 1988 the IMMCs were hoping to obtain a change in the national investment law that would have given their firms a legal foundation and permitted them to join the official economy.

Neither in the level of entrepreneurship nor in perspicacity does there seem to have been much difference between businessmen in the official and parallel economies. Instead, the critical differences seem to have been political rather than economic. When a firm is deciding whether to seek a favorable rent from the state or to avoid state controls entirely, the political connections of its directors may be decisive. Managers with good contacts with the national political elite can play the rent-seeking game with some hope of success. Small firms with humble captains may simply not have this option and thus have to confine themselves to avoiding or bribing local officials. As the IMMCs grew larger and more influential, they found it increasingly easy to pursue some of the profit-guaranteed activities that firms in the official sector had long enjoyed.

Over the long term, a convergence was developing between the money management funds and the official banks. In the short term, however, important differences remained. The companies could pay out larger dividends because they took greater risks. There were no state controls on how much of their capital they laid out in investments. And some of their investments remained highly speculative. This was particularly true of Rayyan. According to Rayyan's own reports, half of its investments remained in foreign currency arbitrage. It also gambled on the price of gold. Rayyan opened a dozen gold retail stores on which it claimed to earn profits of £E 5 million a month.[152]

Some of the IMMCs, particularly the smaller ones, took on more risk than they could handle. A few failed and their owners fled the country.[153] The head of one of the newest companies, Hilal, left the country with much of his company's funds. However, these were small-scale operations; Hilal had total assets of only £E 100 million and eighteen hundred depositors.[154] Instances of fraud and risk among the smaller firms posed no threat to the wider financial system, so long as the public had funds to invest and remained confident that the more prominent companies remained sound. Such tribulations characterize the early development of any financial system, as John Kenneth Galbraith has noted:

> As civilization, or some approximation, came to an Indiana or Michigan crossroads in the 1830s or 1840s, so did a bank. Its notes, when issued and loaned to a farmer to buy land, livestock, seed, feed, food or simple equipment, put him into business. If he and others prospered and paid off their loans, the bank survived. If he and others did not so prosper and pay, the bank failed and someone—perhaps a local creditor, perhaps an eastern supplier—was left holding the worthless notes. But some borrowers from this bank were by now in business. Somewhere someone holding the notes had made an involuntary contribution to the winning of the West. . . . Men of economic wisdom, then as later expressing the views of the reputable business community, spoke of the anarchy of unstable banking. . . . The men of wisdom missed the point. The anarchy served the frontier far better than a more orderly system that kept a tight hand on credit could have done.[155]

Among the larger IMMCs, there were no bankruptcies. Despite government allegations, none were simple pyramid schemes. Rather, they deployed capital among a variety of investments just as any mutual fund would. Yet in developed financial systems, even mutual funds are required to publish balance sheets, to submit themselves to regular audits, and to reserve a portion of their capital to cover unanticipated losses. This is where the Islamic money management companies were genuinely deficient. With the exception of Sharif, these firms had only the most primitive accounting apparatuses. They were still family enterprises which shifted their investments according to crude rules-of-thumb and brooked no outside criticism.

Under this system, there was no way for outsiders to determine how risky investments were. The Islamic companies prospered because thousands of middle class Egyptians took a look at their dividends and service, put their faith in God, and made deposits. But the experts at the IMF and AID were much more skeptical. They tended to believe the allegations about pyramid schemes that they heard from Egyptian officials. Some sympathized with the idea of driving the companies out of business.[156] But the solutions they officially urged on the Egyptian government were cautious. They advocated more stringent accounting of the entire financial sector, which would probably fall most heavily on the Islamic companies. And they also sought wide-ranging liberalization, which they hoped would make the official banks more competitive.

An unprejudiced application of this approach might have produced a balanced solution, some kind of reconciliation of the parallel and official economies. Savings and investment would have been encouraged by the greater accountability of the Islamic money management companies and the rising interest rates offered by the official banks. The best managed firms in both sectors would have survived. But Egyptian bankers did not favor this approach. Their own accounting techniques were not spotless, and they did not want to get into a duel with the Islamic companies over whose portfolios were more solid.[157] Moreover, they remained ambivalent about the value of liberalization, fearing the depression it might produce. Rather than reform the entire financial sector, bankers advocated legislation to penalize the money management companies alone.

The Egyptian government, too, was eager to move against the IMMCs. Yet they were unsure just how to do so. Like government regulators in the American savings and loan crisis, they understood that the entire financial sector, official and parallel, was sutured together and that intervening forcefully against one element might undermine the business of others. A major run on the companies might endanger those banks and government agencies that had done business with them. And bankruptcies among the major companies would endanger the deposits of hundreds of thousands of citizens. Officials hoped to find some way to edge the Islamic companies out of business without provoking a social catastrophe.

In June 1987 the government tried to pass a law that would have forced the IMMCs to place part of their deposits on reserve with official banks and to submit to some regulation by the Central Bank. This provoked strong opposition in Parliament, where the companies were supported by both the Muslim Brothers and the Wafd. The law that eventually emerged had little practical effect.[158] The government then turned to one of its most effective weapons—stealth. It began to try to weaken public confidence in the Islamic companies. A November 1986 article in one of the official newspapers had reported that Rayyan had lost $200 million through gold speculation in London. Followed by an official warning from the Central Bank, this triggered a run by Rayyan depositors. For two weeks depositors demanded their assets, costing Rayyan $11 million a day.[159] But Rayyan covered all requests for withdrawals and business gradually returned to normal. In the fall of 1987 new rumors spread by officials provoked a second run on the deposits of Rayyan.

The IMMCs not only survived these assaults, but their increasingly tight ties to journalists and opposition parties allowed them to turn the debate around and begin questioning the solvency of the official banks. They were thus able to open a public debate over the government's actions. Forced onto the defensive, the government began to prepare a new law that would impose comprehensive regulation on money management funds. In December 1987 it submitted a draft of the new law to Parliament. The draft required the companies to open their books and submit to outside audits. But it also went a step further, requiring that these firms reorganize themselves as joint-stock companies and convert their deposits into shares.[160]

The draft law provoked an even more bitter debate in Parliament, and it terrified the leaders of the IMMCs. If the money managers were forced to operate under the regulations that governed joint-stock companies, they would lose much of their ability to attract deposits and face sharply reduced opportunities for profit. The companies launched a no-holds-barred press campaign against the government. In April 1988, two of the largest companies, Rayyan and Sa'd, decided that they could better confront the government challenge together than alone. They announced a plan to merge.

The merger, however, was hasty and unplanned. It precipitated a split among the Abd al-Fattah brothers who owned Rayyan. Two of the brothers forced Rayyan's director, Fathi Abd al-Fattah, to resign while he lay in a hospital bed. The official press not only played up the confusion within Rayyan's board but also the fact that Fathi was in the hospital for drug rehabilitation. The government issued orders restraining any of the brothers from traveling abroad—lest they abscond with the company's funds. This fiasco provoked a third run of $120 million on Rayyan.[161]

With the largest of the IMMCs in disarray, the government was finally able to act decisively. In May 1988, it railroaded Law 146 through Parliament which drew a dense net of regulations around all money management companies. The new law gave the companies three months to accept one of two options. Either they could accept liquidation, paying off their depositors in two years, or they could be reorganized as joint-stock companies. Deposits would be converted into investment certificates entitling the holders to shares in the companies' profits. Their operations would then be regulated by the Capital Markets Authority and Central Bank. Foreign exchange transfers abroad would be regulated by the Ministry of Economy. The new law also required the companies to maintain specific capital reserves and to publish their balance sheets.[162] It compelled them to submit proposed changes in their boards of directors to the government for approval and to transfer back to Egypt all of their currency deposits abroad. Most important, it placed a moratorium against the companies accepting any new deposits until the law was fully implemented (which would take at least one year).[163]

The Islamic money management companies reacted desperately. The big three—Rayyan, Sa'd, and Huda Misr—tried to put pressure on the financial system by declaring a moratorium on all transactions for a month.[164] They called public meetings of their depositors and told them to blame the government for their lack of dividends.[165] They waged a countercampaign in the press where their position was supported by prominent journalists like Muhsin Muhammad, Anis Mansur, and Muhammad al-Hayawan.[166]

Suspense about whether the companies or the government would prevail in this duel laid a pall over all financial activity.[167] In the summer of 1988 deposits in both Egyptian and hard currency accounts were 70 percent lower than during corresponding periods in earlier years.[168] Official banks too suffered the general depression during this waiting period. There was little new investment in the private sector, save in tourism.[169] To compensate the official banking sector for this stagnation (and to insulate them against the fallout of a possible run on the IMMCs), the government eased official credit restrictions.[170]

Pressure by the IMMCs did win a few concessions. The government decided, for example, to offer the companies "important facilities so they can operate in numerous profitable joint enterprises." Atif Sidqi met with the heads of companies; agreements were to be announced after 'Id al-Adha. The Investment Authority even decided to let the companies continue to operate in the free zones.[171] But the companies generally bungled their public relations campaign. By mid-July the failure to pay dividends had backfired. More than a thousand depositors assembled outside Rayyan to protest.[172] The decline of financial transactions hit the companies hard. In October they were compelled to postpone paying their monthly dividend and announce that in the future such dividends would be cut in half, to 1 percent each month.[173] By this time it was clear that the government was going to execute the new law regardless of its consequences.

In October 1988 the government finally issued the executive decrees that put the new law into effect. All money management companies were ordered to suspend their operations for one year while the government examined—or reconstructed—their books. In the interim, much of their cash was transferred to equity accounts with the official banks. The government promised that when it completed its audit it would decide which firms would be allowed to reorganize as joint-stock companies and which would be forced to liquidate their assets. Bankers were delighted; not only had their competition been put out of business, but the money management firms were ordered to deposit their liquid assets in official banks.

Many of the smallest money management companies folded immediately. Some just could not afford to suspend operations for a year, but many were patently insolvent. Thirty-one small companies accepted application of the new investment law; twenty-one agreed to liquidate themselves. Fifty did not do anything; among them, twenty faced court charges. Fourteen had their cases presented to the socialist prosecutor.[174] All six major companies, however, applied for reorganization.

In November 1989 the government released its verdict on the larger money management companies. Only Rayyan was declared insolvent; its directors were arrested and all of the firm's assets sequestered.[175] Confiscating Rayyan's liquid funds proved difficult. It had remained heavily involved in arbitrage and held much of its funds abroad. Failings in its internal bookkeeping and the silence of its directors made it hard for government accountants to even identify its assets. Despite formal requests to Saudi Arabia and Cyprus, the Egyptian government failed to repatriate most of the firm's funds. The government put its directors on trial and eventually sentenced them to hard labor, hoping that the defendants could be pressured into identifying their accounts in exchange for lighter sentences.

The audit of Rayyan revealed not only sloppy books but instances where depositors were paid their dividends out of principal.[176] However, this appeared to have been an uncommon practice and even hostile accountants did not suggest that the firm relied on pyramid schemes for its regular profits. In June 1989 a lawyer approached the court that was supervising the liquidation of Rayyan and offered to repay the firm's 175,000 depositors $566 million in exchange for control of its assets. This suggested that, while the government audit had highlighted the riskiness of Rayyan's operations, it had not convinced investors that the firm's assets were imaginary.[177]

Most of the other major Islamic money management companies were in much better shape. Sharif, it turned out, had invested the bulk of its assets in a network of profitable domestic industries (particularly plastics and chemicals). Its books showed assets and liabilities of $450 million, including $386 million of investments in companies and financial paper, and $408 million in deposits and profits due to investors of the group; 55 percent of its total investments were in equity of seventeen affiliated companies.[178] It was permitted to convert into a joint-stock company.

The second largest money management company, Sa'd, was also permitted to convert. Its accounts showed 61,000 investors, total deposits of $197 million, and liquid funds of $67 million. After government-mandated restructuring, these were divided among three new companies, specializing in industry, property, and trade.[179] Two of the other major IMMCs were ordered to liquidate their assets and repay their depositors, but neither was shown to be insolvent. The Badr company had come close to meeting the government criteria for staying in business. A European manager who surveyed the operation of the company admitted that he was impressed by Badr's management of projects in industry, tourism, retailing, and trade.[180] Huda Misr also had no trouble coming up with the cash to repay its depositors $136 million, two-thirds of the total claims on it. The government granted both firms generous deadlines within which to liquidate themselves.[181]

By 1990 there was still some mopping up to do in the IMMC crisis, but the denouement of the story was already clear. The winners had been the official banks, which had not only defended their hold on the Egyptian financial system but expanded their assets at the expense of the parallel economy. The money managers finished a distant second. Many of the smallest firms had gone bankrupt and a handful of their directors had even been arrested. But most of the larger firms survived and successfully made the transition to the official economy.

But the money managers did not take last place in the race to control Egypt's financial system. That honor fell to the public. Those who had deposited funds in the smaller firms discovered that their assets had evaporated. Those who had banked on Rayyan learned that it would take years to recover their deposits, even in part. President Mubarak personally warned depositors that the Egyptian government, itself running a £E 10.5 billion budget deficit, could not think of offering compensation for lost deposits.[182]

It can be argued that those people who lost their deposits in insolvent Islamic money management companies were at least prevented from squandering more good money in a bad investment. Yet there was a stiff price to be paid for this gain of security. For a year, all financial activity was subdued while the public awaited the outcome of the struggle. By the time it was over, the financial system had been stripped of some of its most dynamic elements. Only the official banks—with their low interest rates, poor service, and burden of bad debts—remained to meet the financial needs of the Egyptian public.

Conclusion

In the short term, the termination of the Islamic money management companies had only a mild effect on the fortunes of Egyptian agriculture. The companies had been investing in this sector with increasing energy. Badr had extensive investments in food processing and had invested in reclaimed lands in Nubariyya (where, among other things, it had established an experimental ostrich farm).[183] Rayyan had also invested heavily in reclaimed land and had built a sheep farm, an animal feed mill, a cattle farm, a slaughterhouse, a meat processing plant, and a $61 million dairy farm complex.[184] Yet the IMMCs remained largely urban institutions, both in their pattern of investments and in their choice of clientele.

In the long term, however, the liquidation of the money management companies dimmed the chances that agriculture and other sectors of the Egyptian economy would soon be recharged by the development of more sophisticated financial services. The process that had driven the companies into receivership left the official banks without competitors and greatly strengthened their control over the financial system. Supported by the government and protected from foreign and domestic competition, the banks seemed unlikely to put any great energy into improving the financial services they supplied.

Most of the complaints that financial analysts raised about the Islamic firms could have been addressed to the official banks too. In 1984, for example, the state forced four banks to reorganize after they were caught joining in a scheme to launder hard currency for Sami Ali Hasan, the country's largest black market money changer. During the reorganization it was also revealed that one of the bank directors had embezzled £E 600,000. Another bank executive had smuggled $509 million of hard currency into overseas accounts during a twenty-month period. Overall it was estimated that Egypt's official banks kept 53.87 percent of their hard currency deposits abroad.[185]

Nor were the banks necessarily more likely to manage their assets more prudently than the IMMCs. Egyptian banks lost over £E 200 million to businessmen who fled the country. In 1986 customers failed to repay debts of £E 822 million and there were 354 cases of bankruptcy—up from only 173 in 1981.[186] The banks, like the Islamic companies, tended to keep much of their capital abroad; 40 percent of their total liquidity was in dollars and they acted as a net exporter of capital.[187]

And, of course, the official banks were implicated in the wider regime of financial repression. So long as they collaborated with the government in applying directed credit and the inflation tax, they were guaranteed handsome fees and a semimonopoly over finance. When the IMMCs were laid to rest, so was the most formidable challenge to the official system of repression that had ever developed in Egypt.

The whole point of interest rate reform is to lure funds out of the hidden economy or private savings and into financial institutions. To achieve a financial revolution, however, formal banking institutions have to be markedly more reliable, sophisticated, and energetic than their informal counterparts. It is not clear that this is the case in Egypt, where the legacy of cronyism and rent seeking (and not just financial repression) has bred a hidebound and unresponsive banking system.

Those who seek to promote a financial revolution may have legitimate reasons for focusing their attention on the official banks. The banks are public bodies, more susceptible to auditing and control than the amorphous Islamic money management companies. Perhaps official banks will respond more quickly to government efforts aimed at "restoring macroeconomic stability, building better legal, accounting, and regulatory systems, specifying rules for fuller disclosure of information, and levying taxes that do not fall excessively on finance."[188] Higher interest rates may play a role in expediting the modernization of the banking sector. But they are no substitute for opening the system to competition, raising levels of training and service, and providing more thorough regulation and accounting.

Even if the banks are the proper focus of financial development, the recent struggle between them, the IMF, and the Islamic companies cannot be counted as a great advance for reform. The manner in which the campaign against the IMMCs was conducted actually enhanced the political influence of the banks. Egyptian bankers have long used this political power to stifle competition and resist reform. Because of their augmented influence, it may prove tougher to liberalize the financial system and erect better legal, accounting, and regulatory systems.

Until such substantive reforms have been undertaken, it would be unwise to assume that the official banks are superior to their informal counterparts. Transferring funds or power from one sector to another will not stimulate development by itself. In Egypt today there is no special sector of the economy, no special stratum, that is likely to be more entrepreneurial (or less parasitic) than another. Even if the IMF succeeds in forcing Egypt to raise interest rates, this would provide only limited stimulus to the financial system. Most of the official banks are unlikely to employ the funds they lure through higher rates any more productively and responsibly than the parallel economy did. Without radical changes in the way that banks are licensed and audited, without the stimulus of competition and the development of a real service orientation among the banks, a financial revolution hardly seems imminent in Cairo.

The foibles of the official banks also raise questions about the wisdom of AID's hope to convert the Principal Bank for Development and Agricultural Credit into a conventional bank. Until Egypt experiences something like a financial revolution, official banks are not likely to provide an alternative to or a replacement for PBDAC's services in rural areas. Indeed, given the universal volatility of the agricultural economy, rural areas seem likely to be the last area in which official banks will develop large-scale services. For the same reasons, any rush to privatize PBDAC could backfire badly. Under private direction, PBDAC would probably move much of its capital out of agriculture and focus what lending remained on the richest clients with the most tangible collateral. In a crony capitalist system like Egypt's, privatization often replaces public sector bureaucracy and inefficiency with private sector corruption and venality.

This does not mean that there is no hope for financial reform in the rural areas. In other areas of the Third World, both the government and private banks in rural areas have learned to make a valuable contribution to the process of financial revolution. In 1976 Dr. Mohammed Yunus, an American-trained economist, established the Grameen (Village) Bank in Bangladesh. The Grameen Bank required no collateral of its borrowers; in fact, it catered only to landless peasants. It offered small loans (averaging $65) for housing and venture projects such as weaving, rice-husking, and the production of poultry, vegetables, and dairy products. Borrowers had to repay their principal and 16 percent interest in a series of weekly installments stretched out over one year. Grameen Bank employed a variety of subtle techniques to encourage repayment. Borrowers had to apply in groups of five; this not only spread the risk, but created a form of peer pressure against default.

Each group was required to open a savings account with the bank and to make regular deposits equaling a specified fraction of what the members owed. If a group of peasants failed to repay their loan, they were barred from future Grameen credit—which left them at the mercy of local moneylenders, who charged 10 percent a month for their funds.[189]

The Grameen Bank was a success by any measure. As of 1990 it "has 800,000 loans on its books, hands out $6 million a month, has a 98 percent repayment record, and makes enough profit to sustain itself."[190] The example of Grameen encouraged the International Fund of Agricultural Development (IFAD) to sponsor similar experiments in countries as diverse as Mali, Honduras, and Nepal. Credit officers on bicycles or motorbikes were sent into the countryside to market venture capital credit. These IFAD projects, like Grameen, produced very high rates of repayment (85–100 percent), even though some supplied only short-term loans at relatively high rates of interest.[191]

One American who had worked as a mobile credit officer in Burkina Faso later moved to Egypt to work for an AID subcontractor. He won AID support for his proposal to launch a rural small-scale enterprise credit project that would have extended this approach to the Egyptian countryside. Fearing that PBDAC was too corrupted to give this project an honest chance, he chose to work instead with one of the official banks that had more experience in venture capital loans (particularly to the lucrative tourist sector). Managers at this supposedly entrepreneurial bank, however, balked at the project. They thought that the 30–50 percent interest it proposed to charge on short-term loans was usurious and kept insisting that it be reduced. They had little faith in the profitability of rural credit markets and urged that the project sponsor urban business ventures instead. They raised one objection after another, watering down the original proposal, until the project stood little chance of success.

The current environment in Egypt places limits on how receptive the country will be to experiments like the Grameen Bank. So long as bankers feel that they can manipulate government regulations in a manner that assures them profit, there is little chance that many will embrace the risks of pioneering new facilities or absorb the costs of extending their services into local retail banking. Liberalizing interest rates—whether at the macroeconomic level as the IMF urges or within the rural economy as the Agricultural Production and Credit program proposes—might help to wean the official banks from the state. But higher interest rates are not a panacea. They simply facilitate financial development in an environment where government regulation makes banks more reliable, where competition presses them to become more service oriented, and where macroeconomic policy works to preserve the real value of local currency.

CHAPTER 7

Budget Cutting and Economic Reform

ON SEPTEMBER 8, 1988, PRESIDENT HUSNI MUBARAK WENT TO THE village of Mit Birah in his home province of Minufiyya to give his annual speech on the occasion of Farmers Day. He congratulated the assembled crowd of peasants for their contribution to national production and tried to give them a picture of developments in the economy. About halfway through his address he digressed to speak about Egypt's talks with the International Monetary Fund: "The IMF acts like someone in the rural areas in the past who made himself a wiseman—a doctor. He is not a doctor or anything. A patient, for example, needs a treatment for one month. Instead of this doctor telling the patient to take the medicine daily for 1 month, he tells him to take all the medicine today and tomorrow and that he will recover the day after. Of course, he will take the medicine to go to sleep at night and will not wake up in the morning. He dies. This is the IMF. It writes a prescription for those who require prolonged treatment, just as for those who require short treatment. . . . I tell the IMF that economic reform should proceed according to the social and economic situation in the state and according to the people's standard of living. One should not come and say increase the price by 40 percent. Surely, no one will be able to live. This will not be an IMF process: it will be a slaughter. No state can accept such a system, and many states have criticized it."[1]

Mubarak's remarks were extemporaneous and emotional. This was not a scripted ploy; he spoke from the heart. His comparison of the Fund to a quack doctor personally offended the IMF's managing director Michel Camdessus and complicated delicate negotiations over a standby agreement. (A few months later Camdessus gave a scathing interview complaining about the Egyptian government's "pretend"

253

adjustment program.)[2] But Mubarak's words reflected the sentiments of many Egyptians, even those who championed economic reform.

Mubarak spoke at a moment when Washington's official development community—the Fund, the World Bank, the U.S. Agency for International Development (AID), and their various affiliated agencies—was pressing its demands for economic reform with unusual force. The reforms that Cairo had adopted had never been as drastic or as rigorously enforced as those undertaken by Mexico, Ghana, and Nigeria. When the IMF signed its May 1987 standby agreement with Egypt, the Fund's popular director for exchange and trade relations, David Finch, had resigned in protest, charging that Egypt's proposed reform package was inadequate and that it was being given loans solely because of its strategic significance.[3] When the Egyptians then failed not only to implement the reforms they had committed to, but further undermined them by increasing public sector salaries 25 percent, the Fund canceled the second tranche of the standby loan. Long before Mubarak offended Camdessus, the Egyptians had a credibility problem with international financial institutions.

Even the United States government, which in 1987 had lobbied the IMF on Egypt's behalf, had become impatient with the progress of Egyptian reform. In February 1989 the U.S. government turned down Cairo's request for interest relief on its $4.5 billion outstanding military debt.[4] A month later, AID announced its decision to withhold $230 million in economic aid until Egypt showed more progress in policy reform.[5] Later in the year, when it looked as if Egypt would fall more than a year behind in its payments to the United States (which would have been a violation of the Brooke Amendment and triggered an automatic cutoff of all American aid) Washington softened its position— but only a little. In August the Americans released $115 million in cash aid—just enough to allow the Egyptians to keep making their payments and avoid a termination of the aid relationship.[6]

Mubarak and his cabinet thought that the Washington development community demanded too much of Egypt too quickly. Officials in Cairo felt that the Fund was insensitive to the political consequences of the austerity programs it devised. They argued that Fund proposals imposed a heavier burden than the citizens of a poor country could accept. And the results, they noted, were often politically destabilizing. Austerity programs recommended by the IMF had led to major rioting and demonstrations in Tunisia (1984), Morocco (1984), Algeria (1988), and Jordan (1989).[7] Mubarak was fond of saying: "We know our people and there is a limit. I am keen on reforms, but if the people start rioting, it will be a setback for all of the reforms."[8]

But, in addition to these long-standing criticisms, Mubarak's 1988 speech aired newer, deeper doubts about Western development advice. As the Egyptian economy worsened, Fund and AID officials listened less to Cairo's pleas for caution about the pace of reform. Instead they grew more demanding, seeing in Egypt's vulnerability a source of leverage with which to insist on reforms. They demanded deeper budget cuts, more rapid subsidy reductions, and more extensive liberalization of key prices. They began to raise new and more radical demands for privatization of public enterprises, civil service reform, restructuring of the financial system, and a general retreat from state intervention. Like many other African leaders, Mubarak had to listen to lectures from Western economists who complained that Egyptians "have done all the easy reforms like modest devaluation, getting interest rates positive and changing producer prices. But the Government isn't yet willing to go the whole hog and really tackle fundamental change."[9]

While the demands on Cairo were growing harsher, Egyptian officials were beginning to lose confidence that the Fund's proposals constituted a real recipe for development. They brooded over the examples of Ghana and Nigeria, countries that had made enormous sacrifices in response to demands for structural adjustment and were considered model pupils by Western development experts. Between 1980 and 1987 the gross domestic product of Ghana grew at an annual average of only 1.4 percent; in Nigeria the figure was − 1.7 percent. Indeed, in Nigeria per capita income fell from $1,000 to just $300 while $15 billion was drained from the country in the form of debt service and capital flight.[10] Studies commissioned by the World Bank had begun to suggest that the strategy of structural adjustment made a far more marginal contribution to development than had been hoped.[11]

Egyptian politicians on the far left and right of the political spectrum felt that this new atmosphere confirmed old charges that the Washington development community's real agenda in Cairo was to promote opportunities for Western businessmen, not to advance Egyptian development. But even in the middle of the Egyptian spectrum, where support for reform was strongest, new questions festered. The Fund (and the World Bank) had always insisted that its advice to clients did "not take a position on social and political issues, but work[ed] within the existing sociopolitical system of its member countries."[12] But some of the development community's new proposals seemed to imply a wider agenda—not simply to correct the overextension of the state, but to eliminate its central economic functions. The Fund seemed to be edging toward dismantling the state's role in the Egyptian economy and replacing it with a free-market enterprise society. Mubarak and others began to complain that the Fund's reform program was weakening the state, not just circumscribing its role but actually crippling its influence.

Among the new generation of Cairene officials, there were a handful who would have endorsed proposals to convert Egypt into an enterprise economy. But the majority, even of centrists and reformers, had serious doubts about such a strategy. They felt that while the market should govern most aspects of the economy, there were still areas where state intervention was either necessary or desirable. And while they were prepared to redefine the role of the state in the economy, they were not willing to undermine the foundations of its authority.

The Stockman Stratagem

Egyptians' suspicions about the intent of IMF-style reforms are understandable. Some, perhaps even a majority, of the Washington-based economists who advocate these reforms see them as sound macroeconomic policy. But another outspoken group of neoclassical economists also see in them a means to permanently reduce the scope for state intervention and convert Egypt into an enterprise society. Since these two groups often urge substantially the same actions, and since they function as a single bloc in negotiations with Cairo, it is difficult for Egyptian officials to be certain which agenda they are being committed to.

The debates over Cairo's large fiscal deficit illustrate how this confusion arises and why it leaves Egyptian officials anxious. For a decade, the deficit has grown larger both in absolute terms and as a share of GDP (see table 6-2). This government overspending has fostered a host of economic problems, including inflation, trade imbalances, financial repression, and capital flight. Economists at the IMF and other development agencies sometimes argue that bringing the deficit under control is the single most important reform Egypt could undertake. They have made the state budget the first item in the agenda of their discussions in Cairo and have put strong pressure on Egypt to reduce it.

When Egypt opened talks over a second standby accord late in 1988, the IMF insisted on much tougher conditions and began to pay special attention to the size of the budget deficit. The Fund's initial response to the Egyptian request revealed "a barely concealed exasperation at stuttering progress towards economic reform."[13] In fiscal 1988–89, Cairo's budget deficit had equaled 20 percent of GDP; the Fund wanted to see this cut to 10 percent. Egypt could meet this target only by introducing a host of reforms, such as reducing a wide array of subsidies, rapidly raising energy prices, and comprehensively reforming the tax system.[14] The Fund took a very tough stance; long after the Egyptian Parliament passed a budget with a projected deficit in the 10 percent range, IMF officials pored over Egyptian statistics to determine how realistic the projection was. Fund economists determined that the Egyptian projections were overly optimistic, so no accord was signed. This compelled Egypt to postpone talks with the Paris Club about rescheduling its foreign debt.[15]

Continuing pressure from the Fund and the looming prospect of debt default forced more desperate measures by the Egyptian government. In March 1989 the government increased energy prices by 30 percent. In June the Parliament approved a budget for 1989–90 that whittled down real funding for consumer subsidies, increasing appropriations for them by only 14 percent in a year when inflation was running 30–35 percent. In December Cairo leaked news of a plan to raise interest rates.[16] But even taken together these changes did not come close to meeting the IMF's demands. The 1989–90 budget projected a deficit of £E 6.9 billion, but Fund economists remained skeptical. After all, the 1988–89 budget, with a projected shortfall of £E 7.2 billion, had produced a deficit of £E 11 billion.[17]

Egyptian officials could think of many reasons why the IMF would assign such importance to the state budget. And that was precisely the reason they worried. If the Fund was trying to reduce the deficit as a way of promoting the macroeconomic health of the economy, they could sympathize (while disagreeing about the speed and scope of reductions). But many feared that the budget talks concealed a hidden agenda—a plan to strip the state's authority over the economy and to radically alter the balance of public and private power in Egypt.

Some, perhaps most, of the IMF negotiators who urged taking a hard line in Egypt were troubled primarily by the macroeconomic implications of the fiscal shortfall. Cairo's deficit spending increased aggregate demand and helped to trigger inflation. The need to fund the public debt encouraged the government to depress interest rates, employ the inflation tax, and resort to other forms of financial repression. Inflation and high levels of public spending combined to foster overvaluation of the currency, creating a running trade deficit. For these and many other reasons, many economists argued that failure to reduce the fiscal deficit would frustrate reform efforts in finance, trade, and other areas.

Across the Third World, the stabilization programs that IMF officials considered most successful had begun with campaigns to reduce the fiscal deficit. In countries like Chile, reduction of the deficit had been achieved largely through increases in taxation.[18] But few analysts thought such increases were possible in Egypt. Cairo's tax agencies were administratively primitive and too feeble to collect taxes equitably. The bulk of government revenue came from state rents (oil exports and Suez Canal fees) and easily collected excises (customs duties and the profits of agricultural marketing boards like the Cotton Authority).[19] Existing tax laws were routinely evaded and the high level of development of the hidden economy suggested that it would be difficult to widen or deepen the scope of taxation. As a result, most observers thought that the deficit could be reduced only through large cuts in the government's budget.[20]

It was this prospect of budget cuts that intrigued and excited more radical elements in the Washington development community. An influential minority of neoclassical economists was trying to persuade its colleagues within the Fund that the size of the budget itself, and not just the deficit, formed the root of many of Egypt's economic problems. These were the men that Egyptian officials feared were setting the real agenda for the budget talks.

According to these neoclassical radicals (sometimes known as the new political economy school), the lack of budget discipline fostered not only the macroeconomic problems of Egypt, but many of its microeconomic difficulties.[21] They argued that so long as the Egyptian government was willing to run up a large deficit, public sector firms were subject to only soft budgetary constraints. These firms may have wished to turn a profit but they knew that if they did not, the state would underwrite their losses. So long as they obeyed the government's general production instructions, they would not be allowed to go bankrupt. They thus had no incentive to take hard decisions or toy with risky innovations. So public sector firms tended to remain inefficient and the losses from their operations were simply added to the national deficit.[22]

This argument was originally devised to describe the centrally planned economies of Eastern Europe, but it seemed to apply to Egypt too—with a special twist. In Egypt, not only are public sector firms subject to "soft budgetary constraints," but many private firms are as well. If a private firm knows that its losses can be offset by credits, tariffs, and subsidies offered by the state, it too is insulated from the discipline of the market.

Thus, one of the reasons the neoclassical radicals favored a reduction of the Egyptian budget was to impose "hard budgetary constraints" on domestic firms. After cutting the budget (and not just the deficit) Cairo would be unable to accept public sector losses or to underwrite the inefficiency of the private sector. Egyptian firms would be forced to become more competitive, more responsive to market forces. Indeed, budget cutting appeared to be an elegant way to shortcut the entire process of policy reform. As the general budget constricted, the Egyptian government would have to eliminate many of the subsidies that had been targets of AID and the World Bank in the policy dialogue with Egypt. And Egyptian producers would no longer be able to undermine such reforms through shell games, because no funding would be available for alternative, untargeted credits and subventions.

But the neoclassical radicals put forward a second impressive reason for cutting the Egyptian budget. They believed, of course, that subsidies, tariffs, and other forms of state intervention distorted the workings of the market, leading to inefficiency and waste. But they also thought that intervention fostered a special form of political corruption. In the vision of the new political economy, the allure of low-risk profits from state subventions had created a host of special interests that sought to use their political influence to acquire economic entitlements—for instance, "the bureaucracy, public sector functionaries, industrial labor, and those who have been granted the monopolistic protection of the use of their labor or capital by the State's prohibitions on entry and exit of economic enterprises."[23]

Perhaps the most iniquitous form of this corruption was found in its effects on businessmen. Unlike other conservative economists, who clung to a dogmatic optimism about the propriety and virtue of businessmen, the neoclassical radicals argued that businessmen too were subject to the allure of entitlements and that state intervention tended to make them unproductive. These economists invented the concept of rent seeking to describe this form of corruption, in which businessmen tended to divert a growing share of their capital from productive investment into lobbying, bribes, and other inducements designed to elicit subsidies, guaranteed monopolies, and other perquisites from the state. The share of capital that was converted into political influence had to be added to the conventional forms of waste arising from market distortions when tallying the costs of state intervention.[24]

The radicals hoped that budget cutting would greatly restrict the scope of this corruption; they believed that "the best way to limit rent-seeking is to limit government."[25] By reducing the funds necessary to pay for a bloated civil service it would reduce the state's capacity to regulate the economy—and the need for businessmen to use bribes to sustain their operations. By restricting the monies available for subsidies and directed credits, it would reduce the incentive for businessmen to spend their time and capital lobbying politicians for subventions. According to the new political economy, budget cuts, rather than police agencies or better administration, were the most effective tool for rooting out corruption and fostering more honest government.[26]

Economists who argued the case for the benefits of budget cutting did not limit their advice to developing countries, of course. The first analyses of rent seeking were done by students of advanced industrial societies. So were the first arguments that constraining the budget would maximize economic efficiency.[27] In the United States this trend of thought, after many tortuous permutations, gave rise to the campaign for a balanced-budget amendment to the Constitution and rising debate about the economic consequences of the national deficit.

This movement came to fruition under the Reagan administration (1981–89). David Stockman, Ronald Reagan's first director of the Office of Management and Budget, looked at the debate over the budget deficit and saw "the potential leverage it provided to . . . force Congress to shrink the welfare state."[28] Stockman and his liberal opponents still disagree over whether his efforts were successful, but they agree that the core of his strategy was to use pressure on the budget as a means to restrict state intervention, curtail entitlements, and eliminate rents.[29]

Senior officials at AID thought that if the Stockman strategy was good for the United States, it would be even better for Third World countries like Egypt, where the fiscal deficit consumed an even higher share of GDP.[30] The American adoption of budget cutting, however, was hardly pioneering; the Stockman strategy had already been aired by neoclassical economists at the World Bank in the late 1970s and had been a perennial subtheme among thinkers at the IMF.

If the neoclassical radicals were right, the benefits of budget cutting would extend far beyond the macroeconomic virtues of inhibiting inflation and promoting financial liberalization. It would produce microeconomic benefits by improving the efficiency of firms and reducing the incentives for corruption. In the process, it would steadily constrict the scope of state intervention in the economy. This last point is precisely what caused Egyptian officials anxiety.

Horticulture Exports, the Original Political Vegetables

The Stockman strategy is an updated variation of an old liberal dream of so constraining the state that market forces are left free to work their economic magic. The Stockman approach is an especially elegant and appealing variation of this dream, since progress toward balancing the budget in itself offers macroeconomic benefits and cutting state spending across the board appears to be an easier way to administer liberalization than negotiating separate changes in every government subsidy or price control. It may be that the virtues make this strategy an attractive program for advanced, industrialized societies.

But in struggling, developing countries like Egypt, people react to the Stockman proposals with a curious ambivalence. Egyptian businessmen and economic reformers, for example, tend to endorse the idea of liberalization. They want freedom from state controls and regulations, and they want the government to stop mandating and supervising what they produce and for which markets. Yet businessmen and reformers, even the most liberal ones, resist the idea of cutting the state's budget and reducing its centrality in the economy. They believe that the private sector is still too weak to prosper on its own and that it requires massive government support and public investment to develop. As chapter 3 explains, these groups are not etatists (they believe that businessmen and the market should define the direction of economic policy rather than technocrats or officers), but they remain *dirigistes* (who believe that economic development requires the support of a strong state).

What divides Egyptian liberalizers from Western liberals, then, seems to be that the Egyptians think it is the dictatorial, market-insensitive manner or mode by which the state devises policy that hinders development while Westerners tend to think the taproot of the problem is the very size of the state. Reformers in Cairo and Washington who collaborate closely on projects to decontrol prices or to liberalize tariffs tend to turn on each other over this question. Westerners claim that the manner of state operation will change if its size is reduced. Egyptians suspect that if the size of the state diminishes, it will no longer be able to perform many legitimate and desirable economic services.[31]

The Western vision of how the size of the state threatens the economy is a familiar theme of elementary economics textbooks. The Egyptian vision that the growth of the private sector requires a wide array of state supports and services is less familiar. One example of a project where Egyptian and Western reformers agree on the desirability of liberalization but differ over the scope of the state's contribution is the effort to promote Egyptian exports of fruits and vegetables.

For most of the last century, the most popular crop in Egypt was cotton, much of which was grown for export. But from the 1960s onward, many Egyptian farmers grew disenchanted with the cotton market. Overseas markets shrank with the growing popularity of synthetic fabrics and alternative sources of supply, while domestic profits declined as a result of government price controls. Egyptian farmers began to switch to higher-value produce. Poorer peasants devoted their time and energy to raising livestock and cultivating fodder. Richer peasants and agrarian capitalists focused on cultivating fruits and vegetables, whose profits were even higher.[32]

Agricultural economists typically approved of this shift, viewing the cultivation of higher-value crops as a more efficient use of land and labor which would raise both farm and national incomes. They were particularly excited about the development of horticulture.[33] Fruits and vegetables not only fetched high prices domestically, they could be exported. Egypt lay just across the Mediterranean from the European Community (EC), the world's largest importer of fresh and processed horticultural products.[34] Egypt is close enough to Europe to deliver fresh crops quickly, but far enough away to produce fruits and vegetables outside European growing seasons and to raise tropical varieties uncultivable in Europe. European demand for fruits and vegetables is so strong that, even excluding inter-European trade, its market is 80 percent larger than that of the United States.[35]

Private Egyptian farmers understood this and were eager to cash in on the opportunity it presented. Individual farmers, for example, discovered that by hauling their strawberries to Cairo airport during a few weeks in April they could export them to Switzerland (where local stocks were exhausted) at twenty times the normal price. But Egyptian government officials and agronomists were equally enthusiastic, because they saw export horticulture as a means of resolving national problems as well as padding personal profits.

During the early 1980s many economists thought that exports were the key to successful development.[36] They pointed to the examples of South Korea, Taiwan, Hong Kong, and Singapore (the so-called Asian dragons), whose economies had flourished by concentrating on production for overseas trade. By exporting, these countries had greatly expanded the size of the markets available to them, adding Americans and Japanese to their list of local consumers. Of course, consumers in the developed countries demanded higher-quality goods; but this was all right, because they paid more too, and in hard currency. Export-oriented firms in developing countries thus had both the incentive and the means to innovate, to finance technological improvement, and to rationalize their production. Export-led development, economists argued, was not only more lucrative than focusing on the domestic market, it also stimulated producers to become more efficient and modern.[37]

In Egypt, agronomists saw an additional advantage in exporting agricultural products—a solution to the food security problem. In March 1982 Yusuf Wali convened an important conference on the Promotion of Egyptian Exports of Horticulture Crops. Alexander Sarris, one of the American experts invited, delivered a now famous paper on "Cropping Pattern, Food Security, and Exports." Dr. Sarris observed that the crop of vegetables that could be grown on any given feddan in Egypt was several times more valuable than the value of the wheat that the same area might produce. The difference was even greater if the vegetables were exported to high-demand, hard currency markets. As a matter of simple logic, then, land diverted from cereal production into horticulture could earn enough hard currency to more than pay for the forgone wheat crop. Indeed, Dr. Sarris argued, the gap between the value of wheat and vegetables was large enough that if enough land was diverted from the former to the latter, the resulting profits could finance Egypt's wheat import needs.

Dr. Sarris was not certain just how much land would need to be diverted to achieve this form of food security, but he did present an econometric model showing that if Egypt's food import bill averaged $244 million over a ten-year period, then, other things being equal, the diversion of 300,000 feddans from wheat into horticulture could eliminate the food deficit and produce a net agriculture revenue averaging $500 million annually.[38] Later models by Egyptian economists, using more detailed statistics, seemed to bear out his conclusions.[39] Egyptian economists now refer to this application of the doctrine of comparative advantage to the problem of food security as the Davis strategy, named for Dr. Sarris's home institution, the University of California at Davis.

Yusuf Wali (himself a horticulture specialist) was thrilled by what he heard at the 1982 convention. He listened to papers on how Egyptian tomatoes could be exported by switching to varieties that could tolerate low-cost ocean shipping and how Cairo could cash in on peaking European demand for tropical flowers.[40] He incorporated some of the Davis strategy in his own plans for dealing with the food security problem.[41] He left the conference determined to push Egypt into a new era of export agriculture.

Actually, Egyptians had been aware of the potential of the European market for decades. In 1967–68 President Nasser's lieutenants had made a major push to expand fruit and vegetable exports. The Wadi Company, the public sector firm that monopolized horticultural trade, briefly managed to reduce the time that produce spent waiting in Egyptian ports to under forty-eight hours. Its exports to Europe burgeoned from 50,000 tons in 1967 to 220,000 by 1972.[42] This campaign, however, soon faltered. Part of its failure can be attributed to the cutback of agricultural investment under President Sadat. But much of the blame lies in the way that state policies discouraged farmers from expanding production of high-value crops.

Government price controls, of course, limited the incentives for investing in many fruit and vegetable crops. But even in the production of crops whose prices were not regulated, bureaucratic restrictions dampened production. For example, one government official, Bairam Murad, noted the high price of mushrooms in Egypt and decided to try to cultivate these on his family farm. He approached the agriculture minister, Yusuf Wali, for help in securing the necessary bureaucratic approval. Wali told Murad that he himself had considered growing mushrooms but, despite his cabinet position, had been unable to secure all the necessary authorizations. Murad persisted and, with Wali's support, finally won all the necessary permissions. "That effort took three years, an additional forty-two signatures, and eleven further ministerial decrees. It involved departments and agencies at the national and provincial levels and such matters as whether the ministry concerned intended to build a road, canal, or power pylon on or through his farm, as well as issues related specifically to mushrooms and any potentially harmful consequences they might have. . . . After a protracted teething period [Murad] is now successfully producing and marketing his crop. Prices remain high because the labyrinthine procedure of obtaining permission from the state to grow mushrooms has deterred other potential growers."[43]

If Murad had intended to grow mushrooms strictly for domestic markets, he might have been able to ignore state regulations or to begin planting after bribing a few local officials. But since he intended to export part of his crop, he had to win cooperation from a wide array of state agencies. Not surprisingly, then, horticultural exporters in Egypt tend to be a very elite group—men with not only the capital to experiment with new crops, but with the political influence necessary to see them through a host of government marketing restrictions. For the same reasons, they often enjoy the benefits of oligopoly over key crops.

Obviously there is a strong case to be made for deregulating much of horticultural trade. Egyptian state agencies not only discourage farmers, they often bungle their own efforts to organize this trade. For example, in 1983 officials at the Ministry of Supply worried that a rise in exports of onions was going to create domestic shortages, so they abruptly banned exports. The restriction of this market saddled farmers with enormous losses, so they reduced their plantings for the following season by half. The Ministry of Agriculture, which failed to block the interference of the Ministry of Supply in 1983, also failed to anticipate the smaller crop in 1984. It oversold Egyptian onions in world markets and wound up having to negotiate a farmgate price that included an indemnity for the losses of the previous year in order to meet its contracted commitments.[44]

In the early 1980s Yusuf Wali, with heavy support from AID, launched a drive to liberalize the production and trade controls on fruits and vegetables. Under pressure, the Ministry of Economy issued Decree No. 126 of 1983, which permitted private sector exporters to retain foreign exchange earnings and to use the free market rate when buying Egyptian pounds. Law 95 of August 1983 created an Export Development Bank. The following year the export committees that had fixed minimum export prices for fresh produce were abolished. Five new commissions were established to advise the government on how to promote exports by changes in transportation, customs simplification, relaxation of export quotas, planning, and moral and financial incentives. Finally, the government eased its restrictions on the off-season export of fruits and vegetables (which had been banned whenever supplies of domestic produce seemed limited).[45]

In 1985 a major drive to promote exports began. The government summoned a Conference of Egyptian Exporters, which Mubarak himself addressed.[46] The conference evolved into a standing lobby, and vegetable exporters formed an influential caucus within it.[47] Indeed, within a couple of years fruit and vegetable exporters had won independent political standing when the government created a series of commodity councils (*majalis sila'iyya*), the first of which represented the interests of orange and citrus exporters.[48] The government abolished the Wadi Company's monopoly over horticultural exports and began to work directly with the Citrus Commodity Council. Council members gained access to the Wadi Company's eleven plants for washing, stamping, and boxing oranges and won government support for the construction of two new private plants.[49]

These developments stimulated local interest in horticulture but did not boost exports significantly. During the early 1980s, Egypt was producing 6 million tons of vegetables annually, but it exported only 25,000–30,000 tons. Exports of some crops declined in absolute terms; onion exports dropped from 180,000 tons to 5,000 tons, garlic exports from 20,000 tons to 6,000 tons.[50] For all crops only a fraction of the available production was exported. During the years between 1980 and

1984 only 6.3 percent of the tomato crop was exported, 7.9 percent of potatoes, 3.9 percent of onions, 3.7 percent of garlic, and 7.2 percent of green beans.[51] Exports picked up a bit in the later 1980s, but not dramatically.[52]

A variety of factors contributed to this poor-to-modest export performance. Competition between the demands of exports and domestic consumption plagued most crops. Egyptian farmers, merchants, and bureaucrats alike tended to think of exports as a means for disposing of surplus produce, beyond what the domestic market could absorb. But in these years, with rising petroleum revenues inflating personal incomes, local fruit and vegetable consumption increased dramatically, often eliminating whatever surplus had existed for export (see table 7-1). Few entrepreneurs could afford to specialize in export trade, since they could not be confident that there would be any surplus to deal in; and Egyptian exporters probably got poorer terms from European importers since they were an unreliable source of supply.

But the biggest problem was that Egypt lacked the experience and institutions, the infrastructure, necessary to prosper in export horticulture. Exports demanded a completely different agricultural system, employing distinctive techniques of production, handling, and marketing, from that which existed to meet domestic demand. For Egypt, as one expert explained, "entering export markets requires a total marketing effort; special varieties of crops are required; special facilities, such as refrigerated storage and transportation as well as packing and grading houses, must be developed; a wide menu of horticultural crops should be offered to the export market rather than simply the major crop of tomatoes; and professional brokers, market analysts, and marketing specialists must be developed to successfully enter the highly sophisticated international markets."[53] A total marketing effort of this kind would take years to develop and tax the energies of both private firms and the government.

Individual farmers could contribute to developing some of these facilities, but many lay beyond the capacity of farmers. In horticulture, unlike other branches of agriculture, economies of scale are decisive. "Marketing costs are high for fresh products because they may require refrigerated facilities in transit, at collecting points in the producing regions, and at the point of shipment by sea or air. . . . Close coordination of production, processing, and marketing in order to meet the quality requirements of export markets leads to economies of scale;

Table 7-1. Value of Agricultural Exports, 1974–83

Thousands of dollars

Export	1974	1975	1976	1977	1978	1979	1980	1981	1982	1983
Cotton	720,137	523,992	407,410	479,292	354,867	396,856	443,451	477,393	419,456	441,546
Rice	101,573	62,548	79,144	59,775	50,810	31,531	68,000	53,000	11,613	10,200
Potatoes	15,976	8,220	43,848	41,929	15,013	29,901	32,501	25,548	41,100	30,653
Onions	19,402	17,808	26,158	28,320	12,979	4,725	11,646	6,771	5,287	11,723
Oranges	28,534	47,636	48,888	54,974	53,014	22,351	38,940	47,157	82,816	72,444
Sugar, refined	24,978	36,180	25,560	26,196	18,482	12,705	4,307	18,874	12,427	700
Cottonseed cake	3,174	4,363	3,364	2,497	3,857	2,015	1,340	0	0	0
Peanuts	6,496	6,992	5,319	9,739	9,935	5,800	10,434	8,089	10,145	19,670
Flax	4,577	5,100	13,204	20,259	9,009	8,940	6,739	5,310	3,483	3,600
Tomatoes	646	856	1,160	1,697	1,350	1,548	986	1,623	4,254	6,000
Pulses	292	312	3	739	0	334	103	6	639	400
Lemons	21	22	181	243	176	168	157	266	486	650
Grapes	77	72	89	69	24	58	67	49	91	200
Dates	207	483	480	500	560	700	1,000	205	525	0
Beer	561	923	355	58	0	0	30	40	40	50
Wine	400	1,360	1,132	2,645	3	1,011	1,200	1,500	1,400	1,400
Honey	58	112	120	150	463	48	40	178	236	300

Sources: George R. Gardner and John B. Parker, *Agricultural Statistics of Egypt, 1970–84* (U.S. Department of Agriculture, 1985), pp. 81–82; U.S. Department of Agriculture, *Annual Situation Report: Egypt* (1986 and 1988).

such coordination is more easily accomplished when large quantities are marketed or processed. . . . Transaction costs can be reduced by dealing with large shipments and by spreading overhead costs of labeling, packing, and so forth over a large quantity."[54] Theoretically, these economies of scale could be achieved through the formation of either large agricultural estates, large trading firms, or producer cooperatives.

Because of certain legal loopholes, a handful of large estates producing citrus crops already existed on reclaimed lands in Egypt. Certain foreign investors, such as the American Heinz Co. which processed tomatoes, were also permitted to develop large-scale operations.[55] But in general, the clauses of the land reform law prohibited the formation of large estates, and the vast majority of Egyptian farmers would fight to maintain this legislation. This meant that for Egypt, producer cooperatives were the only viable means of obtaining economies of scale.

Large-scale trading firms or agribusinesses (like Continental and Cargill in the United States) might also have enough capital and a large enough stake in the market to justify developing facilities. Unfortunately, the only firms in Egypt that operated on this scale were the wholesaler monopolies at Rawd al-Farag. With overcrowded markets and primitive facilities, their profits still amounted to 7.6 percent of the purchase price of most produce.[56] Locked in a duel with the government over farmgate prices, the wholesalers showed little interest in investing in modern facilities or diversifying into exports. Even if they had shown any talent for efficient marketing, they were not likely to make major new investments to pioneer export trade in a period when the government was searching for ways to break their hold on existing markets.[57]

Egyptians and some foreign advisers, then, thought that producer cooperatives—where individual farmers pool their funds to build common facilities or to take advantage of bulk rates—might be the most viable means for organizing large-scale export trade. Some conservative economists rankle at the very term *cooperative*, but these organizations are not populist pipe dreams. In the United States itself, such nationally recognized brand names as Sunkist (oranges), Diamond (nuts), and Ocean Spray (berries) are marketing labels for producer cooperatives. Cooperatives like Southern States make a vital contribution by purchasing fertilizers and shipping space in bulk.[58] While it may be possible for Egypt's commodity councils to evolve in this direction, they have so far remained primarily lobbies, elite clubs representing not so much the mass of growers as a few influential agricultural capitalists in Cairo.[59]

At the moment, the overhead cost of developing the facilities for profitable export agriculture is simply beyond the capacity of Egyptian private enterprise. It may be years, then, before the Egyptian private sector develops the institutions necessary to finance a total marketing effort in export agriculture. Until then, the burden of pioneering this enterprise falls (or is pushed) on the state. Indeed, growers agree that even after the private sector does begin to develop large-scale institutions, there are certain tasks that require such massive investments of capital and influence that only the state will be able to undertake them.

The existing Egyptian system for transporting, handling, and storing fragile fruits and vegetables is a nightmare. The national system of feeder roads is still underdeveloped, so most crops are dragged from the fields to road heads behind tractors, by donkey, or by hand. Even at the road head, long delays are common before trucks arrive. Manual handling is the norm and techniques are rudimentary; sacks of tomatoes are likely to be treated like sacks of potatoes. Packaging does not help; fruit is crammed into stick crates and burlap bags. Crops for domestic markets are not graded, and the handful of grading facilities that exist can examine only a fraction of the export crops. Refrigeration is a rare luxury. (Tomato growers have found that their crops rot even in the few available refrigerated trucks, since the trucks have no humidity control.) Nor do problems end when crops reach national ports or airports. Scheduling problems and delays at customs and quarantine stations create additional delays.[60]

These delays and rough handling wreak havoc with produce. According to one detailed study, half of the tomato crop and a quarter of the potato and grape crops are either lost or badly damaged before they reach urban markets.[61] Perhaps 35 percent of all vegetables spoil during shipment.[62] The losses for export crops are even higher, both because their journey is longer and because damaged goods which might be acceptable on Egyptian markets have to be culled from export shipments. The damage endured by Egyptian oranges on their way to export, for example, makes them totally unsuitable for European consumers and results in their prices being discounted even in the less fussy markets of the Arab Gulf states.[63] A 1990 conference of Arab agronomists estimated that Egypt loses almost £E 1 billion worth of fruits and vegetables each year because of poor transport and handling techniques.[64] They recommended that Egypt (and other Arab countries) could reasonably try to reduce their rate of post-harvest losses to 20 percent of each crop.

Deficiencies in transportation and storage inhibit Egypt's domestic trade in fruits and vegetables by fostering rot and damage. But the cost is even higher in export trade because of the sensitivity to timeliness in produce deliveries. If Egypt can deliver asparagus to Germany before the Cypriot and Spanish crops arrive, it can make a fortune. If Egypt's crop arrives later than its competitors, there may be no buyers at all.

The problem of timeliness is compounded by the operation of tariff barriers. Most European states offer low out-of-season tariff rates that permit third countries to export produce when local supplies are minimal. For example, the EC encourages imports of potatoes from March to June. During these months Egyptian potato exports compete with crops from Cyprus, Spain, Malta, Italy, and Israel. If Egypt could deliver potatoes before Spain, whose crop is not available until the middle of April, Cairo would win a much bigger market share. This would also lower the tariff cost to Egypt since European duties on potatoes rise from 9 percent at the end of March to 15 percent on the first of April.[65]

But getting crops to market on time requires a complex system of collaboration among farmers, distributors, and importers. The irregular performance of the potato crop (which, strange as it sounds, is Egypt's most valuable vegetable export) illustrates how many things can go wrong.[66] Egypt grows a special variety of potato (King Edward) for export and must import the seed from England. But in 1986 the mission from the Association of Potato Producers that was supposed to procure seed was delayed in London for more than a month. (According to some farmers the delegates were having such a good time abroad they just forgot themselves.) When the seed arrived at Alexandria, port congestion delayed its shipment for another month. As a result 8,000 feddans that had been prepared for potatoes lay fallow and there was no winter export crop.[67]

The Egyptian state could go a long way toward alleviating these problems by investing in transportation. On paper, Egypt looks like an easy country for which to develop a national transportation system. The population is concentrated along a single axis, within the narrow confines and gentle slope of the Nile Valley. Yet in practice, Egypt's transportation services have decayed over the last twenty years for lack of government investment.[68]

Many of Egypt's bulk crops (cereals, for example) could be moved by river barge. But domestic shipping has stagnated because the existing river ports are commonly crude wharves, lacking modern loading facilities (even the newest river port, built by the government at Aswan, can handle only 100,000 tons of cargo a year). Many of the Nile's navigation channels need to be dredged and marked with buoys and lights. Forty-two percent of Egypt's steamers are twenty or more years old; they work only an average of three months a year because of poor maintenance, delays in repairs, and inadequate ports.[69]

The railroad system is in no better shape. Until 1979, after a major accident provoked a budget increase, the Egyptian Railroad Authority was literally starved for funds. Government price regulations, designed to keep fares low for passengers and shippers, forced the authority to accept increasing annual losses. It was unable to fund even the most routine maintenance. A third of the operating track was long overdue for replacement; 40 percent of passenger and freight cars were over thirty years old and were in poor shape.[70]

As a result, more and more shippers turned to trucks and highways to carry their crops. Freight traffic on the railways declined from more than 11 million tons a year to only 5 million tons in 1979; and although the absolute volume carried by train began to slowly recover thereafter, highways carried a growing share of the transport burden. Yet only half of Egypt's 26,000 kilometers of road are paved.[71] Traffic control systems are woefully inadequate. The competition for space between speeding trucks and crawling donkey carts on the unlit Delta highway between Cairo and Alexandria makes it one of the most dangerous roads in the world. Under the best of circumstances, road transport in Egypt costs up to 65 percent more than rail shipping.[72]

A handful of agricultural capitalists do have the funds to buy the trucks necessary to carry their crops to port. But since their transport costs are high, they can only afford to ship the highest-value crops, and in relatively small volumes. And the bulk of Egypt's fruit and vegetable producers, who are not agrarian capitalists but capital-poor peasants, cannot afford to enter the export market at all. If horticultural exports are to be more than a marginal activity, if they are to make a contribution to the national economy as envisaged by the Davis strategy, the state will have to get the ball rolling by heavy investment in transportation and handling facilities.

Expanded public investment in transportation could have a salutary effect on Egypt's horticultural (and other) exports. By lowering transportation costs and improving the timeliness of crop deliveries, it would free capital that private firms might then invest in other facilities necessary for export agriculture. Private firms might be able to absorb the costs of experimenting with new seeds and cultivation techniques necessary to be competitive in foreign markets. (In practice, cultivators rely heavily on the state agricultural extension service to absorb the costs of these experiments.) They might be able to invest collectively in new processing facilities, and to work out their own rules about quality control and grading crops. (Health and quality standards are critical in export horticulture. Europeans refuse to import many kinds of Egyptian produce because of the high levels of pesticides used in its cultivation.)[73] But they cannot even begin to raise the kinds of funds necessary to significantly lower transportation costs. That, Egyptian growers agree, must be left to the state.

With a pooling of public and private investment, Egypt might be able to construct the complex network of mechanized loading docks, refrigerated storage units, and sanitary processing facilities necessary to produce fruits and vegetables that are salable on international markets. Even this investment, however, will not assure the success of export horticulture. Winning export markets, in practice, requires as much political influence as economic savvy. Here, too, Egyptian exporters think that the state will have to play a leading role.

A German merchant, addressing a conference of Egyptian exporters, insisted that the key to success in European markets was to "present the right product to the right consumer for the right price at the right place and time."[74] Unfortunately, these are only necessary, not sufficient, conditions for successful marketing of Egyptian produce in the West. European agricultural markets are heavily protected by the European Community's common agricultural policy (CAP). The CAP, in operation since 1967, consists of an ever-expanding body of regulations, tariffs, and subsidies designed to stabilize agricultural prices while promoting trade between members of the Community. Members agree on a basic price at which they think specific agricultural commodities should trade. To defend this price, the Community subsidizes a series of storage, processing, and export programs that absorb any surplus supply that threatens to depress prices.[75]

It is precisely the stable and relatively high prices created by these programs that make the Community so alluring as a market for Egypt and other countries outside the Community. But to prevent third countries from rushing into European markets and edging out local producers, the CAP also includes an array of minimum import prices, ad valorem tariffs, and countervailing duties. These barriers vary seasonally, ensuring protection for Community producers while limiting the damage to consumers.[76]

Egypt's problem in penetrating the CAP has been compounded by competition with its neighbors. Israel, Turkey, Morocco, and other southern Mediterranean states produce the same crops that Egypt hoped to export. The problem of competition mushroomed in the mid-1980s when Greece, Spain, and Portugal joined the European Community.[77] The entry of these states increases the Community's volume of agricultural production by 24 percent, its cultivated area by 49 percent, and the number of its farms by 57 percent. (Spain supplied most of this increase.) But the Community's demand for agricultural products did not increase proportionally; the average per capita income in Spain was only half that of the rest of the Community. Spain's addition to the Community is expected to drastically reduce Community imports from southern Mediterranean countries, including Egypt.[78]

The EC does allow certain exceptions to CAP restrictions, and Egypt already enjoys a moderate reduction of tariffs. If it is able to establish an industry, it might be able to press for improved entry terms as a political favor. Europe (especially France) is not insensitive to the need to keep Egypt stable as part of its relations with the Arab world. Members of the Community fully understand that success in export horticulture is as much a matter of politics as economics.[79]

The European Community has signed a variety of preferential agreements, including tariff reductions, with Third World countries. The most important of these, the Lomé Convention, gives tariff concessions for horticultural products to sixty-four African, Caribbean, and Pacific countries. Countries covered by the convention can supply potatoes, pears, beans, sweet peppers, eggplant, and zucchini in unlimited amounts. Tomatoes, onions, carrots, and asparagus are subject to volume and season controls. Certain countries, notably

Morocco, have been able to negotiate bilateral or multilateral accords that make it relatively easy for their produce to enter European markets.

Egypt is party to a number of similar agreements. It has a bilateral agreement governing potatoes with England, which takes most of its export crop.[80] It is covered by the Community's multilateral agricultural trade agreement with Mashreq (eastern Arab) states. The 1977 cooperation agreement between Egypt and the EC gave Egypt exemptions from certain tariffs, primarily on metal products, vegetables, leather goods, and fish.[81] Even taken together, however, these concords do not give Egypt anything like the access enjoyed by Morocco.[82] Moroccan citrus fruits have duties reduced by 80 percent, Egyptian ones only by 40–60 percent.[83]

The Davis strategy simply will not work unless Egypt can negotiate better trade terms with the European Community. Cairo's exporters do not dream that this is something they could win by themselves. Their fondest hope has been that the government would open up foreign markets on their behalf. (Some, in fact, have urged their government to imitate Israel's extensive and efficient network of overseas marketing contacts.) But the Cairo regime, although sympathetic to their pleas, has not been well positioned to respond. Mubarak lacks any real leverage in his negotiations with European leaders and needs to conserve what little influence he has for more pressing tasks like seeking debt relief or winning additional cash aid.[84]

There is still some hope that Egyptian exporters may win access to European markets by riding the coattails of more powerful governments than their own. Egypt is not the only country seeking to lower Europe's agricultural trade barriers. The United States, the largest agricultural exporter in the world, has been pressing the Community for freer trade policies. Throughout the Uruguay Round of the General Agreement on Tariffs and Trade (GATT) the Americans urged the Europeans to reform and even threatened a trade war if they did not. If the developed countries agree upon a formula for lifting tariffs on horticultural products, their imports could grow by 6–9 percent (between $570 million and $850 million). Removing nontariff barriers would stimulate trade even more, expanding imports by 24–36 percent ($2–3 billion).[85] It seems probable that Europe will open its markets eventually, although all the Community's proposals so far have envisaged only a slow and limited reduction of trade restrictions.[86]

There is still a chance that the Egyptian state might play some role in opening horticultural markets for its exporters, but not in Europe. In some of the Arab Gulf states consumers will pay high prices for fruits and vegetables. These markets are not particularly large, but they are profitable and culturally accessible to Egyptian entrepreneurs.[87] Egyptians have not had much success penetrating these markets in part because the quality of their exports falls below that demanded in the Gulf. This could be corrected through new investment in Egypt's processing and transport facilities.

A second reason that horticultural exports have not prospered in the Gulf is that countries like Saudi Arabia share Egypt's obsession with food security (after the Arab oil embargo of 1973 they feared the industrialized nations might retaliate with a food embargo). They have offered local farmers lavish subsidies which successfully stimulated production. Saudi Arabia, for example, is now a net exporter of wheat. These subsidies also enabled local farmers to sell their vegetables at prices much lower than those of any competing imports. The Egyptian government, particularly in the wake of Iraq's invasion of Kuwait, has much more leverage in the Gulf than in Europe. It is just plausible that it might persuade the Saudi government to cut back its own farm subsidies, or to offer Egyptian exporters special trade concessions.

This window of opportunity, however, is not large enough to sustain the promise of the Davis strategy. Even with full government support, the income from Egyptian horticultural exports will remain dramatically smaller than the payments for the country's cereal imports. This does not mean that the government will not remain wedded to the program. Even though it is apparent that investment in this area will make only a small contribution to national economic development, fruit and vegetable exporters may have enough political clout to sustain it.

Moreover, Egyptians may decide that government investment in food processing and transportation facilities is a genuine priority for domestic development. Such facilities could raise profits even among capital-poor farmers who stand little chance of breaking into export markets. They would also lower produce prices in urban markets, thereby raising the standard of living and slowing the rise of wages. Some of these facilities will be needed in any case to reduce the waste common in such mainstream crops as wheat, cotton, and rice.

Most of the Western advisers who favor slashing Egypt's state budget would not mind if investments in transportation and other infrastructure survived the cuts. As David Stockman himself put it, "We are interested in curtailing weak claims rather than weak clients."[88] In many cases, however, Egyptians and their Western advisers do not agree about which claims are weak and which are strong.

Market Failures in Agriculture

Agriculture possesses special characteristics that may make state intervention more alluring than in other branches of production. On the one hand, agriculture is more volatile than many sectors of the economy. The weather, insect infestations, and a host of other organic vagaries conspire to stimulate crops one year and devastate them the next. These vicissitudes are compounded by the operations of the global economy. There are many more countries growing rice than manufacturing machine tools, so the price of Egyptian rice can vary not only in response to crop conditions in the United States and Japan, but in Thailand, India, Iraq, and Mexico. Moreover, there are more economies producing competing goods, so that sudden changes in international production and stocks are commonplace. Sudden, unpredictable surges and collapses of crop prices are normal conditions in agriculture.[89]

On the other hand, agriculturalists are more poorly positioned to respond to these vicissitudes than their counterparts in industry or trade. They have no control over the weather; the only thing that may help them adjust to changes in the availability of rain or sunlight is a religious sense of resignation. In countries like Egypt, the volume of available water and land is essentially fixed in the short term; it can be enhanced in the long term only through extremely expensive and time-consuming work on irrigation and reclamation projects. Even changing the crop choices is not much help in adjusting to short-term changes of demand and price. Once a wheat crop is in the ground, the land is tied up for at least six months; farmers cannot "unplant" it and switch to an alternative crop that would fetch a fairer price. In fact, a single cropping decision may tie up the land for years.

When an Egyptian farmer plants cotton, it occupies the fields for a full eight months. Even after this crop is harvested it restricts the options for succeeding plantings, because cotton drains nitrogen from the soil. So a cotton planting is commonly succeeded by a crop of *birsim* or beans which replace the soil's nitrogen. Then, to allow time for other soil nutrients to be replenished, the field must be left fallow for a season. This cycle of crop rotations means that a farmer can decide whether or not to grow another crop of cotton only once every two or three years. Other crops are even more restrictive; once a fruit orchard is planted, it can take seven years to reach maturity. The natural requirements of agriculture leave no opportunities for midyear corrections. If prices have not been anticipated correctly, or if the weather does not cooperate, several years of labor and investment can evaporate overnight.

These factors make agriculture an exceptionally risky and volatile business. A profitable matching of supply with demand is very hard to achieve. All too often, it turns out that farmers have planted insufficient or excessive quantities of some crop. In the public imagination, shortage seems the more pressing problem. If farmers lose too much of their crop to drought or pests, they may go broke even while consumers are forced to pay ludicrous prices for the surviving produce. But overproduction is also a menace to farmers. If they plant too much of some crop, its price may be driven below the level at which they recoup the cost of their investment in it. Viewed from the farm, either glut or dearth may be disastrous.[90]

These vicissitudes of the agricultural product cycle affect farmers seeking profits, consumers concerned about supply, businessmen hoping for predictable prices, and state officials concerned about food security. They trigger a public quest for ways to stabilize the product cycle, to minimize its volatility and the risks that entails. This is as true of China or the United States as it is of Egypt.

Most countries have devised food security programs to cope with dearth, stockpiling crops during good years to hedge against the bad. Sometimes these programs are supplemented by private crop insurance plans which reimburse farmers for their losses. Many also enforce production controls to head off glut and support prices. Land retirement programs, which pay farmers not to plant certain crops, and formal price controls are two of the most common means to this end. These programs can often be complementary: by buying up food during years of glut, states can both stabilize prices and accumulate a reserve against years of dearth.

Such schemes to protect farmers from the risks of environmental change are commonly interwoven with programs to protect them from economic competition. For example, many developed countries consider sugar, rice, and other basic foodstuffs to be strategic crops and restrict their import through high tariffs, quotas, or health regulations to protect domestic sources of supply. The restrictions that developed countries impose on tea, coffee, and tropical crops (like bananas, litchi nuts, jute, chestnuts, and spices) cost developing countries $26 billion each year in trade.[91] Moreover, wealthier countries can afford to promote the competitiveness of their farmers in international markets through export subsidies on wheat, beef, poultry, and dairy products. In 1988, for example, the United States planned to use both its Food for Peace program and a $2.5 billion export enhancement program to pry open foreign markets. In the same year, the European Community spent $26 billion on export subsidies.[92]

In 1987 the distorting and wasteful effects of these agricultural policies emerged as the central topic in the Uruguay Round of GATT talks. Estimates suggested that Western taxpayers alone paid $245 billion a year for agricultural subsidies.[93] In Japan, government subsidies amounted to 74 percent of producer income for sugar, 99 percent for wheat, and 100 percent for dairy products.[94] Sixty to eighty percent of the budget of the European Community went to support its common agricultural policy, a lavish network of subsidies and price supports which kept prices for corn, soybeans, and other key crops in Europe more than double those on international markets.[95] Even the United States, which prided itself as the home of free enterprise and was quick to criticize state intervention in other societies, supported its farmers through elaborate programs of acreage reduction, advance crop loans, conservation reserve, deficiency payments, export enhancements, Public Law 480 foreign aid, payments in kind, and whole-herd buyouts. In 1986 American price support programs cost roughly $26 billion, more than Egypt's entire gross domestic product (estimated at £E 38 billion, or about $19 billion) for the same year.[96]

The GATT negotiations on reducing the impediments to international trade proved arduous and confrontational. Yet there was widespread agreement that such impediments were both expensive and counterproductive, so high hope remained that a compromise solution was possible. Talks were urged on by the so-called Cairns Group, a dozen states (led by Australia, New Zealand, Brazil, and Mexico) that had already proved they could compete in global agriculture without recourse to export subsidies.[97] However, even most of the countries in the Cairns Group maintained some domestic subsidies, stockpiles, or price supports to cope with the vicissitudes of the agricultural product cycle. Neoclassical economists, who were critical of farm support programs, had difficulty proposing market mechanisms that would mitigate natural price volatility.[98] If a society wishes to ensure both that farmers receive a return equal to their investment in production and that consumers are able to buy food for reasonably stable prices, state intervention appears almost inevitable.

Egyptians discovered this fact decades ago. They resorted to state intervention to promote price stability and food security long before the military coup of 1952. This has been particularly evident in government regulation of cotton that has dominated Egyptian agriculture for the past hundred years. In the nineteenth century, Egypt was the second largest exporter of cotton (after the United States) and its economy was virtually a cotton monoculture. Until the 1970s, when it was eclipsed by oil, cotton supplied the vast majority of Egypt's hard currency revenues; Egyptians nicknamed this crop "white gold." While Egypt's share of the world market has declined, cotton remains a very important crop. It still accounts for 25 percent of the value of all Egypt's field crops. Cottonseed oil supplies 90 percent of Egyptian domestic vegetable oil production. In 1988, a year when Egyptian cotton production was down by 30 percent, cotton exports were still estimated to be worth $340 million.[99] Not only is cotton a key source of hard currency revenues, it plays a critical role in local industry. Egyptian textile plants account for 36.6 percent of all manufacturing production, employ 76.8 percent of all industrial labor, and realize 43.5 percent of all foreign currency earned by manufactures.[100]

Cotton has always been a volatile crop (see table 7-2). During the decade beginning in 1974, the average price that Egyptian cotton fetched on the world market vacillated between $2,000 and $3,000 a ton. Cairo's cotton export revenues, in turn, wobbled between $400 million and over $700 million. A host of factors affected these figures. The rise in oil prices after 1973 made synthetic fibers more expensive, thus increasing the market for natural cotton. The American decision to begin a massive export of cotton to China then reduced the market. Drought, changes in world acreage, stockpiling, textile trade agreements, and myriad other forces also pressed prices up and down.[101]

Egyptian farmers have long searched for a way to cope with this

Table 7-2. **Fluctuation of Cotton Exports, 1974–83**

Year	Volume (thousands of metric tons)	Value (millions of dollars)	Average price (dollars per metric ton)
1974	241.90	720.10	2,976.85
1975	202.50	523.90	2,587.16
1976	180.70	407.40	2,254.57
1977	158.70	479.20	3,019.53
1978	153.90	354.80	2,305.39
1979	161.00	396.80	2,464.60
1980	179.60	443.40	2,468.82
1981	193.00	477.30	2,473.06
1982	209.80	419.40	1,999.05
1983	208.80	441.50	2,114.45

Source: George R. Gardner and John B. Parker, *Agricultural Statistics of Egypt, 1970–84* (U.S. Department of Agriculture, 1985), pp. 81–82.

volatility. As early as 1916 the Egyptian government proscribed any import of cotton, thereby turning the domestic textile industry into a captive market for farmers.[102] In 1921 large landowners banded together and formed the General Agricultural Syndicate to lobby the state to buy cotton to support prices when the market fell.[103] They finally attained this dream during World War II. In 1940 all activities of the Cotton Futures Market were suspended (activity only resumed briefly after 1948.)[104] In 1941, fear that the wartime scarcity of shipping would constrict Egyptian wheat imports led the government to decree a reduction of cotton acreage and encourage additional wheat planting. At the same time the British set up a Government Cotton Buying Commission which eagerly bought the entire Egyptian crop at premium prices. The commission's price remained the effective floor price for Egyptian cotton. After the war Cairo set up its own Cotton Commission to continue this function. The commission regularly bought large quantities at fixed prices and stored its cotton in anticipation of price increases. As a result, the Egyptian government built up a large buffer stock of cotton between 1953 and 1961.[105]

The ability of the Egyptian government to regulate prices reached its apogee, of course, after 1961 when it nationalized all trade in cotton. It consolidated all private cotton export companies into six public sector firms, put control over all gins under another five agencies, and placed all these institutions under the direction of an overarching General Authority for the Cotton Sector.[106] The government not only fixed the farmgate and border price of cotton, but in 1966 it also began to decree how much acreage farmers must devote to this crop.

Over the years, state intervention radically altered the character of cotton production. After the coup of 1952 the General Agricultural Syndicate was abolished. The landed magnates who had dominated cotton production were shattered by the land reform. Yet the government's commitment to the policy of price stabilization remained undiminished. This was partly because the policy had simply been institutionalized, had become part of the pattern of bureaucratic behavior. But the new regime also promoted price stability both to help protect the small peasants, who now produced most of Egypt's cotton, and to stabilize the input price of cotton available to the textile industry, which it had also nationalized.

Of course, price stability was not the only objective that the state sought through its nationalization of cotton production. The decrees of 1961 had been part of a political campaign against the power of the visible feudalist elite and the invisible commercial middlemen who contested the military regime's authority. At the same time, control over the cotton crop must have seemed an easy means to enhance the government's power of taxation. Cotton export was not only a large source of potential revenue, it was also unusually easy to supervise. Cotton is entirely a cash crop (peasants cannot just consume it whenever they feel prices are too low); and the large gins needed to prepare cotton for the market are easily supervised by the state.

State intervention served a variety of purposes, but price stabilization remained the government's overriding priority. In the early 1960s the government actually paid the farmers more than the export price for cotton. The implicit tax on cotton only made a net contribution to the general budget during a brief period in the late 1960s and early 1970s. Since 1974 most of the revenue the government has extracted from cotton producers through controlled prices has been remitted to cotton consumers in the form of subsidized domestic textiles. On numerous occasions, the government's efforts to keep the cotton prices stable have taken precedence over the fiscal objectives of the Cotton Authority.[107]

The Egyptian experience is not unusual. Stabilization and taxation incentives have prompted state intervention in cotton production in most countries. Less than 8 percent of world cotton production is affected solely by market forces. Most countries employ fixed whole-saler prices, fixed producer prices, or both.[108] Yet in Egypt there is another, more unusual, motive for intervention—the prospect of monopoly profits.

Since 1985 Egypt has provided only about 2 percent of the world's annual cotton trade. However, it has been supplying around 45 percent of the world's trade in extra-long staple cotton. Extra-long staple cotton (whose fibers are 1.29 inches or longer) is prized because the longer the staple, the finer and stronger the yarn it yields. Thus, Egypt's exports of ELS cotton earn a premium in the export market. In 1984 when the average price of a ton of cotton was $1,780, Egypt's ELS was earning $3,610.[109] Egypt is ideally situated to exploit this market. Although a handful of other countries (the United States, India, China, and Peru) grow small ELS crops, only the Sudan exports ELS in volumes comparable to Egypt—and Cairo has long coordinated its cotton policy with Khartoum. Between them, Egypt and Sudan account for 88 percent of international trade in ELS cotton; they enjoy a virtual monopoly.[110]

Egyptians must be careful, however, how they manage this monopoly. Because of its unusual qualities, the price of ELS cotton can rise considerably before consumers will choose to switch to alternatives like short-staple or synthetic fibers. The prospect of high prices (other things being equal) encourages farmers to plant large volumes of cotton. But the price of ELS is extremely sensitive to supply, so if they grow too much ELS, creating supply in excess of demand, the crop's price collapses. In such a monopoly situation, Egyptian farmers cannot rely on the market to coordinate how much they produce. To ensure that they produce just enough to maximize their revenues, they rely on the state to carefully gauge the world demand for ELS cotton and regulate production accordingly.[111]

The prospect of an ELS price collapse shadowed Egypt in the late 1970s. In 1977 higher domestic producer prices and dissemination of new seed varieties triggered sharp increases of Egyptian cotton production. Over the next five years, cotton yields reached record levels, with annual increases in the range of 13 percent. The Egyptian Cotton Authority struggled to keep this surplus production from sparking a fall of prices. Initially they sought to do this by marketing only as much cotton as was compatible with maximum prices and

Figure 7-1. Cotton Performance, 1975–86

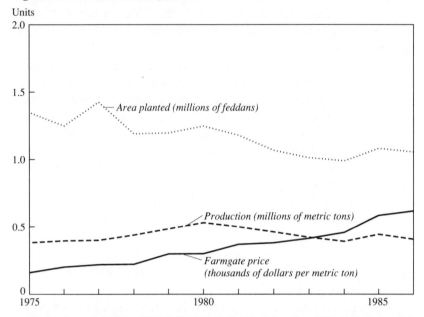

Units

Sources: George R. Gardner and John B. Parker, *Agricultural Statistics of Egypt, 1970–84* (Washington: U.S. Department of Agriculture, 1985), pp. 37–38; Jean-Jacques Dethier, *Trade, Exchange Rate, and Agricultural Pricing Policies in Egypt* vol. 2 (Washington: World Bank, 1989), p. 53; and USDA (U.S. Department of Agriculture) Foreign Agricultural Service, *Annual Situation Report: Egypt, 1986* and *1988*.

withholding the rest. As a result, between 1978 and 1981 Egypt's surplus stock of cotton rose from 36,000 to 183,000 metric tons. By 1981 the excess stock was as large as annual export sales.[112]

As stockpiles swelled, Egyptian officials agreed that they needed to switch strategies. They decided to try to reduce the volume of cotton produced by lowering the price the government paid for the crop. A debate erupted over how much of a cut was desirable; some wanted to reduce the $1.10 price to $1.00, others to $0.80. In the end, the median figure of $0.90 was adopted, which meant a resulting 25 percent drop in Egyptian prices.[113] It was hoped that this price cut would liquidate both the current large crop and the preceding year's stocks. But sales fell far short of expectations, rising only 10 percent.

Still, during the 1980s farmers planted smaller crops of cotton (figure 7-1). In fact, between 1980 and 1990 Egyptian cotton production declined 44 percent, from 2.4 million bales to 1.4 million bales.[114] At the same time, world demand for cotton had been rising. Global stockpiles of cotton, including Egypt's, were drawn down. In 1989–90 they dropped to 33 percent of world consumption, the first time they had dropped under 35 percent since World War II.[115] Egypt was again in a position to command optimal prices for its white gold.

Egyptian cotton production had declined so much, however, that more could have been exported without imperiling prices. Sales opportunities went begging because of insufficient supply. By 1988 the Cotton Authority wanted to stimulate additional production but faced real difficulties in doing so. Although cuts in official prices had encouraged the trend toward smaller plantings, the reduction of cotton acreage was primarily the result of the rising relative prices of alternative crops. As local demand for red meat had expanded during the 1980s, so had the price of *birsim* clover. Egyptian peasants began to plant cotton later in the season so that they could take additional cuttings of *birsim*.[116] After the price of wheat began to rise in 1988, some farmers abandoned cotton entirely and shifted into cereals. Those who could not afford to switch cut their losses by selling state-supplied pesticides on the black market and putting as little labor as possible into their crops.[117]

The problem of relative prices is largely ignored in the AID and World Bank literature on Egypt. The reports of these organizations suggest that low official prices are solely responsible for declining crop acreages and that a return to market prices will solve this problem.[118] It is true that official prices often offer only small incentives, but even under a free market system that offered cultivators a larger share of the border price of cotton, many farmers would have resisted planting more. In 1985 the net return on a feddan of land for a peasant who planted cotton was £E 274; one who cultivated corn, which required "less time and headaches," could earn £E 344.[119] The returns on *birsim* were astronomically higher. In the late 1980s, cotton acreages continued to stagnate despite rising official prices.

State intervention to maximize cotton revenues, obviously, led to certain inefficiencies. Egyptian farmers grew too much cotton in the late 1970s and too little in the late 1980s. The Egyptian Cotton Authority was often left holding the bag; in 1989 it showed losses of £E 40 million.[120] But it is not clear that a pure market system would have been preferable. Market forces might have signaled peasants to adjust their acreages more rapidly but, because of the rigors of the cropping cycle, it also would have saddled them with enormous liabilities during the transition. In the late 1970s peasants would inevitably have lost millions of pounds because they had planted too much, triggering a wave of bankruptcies and hardships for a section of the Egyptian population that was already economically vulnerable. If this had translated into political discontent in rural areas, the urban food riots (and the 1986 revolt of Central Security Forces) might have triggered national political instability.

Cairo's effort to maximize cotton revenues, then, attempts to serve a legitimate public purpose. This does not mean that the system is perfect, or that reform is unnecessary. Some observers note that Egypt's public-sector cotton export companies use a sealed-bid sales system, which probably means foreign sales are underpriced. Others argue that the current tools the government uses to regulate cotton production (price and acreage controls) not only are expensive to administer but constrain producers unnecessarily. They suggest that a national tax on the cotton crop could be constructed so that it would discourage over- and underproduction while freeing farmers to make market-responsive decisions on their own. (For example, under a cotton tax farmers, and not the state, would decide how much of the ELS crop to sell to local textile firms rather than on the international market.)[121]

The Egyptian government is aware of some of these inefficiencies and continues to tinker with the system in hopes of improving it. In 1990, for example, the Cotton Authority offered peasants bonus prices and discounts on fertilizers if they planted and harvested their crops by specified, yield-optimizing dates. This proved an effective means of discouraging the prevailing practice of planting cotton late to take advantage of extra *birsim* cuttings.[122]

What is true of cotton is also true of many other crops. Market mechanisms alone imperfectly match supply and demand in agriculture. Sugar and other crops are subject to problems of overproduction that require acreage regulations very similar to those applied on cotton. In the early 1980s Egyptian farmers, responding to high prices in foreign markets, consistently planted too many strawberries, driving down prices and leading to many bankruptcies.[123] For many different crops, the operation of market forces alone does not seem to promote either private profits or the public interest.

This problem becomes aggravated whenever choices must be made among alternative crops. When farmers plant too much cotton, they may fail to plant enough corn; one crop crowds out another. This has been a major source of Egypt's food security problems (described in chapter 2). In Egypt this problem of crowding becomes particularly acute because crops compete with each other not only for land but for water. Rice, which is usually Egypt's second most valuable export crop (after cotton), is a very thirsty plant. Every feddan planted in rice consumes about 10,000 cubic meters of water.[124] Each year, Egypt draws 55 billion cubic meters of water from its only source, the Nile.[125] About 48 billion cubic meters of this are used in agriculture, about a third of which is devoted to rice.

Starting in 1979, the volume of rain falling on the Nile's drainage basin in Central Africa began to decline. In that year the water level in Egypt's Lake Nasser reservoir behind the Aswan Dam stood at 528 feet. By 1985 it had fallen to a record low of 468 feet.[126] By 1987 the drop in the water level had reduced pressure behind the High Dam, cutting its power production by 20 percent.[127] If this trend had continued for another year or two, Egypt would have faced an agricultural disaster.

Fortunately, the state controls water distribution in Egypt. There have been periodic proposals, from Western advisers, that Egypt privatize or at least "marketize" this service, but they have come to naught.[128] Egypt's irrigation system is too complex and expensive for private businesses to maintain. (Similarly, state control of irrigation is a necessity in the western states of the United States, where organizations like the Los Angeles Department of Water and Power, the Army Corps of Engineers, and the Federal Bureau of Reclamation have long exercised the kinds of power that Westerners associate with oriental despotism.)[129] No private agency has the resources to build massive works like the High Dam. Individual farmers do not even have the capital necessary to drain their plots properly, without which the soil becomes waterlogged and salinization begins to erode crop yields. So the Egyptian government has organized a costly long-term program of drain construction.[130]

In 1987 the Egyptian government scrambled to reduce water consumption. It ordered an 8 percent cut in the area devoted to rice, reducing plantings from 1,150,000 to 900,000 feddans. It mandated a cut of 5–10 percent in the use of water for all irrigation purposes. To reduce the water used to drive the High Dam's generators, it raised electricity prices and arranged periodic brownouts.[131] Happily, in August 1988 the rains returned to Central Africa, flooding the city of

Khartoum and raising the water level in Lake Nasser back to 514 feet.[132] This removed the immediate threat of drought and gave Egypt a respite during which the government launched a series of long-term water conservation measures. The government inaugurated or stepped up programs like laser land-leveling, surge furrow irrigation, requiring farmers to irrigate at night, and recycling agricultural drainage water.[133]

The demand for conservation measures seemed likely to increase in the future. In 1989 the rains were once again 10 percent below average, and Egypt was only able to draw 53 billion cubic meters from the Nile.[134] Hydrologists differed over why Egypt's water sources were drying up, but they agreed about the long-term trend. Some argued that the rising cost of technological conservation measures would eventually force Egyptians to alter their crop choices, to reduce their plantings of thirsty crops like rice, sugarcane, and cotton and switch to less water-hungry plants like wheat and corn.[135] Since the state, rather than the farmer, bears the immediate cost of sustaining irrigation, the government would probably wind up mandating the change in cropping patterns.

This being the case, the current strategy of the Washington development community seems to be misdirected. By seeking to confine the state to providing infrastructure and eliminating all programs that result in market distortions, it is trying to strip Egypt of policies that provide, overall, real economic benefits. The dogma that all price controls are bad needs to be tempered by recognition of important exceptions.

This does not mean that the current pattern of state intervention in Egypt is sacrosanct. The rationale offered to justify many price control programs does not outweigh the harm they do. But even acknowledging that such interventions have some rationale suggests a need to rethink the prevailing dogma. A cost-benefit analysis of specific price interventions is needed to determine which ones, on the whole, are beneficial. Even in cases where a policy's net benefits are positive, Egypt can improve its mode of intervention in a manner that reduces the resulting market distortions. The abolition of acreage controls on cotton and the switch to taxation as a means of adjusting production provide a good example of how state intervention could be made more efficient.

Officials at the IMF and other institutions who have embraced the Stockman strategy are unlikely to teach Egypt how to make state intervention more efficient. They suspect that cost-benefit analyses and policy-by-policy review will play into the hands of special interests who seek to defend policy-enshrined entitlements. They hope that radical, across-the-board budget cuts will remove the element of political discretion and compel a universal constriction of state interventions. Unfortunately, they are wrong.

Land Rent and Property Rights

Faith that budget cuts will fall on "weak claims, not weak clients" is essential to the Stockman strategy. Even the most hardened neoclassical radical concedes that some state services are desirable and that budget cuts should not reduce these but be concentrated on iniquitous, market-distorting interventions. If Third World governments were formed from an alliance of IMF-inspired economists and patriotic military officers, the Stockman strategy might work. The economists, like Platonic philosopher-kings, would decree which budget cuts were in the national economic interest and the officers would machine-gun those groups that objected.

Too often, members of the Washington development community privately speak as if such developmental authoritarianism were the optimal form of government for developing countries. Fortunately or unfortunately, real governments in countries like Egypt are very different. Egyptian economists, even those who embrace neoclassical doctrine, tend to align themselves with specific political factions and interest groups. Egyptian officers remain reluctant to shoot down their compatriots—except when the very survival of the regime is at stake. In Cairo, certainly, where a weak state and crony capitalism prevail, there is not much chance that the Stockman strategy would lead to an economically rational distribution of budget cuts.

The case of cotton provides one example of this. Washington-based economists have accustomed themselves to thinking of price and acreage controls on cotton as a form of cross-subsidization, in which income that might have accrued to farmers is transferred to the government and the public-sector textile industry. As a subsidy, these controls should be affected by budget cuts. Viewed from the perspective of the Egyptian Parliament, however, cotton controls are not a subsidy but a tax; they bring in revenue for the government. As Cairo faces increasing budgetary pressure, its natural instinct may be to increase the revenue generated by cotton controls, not to eliminate the controls.

This may partly account for the fact that, despite AID pressure to liberalize price controls which has resulted in higher farmgate prices for cotton, the Egyptian government has stiffly resisted eliminating them.

Again, what is true of cotton is true of many other state interventions. Price controls, tariffs, and discriminatory taxes can be understood as de facto subsidies to certain groups, but when viewed from the perspective of the budget they are income, not outlays. Pressure on the budget not only does nothing to enhance the case for eliminating these controls, it may actually encourage their extension. Ironically, the Stockman strategy may make the pattern of state intervention less, rather than more, economically rational. This is true not only of those state interventions that do not require budgetary appropriations. Even in the case of genuine subsidies, the extant pattern of politics in Egypt is likely to make the distribution of budget cuts economically suboptimal. Politics, not neoclassical economic wisdom, will determine where the budget-cutting axe will fall.

One of the terrible facts about political life is that the amount of organized support a policy receives is often inversely proportional to the public good it accomplishes. Iniquitous rents, monopolies, and subsidies often enjoy the support of well-organized minorities who expect to benefit from them. In contrast, precisely because genuine collective goods, like education or roads, benefit so many people it is often unclear who should be responsible for lobbying for them. Even in industrialized societies with relatively open political systems, this means that policy tends to reflect the distribution of power rather than social need.[136] And in countries like Egypt, where the distribution of power is highly inequitable and only the most privileged elements of society can afford to support lobbies, the gap between political support for a policy and its public welfare consequences yawns even wider.

Contrary to the dreams of Stockman strategists, in Cairo strong clients tend to crowd out strong causes. The long debate over whether or how to reform the agricultural rent control law illuminates this point. In the 1980s that debate emerged as one of the most contentious issues in Egyptian politics. Parliament deadlocked over the question. The issue had been raised by parties purporting to represent landowners, who claimed that the existing law kept rental revenues unfairly low, diminishing profits and discouraging investment. They argued for revising the law to raise or decontrol rents, and contemplated offering renters some monetary compensation for their diminished rights. Other parties argued against revision, claiming that the existing law guaranteed access to land for millions of economically vulnerable peasants. They proposed that the state should pay to transfer title from lessors to lessees. If either of these contending positions prevailed, the cost to the taxpayer could run into millions of pounds.

Economists working for Washington development agencies tended to view this whole debate with suspicion. They saw rent control as a distortion of prices and, as a matter of principle, inclined to favor its abolition. But they were also dubious about the need to indemnify whichever party suffered from resolution of the rent law debate. They saw such compensation as a form of entitlement, a rent or bribe paid in exchange for political quiescence. Some, particularly those who had never studied Egypt in detail, thought the Stockman strategy might help to resolve the issue by ruling out the possibility of indemnities and forcing Egyptians to frame the issue in terms of its economic merits alone.

But those who were familiar with the background of the question understood that in Egypt the debate over rent control was not about prices, it was about property. It reflected a long-standing ambiguity about who really owned land. Did it belong to those who cultivated it or to those who happened to have registered title with the state?

To Westerners, who live in societies where property rights have been well defined for centuries, this may seem to be a peculiar question. But in Egypt, the first law conferring an absolute private right of ownership of land was only issued in 1856. (Before that time, three distinct property systems—village rights, tax-collector rights, and state rights—had operated concurrently.)[137] And in the century and a half since this law was issued, land rights have still not fully congealed. Part of the problem is political. Peasants often resisted registering their title with the state in the (well-founded) belief that such registration would lay them open to military and labor conscription. More recently, wealthier farmers have resisted land registration in order to evade taxes and land reform.[138]

The convolutions of the agrarian economy have compounded the problem. Volatile agricultural prices lead to periods of bust in which thousands of cultivators are driven into debt or default. At the edge of bankruptcy, the victims of these cycles are forced to sell their lands to more fortunate neighbors. If these cycles afflicted only a small fraction of the rural community, they might be accepted as a Darwinian way of transferring land from inefficient cultivators to the fittest farmers. But the vagaries of the agricultural product cycle often compel huge blocs of the rural community to face bankruptcy at the same time. If the rains do not come or if cotton prices fall for several years, entire villages, sometimes entire classes, share in the disaster.[139]

When the livelihood of masses of people is at stake, their anger and anxiety become a political force. State intervention is a common result. In this century, misery in the countryside has forced the Egyptian state to contemplate important changes in property relations three times.[140] In the 1930s, high debt burdens aggravated by an agricultural depression threatened the owners of many large estates with bankruptcy. The government intervened to save this class, expanding the flow of agricultural credit and altering the mortgage law to make foreclosure more difficult.[141] After World War II, declining rural incomes and spreading violence in the villages compelled the government to attend to the plight of smaller peasants, resulting in the agrarian reform of 1952. The legacy of land distribution, refracted by a labor shortage in the late 1970s, set the stage for the third great debate about redistributing property, rent law reform.

During the land reforms of the 1950s and 1960s, the Egyptian state confiscated 900,000 feddans of farmland and redistributed them to 318,000 families.[142] While this was a major blow to owners, not enough land was involved to begin to assuage the demands of millions of landless peasants. In an effort to address the needs of poor villagers, Nasser's regime enacted a series of rent laws that beefed up tenant rights. In 1952 it defined the maximum annual rent that could be levied as seven times the value of the land tax assessed for a given plot. In 1963 it issued Law 17, which declared that tenants had the right to remain on any plot they were actually farming, even if their rent was in arrears. Law 52 of 1966 added further details about the resolution of rent disputes. It prohibited owners from evicting tenants for any reason other than voluntary default on their obligations. It redefined sharecropping contracts so that the owner was forced to share the costs of harvest and preparation, previously borne by the tenants. In effect, it made all long-term (longer than one year) rent contracts permanent and inheritable. To enforce these rights, a supplementary law created the committees for the settlement of agricultural disputes, special rural courts for adjudicating tenancy disputes.[143]

In speech after speech, Nasser told poor peasants that they were as valuable citizens as any other Egyptians. His rhetoric encouraged tenants to become more assertive. The police were increasingly reluctant to enforce the rights of absentee owners. The powers conferred by (and revenue derived from) title to a piece of rented land steadily declined. Taken together, the new renters' rights decrees effectively transferred control of the land to tenants. Since rent contracts could be inherited by children of the original tenant, the transfer seemed to be permanent. Unlike an actual confiscation, these measures were self-administering and required very little action from Cairo. In most cases peasants could defend their own rights, with marginal help from village councils. Moreover, since no transfer of title was involved, the government did not have to dip into its coffers to compensate the dispossessed title holders.

As an aspect of land reform, rent control affected many more people than redistribution. In 1952 some 60 percent of Egypt's cultivated area was under rent and the vast majority of peasants rented all or some of their land.[144] Rent control was thus the most popular and arguably the most important element of the entire land reform program. Years after its implementation, Yusuf Wali, who believed that the rent control laws were outdated, still conceded that "the Law of the Owner and the Renter, in spite of its negative aspects, led to stability in political conditions for a long period."[145]

When rent controls were first instituted in the 1960s they did not provoke major complaint. Landless peasants who had to rent land were pleased; so, more surprisingly, were rich peasants (those cultivating between five and ten feddans).[146] Rich peasants rented more land than any other group; their total holdings (owned and leased) were twice as large as the area they owned outright.[147] Since they avoided cultivating low-profit, state-regulated crops like cotton and specialized in the production of high-value produce, they could make very profitable use of the extra land. The land they rented came mostly from land-poor peasants (who farmed less than three feddans), particularly from those with dwarf holdings of one feddan or less.[148] Land-poor peasants controlled plots too small to support a family by themselves, so they often chose to rent out their lands and live on what they earned from a combination of rent and wages as agricultural workers.

By the early 1970s, however, a new pattern of land distribution had begun to evolve which almost completely reversed earlier conditions.

In 1961 peasant smallholders (farming five feddans or less) owned or leased 38 percent of agricultural land. By 1975 they controlled 66 percent of the total registered area. Smallholders acquired this additional area by leasing the lands of richer farmers. According to one study, between 1961 and 1977 the land area controlled by rich peasants decreased from 1,100,000 to 785,000 feddans. The holdings of the largest landowners, who owned or leased ten feddans or more, dropped from 44 percent to 20 percent of the total registered land area.[149] This transfer permitted smallholders to continue farming plots of roughly the same size throughout this period, even though their numbers had expanded dramatically while the total area available for farming remained virtually constant.[150] The surrender of land by rich peasants and wealthy farmers was so dramatic, and in such stark contrast to the trend of the preceding seventy years, that some leading scholars were inclined to dismiss it as a glitch in the statistics.[151]

Studies at the village level, however, documented the mechanisms of this transfer. In the 1970s villagers (particularly landless peasants) began to migrate abroad in large numbers, driving wages up and making it more costly for owners of larger farms to hire the labor needed to cultivate their plots. Rich peasants and farmers (holding more than ten feddans) faced a squeeze on profits. But smallholding peasants, who relied on family labor rather than wage hiring, did not face this squeeze since they often had more labor available than land. As smallholders began to enjoy a flow of cash sent home by workers abroad, they began to bid for the surplus lands of rich farmers, steadily driving up prices.[152] This dynamic steadily transferred lands into the hands of smallholding peasants.[153]

This change in the pattern of landholding did not diminish the economic, much less the political, influence of rich farmers and other rural notables. They simply shifted their capital out of land and into other ventures. Some discovered that real estate sales were more profitable than working the land itself. Many invested in agricultural machinery (pumps, tractors, threshers) and derived a handsome income from renting it to other peasants.[154] Some deserted agriculture entirely and shifted their attention to local commercial ventures. The power and privilege of the rich peasants survived, although it was exercised through different instruments.

As rich peasants ceased to be the beneficiaries and became the victims of rent control, their attitudes changed. Increasingly they were irritated by the inequity of the rent control system. Even though crop prices and land values increased throughout the 1970s, the maximum legal rent had not been adjusted to keep pace. In real terms, the income derived from rents declined steadily.[155] Yet as farm incomes rose, rents formed a relatively smaller share of tenant budgets and it seemed that renters ought to be able to pay more. Increasingly there were complaints that typically tenants earned three times what they paid in rent.[156] Owners became eager to either raise rents or reclaim their plots for sale, but the rent law stood in their way.

During Anwar Sadat's rule, owners were increasingly encouraged to air these complaints about rent control.[157] In the early 1970s Sadat even restored title to a number of owners whose lands had been improperly sequestered. The police were again encouraged to protect the rights of owners. In his attempt to build a reliable conservative constituency, Sadat packed the Parliament with rural notables. This parliamentary gentry began to explore various proposals to strengthen the position of landowners.

In 1975 this new Parliament passed Law 67, a fairly bold revision of the rent control law which strengthened the hand of landlords. It adjusted land tax assessments to give owners the ability to raise rents. It also gave the owner the right to petition for cancellation of the rent contract if the renter was repeatedly late in payment. Most important, it canceled the settlement committees, forcing tenants to refer rent disputes to regular provincial courts where they would receive a far less sympathetic hearing.[158] This limited victory appeased landowners temporarily, but within a few years they were clamoring for further changes.

Landlords had a long list of additional revisions they wanted in the rent law. First, they wanted the right to increase rents, so they proposed raising the maximum rent from seven to nearly ten times the value of the land tax. Second, they wanted to give owners of fewer than five feddans the right to terminate rent contracts unilaterally. Third, they wanted the right to expel tenants who were either delinquent in paying rent or refused to switch from traditional to high-value crops. Fourth, they wanted the right to turn land from cash rent to sharecropping.[159] The public was sympathetic to some of these demands. Most Egyptians felt that landowners were entitled to raise rents in proportion to increases in production. As incomes from farming rose in the late 1970s, many felt that renters could afford to pay more. Even some of the luminaries of the left, like Ibrahim Shukri and Mustafa al-Gabali, agreed that "it is absolutely unreasonable that the value of rents should continue for more than thirty years without an increase."[160]

However, the public did not want to see renters evicted or dispossessed. And this was a problem, since to make new rents effective, owners had to be able to expel tenants who refused to pay them. Even many prominent politicians on the right, who favored market determination of rents, understood that any change in the rent law that aggravated rural landlessness would offend public opinion and be socially destabilizing. For example, Sa'd Hagras, the chairman of the parliamentary committee on agriculture and a former deputy of Sayyid Mar'i, urged landowners to drop their demands that the rent law be revised to permit eviction of owners of five feddans or less. Such a revised law would permit evictions on 90 percent of Egypt's cultivated land and would encourage landowners to re-register their plots in smaller fragments so that they could evict their tenants. This revision would transform most renters from permanent and productive cultivators into an angry agricultural proletariat.[161]

Most Egyptians, then, saw the need for a compromise. They wanted a rent control law that would allow owners to raise rents proportionately with increases in production but would not undermine the tenancy rights of renters. All the various proposals advanced by advocates for owners and renters claimed to achieve this compromise, but in practice neither side found it easy to accept the other's definition of a fair and equitable solution. After 1979, landowners' demands for revision of the rent law were voiced in Parliament primarily by delegates of the New Wafd party. Many leading Wafdists had been large landowners before 1952 and remained very hostile to the idea of land reform. The party's program called for giving owners of five feddans or less the right to reassume direct control of their plots after paying their tenants the equivalent of seven times the annual rent. The party wanted the government to facilitate this buyout by ordering banks to extend low-interest loans to qualified landowners.[162] Wafdists sought to portray this proposal as a measure of assistance to the helpless, claiming that the owners of such small plots were mostly widows and poor peasants, who desperately needed the power to increase their rents, although no one presented any statistics to prove this assertion.[163]

Inside Parliament the Wafd was opposed by the Tagammu' party, which attempted to speak on behalf of renters. Scholars affiliated with the party developed an elaborate critique of landowner complaints. They noted that although renters paid a smaller share of their income in rents, they had to pay a growing share in costs of production, particularly in pesticide and fertilizer prices. They argued that landowners had succeeded in raising rents, either in direct violation of the law or through semi-legal mechanisms like short-term contracts on which rent controls did not apply.[164] The Tagammu' party program espoused a solution to the rent problem that totally inverted the recommendations of the Wafd. It wanted to create a special state fund that would advance capital (at interest rates of 2–5 percent) to peasants so that they could buy full title to their plots from absentee owners.[165] These buyouts would immediately give owners the full market value of their lands, although repayment of the state's loans would be stretched out over thirty years.[166]

This recommendation, interestingly, was echoed in the proposal of an American expert on land reform, Roy Prosterman.[167] He argued that Egyptian landlords, who collected a small fixed rent, often lived far from the land, and had little experience or authority in agricultural management, were little more then tax collectors. He favored helping tenants, who were positioned to make the most effective economic use of the land, to buy full title rights.[168] Prosterman tried to determine, through an elaborate series of calculations estimating the value of rents and the resale value of the land, just how much it would cost to finance such a buyout. He proposed offering owners £E 7,500 per feddan, with £E 1,500 to be paid up front and the remainder to be paid over thirty years. To help tenants make these payments (under which they would pay owners £E 200 annually, roughly triple the prevailing rent), he recommended that the Egyptian government double its procurement price for cotton. He also suggested that AID facilitate the program by supplying $100 million each year which would just cover the interest charges the Egyptian government would sustain if it lent tenants the initial £E 1,500 down-payment for their title purchase.

The Egyptian government gave these recommendations serious consideration.[169] However, AID never endorsed the Prosterman proposal and the Egyptian government was reluctant to raise cotton prices by the required amount. Under the pinched budget conditions of the 1980s, then, both the Wafdist and Tagammu' versions of a buyout program remained beyond the fiscal capacity of the state. Both were also politically unattractive to the Mubarak regime. They required a clear choice in favor of landlords or tenants which, either way, would have alienated an important public constituency. Mubarak's advisers chose instead to search for some type of compromise. Over the years, they considered several solutions.

The first proposal floated by the Ministry of Agriculture was to convert most rental contracts into sharecropping arrangements.[170] This would leave tenants on the land but would give owners a chance to increase their income by negotiating with renters over the subdivision of the crop at the beginning of each season. Sharecropping was already practiced on 18.5 percent of the rented area.[171] In addition to its appeal as a compromise between owners and renters, sharecropping attracted government interest for two reasons. First, it gave both landlords and tenants a stake in raising the productivity of land. Second, the conversion of rent contracts into sharecropping deals would cost the state nothing. Yet this idea never caught on because of serious questions about how the conversion would be administered and tenants' worries that sharecropping would leave them vulnerable to abuse by landlords.

Another proposal that was popular with certain cabinet ministers suggested letting owners reclaim half their rented lands on the condition that they give the other half to their tenants. But when this formula had been applied experimentally during the 1950s' land reform, owners tended to give their renters those lands that were least suitable for farming, whether poorly irrigated or of low soil quality.[172]

Gradually, landowners began to push for more radical programs. Rural notables, including many of those who had voted for the 1975 revision of rent control, formed a critical element of Mubarak's own party, the NDP. In 1982 this agricultural lobby within the party succeeded in making the right of landowners to evict tenants and resume farming themselves a centerpiece of the NDP's agrarian program.[173] Mubarak was concerned that this bloc might be lured away from the party by the Wafd's proposal to buy out tenants. This fear became especially acute in 1984 when the Wafd won 58 seats (from a total of 448) in parliamentary elections.[174] After the elections, Mubarak permitted NDP parliamentary delegates to start drafting a comprehensive reform of the rent law.[175]

The NDP took its draft of a new rent control law, which would have greatly expanded the power of landlords, to Parliament's Agriculture and Irrigation Committee. The proposal would have given owners the right to raise rents to keep pace with prices and to convert contracts from cash payment to sharecropping, even without the consent of the renter. Landlords would also have acquired the right to evict renters from lands about to be sold, after paying them just compensation. All rent contracts would be for fixed durations and tenants would have been forbidden to inherit rent contracts, except for males actually working on the land.[176]

This draft legislation provoked a scathing counterattack by the Tagammu' party. It accused the NDP of appropriating the Wafd's position on rent control and charged that the two were conspiring to overturn the land reform. The Tagammu' party's influential newspaper ran the headline, "NDP and Wafd Have Agreed on Evicting Renters."[177] The left launched a propaganda campaign that suggested that revision of the rural rent control law was only the first step in a drive that would abolish urban rent controls as well. They argued that if rural renters could be evicted, it would not be long before urban landlords began expelling tenants too. This turned millions of Cairene renters against the draft legislation and placed the government under enormous pressure.

The task of defending the NDP's position fell to Yusuf Wali. He claimed that the draft legislation sought solely to ensure that cash rents from land keep up with rises in profits and costs, and that it would not give owners a free hand over renters.[178] Wali was not persuasive, however, and the government was forced to alter its stance. By the end of the year Wali was assuring businessmen that the Parliament would prepare a bill that would "protect social peace."[179]

The Agriculture and Irrigation Committee abandoned the NDP's draft and began considering an array of more moderate measures. It agreed to place limitations on the inheritance of rental contracts and debated various schemes to raise the maximum rent, either by doubling assessments or permitting landlords to charge rents equal to fourteen, rather than seven, times the prevailing tax.[180] Even these proposals, which like the 1975 rent law simply sidestepped the key questions of default and eviction, never became law. Parliament entertained different suggestions every year, but Mubarak declined to endorse any of them. And in the absence of presidential support, Parliament was too badly divided internally to guarantee the passage of any resolution of this contentious issue.

While the government dithered over this question, landowners

Table 7-3. Percentage of Area Owned and Leased by Size of Landholdings, 1961 and 1982

Size of holding (feddans)	Purely owned holdings		Purely leased holdings		Mixed or other holdings	
	1961	1982	1961	1982	1961	1982
Less than 1	47	71	39	22	14	7
1–2	32	57	36	22	32	21
2–3	37	55	30	22	33	23
3–4	34	57	29	17	37	26
4–5	32	57	27	14	41	29
5–10	33	59	24	13	43	28
10–20	41	67	15	5	44	28
20–50	48	72	8	4	44	24
50–100	54	70	7	2	39	28
More than 100	59	71	7	5	34	24
Total	38	62	32	20	30	18

Source: Robert Springborg, "Rolling Back Agrarian Reforms in Egypt," Macquarie University, 1989, p. 29.

slowly took matters into their own hands. Lured by the opportunity to enhance their incomes, owners began to circumvent the rent law in various ways. Nearly half refused to give their tenants a written contract, preferring a simple oral agreement which was much easier to revise. Others adopted single-season contracts, which were exempt from the rent laws.[181] Before they could adopt either of these tactics, many owners had to find a way to break the contract of the existing tenants, who were covered by the full protection of the rent law. The most common way of doing this was for the owner to pay the renter a fee called *khalawat rigl* (literally, "remove a foot"). This mechanism was also used when the owner wanted to vacate a plot of land so that he could sell it unencumbered. The fee typically varied between a quarter and a half of the value of the land sold.[182]

As a result of devices like *khalawat rigl*, the share of land farmed directly by its owners rose from 25 percent in 1952 to 57.6 percent by 1983.[183] Among all categories of agriculturalists, ownership increased while rentals declined (see table 7-3). The result was a significant transformation in land distribution. Rich peasants increased their holdings to 18 percent of the total registered area, up from 13 percent in 1977. And farmers (owning more than ten feddans) enlarged their holdings from 20 percent to 25 percent of the total registered area (table 7-4).[184]

Table 7-4. Distribution of Farmland, Various Years, 1961–82

Size of holding (feddans)	Number of holdings		Area of holdings		Average plot size (feddans)
	Thousands	Percent of total	Thousands of feddans	Percent of total	
1961	1,642.1	100	6,222.8	100	3.79
Less than 3	1,106.9	67	1,364.4	22	1.23
3–5	274.3	17	990.0	16	3.61
5–10	170.0	10	1,100.7	18	4.47
More than 10	90.9	6	2,767.7	44	30.45
1965	2,082.0	100	5,921.2	100	2.84
Less than 3	1,564.6	75	2,017.2	34	1.29
3–5	283.2	14	1,041.6	18	3.68
5–10	147.5	7	970.7	16	6.58
More than 10	86.7	4	1,891.7	32	21.82
1975	2,642.0	100	5,983.4	100	2.26
Less than 3	2,073.5	79	2,762.5	46	1.21
3–5	354.8	13	1,185.5	20	3.34
5–10	148.4	6	944.4	16	6.36
More than 10	65.2	2	1,091.1	18	16.73
1978	2,989.3	100	6,015.7	100	2.01
Less than 3	2,443.1	82	2,937.3	48	1.20
3–5	348.7	12	1,165.6	19	3.34
5–10	127.6	4	785.9	13	6.16
More than 10	69.9	2	1,126.9	20	17.55
1982	2,466.9	100	6,072.5	100	2.48
Less than 3	1,892.5	77	2,302.1	38	1.22
3–5	330.6	13	1,180.8	19	3.57
5–10	173.1	7	1,097.3	18	6.34
More than 10	70.7	3	1,492.3	25	21.11

Source: Springborg, "Rolling Back Agrarian Reforms," p. 26. Figures are rounded.

At first glance it might seem that this shift in landholding resolved the problem of rent control. By the mid-1980s a majority of cultivators owned the lands they tended and rent contracts were of diminished importance. Cultivators had bought out full rights to their land with results quite similar to those anticipated in the Wafd's buyout proposal, yet without expensive government intervention. Some Egyptian officials hoped that this would eliminate the need for further debate about the rent control law.

But detailed analysis of the most recent cadastral survey leaves less reason to be sanguine. In 1982 some 3,765,000 feddans (62 percent of the total farmed area) were owned freehold, with no rent involved. Only 5 percent of this was held in plots of one feddan or less. This was a big change when compared to 1961, when only 38 percent of land was worked as wholly owned farms. In 1982, 62 percent of all farmers (amounting to 1,529,000) worked entirely on their own lands, compared with only 38 percent in 1961.

This does not mean that rents were no longer an important means of access to land; 937,000 peasants, or 36 percent of the farming population, still relied on rented plots. Furthermore, 565,000 peasants who owned their own land worked plots of one feddan or less. Since they could not sustain a family on such small farms, they had to supplement their incomes by taking work as laborers, and many of them also leased out the plots they owned.[185] Such smallholders constituted 37.2 percent of all freeholders. If the freeholders who owned less than a feddan are added to the others who rented, it appears that 1,512,000 farmers, or 61 percent of the households, were probably still dependent on rents in some way. Hardly enough to suggest that the market was taking care of the problem.

Even this does not fully describe the ongoing importance of rental property in rural Egypt. Egyptian cadastres tally only long-term leases (one year or more). Many peasants rent on short-term leases, an increasingly popular mechanism that landowners used because the land was not subject to rent control. The share of peasants who augment their plots through short-term leases is significant although, since they are uncounted, there is no way to be certain just how significant.

The 1982 data do show an increase in the area owned outright by peasants. This is what would be expected after twenty years of applying a rent control law that made leasing unprofitable. The combination of land reform and peasants buying out lease rights did reduce the total share of land rented. But rents remained critical for the two-thirds of the farming population that did not own enough land to subsist on their own plots. In fact, the problem of access to land seemed likely to increase.

Land hunger remained a serious problem. The land transfers of the 1980s left smallholders with dramatically less land than at any time since 1965. Two million peasants with small holdings saw their access to land drop by 634,000 feddans.[186] Under the new distribution the land available to the millions of peasants who farm less than three feddans dropped from 48 percent to 38 percent of the total area. This situation was only tolerable for the poorer peasants because of the massive growth of nonagricultural sources of income. By the 1980s farming was no longer the primary source of income for most villagers. In one detailed survey only slightly over one-third of male villagers listed agriculture as their primary occupation. And even among farm households around 30 percent of the family budget was derived from employment outside agriculture.[187]

In the same survey, 35 percent of male villagers claimed to work in public service or government employment and another 13 percent in the army or police force.[188] As the state budget is squeezed by declining hard currency revenues and stricter lending terms, opportunities (and salaries) in public employment will decline. Public sector employees in rural areas, who contribute little to the operation of line ministries, may be the first to be let go.

Yet the opportunities to ameliorate land hunger through labor migration are diminishing. The largest contingent of Egyptian workers abroad (between 1.5 million and 2 million) was in Iraq, where they had worked as replacements for the million young Iraqis conscripted for service in the Gulf War. In 1989, after the war ended, 500,000 of these Iraqis were demobilized, returned home, and discovered their old jobs occupied. To vacate these positions for Iraqi nationals, the Iraqi government announced in August 1989 a series of measures to encourage Egyptian workers to return home. Skilled Egyptian workers who paid social insurance fees in Iraq were henceforth restricted to sending home 30 dinars a month ($90). Unskilled workers could remit only 10 dinars ($30). Five dinars a day was considered low wages in Iraq; so unskilled Egyptians who earned 150 dinars a month were being allowed to remit only a fifteenth of their income.[189] Even those remittances permitted by law became subject to long delays at Baghdad's central bank. By November Egyptian officials complained that $350 million in remittances had been held up by the Iraqis.[190]

As if this were not bad enough, individual Iraqis began to murder Egyptians in quarrels over jobs and money. The Cairo daily *al-Akhbar* reported that in October 1989 alone the corpses of more than a thousand Egyptian workers had been returned from Baghdad. Many of them showed bullet holes.[191] This violence triggered a panic among the remaining Egyptian workers. Political sources estimated that in the summer of 1989, 70,000 Egyptian workers fled Iraq, and 150,000 were expected to leave by the end of the year.[192] Egypt's leading daily, *al-Ahram*, reported that 10,000 workers a day were leaving by air (ten extra daily flights had to be added for the Baghdad-Cairo route) and many more were returning overland.[193] The exodus accelerated after November 17 when a number of Egyptians were killed by Iraqis during a riot following a soccer match in Baghdad.[194]

There were no quick tallies of how badly Iraqi restrictions and Egyptian worker flight would cut into the value of remittances to Cairo. But these incidents in Baghdad demonstrated how vulnerable and unreliable remittances might be as a source of nonfarm income.

In August 1990 the system of labor remittances, which had sustained the Egyptian economy during the preceding decade while oil prices declined and debts piled up, collapsed. On August 2, the government of Iraq (where 850,000 Egyptians still worked) invaded Kuwait (where another 150,000 Egyptians labored). Suddenly, neither the Iraqi nor the Kuwaiti government had the cash to pay their Egyptian guest workers and the specter of war hung over the Gulf. A flood of Egyptian laborers began to flee back to Cairo. By August 20 some 100,000 had already left the Gulf, although 40,000 remained stuck with other Gulf refugees while trying to cross Jordan.[195] By mid-September 255,000 had returned to Egypt and the government in Cairo was expecting to have to reabsorb at least half a million refugees.[196]

This was going to be a painful task. Even before the Gulf crisis unemployment afflicted 20 percent of Egypt's 15 million workers and housing was in short supply. Although the crisis augmented government revenues by prompting debt forgiveness and raising oil prices, it savaged the private sector. Losses in the tourist sector alone were expected to exceed $1 billion.[197] The return of workers in the Gulf and the disruption of communications in the region was expected to cost the country $2.4 billion in annual remittances.[198] At the same time, IMF-mandated price rises continued to erode the standard of living.[199]

These dislocations would be especially painful in rural areas. The return of the migrants meant that peasant farms would be saddled with more labor than they could absorb. This would depress wages. The cost of land, whether rented or sold, would probably be driven up by competitive bidding between returning migrants and prosperous farmers (the latter would want more land now that it was cheaper to hire labor). The pressure from both owners and tenants to resolve who controlled the land would grow more intense.

As pressure on the land regime grew, the Egyptian government appeared to confront a painful and complicated choice. If it transferred land titles to lessees, it might be closing the door to much-needed investment in agriculture by absentee landowners. If it restored full title to the landowners, it might both aggravate the problem of landlessness and trigger a decline in yields (agronomists agree that peasants work much harder on plots they own than on those they work as sharecroppers or hired hands). Government data on landholding was too old and unreliable to indicate just what the economic effects of either decision would be. Yet it was clear that failing to make a decision and leaving the question of title ambiguous or uncertain would aggravate all of these problems, stifling investment, reducing work incentives, and promoting landlessness.

In terms of the state budget, the cheapest course for the government would be to choose sides and then transfer title between title holders and lessees by legislative fiat. The losing party would complain, but those who refused to cooperate could be arrested. Historically, many title disputes have been settled in this way—for example, the enclosure movement in England and the dispossession of the Native Americans in the West.

For the soft state in Cairo, however, such bold action was not politically viable. The government was not confident that it had the authority or coercive capacity to effectively strip peasant lessees of their rights. Certainly, this was a confrontation it wanted to avoid. On the other hand, it could not afford to alienate title holders either, particularly when they formed an influential element of the agrarian elite within the National Democratic party itself.

It was the political influence of these groups, after all, that had forced the question of the rural rent law onto the government's agenda. Few government officials wanted to tackle this painful issue; they would have preferred to focus attention on less contentious questions like funding transportation, irrigation, and other programs of general social benefit. But such public goods, while receiving universal acclamation, often receive surprisingly little concerted support. Issues like the rent law, which affect a discrete, influential, and organizable section of the population, are much more likely to be pressed by lobbyists and parliamentarians. Landlords were just such an organized minority. They had put the rent law at the top of the parliamentary agenda in the 1980s, and they would keep it there until the question was resolved.

The government had, of course, alternatives to deciding the question by fiat. It could choose between title holders and lessees, then soften the blow to the losing party through a program of indemnities. This is the solution that both the Wafd and Tagammu' parties, from different sides, had urged on the government—to buy out one party to the dispute. Mubarak could offer subsidized credits to rural landowners who wished to buy out their tenants; or he could embrace the Prosterman proposal and raise cotton prices, enabling renters to buy out their landlords. But neither of these alternatives was cheap; either required a multimillion-dollar appropriation by the government.

Under the best of circumstances, the Egyptian government might shy away from such expensive programs. Its austere fiscal straits in the early 1990s stiffen this reluctance. The government budget is being sapped by the economic fallout of the Iraqi invasion of Kuwait—a sharp decline of workers' remittances, tourist receipts, and Suez Canal revenues. In addition there is pressure from the IMF to cut the budget deficit. The Stockman strategy does not allow Egypt funds for "nonessential" state services like defining landed property rights.

Prevented by political considerations from imposing a solution to the rent law debate, and restrained by economic limitations from buying one, the Egyptian government seemed to have only one option left, to fudge. It could drag out the debate over the law without resolving anything, hoping that the affected parties would accommodate as best they could. It could propose various half-measures (like Yusuf Wali's sharecropping proposal), knowing that none would be adopted or make any difference. It could even offer minor emoluments to the aggrieved parties (marginal increases in cotton prices for peasants; directed credits for landlords), hoping that a few cheap subsidies would help them resign themselves to the persistence of an uncomfortable and uncertain situation.

Of course, Egypt would pay a price for this indecision. Farmers would continue to delay investments of capital and labor until their title became clearer. Even worse, perhaps, the ability of the government to command respect and implement policy would erode a notch further. But, strapped and hamstrung, the best the government could hope for was to ride its fiscal crisis out, with the intention of restoring services and behaving more decisively at some future moment when resources were less scarce. There was nothing peculiarly Egyptian about this behavior. As the American budget debates in the late 1980s demonstrated, in times of fiscal crisis many societies have difficulty finding the leadership necessary to distribute the inevitable budget sacrifices rationally and equitably.

Despite the high hopes of neoclassical economists, fiscal austerity does not create compelling incentives for economic rationalization. It might force a state to face hard questions, but it does not guarantee that the government will answer them, let alone make the most economically efficient choice. If the Egyptian government, ruling a soft state and on behalf of factionalized elites, could not stand up to a few landlords and peasants, what were the odds that it could impose serious budget cuts on those who consumed the lion's share of the budget, the officer corps?

David Stockman himself claims to have learned that the choice between strong clients and strong causes in budget battles is not determined by economic efficiency. It is decided by political influence.[200]

Conclusion

The Egyptian economy would clearly benefit from moves to balance the fiscal budget. Any steps in this direction would curb inflation, reduce government pressure on the financial system, and improve the value of Egypt's currency. Budget cuts could make an important contribution to this end. An improved and expanded tax collection system would also help.[201] Yet many of the officials in the Washington development community show little enthusiasm for expanding Egypt's tax revenues. They firmly believe that the scope of the Egyptian state's economic activities is already too large. They do not want to see it sustained or expanded by tax hikes. Instead, they hope that putting pressure on Cairo to make budget cuts will constrict the state's scope.

Budget cuts are not the only tool that Washington's experts use to constrict the Egyptian state. They also favor privatization (which would transfer public sector enterprises to the hands of more efficient private entrepreneurs), price liberalization (which would terminate market distortions and sometimes cut government revenues), and deregulation (which would eliminate bureaucratic obstructions to routine business practices). In many specific cases these reforms would promote economic development. But the more radical economists in Washington are less interested in the immediate sectoral benefits of such changes than in their wider effect on the entire economy. Taken together, these reforms could pry the state out of many activities where it is currently active.

Many neoclassical economists believe that the size of the state largely determines its contribution to the economy. They contend that states, which rely basically on collective sanctions rather than individual incentives, are intrinsically less efficient than markets.[202] Given a choice, they would always prefer to leave economic activities to the private sector. Yet they concede that this is not always possible. There are certain public goods, such as provision for the national defense, regulating pollution, and investing in massive infrastructural projects, that cannot be supplied by private corporations alone. These must be left to the state, and they form its proper sphere of operations.[203]

Whenever the state extends its activities beyond this core, however, society pays a price. It means that the state is wasting resources, because some private firm could supply the same good more efficiently. It also means that the private sector is producing less than it could, since it must cope with the loss of capital, the regulations, and the market distortions that state intervention inevitably entails. Given this vision, neoclassical economists believe that the first task of economic reform should be to shrink the scope of the state to its proper domain, constricting the bureaucrats and liberating the businessmen. They would endorse Thoreau's motto: "That government is best which governs least."[204]

This vision that among states "small is beautiful" is elegant and compelling. Unfortunately, it provides a poor guide to how to conduct economic reform in the Third World. It is crippled by three main flaws. First, restraints on the fiscal budget do not always shrink the state in the manner neoclassical economists hope. Sometimes the budget axe passes over rents and privileges and falls on legitimate state activities.

In practice, politics always influences the way that budget cuts are made. Economists might consider rural education a legitimate form of state investment in infrastructure. But in countries like Egypt, who lobbies for rural education? Many parents, needing all the labor they can get to bring in their crops, take their children out of school at a very early age. They are hardly in a position to march on Cairo to demand more investment in human capital. Partly as a result, between 1970 and 1985—years when foreign aid and credits were flowing into Egypt—the adult literacy rate only rose from 35 percent to 45 percent.[205]

In contrast, who lobbies for reform of the rent law, or for profitable controls on banking competition, or for corn subsidies? These causes enlist the most influential parties, articulate journalists, and richest businessmen in Cairo. The difference between the political influence commanded by these elites and the poor, disorganized proponents of many infrastructural projects inevitably skews the distribution of budget cuts. Strong clients crowd out strong causes.

Even if these political distortions in budget cutting could be eliminated, a second problem would remain. Most Egyptians, and some economists, differ with the neoclassicists over which forms of state intervention are legitimate and which are not. The former contend that some of the activities that the Washington radicals would like to see cut from the budget are actually useful and desirable.

Operating on its own, the private sector does not always produce the most efficient or optimal results. There is such a thing as market failure. Private monopolies distort prices. Private firms do not produce public goods because they cannot be made profitable. Externalities (like pollution) do not appear in corporate balance sheets. When markets fail, collective or political remedies are often legitimate. It seems likely that such market failures are more common in developing countries than in developed ones. The entry costs of pioneering a modern business are higher, making monopolies easier to defend. Certain services that might be supplied privately in a more developed economy take on the character of public goods, since the cost of supplying them looms so large relative to the capital of the average firm. And much of the expensive infrastructure that firms in developed countries take for granted—including the definition of property rights—still has to be built.

In Cairo the scope of legitimate state action may be larger than economists in offices on the far side of the Atlantic may presume. Conditions in agriculture suggest that this is so. Egyptians may have a case for distorting the price of imports in order to discourage overproduction of cotton. They may properly want government ministries to absorb the costs of pioneering new transportation and storage facilities. They may have legitimate reasons for demanding national antitrust regulations that discourage the consolidation of monopolies like Rawd al-Farag. They may even be able to justify deliberately creating rents (by subsidies, tariffs, or other means) to encourage private firms to pioneer certain enterprises.

Finally, there is a third problem with the Stockman stratagem, an error of omission rather than commission. Because neoclassical economists expect all states to be inefficient, they neglect or inadvertently discourage reforms that might cut waste and minimize distortions by improving the efficiency of states. It may be true, as many economists suppose, that states are universally less efficient at providing goods and services than private firms. But this does not mean that all states are equally inefficient. Some seem to waste less and accomplish more using roughly the same level of resources.

In 1980 Egyptian public sector employees formed about 9 percent of the nonagricultural work force and their wages consumed about 9 percent of the national income. The size of the Egyptian public sector work force was roughly the same as that of South Korea (10 percent of the labor force, with wages equaling 16 percent of the national income) and Great Britain (10 percent of labor; wages equaling 9 percent of income).[206] Yet British and Korean civil servants and state enterprises enjoyed a reputation for being vastly more efficient than their Egyptian counterparts. How were these countries able to do more with less?

Even within the Egyptian government, certain ministries and bureaus have the reputation of being better managed, less corruption-prone, and more effective than others. The Suez Canal Authority seems to be much more efficient and honest than the Customs Authority. Obviously, the efficiency and efficacy of Egyptian government agencies could be vastly improved.

This is a fact of considerable importance. Given that there are many areas where the market cannot—or for political reasons will not—deliver the goods, improving the efficiency of the state in taking up those tasks could save billions of dollars. Certainly some government subsidies and interventions need to be curbed, but it may prove no less important to allocate subsidies efficiently and conduct interventions effectively.

The literature of neoclassical economists contains some suggestions as to how this might be done by demonstrating that certain types of state intervention are intrinsically less efficient or more distorting than others. For example, if the Egyptian government insists on protecting local poultry producers, it is preferable that it do this through tariffs than through quotas or nontariff trade barriers. Tariffs may discourage trade, but they leave consumers free to make choices—if they demand imported chickens they can get them by paying more. Quotas, on the other hand, undercut market mechanisms entirely; they limit how much imported chicken is available at any price.[207] In a similar manner, if the Egyptian government insists on lowering the cost of food, it is preferable that it employ subsidies rather than price controls. Subsidies distort demand, but price controls restrain production. Some forms of state intervention are less distorting, more market conforming, than others.[208]

The neoclassical element within the Washington development community, however, has avoided pressing for changes in the efficiency of government intervention. Its adherents oppose, as a matter of principle, all forms of protectionism and state intervention; they do not want to make it easier for the Egyptians to cling to these iniquitous practices by suggesting that some versions are less harmful than others. In their agenda, not only do they not assign improving the efficiency of state intervention a priority comparable to that of cutting the scope of state activities, they fear that even discussing the former might divert attention from the latter.

In practice, state-curbing programs like the Stockman stratagem seem likely to make the Egyptian government less efficient, not more. As the budget is cut, politically entrenched subsidies will persist while general-interest public goods will be cut. Government agencies, strapped for resources and preoccupied with defending existing programs, will have little opportunity to experiment with new approaches that might cut waste and distortions. Compounding the budget crisis in Cairo seems more likely to confuse and demoralize state officials than to prompt them to take bold and innovative measures.

In Egypt, application of the Stockman stratagem has not led to the breakthrough in economic liberalization that its proponents had hoped for. Partly this is because Egyptians have resisted and frustrated IMF reform efforts. But it is also partly because the assumption that smaller states are better states is flawed. How much benefit or damage state interventions inflict on an economy is as much a product of their quality as of their quantity.

CHAPTER 8

Reorienting Egypt's Reform Agenda

THE EXPERTS OF THE WASHINGTON DEVELOPMENT COMMUNITY HAVE forged certain powerful and (largely) accurate insights into the dynamics of economic development. They understand that no amount of moralizing or state coercion can generate the level of energy and innovation that the profit motive and market forces tap. They see that Egypt's economic policies have blunted and dissipated the energy that private initiative provides, seriously handicapping reform efforts. They have proposed many sound, constructive changes in economic policy which—if adopted—would put Egypt on the road to economic recovery.

Unfortunately, their campaign to reform Egypt has been systematically marred by misunderstandings of the social and political environment in which their reform program must be implemented. For example, they have projected their own ideas about the antinomy of businessman and bureaucrat onto countries like Egypt. They presume that the two groups are intrinsically and eternally opposed, that businessmen seek to liberate markets while bureaucrats hope to maintain state controls. But this vision bears little resemblance to actual practice in Egypt or most of the Third World. In the less developed countries the boundary between the public and the private sector is much more permeable, more fuzzy, than in already industrialized states. In the Third World "state-private relationships are generally symbiotic. The returns to a new factory, for example, may depend crucially on investment by the state in a new road—and the economic viability of that road may depend no less crucially on its use by the factory. In terms of personnel, too, it can be hard to know private from public agents, as in governments and public administrations many of whose members are actively engaged in business; or where private agents are so beholden to the state for their incomes as to effectively eliminate their independence."[1]

This interpenetration of the public and the private is evident in the behavior of Egyptian businessmen. On the one hand most Cairo capitalists extol the profit motive and the efficiency of markets. On the other, their enthusiasm is tempered by a conviction that the state should intervene to limit foreign competition, moderate business cycles, and invest massively in the infrastructure necessary for economic development. Egyptian businessmen are eager to invest in productive ventures and hope to make them competitive and profitable; but they also seek to ensure the success of their ventures by cultivating state-created rents. They understand that the totality of state-created rents and market distortions is stifling the economy; but they are reluctant to abandon the specific subsidies and controls that boost the profits of their own firms. Egyptian businessmen thus play an ambivalent role in the process of economic reform. They applaud reform in principle, while often resisting or undermining its specific applications. The general blindness of development economists to this ambivalence has actually compounded the difficulty of reform.

Working on the assumption that businessmen are wholehearted allies of economic reform, the Washington development community has sought to bolster the political influence of Egyptian businessmen. They have sponsored the formation of lobbies like the American-Egyptian Chamber of Commerce. They have shipped Egyptian bureaucrats to Washington to attend seminars on "the virtues of privatization." They have allocated their economic aid to encourage private projects and joint ventures. This foreign support has not been the only factor promoting the influence of Egyptian businessmen, but it dramatically enhanced their power.

Sometimes Egyptian businessmen have used this enhanced power to promote market-oriented reforms. But on other occasions they have employed it to win additional rents from the state (as happened in the case of poultry producers), to resist economic reforms (the official banks), or to alter policies so that they transferred income from other segments of the population to themselves (absentee landowners). Bolstering the power of businessmen did not make them any less *dirigiste* or more market-oriented. The Washington development community has tried to transfer power from bureaucrats to businessmen;

but this has not in itself altered the quality of the ties that bind the two groups. It is as if development economists expect to transform water into wine by pouring it from one bucket into another. The miracle of transubstantiation does not occur so easily.

The Washington development community's faith in the businessman has been mirrored in its suspicion of the bureaucrat. If the private sector is good, the state must be evil. So the U.S. Agency for International Development (AID), the International Monetary Fund (IMF), and the World Bank have each sought to master the Egyptian government, to check its wicked ways so that the private sector might be made free to thrive. They have moralized and indoctrinated Egyptian bureaucrats, seeking to convert them to the idea of "limited government." They have made the release of credit, aid, and debt rescheduling conditional on the termination of state economic controls. And they have believed that the pressure of a fiscal crisis might have the salutary effect of compelling the state to curtail its activities and trim its waste.

It is true that when the state does not respect the sanctity of private property, the business community will not make its irreplaceable contribution to development. It is also true that when the state intervenes in the wrong areas, it suppresses private initiative and encourages waste. Certainly many of the specific policy reforms that the Washington development community has urged on Egypt could be quite helpful. But it does not follow that a general assault on the state budget, on the powers of public officials, on the morale of the bureaucrats, is a good way to bring about these changes.

When the Egyptian state ran short of funds in the late 1980s, programs that resulted in rents and waste were not the only (or even the primary) ones that suffered. Rail lines eroded, public health care decayed, literacy rates continued to lag. The flow of bureaucratic paperwork slowed, making private investment even more difficult to launch. Even if these hardships had provoked the government to adopt economic reform, the new funds made available by the Washington development community would have been largely absorbed reviving facilities that had corroded during the preceding crisis.

The economic crunch, moreover, caused disturbing changes in the pattern of politics. Egyptian officials entered a crisis mode in which they had little time to contemplate long-term development issues. Their energy was sapped by the struggle for daily survival. The groups that lobbied ministries or raised their voices in Parliament became less receptive to the promise that short-term sacrifices would lay the groundwork for future prosperity and became more insistent on preserving subsidies and policies that bolstered their immediate standard of living. Everyone became more defensive and conservative, and faith that the government might sustain a program of economic reform evaporated.

Worst of all, the crisis aggravated the problems of corruption and rent seeking. Public officials, watching the ship of state slowly sink, became more eager to use the remaining powers of their office on behalf of business constituencies; such favors could prepare the way for their own careers in the private sector after they left government service. Civil servants, unable to maintain their standard of living on existing salaries, became more susceptible to corruption. In 1990 one journalist reported: "'A year ago you paid a little baksheesh to avoid a parking ticket,' a professor said, using the Egyptian term that denotes something less than a bribe and something more than a tip. 'Now you pay a little baksheesh to park legally.'"[2] Foreign experts have put pressure on the Egyptian state in hopes of making it "smaller" and less intrusive on the market. But the practical effect of their policies has been to make the state "softer" and thus less resistant to the confusion of public and private purposes.

The Egyptian experience highlights the force of what Miles Kahler has dubbed "the orthodox paradox."[3] The Washington development community seeks to enlist the collaboration of Egyptian officials to reform economic policy. Yet the policy reforms it seeks and the means it employs to pursue them steadily reduce the authority of state officials. In general, it is surprising that Cairo's bureaucrats have not done more to resist implementation of the development community's reforms. The irony is that the economic pressure that foreign aid agencies have laid on the Egyptian state has undermined the power of those officials whom they hope to use as instruments of reform.

The Pitfalls of Crony Capitalism

The "good market, bad state," interpretation of political economy offered by neoclassical economists is mistaken. In most Third World countries neither businessmen nor bureaucrats are, in themselves, obstacles to development. The quality of the relationship between these groups, however, makes a profound difference to a country's economic fortunes. If bureaucrats and businessmen are too hostile to each other, their feuds can do more to cripple the national economy than any natural disaster. But when bureaucrats and businessmen become allies, their collaboration can be equally debilitating. Through various forms of rent seeking, businessmen can divert public resources to their private benefit, feeding their profits without producing economic growth (much less development).

Twenty years ago, antagonism between businessmen and bureaucrats was a major problem in Egypt and many developing countries. But the world has changed. The example of successful capitalist growth in Taiwan and Chile, reinforced by constant pressure from the Washington development community, has fostered a new atmosphere of collaboration between public and private authorities in much of the Third World. Today it is crony capitalism—the corruption of this collaboration—that may be the most common obstacle to development.

It has been hard for development experts to grapple with the problem of crony capitalism because it is not solely an economic or a political problem. It is both. It arises not just from bad economic policies nor from weak political institutions, but from the relationship between the two. To understand this problem, much less to treat it, requires some expertise in both economic and political analysis and some attempt to ferret out the dynamics that link these two spheres of society. It requires some understanding of political economy.

Of course, crony capitalism is not the only way in which the interaction of politics and economics plagues the development process; other political-economic problems abound. There is always some tension between the political agenda of promoting stability and security and the economic agenda of fostering growth. When subsidies are slashed in order to liberate market forces, the government's objective of promoting stability becomes more difficult to achieve. When a Third World regime spends more than half of its budget on building a modern military apparatus, this drains funds away from economic development.

But among all the political economic problems that assault the Third World, crony capitalism may deserve pride of place. It alone both fosters resistance to economic reform and undermines the effects of reforms after they have been implemented. The example of Egypt illustrates how crony capitalism can retard attempts to adopt and implement economic reforms. Bankers, money changers, poultry farmers, cotton growers, and vegetable wholesalers may all have strong incentives to resist attempts to build a more market-oriented economy. Under these conditions, efforts by AID and the IMF to bolster the political influence of Egyptian businessmen may backfire, actually stiffening the resistance to reform.

Yet even if Egypt managed to clear these hurdles and adopt a far-reaching economic reform program, there is every reason to believe that crony capitalism would continue to hamper growth. The recent experience of Eastern European countries demonstrates this. In 1989 and 1990 the governments of Eastern Europe launched economic reform plans that set far more ambitious objectives and were implemented with far greater energy than any of the adjustment programs Cairo has ever contemplated. The formerly communist countries radically devalued their currencies, opened their markets to foreign trade and investment, and began a large-scale transfer of public assets to the private sector. Yet despite these changes, the basic institutions of crony capitalism survived and obstructed growth.

One recurrent problem in Eastern Europe has been the persistence of monopolies. In the Soviet Union, for example, a single factory often produces 90–100 percent of the national output of particular goods. Privatizing such factories does not create market incentives to produce more efficiently because the factory managers are still in a position to set monopoly prices. The Soviets have discovered that even where there is more than one factory producing a good, the "new capitalists" who control these enterprises tend to band together into businessmen's associations that behave as monopolies.[4] One factor that reinforces this monopolistic behavior is the identity of the new capitalists who manage such enterprises. They are commonly the same members of the *nomenklatura*, the "priviligentsia" of party functionaries, who controlled these firms before reform. Using the same techniques of patronage, insider information, and backdoor deals that are common to any crony system, this elite has manipulated the reform process to ensure that they retain their privileged positions in the postcommunist economy. Marek Ogrodzki, chairman of Poland's Omig Company (which manufactures electronic components), is one of the wealthiest businessmen men in post-reform Poland. Before reform Ogrodzki was the state functionary in charge of Omig and one of the most influential communist bureaucrats. In East Germany, "the several dozen restaurants, cafes and cafeterias in the center of East Berlin that used to be run by a state trading organization headed by a Communist functionary named Erich Weber are now being leased or sold by the new privatization trustee, a former Communist named—Erich Weber."[5]

Not only do the same men (and women) often control Eastern European firms after privatization, they often derive their profits from the same rent-seeking mechanisms that were employed under the old regime. In Poland this has developed into a major scandal. Managers of privatized firms have cashed in on the incentives that the government has offered to stimulate the private sector, such as reduced tax rates and more relaxed employment regulations. Yet they have continued, often quite illegally, to draw on the same privileges that the state formerly offered to public sector firms. They often buy their raw materials and machinery, or even lease their workshops and work force, from state enterprises at the highly subsidized prices prevailing in the public sector. In some cases this amounts to outright theft. Managers of public sector firms have established private sector enterprises, then transferred the assets of the former to the latter either at ridiculously low prices or without any payment at all.[6]

The governments in Moscow, Warsaw, and Berlin have shown genuine enthusiasm for economic reform and a strong will to change. Their plans have been inspected, and sometimes drafted, by the best talents in the Washington development community. Yet they have not tackled the problem of cronyism. As a result, crony communism has been transformed into crony capitalism, without any apparent improvement of national economic performance.

Pegging Privilege to Performance

The disappointing result of economic liberalization in Eastern Europe is beginning to provoke a reassessment within the Washington development community. It has led some of the leading proponents of policy reform to question whether the orthodox tenets of reform, such as radical currency devaluation and eliminating trade barriers, necessarily foster growth.[7] And it has forced a growing body of scholars to emphasize the importance of political change as a requisite of economic development. The commitment of the regimes in Warsaw, Berlin, and Moscow to economic reform is so obviously sincere and enthusiastic that the Washington development community can no longer blame their failing on a lack of political will.

No consensus has congealed within the development community about precisely what political changes are necessary to stimulate and sustain economic growth. Anders Aslund, one of the world's leading authorities on Soviet reform efforts, has argued that a radical turn to democracy is required. Other experts, rather less boldly, suggest that a temporary return to "developmental dictatorship" may be helpful. Inside Eastern Europe the debate is similarly contentious. Both democratizers like Boris Yeltsin and economists from dictatorships like Chile and South Korea are held in high esteem.[8]

In Egypt, desperation over the stagnant economy has produced a similar political debate. Islamists, army officers, and Western-trained technocrats all insist that radical political changes are necessary to spur development. Both democracy and dictatorship appear increasingly alluring as alternatives to the current "soft state." The idea of political revolution has gained momentum on both the left and the right. Radical democratization might reduce the power of cronies over Egyptian economic policy. Acting through the polls, the people might be able to insist on more honest and responsible performance from their officials. A freer press might expose the existence of businessman-bureaucrat cabals, and a more independent judiciary might act to curb malfeasance. But a more potent dictatorship might be able to achieve similar results. An autocrat might unleash the secret police to ferret out corruption, insulate the bureaucracy from economic pressure groups, and be able to impose on the public the sacrifices necessary to stimulate the economy.

The handful of existing high-quality studies of the politics of economic adjustment suggest that either democracy or dictatorship can, under the right conditions, provide the political framework for economic growth.[9] In countries as diverse as Thailand, Costa Rica, and Ghana, both kinds of regime have made a contribution to growth. In politics, as in economics, there may be more than one legitimate road to development. Very different means may be employed to accomplish similar ends. This does not mean that any particular cluster of political changes will work. To break the vicious circle of rent seeking and create a political atmosphere conducive to development, a regime—whether democratic or authoritarian—must undertake certain specific functions. In a phrase, they must learn to peg privileges to performance.

Just what this means emerged very clearly in Alice Amsden's recent study of South Korea, *Asia's Next Giant*. "In late-industrializing countries, *the state intervenes with subsidies deliberately to distort relative prices in order to stimulate economic activity*. This has been true in Korea, Japan, and Taiwan as it has been in Brazil, India, and Turkey. In Korea, Japan, and Taiwan, however, the state has exercised discipline over subsidy recipients. *In exchange for subsidies, the state has imposed performance standards on private firms*. Subsidies have not been giveaways, but instead have been dispensed on the principle of reciprocity. With more disciplined firms, subsidies and protection have been lower and more effective than otherwise."[10]

In other words, officials in Seoul have been able to distribute and redistribute rents according to the promise of an enterprise. When a venture thrives and develops it continues to receive state support, but if its management cannot make it profitable its privileges are withdrawn. This contrasts starkly with the operation of Egypt's "crony capitalism" where the translation of political power into economic privilege is far more facile. In Cairo whether an enterprise receives state rents depends overwhelmingly on the political influence of its proponents rather than on its contribution to national economic development. Bureaucrats often distribute rents in exchange for either political loyalty or personal profit. Businessmen often find it easy to shape government policy and secure rents even when they cannot demonstrate that state intervention contributes to national development.

The South Korean government's nuanced control over the extension of economic privileges has contributed to development in a number of ways. Experts on East Asia continue to debate whether subsidies like those offered in Seoul have been necessary to promote development or have been a marginal lapse in a strategy whose real motor is the market. But they would agree that the social cost of such subsidies has been minimized by the way they are targeted on specific enterprises. This, again, contrasts with Egypt, where state-created rents support broad categories of economic activity rather than focus on a few pioneering ventures. The policy instruments that Cairo uses to create rents (price controls or general input subsidies) often lead to wider market distortions than do the instruments preferred in East Asia (targeted credits and special licensing arrangements). Subsidies and other rents consume a much higher share of the gross national product in Egypt than in Korea.[11]

Another benefit South Korea has derived from its government's control over the pattern of economic privilege is the ability to experiment and to learn from experience. In the 1950s officials in Seoul were no wiser than their counterparts in Cairo about which economic policies would prove successful. In fact, the regimes in both countries were committed to a similar program of import-substitution industrialization. Over the following decades, however, Korean officials steadily revised their policies, learning from experience which enterprises were likely to succeed and which were not. In this way, they gradually shifted toward their now famous strategy of export-led development.[12] "It is important to note that there were significant mistakes made by Korean policy makers. It is not that economic policy in one country was 'right,' and the other 'wrong.' If there was a difference in policy formulation itself, it rather lay in the speed with which policy makers recognized their mistakes and dealt with them."[13]

Egyptian officials did not make similar adjustments. As time passed, economic policy grew, if anything, more rigid. Pressure from consumers, businessmen, and other constituencies steadily reduced the options open to weak and harassed officials. The burden of short-term subventions gradually crowded out the opportunities for long-term development. This lack of flexibility exacted a terrible price. There probably is no single miracle recipe for economic development, but even if there were its application would have to be constantly adjusted to changes in international oil prices, interest rates, and so forth. Seoul has been able to make these adjustments speedily and effectively; Cairo has not.

The Korean approach to pegging privileges to performance may seem counterintuitive at first. Those who urge radical democratization or developmental dictatorship on developing countries argue (in part) that these regimes will sweep cronies from their positions of power and open access to government support to all citizens with legitimate demands. They seek to promote "good government"—honest, impartial, and law-abiding.[14] South Korea has not done this. Seoul has tolerated cliques of businessmen and bureaucrats so long as they contribute to national development. Yet while this approach has not eliminated the politics of patronage, it has obstructed pressure for universalizing the system of rent seeking.

The critical advantage of the Korean system is obvious. It can be made to work more rapidly, with fewer changes, than more radical political reforms. Countries like Egypt may not yet possess the requisites for building a really effective democracy or dictatorship. The transformation of a soft state into a strong state anywhere is long and arduous. But even soft states may possess the resources to exercise greater control over the distribution of economic privilege. In 1985 the government of Indonesia, frustrated by the way corruption in its customs authority was undermining trade policy, simply transferred the army officers who controlled its ports and called in a firm of Swiss accountants to replace them. In 1989 the government of Mexico liberated its petroleum industry from the hegemony of corrupt officials of the Oil Workers' Union through the simple expedient of imprisoning the union's chief officers. In both countries, controlling the cronies was a critical part of a wider package of reforms that substantially improved economic performance.[15]

Indonesia and Mexico's actions were not especially subtle or sophisticated. But by eliminating cronyism in key sectors they reasserted some government control over the distribution of rents and privileges. They demonstrated to cronies throughout the economy that the cost of their behavior was rising. They created an opportunity to erect more durable procedures for pegging privilege to performance. Even the Egyptian government possesses the resources to undertake similar actions.

The strategy the Washington development community has urged on Egypt has been to eliminate all rents and curb the scope of state intervention. Whether this is a desirable objective over the long run or not, the example of South Korea suggests that it is not a necessary condition for development. Instead, the critical lesson from Seoul seems to be that Egypt needs to develop the capacity to select among rents, to make their allocation more effective by concentrating resources on the most promising projects. Orthodox development experts have claimed, in effect, that liberalization or privatization, in itself, is enough to transform the businessmen who act as cronies in a *dirigiste* system into productive capitalists. Experience does not support this claim.

Cronyism is not the only obstacle that Cairo will have to surmount on the road to development. But until Egypt leaps beyond the hurdle of cronyism, it will never even discover the others.

Notes

CHAPTER 1

1. William B. Quandt, *The United States and Egypt* (Brookings, 1990), p. 41.

2. For a history of the Fund's activities in Egypt and its relationship to foreign borrowing, see Adil Husayn, *al-Iqtisad al-Misri min al-Istiqlal ila al-Taba'iyya 1974–1979* (Beirut: Dar al-Kalima, 1981).

3. The new orientation at the World Bank began in 1980 when the Bank switched to an approach of policy-based lending, which made loans "conditional" on reforms in economic policy. See Joan M. Nelson, "The Diplomacy of Policy-Based Lending," in Richard E. Feinberg, ed., *Between Two Worlds: The World Bank's Next Decade* (New Brunswick, N.J.: Transaction Books, 1986), pp. 67–86. As soon as the Reagan administration took office in 1981, AID philosophy began to evolve in the same direction. The approach of the IMF did not change as much; it had always made its standby agreements conditional on the adoption of sound financial policies by the recipient government. But the Fund's conservative voice in development lending grew far more influential after 1982 when it assembled the package that staved off Mexico's impending default and emerged as the central player in negotiations over the looming Third World debt crisis. For an assessment of the Fund's new role, see Tony Killick, Graham Bird, Jennifer Sharpley, and Mary Sutton, "The IMF: Case for a Change in Emphasis," in Richard E. Feinberg and Valeriana Kallab, eds., *Adjustment Crisis in the Third World* (New Brunswick, N.J.: Transaction Books, 1984), pp. 59–81.

4. For a summary and critique of this counterrevolution, see John Toye, *Dilemmas of Development* (Oxford: Blackwell, 1987).

5. Deepak Lal, *The Poverty of 'Development Economics'* (Harvard University Press, 1985), p. 107.

6. U.S. Embassy, *Egyptian Economic Trends* (Cairo, March 1989), p. 3.

7. For an analysis of the changes in Egypt's gross domestic product, see Economist Intelligence Unit, *Country Profile: Egypt, 1988–89* (London, 1988), pp. 15–17.

8. World Bank, Country Operations Division, *Egypt: Country Economic Memorandum* (Washington, January 5, 1989), vol. 2, p. 23.

9. World Bank, *World Development Report 1989* (New York: Oxford University Press, 1989), p. 166.

10. The first outline of Egypt's agricultural potential by AID is in its 1976 report *Major Constraints to Increasing Agricultural Productivity* (U.S. Agency for International Development, 1976).

11. Agriculture in the Indian Punjab was markedly more productive than in the Pakistani Punjab, despite nearly identical environments and land endowments. Experts attributed the difference to distinct government policies; see Holly Sims, *Political Regimes, Public Policy and Economic Development: Agricultural Performance and Rural Change in Two Punjabs* (Sage, 1988). A similar correlation of policy and performance seemed evident in the contrast between Kenya and Tanzania; see Michael F. Lofchie, *The Policy Factor: Agricultural Performance in Kenya and Tanzania* (Boulder, Colo.: Lynne Rienner, 1988).

12. Dr. Wali's campaign is discussed in chap. 5.

13. Yahya Sadowski, "The Sphinx's New Riddle: Why Does Egypt Delay Economic Reform?" *American-Arab Affairs*, no. 22 (Fall 1987), p. 39.

14. "The 'Soft State' and the Open Door: Egypt's Experience with Economic Liberalization, 1974–1984," *Comparative Politics*, vol. 18 (October 1985), p. 65.

15. Lanham, Md.: University Press of America, 1988.

16. Quoted in Lawrence E. Harrison, "Cultural Obstacles to Progress in the Third World—and at Home," *Fletcher Forum*, vol. 13 (Summer 1989), p. 243. A host of popular studies blame culture for the backwardness of Egypt and the Arab world; the most recent major contribution is David Pryce-Jones, *The Closed Circle: An Interpretation of the Arabs* (Harper and Row, 1989).

17. Charles William Maynes, "America's Third World Hang-Ups," *Foreign Policy*, no. 71 (Summer 1988), p. 124.

18. David Ottaway, "U.S. Withholds $230 Million from Egypt," *Washington Post*, March 8, 1989; and Melanie Tammen, "Inept Aid to Egypt," *Wall Street Journal*, January 24, 1989.

19. For the structure of Mubarak's work day, see Ahmad al-Jarallah, "Interview with President Husni Mubarak," *al-Dustur*, October 28, 1987, pp. 14–15, in Foreign Broadcast Information Service, *Daily Report: Near East & South Asia*, October 29, 1987, p. 9. (Hereafter FBIS, *Near East.*)

20. Some sense of just how arduous life is for the Egyptian peasant can be grasped from films like Sharqawi's *al-Ard* or even Robert Benton's *Places in the Heart*.

21. Labib al-Siba'i, "Wazir al-Sina'a Yutliq al-Rasas 'ala al-Sina'a al-Misriyya," *al-Ahram al-Iqtisadi*, June 4, 1990, pp. 12–15.

22. "MENA Carries Sidqi Biography," in FBIS, *Near East*, November 10, 1986, p. D1; and Thomas Koszinowski, "Ali Lutfi," *Orient*, vol. 26 (September 1985), pp. 295–98.

23. "Min Khariji Jami'at al-Wilayat al-Mutahhida fi al-'Alam al-'Arabi wa-Tullabiha," *al-Majalla*, October 17, 1989, pp. 72–73.

CHAPTER 2

1. "Nastawrid 78 fi al-Mi'a min Ihtiyajatina al-Ghidha'iyya," *al-Ahram al-Iqtisadi*, April 11, 1988, pp. 42–43. (Hereafter *AI*.)

2. *AI*, February 29, 1988, p. 96.

3. "Drought's Little Local Difficulty," *Economist*, July 2–8, 1988, p. 10.

4. It constitutes 63 percent of urban diets, according to Ibrahim Soliman and Shahla Shapouri, "The Impact of Wheat Price Policy Change on Nutritional Status in Egypt" (U.S. Department of Agriculture, Economic Research Service, February 1984), cited in Jean-Jacques Dethier and Kathy Funk, "The Language of Food: PL 480 in Egypt," *Middle East Report*, vol. 17 (March–April 1987), p. 23.

5. Harold Alderman, Joachim von Braun, and Sakr Ahmed Sakr, *Egypt's Food Subsidy and Rationing System: A Description* (Washington: International Food Policy Research Institute, October 1982), p. 29. According to International Wheat Council, *World Wheat Statistics* (London, 1987), p. 94, only in Bolivia and Pakistan, where subsidies bring the price of bread down to 3 cents a loaf, are bread prices remotely comparable to Egypt's.

6. World Bank, *World Development Report 1989* (Oxford University Press, 1989), p. 164.

7. A. D. Little & Co., *Investment Opportunities in Egypt: Project Listings and Profiles* (Cairo, 1981), cited in U. S. Agency for International Development, *Country Development Strategy Statement: Egypt, Fiscal Year 1984, Annex: Policy Issues Facing Egypt* (Washington, 1982), p. 5.

8. See, for example, Ali Khamis, "al-Fallah Ya'mal, al-Hukuma Taksib . . . al-Zira'a Tadahwara," *al-Wafd*, March 14, 1987; and Muhammad al-Fiqqi, "Hukumat al-Hizb al-Watani . . . wal-Fallah al-Mazlum," *al-Ahrar*, March 9, 1987.

9. The best analysis of the military's role in the Egyptian economy is Robert Springborg, "The President and the Field Marshal: Civil-Military Relations in Egypt Today," *Middle East Report*, vol. 17 (July–August 1987), pp. 4–16. Also see Misbah Qutb, "Hal Huwa Infitah 'Askari Ba'd Fashl al-Infitah al-Iqtisadi?" *al-Ahali*, June 4, 1986.

10. Discussed in detail in Edward Hoyt, "Taming the Desert with the Military," *Business Monthly*, vol. 4 (January 1988), pp. 16 and 28.

11. Middle East News Agency, "Ministers Review Wheat Consumption, Subsidies," July 16, 1988, in Foreign Broadcast Information Service, *Daily Report: Near East & South Asia*, July 20, 1988, p. 9. (Hereafter FBIS, *Near East*.)

12. Ibid.; and John Parker, "Egypt: Wheat," *USDA Market Fundamentals*, April 28, 1989, p. 1.

13. "Mubarak 23 July Revolution Anniversary Speech," cited in FBIS, *Near East*, July 21, 1988, p. 13.

14. Lester R. Brown, "The Browning of the Green Revolution," *Washington Post*, July 3, 1988.

15. *Agricultural Outlook* (U.S. Department of Agriculture), no. 146 (October 1988), pp. 19–21.

16. U.S. Agency for International Development, *Status Report: United States Economic Assistance to Egypt* (Cairo, September 1988), p. 2.

17. For an account of the trade war, see Robert L. Paarlberg, *Fixing Farm Trade* (Cambridge, Mass.: Ballinger, 1988), pp. 91–97.

18. *Middle East Economic Digest*, May 5, 1989, p. 21. (Hereafter *MEED*.)

19. Tony Walker, "Mubarak Tries to Rally Egypt's Frustrated Creditors," *Financial Times*, September 21, 1988.

20. "Special Report Australia," *MEED*, March 24, 1989, p. 11; and *MEED*, September 23, 1988, p. 14.

21. Markaz al-Dirasat al-Siyasiyya wal-Istratijiyya bil-Ahram, *al-Taqrir al-Istratiji al-'Arabi 1986* (Cairo: al-Ahram, 1987), p. 427.

22. Andrew Cunningham, "Leaving Debtors Out in the Cold," *MEED*, January 12, 1990, pp. 4–6.

23. "Debtor Countries Face Tough 1989," *MEED*, December 23, 1988, p. 18; and figures supplied by the U.S. Office of Management and Budget.

24. Egyptians consumed 1.5 million tons of sugar annually, one-third of it imported. At the end of 1987 the price of sugar shot from $169 a ton to $310. David Butter, "Supply Minister Faces the People's Wrath," *MEED*, March 19, 1988, p. 4.

25. Ibid.; "Dr. Galal Abu al-Dhahab Wazir al-Tamwin li-'Uktubir'," *Uktubir*, May 22, 1988, p. 16; and "Qabla Munaqashat al-Lajna al-Iqtisadiyya bi-Majlis al-Sha'b lil-'Azma al-Tamwiniyya," *AI*, April 4, 1988, pp. 12–13.

26. For a sympathetic analysis of what population growth has cost Egypt in recent years, see René Dumont and Marcel Mazoyer, *Socialisms and Development* (Praeger, 1973), pp. 185–207.

27. John Waterbury, *Egypt: Burdens of the Past/Options for the Future* (Indiana University Press, 1978), pp. 121 and 126. Figures from Population Reference Bureau, *1990 World Population Data Sheet* (Washington, 1990).

28. The classic work on Egypt's housing problems is Milad Hanna, *Uridu Maskanan: Mushkila laha Hall* (Cairo: Ruz al-Yusuf, 1978). For an update on the problem, see Anwar al-Himaqi, "Azmat Iskan," and Muhammad Abu al-Shuhud, "Mi'at al-Malayin Mukhassasa lil-Iskan Mujammida," *AI*, August 8, 1988, pp. 16–17 and 18–20.

29. John Kifner, "Cairo's Flood of People Destroys Nile Farmlands," *New York Times*, November 6, 1986.

30. Saad Eddin Ibrahim, "Urbanization in the Arab World: The Need for an Urban Strategy," in Nicholas S. Hopkins and Saad Eddin Ibrahim, eds., *Arab Society: Social Science Perspectives* (Cairo: American University in Cairo Press, 1985), p. 127; "Cairo's Middle Class Faces Severe Housing Shortage," *Christian Science Monitor*, May 22, 1989.

31. Andrew Gowers, "More and Still More Mouths to Feed," *Financial Times*, June 27, 1988; Sa'd al-Din Ibrahim, "Hawla Zahirat al-Batala fi Awakhir al-Thamaninat," *AI*, August 22, 1988, pp. 19–21; "Kayf Tuwajih Misr Mushkilat 3 Malayin 'Atil Yabhathun 'An 'Amal," *al-Majalla*, August 30–September 5,

1989, pp. 46–48; and Adalat Hammad, "Unemployment in Egypt," *Japan Institute of Middle Eastern Economies*, no. 5 (Spring 1989), pp. 83–97.

32. Allen C. Kelley, Atef M. Khalifa, and M. Nabil El-Khorazaty, *Population and Development in Rural Egypt* (Duke University Press, 1982), pp. 8–12, 23, 27, and 36. Also see J. Mayone Stycos, Hussein Abdel Aziz Sayed, Roger Avery, and Samuel Fridman, *Community Development and Family Planning: An Egyptian Experiment* (Boulder, Colo.: Westview Press, 1988).

33. For an illuminating history of family planning programs in Egypt, see Charles F. Gallagher, "Population and Development in Egypt. Part II: New Hopes for Old Problems," *American University Field Staff Reports*, 32 (1981), pp. 1–21; and Saad M. Gadalla, *Is There Hope? Fertility and Family Planning in a Rural Egyptian Community* (Cairo: American University in Cairo Press, 1978).

34. Most studies suggest this was the result of the 1967 War and economic austerity, rather than family planning.

35. For the Islamists' family politics, see the excellent article by Mervat Hatem, "Egypt's Middle Class in Crisis: The Sexual Division of Labor," *Middle East Journal*, vol. 42 (Summer 1988), pp. 407–22; and Fauzi M. Najjar, "Egypt's Laws of Personal Status," *Arab Studies Quarterly*, vol. 10 (Summer 1988), pp. 319 and 345.

36. See Yahya Sadowski, "Egypt's Islamist Movement: A New Political and Economic Force," *Middle East Insight*, vol. 5 (November–December 1987), pp. 37–45.

37. George D. Moffett III, "Egypt Intensifies Population Battle," *Christian Science Monitor*, March 7, 1989.

38. Alan Richards, *Food Problems and Prospects in the Middle East* (Georgetown University, Center for Contemporary Arab Studies, 1984).

39. Abd al-Magid Farag, "al-10 al-Kubar: al-Misaha al-Mazru'a," *AI*, November 7, 1988, p. 91.

40. Calculated from table 2–3 using 6 million feddans (2.52 million hectares) as the approximate arable surface for Egypt.

41. See table 7–4.

42. World Bank, *Arab Republic of Egypt: Current Economic Situation and Economic Reform Program* (Washington, October 22, 1986), p. 27.

43. Christopher S. Wren, "The Greening of Sinai Mixes Water and Hope," *New York Times*, August 10, 1986; and Isam Rif'at, "al-Khuruj min Da'irat al-Dhull al-Qamhi," *AI*, May 22, 1989, pp. 8–9.

44. Sarah P. Voll, "Egyptian Land Reclamation Since the Revolution," *Middle East Journal*, vol. 34 (Spring 1980), p. 128.

45. Carl H. Gotsch and Wayne M. Dyer, "Rhetoric and Reason in the Egyptian 'New Lands' Debate," *Food Research Institute Studies*, vol. 18 (1982), pp. 129–47.

46. Pacific Consultants, *New Lands Productivity in Egypt: Technical and Economic Feasibility* (Cairo: U.S. Agency for International Development, 1980). The conclusions of this report remain quite controversial. For an Egyptian critique, see Dina Galal, "Amrika wa-Misr: al-Ma'una wal-'Alaqa,"

AI, August 3, 1987, pp. 32–34. For an American critique, see Jennifer Bremer, *New Lands Concepts Paper II: Rethinking an AID Assistance Strategy for the New Lands of Egypt* (Washington: Development Alternatives, 1981).

47. For discussion of new irrigation techniques and their economics, see Ahmad Ali Kamal, "Taqyim Mashru'at al-Rayy fi Misr," *l'Egypte contemporaine*, vol. 76 (April 1985), pp. 69–92.

48. Anne Charnock, "The Greening of Egypt," *New Scientist*, vol. 109 (January 23, 1986), pp. 44–47. For an evaluation of plasticulture technologies, see Sharif S. Elmusa, "A Multilevel Analysis of the Characteristics, Determinants, and Impact of Technological Change in East Jordan Valley Agriculture (1950–1980): A Study in Development and Dependence," Ph.D. dissertation, M.I.T., May 1986.

49. On the loss of agricultural land through urban sprawl, brickmaking, and erosion, see Usama Rashid, "Man Yahmi al-Ard al-Zira'iyya?" *al-Ahali*, September 19, 1984; and Galila Gamal al-Qadi, "al-Numuw al-'Umrani 'ala al-Aradi al-Zira'iyya wa-Azmat al-Iskan fi Madinat al-Qahira," *Le Monde Diplomatique* (Arabic Edition) (June 1990), p. 7.

50. Mohammed Salah Zohar, "If Egypt Is to Develop There Must Be Massive Relocation, Study Says," *Middle East Times*, May 20–26, 1988; and John King, "Letter from Sadat City," *Middle East International*, June 12, 1987, p. 20.

51. Fred Wendorf, Romuald Schild, and Angela E. Close, "An Ancient Harvest on the Nile," *Science 82*, vol. 3 (November 1982), pp. 68–73.

52. Alan Richards, "The Agricultural Crisis in Egypt," *Journal of Development Studies*, vol. 16 (1980), p. 304.

53. "Rice Self-Sufficiency: An Ambitious Plan," *Middle East Times*, June 18–24, 1988.

54. See the excellent survey by Richard H. Adams, Jr., "Development and Structural Change in Rural Egypt, 1952 to 1982," *World Development*, vol. 13 (June 1985), p. 713.

55. Youssef A. Wally, "Dedication," in *Rice Farming Systems: New Directions* (Manila: International Rice Research Institute, 1989), p. 5.

56. The seminal study was ERA 2000, "Further Mechanization of Egyptian Agriculture," report prepared for U.S. Agency for International Development, Gaithersburg, 1979.

57. The area of arable land—suitable for cultivation—in Egypt is relatively fixed at about 6 million feddans. But by planting in different seasons, farmers can produce two or even three crops on the same piece of land, resulting in a much larger, and potentially expandable, cropped area.

58. See the studies assembled in Alan Richards and Philip L. Martin, eds., *Migration, Mechanization, and Agricultural Labor Markets in Egypt* (Boulder, Colo.: Westview Press, 1983).

59. John Kerr, "The Egyptian Agricultural Machinery Market: A Case Study of the Turkish Thresher," Master's thesis, Stanford University, August 1988. For a full discussion of the debate over the economics of agricultural mechanization in Egypt, see Richards and Martin, *Migration, Mechaniza-*

tion, pp. 1–17. An excellent update is Simon Commander, *The State and Agricultural Development in Egypt since 1973* (London: Ithaca Press, 1987), pp. 233–76.

60. "Dr. Ibrahim Antar fi Jami'at al-Mansura: Amam Misr Fursat Ziyadat al-Intaj al-Zira'i bi-Nisbat 80% bi-Tahwil al-Dalta ila Aradi min al-Daraja al-Uwla," *AI*, January 25, 1988, p. 16; and Ibrahim Antar, "Comprehensive Plan to Rejuvenate Egypt's Agricultural Land," *Middle East Times*, October 4–10, 1987. For a critique of the program, see Adil al-Qadi, "Hay'at Tahsin al-Aradi Tusahim bi-Malayin al-Junayh," *al-Wafd*, March 13, 1988.

61. John Jeavons, *How to Grow More Vegetables Than You Ever Thought Possible on Less Land Than You Can Imagine* (Willits, Calif.: Ecology Action, 1982).

62. Mustafa al-Gabali, *Nazra 'Asriyya 'ala al-Zira'a fi Misr* (Cairo: Dar al-Ta'awun, 1984).

63. For the rationale of this approach, see the interview with Sayyid Mar'i in Gamal al-Sharqawi, *Misr Tastati'u Tasdir al-Qamh* (Cairo: Dar al-Thaqafa al-Jadida, 1986), pp. 9–14.

64. Jerry Foytik and Nabil Habashy, "Minimizing Egypt's Foreign Exchange Deficit for 18 Crops," Economics Working Paper 170 (Davis, Calif.: Agricultural Development Systems—Egypt Project, July 1983).

65. Abd al-Azim Muhammad Mustafa and Sa'd Nassar, "Dawr al-Zira'a al-Misriyya fi Tahqiq al-Amn al-Ghidha'i," *l'Egypte contemporaine*, vol. 72 (October 1981), pp. 105–19.

66. al-Sharqawi, *Misr Tastati'u Tasdir al-Qamh*, p. 27.

67. Adams, "Development and Structural Change," pp. 705–23.

68. Dana G. Dalrymple, *Development and Spread of High-Yielding Wheat Varieties in Developing Countries* (U.S. Agency for International Development, 1986), pp. 44–45. After 1984 there were some gains in rice production as a result of employing an early-maturing Japanese variety.

69. Jack Doyle, *Altered Harvest* (Penguin Books, 1985). Additional questions have been raised about ecological effects and the gene pool.

70. For excellent discussions of the social and economic impact of the Green Revolution, see Keith Griffin, *Alternative Strategies for Economic Development* (London: Macmillan, 1989), pp. 132–63; and Michael Lipton and Richard Longhurst, *Modern Varieties, International Agricultural Research, and the Poor* (Washington: World Bank, 1985).

71. Wendy L. Wall, "Growing Pains: In Indonesia's Paddies, the Rice Revolution Loses Some Ground," *Wall Street Journal*, April 1, 1988.

72. Roy L. Prosterman and Jeffrey M. Riedinger, *Egyptian Development and U.S. Aid: A 6-Year Report* (Seattle: Rural Development Institute, November 1985), p. 14.

73. Ibid., pp. 15–16.

74. The most important of these studies are al-Gabali, *Nazra 'Asriyya*; E.T. York and others, *Strategies for Accelerating Agricultural Development* (U.S. Agency for International Development and U.S. Department of Agriculture, July 1982); and Youssef Wally, *Strategy of Agricultural Development in the*

Eighties (Arab Republic of Egypt, Ministry of Agriculture and Food Security, February 1982).

75. Abd al-Magid Farag, "al-10 al-Kubar: Numuw al-Intaj al-Ghidha'i," *AI*, June 12, 1989, p. 51.

76. M. Mohiey Nasrat and A. Ahmed Goueli, "The Productivity of the Human Work Force in Traditional Agriculture with Special Reference to Egypt," in *Proceedings of the World Food Conference of 1976* (Iowa State University Press, 1977), pp. 331–37; and John M. Antle and Ali S. Aitah, "Rice Technology, Farmer Rationality, and Agricultural Policy in Egypt," *American Journal of Agricultural Economics*, vol. 65 (November 1983), pp. 667–74.

77. This is the sentiment of Richard H. Adams, Jr., *Development and Social Change in Rural Egypt* (Syracuse University Press, 1986).

78. Dan Morgan, *Merchants of Grain* (Penguin Books, 1980), pp. 38–39.

79. For the structural factors that led to the 1972 food crisis, see Harriet Friedmann, "The Political Economy of Food: The Rise and Fall of the Postwar International Food Order," *American Journal of Sociology*, vol. 88 (1982), pp. S248–86. The outstanding study of the discrete forces that led to famine in the Sahel is Richard W. Franke and Barbara H. Chasin, *Seeds of Famine* (Montclair, N.J.: Allanheld Osmun and Co., 1980).

80. Waterbury, *Egypt*, p. 121.

81. Jean-Jacques Dethier, *Trade, Exchange Rate, and Agricultural Pricing Policies in Egypt* (Washington: World Bank, 1989), vol. 2, p. 96.

82. "President Makes May Day Speech at Rally," May 1, 1988, in FBIS, *Near East*, May 3, 1988, p. 15.

83. Ibid., p. 13.

84. Speech at Mit Birah village on the occasion of Farmers Day, September 8, 1988, in FBIS, *Near East*, September 13, 1988, pp. 14 ff.

85. Gamal Fadil, "Misr: Kayf Tushfiya min Idman al-Qamh?" *AI*, March 7, 1988, p. 27. For a long discussion of how varying techniques for processing flour and cereal might affect wheat consumption, see Sa'd Taha Allam and others, "Istihlak al-Fard 183 Kg . . . Limadha?" *AI*, September 18, 1989, pp. 70–76.

86. Foreign Agricultural Service, *Annual Situation Report: Egypt* (U.S. Department of Agriculture, March 6, 1986), p. 13.

87. *Africa Research Bulletin*, June 30, 1989, p. 9582.

88. al-Sharqawi, *Misr Tastati'u Tasdir al-Qamh*, p. 19.

89. Ashraf Khalil, "Baker Makes 200-Pounds-a-Day Profit on Black Market," *al-Sha'b*, April 4, 1989, in FBIS, *Near East*, April 11, 1989, p. 9.

90. Fikriya Ahmad, "Demonstrations Over Bread Prices in al-Minya," *al-Wafd*, February 6, 1989, in FBIS, *Near East*, February 8, 1989, p. 10.

91. Nihad Muhammad, "Arrests Reported for Protests Over Bread Price," *al-Wafd*, April 10, 1989, in FBIS, *Near East*, April 13, 1989, p. 14; Muhammad Asfur, "Anyone Who Does Not Lose His Life in the Bread Queue Can Lose his Freedom," *al-Wafd*, April 17, 1989, in FBIS, *Near East*, April 20, 1989, p. 12.

92. Tony Walker, "Mubarak Tries to Rally Egypt's Frustrated Creditors," *Financial Times*, September 21, 1988.

93. Keith Schneider, "World Grain Supplies Are Dropping," *New York Times*, August 4, 1988.

94. Nazira al-Afandi, "Ghidha'una al-Yawmi wal-Taqallubat al-Duwaliyya," *AI*, August 1, 1988, p. 58.

95. Mustafa Kamil Murad, "The Opposition's Opinion: Bread Crisis!" *al-Ahrar*, April 10, 1989, in FBIS, *Near East*, April 13, 1989, pp. 14–15.

96. Alderman, von Braun, and Sakr, *Egypt's Food Subsidy*, p. 24.

97. Abd al-Aziz Hilali, *al-Akhbar*, April 18, 1989, in FBIS, *Near East*, April 21, 1989, p. 9.

98. *MEED*, April 14, 1989, p. 11.

99. FBIS, *Near East*, April 11, 1989, p. 10.

100. Diana deTreville, *Food Processing and Distribution Systems in Rural Egypt: Grain, Bread and Dairy Products* (Cairo: U.S. Agency for International Development, 1983), pp. 67–68. For a typical statement of the anti-subsidy position, see Isam Rif'at, "Raghif al-Khubz: Azma min al-Intaj am al-Istihlak?" *AI*, August 15, 1978, pp. 4–11.

101. al-Sharqawi, *Misr Tastati'u Tasdir al-Qamh*, p. 19.

102. Harold Alderman and Joachim von Braun, *The Effects of the Egyptian Food Ration and Subsidy System on Income Distribution and Consumption* (Washington: International Food Policy Research Institute, 1984), pp. 20–22.

103. Shahla Shapouri and Ibrahim Soliman, *Egyptian Meat Market: Policy Issues in Trade, Prices and Expected Market Performance* (U.S. Department of Agriculture, 1985), pp. 11, 12, and 14.

104. "The major inefficiencies in allocation were inherent in Egyptian agricultural policy before the budget outlays for food subsidies began to expand in the 1970s. The net social loss in the production and consumption of all the commodities considered in this study accounted for 1.5 percent of national income in 1979/80. The bulk of the social costs result from the protection of livestock production, the taxation of cotton and depressed cereal prices, with only the latter being partly a result of explicit and implicit food subsidies." Harold Alderman and Joachim von Braun, "Egypt's Food Subsidy Policy: Lessons and Options," *Food Policy*, vol. 11 (August 1986), pp. 233–34.

105. Mahmud Abd al-Fadil, "al-Jadid fi Rif al-Saba'inat wal-Thamaninat," *al-Ahali*, January 4, 1984.

106. Frances Moore Lappé, *Diet for a Small Planet* (Ballantine Books, 1971), pp. 6–8.

107. James Fitch and Ibrahim Soliman, "The Livestock Economy in Egypt: An Appraisal of the Current Situation," Economics Working Paper 29 (Davis, Calif.: Agricultural Development Systems—Egypt Project, 1981), p. 6. Volumes are mistakenly given in millions of tons. For 1985 imports, see Foreign Agricultural Service, *Annual Situation Report: Egypt*, p. 21.

108. Alan Richards, "Agricultural Crisis in Egypt," *Journal of Development Studies*, vol. 16 (1980). For additional research on the impact of livestock

production, see Shala Shapouri and Ibrahim Soliman, "The Role of Meat in the Egyptian Food Economy," Economics Working Paper 119 (Davis, Calif.: Agricultural Development Systems—Egypt Project, February 1983), p. 3. Also see James B. Fitch and Ibrahim A. Soliman, "Livestock and Small Farmer Labor Supply," in Richards and Martin, eds., *Migration, Mechanization*, pp. 45–78.

109. al-Sharqawi, *Misr Tastati'u Tasdir al-Qamh*, p. 9.

110. The best introduction to cotton in the history of Egyptian agricultural policy is Alan Richards, *Egypt's Agricultural Development, 1800–1980* (Boulder, Colo.: Westview Press, 1982).

111. William Cuddihy, *Agricultural Price Management in Egypt* (Washington: World Bank, 1980), pp. iv and 89.

112. The most famous statement of this argument that state intervention suppresses yields is the so-called Berg report: *Accelerated Development in Sub-Saharan Africa: An Agenda for Action* (Washington: World Bank, 1981), pp. 45–69.

113. For a discussion of some of the factors that lead to sluggish supply responses to price changes in Egyptian agriculture, see Hadi S. Esfahani, "Growth, Employment and Income Distribution in Egyptian Agriculture, 1964–79," especially p. 1205; and Harold Alderman, "Food Subsidies and State Policies in Egypt," in Alan Richards, ed., *Food, States, and Peasants: Analyses of the Agrarian Question in the Middle East* (Boulder, Colo.: Westview Press, 1986), p. 187. For a global statement of the argument, see Raj Krisna, "Some Aspects of Agricultural Growth, Price Policy, and Equity in Developing Countries," *Food Research Institute Studies*, vol. 18 (1982), pp. 1–34.

114. Also, see Joachim von Braun and Hartwig de Haen, *The Effects of Food Price and Subsidy Policies on Egyptian Agriculture* (Washington: International Food Policy Research Institute, 1983), p. 77.

115. Alderman and von Braun, "Egypt's Food Subsidy Policy," p. 234.

116. Usama Saraya, "al-Zira'a Ma Zalat Tahtall al-Muqaddima fi al-Nashat al-Iqtisadi bi Misr," *AI*, June 26, 1989, p. 16.

117. Alderman and von Braun, "Egypt's Food Subsidy Policy," p. 227.

118. Quoted in John Waterbury, "'Aish: Egypt's Growing Food Crisis," *Northeast Africa Series*, vol. 19, no. 3 (American Universities Field Staff, Inc., 1974), p. 10.

119. World Bank, *Arab Republic of Egypt*, p. 28.

120. *The Strategy of Economic Development* (Yale University Press, 1958), pp. 109–10.

121. World Bank, *Egypt: Fertilizer Industry Review* (Washington, January 1988), p. ii.

122. The beginnings of this reassessment may be credited to John W. Mellor, *The New Economics of Growth* (Cornell University Press, 1976). For a recent summary of the debate, see Bob Sutcliffe, "Industry and Underdevelopment Re-examined," *Journal of Development Studies*, vol. 21 (October 1984), pp. 121–33.

123. Strong forward linkages characterize cotton production in many parts

of the world; see Prem S. Laumas and Martin Williams, "Cotton Textiles— An Agro-Industry," *World Development*, vol. 15 (June 1987), pp. 841–45.

124. From the 1930s into the 1970s Egypt did just the reverse, reserving ELS cotton for inefficient local firms and thereby sacrificing millions of dollars in potential export profits.

125. World Bank, *Egypt: Review of the Finances of the Decentralized Public Sector* (Washington, March 1987), vol. 1, p. 97.

126. James Bedding, "From Bulk to Boutiques," *Middle East*, May 1988, pp. 27–28.

127. Peter B.R. Hazell and Ailsa Roell, *Rural Growth Linkages: Household Expenditure Patterns in Malaysia and Nigeria* (Washington: International Food Policy Research Institute, 1983), p. 12. Also see Barbara Harriss, "Regional Growth Linkages from Agriculture," *Journal of Development Studies*, vol. 23 (January 1987), pp. 275–89.

128. Bent Hansen and Samir Radwan, *Employment Opportunities and Equity in a Changing Economy: Egypt in the 1980s* (Geneva: International Labour Office, 1982), pp. 64–65.

129. Donald C. Mead and others, *Small Enterprises in Egypt: A Study of Two Governorates*, Working Paper 16 (Michigan State University, April 1984).

130. David Freidman's *The Misunderstood Miracle: Industrial Development and Political Change in Japan* (Cornell University Press, 1988) highlights the role of small firms in the Japanese economy and debunks the myth that large-scale enterprises have been the key to development.

131. Gunter Meyer, "Socioeconomic Structure and Development of Small-Scale Manufacturing in Old Quarters of Cairo," paper presented at the annual meeting of the Middle East Studies Association in Baltimore, November 15–17, 1987.

132. Nigel Harris, *The End of the Third World: Newly Industrializing Countries and the Decline of Ideology* (Penguin Books, 1986), pp. 56–59.

133. For a detailed analysis of the economics of scale, see Frances Stewart, *Technology and Underdevelopment* (London: Macmillan, 1977).

134. The common wisdom among development economists has been that the experience of Taiwan testifies to the importance of policy reform as a trigger to economic growth. For penetrating alternative analyses, particularly relevant for Egypt, see Gustav Ranis, "The Role of Institutions in Transition Growth: The East Asian Newly Industrializing Countries," *World Development*, vol. 17 (1989), pp. 1443–53; and Alice H. Amsden, "Taiwan's Economic History: A Case of *Etatisme* and a Challenge to Dependency Theory," in Robert H. Bates, ed., *Toward a Political Economy of Development* (University of California Press, 1988), pp. 142–75.

135. Harris, *End of the Third World*, p. 48.

136. Carl Liedholm and Donald Mead, *Small Scale Industries in Developing Countries: Empirical Evidence & Policy Implications* (Michigan State University, 1987), pp. 91–93.

137. This is the central point in a new wave of studies, including Tom Peters, *Beyond Hierarchy: Organizations in the 1990s* (Knopf, 1991); and

Michael J. Piore and Charles F. Sabel, *The Second Industrial Divide: Possibilities For Prosperity* (Basic Books, 1984).

138. "The Rural Crisis, and What to Do About It," *Economic Development Quarterly*, vol. 2 (1988), p. 5.

139. Paul Bairoch, "Agriculture and the Industrial Revolution, 1700–1914," in Carlo M. Cipolla, ed., *The Fontana Economic History of Europe: The Industrial Revolution* (London: Fontana Books, 1973), pp. 452–506.

140. *Can the Third World Survive?* (Johns Hopkins University Press, 1983), p. 147.

141. Irma Adelman, "Beyond Export-Led Growth," *World Development*, vol. 12 (September 1984), p. 939.

142. For a discussion of the respective merits of agriculture and industry as leading sectors in economic development, see Gavin Kitching, *Development and Underdevelopment in Historical Perspective* (London: Methuen, 1982).

143. The rural constituency for reform is a latent one at best. Chapter 3 discusses one of the obstacles to its mobilization—the difference of interests that divides rich and poor peasants. Chapter 5 analyzes another obstacle, the existence of anti-reform lobbies among agricultural capitalists.

144. Cuddihy, *Agricultural Price Management*, p. v.

CHAPTER 3

1. Usama Rashid, "Zuwwar al-Fajr Yuhajimun al-Qura," *al-Ahali*, May 19, 1982.

2. James A. Phillips, "Options for the U.S. as Egypt's Time of Reckoning Nears," *Heritage Foundation Backgrounder*, no. 546 (November 10, 1986), p. 3.

3. It draws heavily on several excellent accounts of Egyptian agricultural policy, particularly John Waterbury, *The Egypt of Nasser and Sadat: The Political Economy of Two Regimes* (Princeton University Press, 1983) chap. 12; Alan Richards, *Egypt's Agricultural Development, 1800–1980* (Boulder, Colo.: Westview Press, 1982); Simon Commander, *The State & Agricultural Development in Egypt since 1973* (London: Ithaca Press, 1987); and Jean-Jacques Dethier, *Trade, Exchange Rate, and Agricultural Pricing Policies in Egypt*, 2 vols. (Washington: World Bank, 1989).

4. For the development of the debate over land reform, see Gabriel Baer, "Egyptian Attitudes Toward Land Reform, 1922–1955," in Walter Z. Laqueur, ed., *The Middle East in Transition* (London: Routledge, 1958), pp. 80–99.

5. Mahmoud Abdel-Fadil, *Development, Income Distribution, and Social Change in Rural Egypt (1952–1970)* (Cambridge University Press, 1975), pp. 4–5.

6. Ibid., p. 5.

7. Ibid., pp. 14 and 44.

8. On the rising tide of rural violence, see Nathan J. Brown, *Peasant Politics in Modern Egypt* (Yale University Press, 1990), pp. 141–47. On the growth of elite anxiety, see Baer, "Egyptian Attitudes," pp. 80–99.

9. After the coup of 1952 all political parties in Egypt were suppressed. When political competition was permitted again in the 1980s, most of the prerevolutionary parties renewed their activities. The same parties that debated the question of agrarian reform in the 1940s tussled over the issue of revising the Land Law thirty years later. See Roel Meijer, "Contemporary Egyptian Historiography of the Period 1936–1952: A Study of Its Scientific and Political Character," Ph.D. dissertation, Amsterdam, 1985, pp. xii–xv.

10. See Brown, *Peasant Politics*; and Aziz Khanqi, "Hawadith al-Ightiyal fi al-Rif," *al-Ahram*, October 23, 1944, in Baer, *Egyptian Attitudes*, p. 85. There were insurrections on estates in Gharbiyya, Sharqiyya, and Daqhiliyya.

11. Hanna Batatu, *The Egyptian, Syrian, and Iraqi Revolutions: Some Observations on Their Underlying Causes and Social Character* (Georgetown University, Center for Contemporary Arab Studies, 1983), p. 8.

12. Baer even suggests that the Free Officers may have worried that rural unrest might fuel movement toward a "Communist revolution"; *Egyptian Attitudes*, p. 98.

13. Robert Mabro, *The Egyptian Economy: 1952–1972* (Oxford University Press, 1974), pp. 61 and 73.

14. The classic study of the landowning elite in Egypt before 1952 is Asim al-Dissuqi, *Kibar Mullak al-Aradi al-Zira'iyya wa-Dawruhum fi al-Mujtama' al-Misri 1914–1952* (Cairo, 1975). For additional details, see Doreen Warriner, *Land Reform and Development in the Middle East: A Study of Egypt, Syria and Iraq* (Westport, Conn.: Greenwood Press, 1962).

15. The best description of how the Free Officers implemented land reform is Ahmad Hamrush, *Qissat Thawrat 23 Yuliyu*, vol. 1 (Cairo: Madbuli, 1983), pp. 249–62. Hamrush was one of two Free Officers who supervised the civilians who drafted the land reform law.

16. Five feddans was considered an adequate plot for a peasant household, since it would produce £E 128 in an average year, or enough to support a family of eight; see Sayed Marii, "The Agrarian Reform in Egypt," *International Labour Review*, vol. 69 (February 1954), pp. 145–46.

17. Even Michael Lipton, a passionate defender of small peasant farms, admits that the economics of redistributing land to the landless tends to inhibit production and promote poverty; "Towards a Theory of Land Reform," in David Lehmann, ed., *Agrarian Reform & Agrarian Reformism* (London: Faber and Faber, 1974), p. 284.

18. Gabriel S. Saab, *The Egyptian Agrarian Reform, 1952–1962* (Oxford University Press, 1967), pp. 20–21.

19. Ibid., p. 54.

20. Mohammed Heikal, *The Cairo Documents* (Doubleday, 1973), p. 26.

21. Doreen Warriner, *Agrarian Reform and Community Development in U.A.R.* (Cairo: Dar al-Ta'awun), pp. 30–31.

22. Abdel-Fadil, *Development, Income Distribution*, p. 10.

23. Salah Mansi, *al-Musharaka al-Siyasiyya lil-Fallahin* (Cairo: Dar al-Mawqif al-'Arabi, 1984), p. 87.

24. Alain de Janvry, *The Agrarian Question and Reformism in Latin America* (Johns Hopkins University Press, 1981), p. 218.

25. Mar'i's rising influence is detailed in Robert Springborg, *Family, Power and Politics in Egypt* (University of Pennsylvania Press, 1982), pp. 144–54. Practically the only aspect of agriculture that remained beyond his control was irrigation, which was dominated by an ancient and well-entrenched ministry of its own.

26. Magdi Hasanayn, one of the minority of socialist-oriented Free Officers, acknowledged that whatever chance there might have been for movement toward collective agriculture had been demolished by consolidation of small property rights under the land reform; *al-Sahra' . . . al-Thawra wal-Tharwa* (Cairo: al-Hay'a al-Misriyya al-'Amma lil-Kuttab, 1975), p. 76.

27. Land reform (or agrarian reform) is the redistribution of existing plots in order to improve productivity or social equity. Land reclamation is the use of technology to permit farming on previously uncultivable plots.

28. Hasanayn, *al-Sahra'*, p. 154.

29. Warriner, *Agrarian Reform*, p. 53.

30. Samir Radwan, *Agrarian Reform and Rural Poverty in Egypt, 1952–1975* (Geneva: International Labour Office, 1977), pp. 45–46.

31. Anouar Abdel-Malek, *Egypt: Military Society* (Random House, 1968), pp. 124 and 131.

32. A series of factors was at work, pushing Nasser in this direction—advice from Marshal Tito of Yugoslavia and Jawaharlal Nehru of India, aid from the Soviet Union, taunts from his Ba'thist rivals in Syria, and the threat of business power centers at home. The most detailed effort to sort out the mixture of these motives is Patrick O'Brien, *The Revolution in Egypt's Economic System: From Private Enterprise to Socialism 1952–1965* (Oxford University Press, 1966), pp. 199–240. For an updated account making use of more recently available memoirs, see Waterbury, *Egypt of Nasser and Sadat, pp. 57–82.*

33. For a fascinating account of these debates, written by one of the Free Officers who favored retaining a more market-oriented economy, see Abd al-Latif al-Baghdadi, *Mudhakkirat Abd al-Latif al-Baghdadi* (Cairo: al-Maktab al-Misri al-Hadith, 1977). Also see Hamrush, *Qissat Thawrat 23 Yuliyu*.

34. For the history of Nasser's evolving ideological commitments, see Jean Lacouture, *Nasser* (Knopf, 1973), pp. 221–58.

35. A major factor in Mar'i's downfall was the poor performance of the Ministry of Agriculture in combating a devastating outbreak of cotton worm in 1960. For Mar'i's own version of these events, see his *Awraq Siyasiyya*, pt. 2 (Cairo: al-Ahram Press, 1979), pp. 424–51.

36. Warriner, *Agrarian Reform*, pp. 44–45.

37. For the details of the rotation schemes, see Richards, *Egypt's Agricultural Development*.

38. Saab, *Egyptian Agrarian Reform*, pp. 148–50 and 190–96.

39. Mabro, *Egyptian Economy*, p. 69.

40. Saab, *Egyptian Agrarian Reform*, pp. 154–55.

41. Fathi Abd al-Fattah, *al-Nasiriyya wa-Tajribat al-Thawra min A'la* (Cairo: Dar al-Fikr, 1987), pp. 64–66.

42. Radwan, *Agrarian Reform*, pp. 62–63.

43. Ibid., p. 66.

44. O'Brien, *Revolution*, p. 141.

45. Charles Issawi, *Egypt in Revolution* (Oxford University Press, 1963), p. 28. Through the 1950s the regime still enjoyed £425 million of sterling assets built up during the war; Waterbury, *Egypt of Nasser and Sadat*, p. 61.

46. See Richard H. Adams, Jr., *Development and Social Change in Rural Egypt* (Syracuse University Press, 1986), chap. 2.

47. Joel S. Migdal, *Strong Societies and Weak States* (Princeton University Press, 1988), p. 204; quoting Malcolm H. Kerr's *The Arab Cold War*.

48. Robert L. Tignor, *State, Private Enterprise, and Economic Change in Egypt 1918–1952* (Princeton University Press, 1984), p. 236.

49. For a polished version of Uthman's critique, see Uthman Ahmad Uthman, *Safahat min Tajribati* (Cairo: al-Maktab al-Misri al-Hadith, 1981). For a Nasserist response, see Abdallah Imam, *Tajribat Uthman* (Cairo: Dar al-Mawqif al-'Arabi, 1981).

50. This is certainly the case in the analysis of Richard Adams's trenchant critique of Nasser, "Taxation, Control, and Agrarian Transition in Rural Egypt: A Local-Level View," in Alan Richards, ed., *Food, States, and Peasants* (Boulder, Colo.: Westview Press, 1986), pp. 159–82.

51. This section relies heavily on the work of Dethier, *Trade, Exchange Rate*, a rigorous analysis which promises to be the definitive work on this subject.

52. For details on the mechanisms by which Egypt overvalued its currency, see Giacomo Luciani, "Multiple Puzzle: Egypt's Exchange Rate Regime Controversy," *Journal of Arab Affairs*, vol. 5 (1986), pp. 111–30. For an attempt to analyze the actual prices various commodities (including cotton) would have commanded in the absence of such distortions, see John M. Page, Jr., *Shadow Prices for Trade Strategy and Investment Planning in Egypt*, World Bank Staff Working Papers 521 (Washington: World Bank, 1982).

53. For a detailed study, see Bruce Glassburner, "Exchange Rate Policy in Egypt Since 1975 and Its Significance for Cotton," in paper presented at the ADS Egypt-California Project Conference, "The Future of Cotton in the Egyptian Economy," Economics Working Paper 116 (December 18–19, 1982).

54. Dethier, *Trade, Exchange Rate*, vol. 1, pp. 191–97.

55. Simon Commander, "Land Management and Constraints: Some Issues in Agricultural Sector Policy," paper prepared for a conference on Politics and the Economy under Mubarak at the School of Oriental and African Studies (London, May 18, 1987), p. 7.

56. Nemat Shafik, "Private Investment in Egypt under the Infitah" (Oxford University, November 1988), pp. 10–11.

57. Michael Lipton, "Why Poor People Stay Poor," in John Harriss, ed.,

Rural Development: Theories of Peasant Economy and Agrarian Change (London: Hutchinson University Library, 1982), p. 67.

58. *Les fondements géographiques de l'histoire de l'Islam* (Paris: Flammarion, 1968).

59. See, for example, Karima Korayem, "The Rural-Urban Income Gap in Egypt and Biased Agricultural Pricing Policy," *Social Problems*, vol. 28 (April 1981), pp. 417–29; and the comments by Atif Sidqi (who later became prime minister) and Abd al-Aziz Hijazi (former prime minister) following Karima Kurayyim, "Tawzi' al-Dakhl Bayn al-Hadar wal-Rif fi Misr, 1952–1975," in *al-Iqtisad al-Misri fi Rub' Qarn, 1952–1977* (Cairo: al-Hay'a al-Misriyya al-'Amma lil-Kuttab, 1978), pp. 65–120.

60. Mabro, *Egyptian Economy*, pp. 115–24.

61. "Agricultural Prices, Growth and Sectoral Terms of Trade in Egypt," FAO/SIDA Seminar on Agricultural Sector Analysis in the Near East and North Africa, Cairo, October 20–26, 1975, cited in John Waterbury, "Egyptian Agriculture Adrift," in Barbara Huddleston and Jon McLin, eds., *Political Investments in Food Production* (Indiana University Press, 1979), pp. 63, 75.

62. For a revealing analysis of agricultural policies in Latin America which were quite similar to Egypt's in both their strengths and weaknesses, see Alain de Janvry, "Latin American Agriculture from Import Substitution Industrialization to Debt Crisis," in W. Ladd Hollist and F. LaMond Tullis, eds., *Pursuing Food Security Strategies and Obstacles in Africa, Asia, Latin America and the Middle East* (Boulder, Colo.: Lynne Rienner, 1987), pp. 197–229.

63. Ahmed H. Ibrahim, "Impact of Agricultural Policies on Income Distribution," in Gouda Abdel-Khalek and Robert Tignor, eds., *The Political Economy of Income Distribution in Egypt* (New York: Holmes & Meier, 1982), p. 227.

64. Hadi S. Esfahani, "Growth, Employment and Income Distribution in Egyptian Agriculture, 1964–1979," *World Development*, vol. 15 (September 1987), p. 1214.

65. *al-Ahram*, October 27, 1974, cited in David Hirst and Irene Beeson, *Sadat* (London: Faber and Faber, 1981), p. 202.

66. Esfahani, "Growth, Employment and Income Distribution," p. 1215.

67. George R. Gardner and John G. Parker, *Agricultural Statistics of Egypt, 1970–84* (U.S. Department of Agriculture, 1985), p. 38.

68. Radwan, *Agrarian Reform*, pp. 45–46.

69. Karl Marx, "The Eighteenth Brumaire of Louis Bonaparte," in David Fernbach, ed., *Karl Marx: Surveys from Exile* (Random House, 1974), p. 239.

70. Esfahani, "Growth, Employment and Income Distribution," p. 1207; and Dethier, *Trade, Exchange Rate*, vol. 1, pp. 126–27 and 253.

71. For a detailed description of how a rich peasant farm is likely to be organized—cropping patterns, labor organization, and so on—see Georg Stauth, "Capitalist Farming and Small Peasant Households in Egypt," *Review*, vol. 7 (Fall 1983), pp. 285–313. Also see Richard's magisterial *Egypt's Agricultural Development*, p. 205.

72. Abdel-Fadil, *Development, Income Distribution*, pp. 38–39.

73. Izzat al-Sa'adni, "La'nat al-Qutn Asabat al-Fallah al-Misri," *al-Ahram al-Iqtisadi*, November 15, 1975, pp. 13–15. (Hereafter *AI*.)

74. Abdel-Fadil, *Development, Income Distribution*, p. 23.

75. Éprime Eshag and M.A. Kamal, "Agrarian Reform in the United Arab Republic (Egypt)," *Bulletin of the Oxford University Institute of Economics and Statistics*, vol. 30 (May 1968), p. 78.

76. Jennifer Bremer, "Privatization of Agricultural Input Supply: Constraints and Opportunities for Reform," report prepared for U.S. AID (Robert Nathan Associates, February 11, 1986), p. II-8.

77. Ibrahim, "Impact of Agricultural Policies," pp. 215 and 217.

78. Radwan, *Agrarian Reform*, p. 69.

79. Waterbury, *Egypt of Nasser and Sadat*, p. 289.

80. Abdel-Fadil, *Development, Income Distribution*, p. 42, categorizes holders of five to twenty feddans as "middle peasants." But rural sociologists tend to define middle peasants as "a peasant population which has secure access to land of its own and cultivates it with family labor." See Eric R. Wolf, *Peasant Wars of the Twentieth Century* (Harper and Row, 1969), p. 291. In the Egyptian case, then, this means those who own three to five feddans. The group that Abdel-Fadil calls middle peasants (owners of five to twenty feddans) are, in the classical vocabulary of rural sociology, "rich peasants."

81. Among the richer cultivators, owning ten feddans or more, size of holding ceases to be a reliable guide to economic and political behavior. Instead, patterns of residence, officeholding, and access to capital become more important. Three subgroups are discernible. For a general discussion of the contribution of village notables, the rural gentry, and agrarian capitalists to economic development, see T.J. Byres, "Agrarian Transition and the Agrarian Question," *Journal of Peasant Studies*, vol. 4 (1977), pp. 258–74.

82. For a perceptive analysis of the rural elite in the nineteenth century, see Kenneth M. Cuno, "Landholding, Society and Economy in Rural Egypt, 1740–1850: A Case Study of Al-Daqahliyya Province," Ph.D. dissertation, University of California at Los Angeles, 1985.

83. Hamied Ansari, *Egypt: The Stalled Society* (State University of New York Press, 1986), pp. 263–65, gives a list of these clans.

84. Ibid., pp. 113–15.

85. Richard H. Adams, Jr., "Bureaucrats, Peasants and the Dominant Coalition: An Egyptian Case Study," *Journal of Development Studies*, vol. 22 (January 1986), pp. 336–54.

86. See Sohair Mehanna, Richard Huntington, and Rachad Antonius, *Irrigation and Society in Rural Egypt* (Cairo: American University Press, 1984).

87. Ansari, *Egypt*, p. 131.

88. Ibid., p. 106. Also see Muhammad Rashad, *Sirri Jiddan: Min Malafat Lajnat Tasfiyat al-'Iqta'* (Cairo: Dar al-Ta'awun, 1977).

89. Ansari, *Egypt*, pp. 101–02.

90. This argument is presented in Leonard Binder, *In a Moment of Enthusiasm: Political Power and the Second Stratum in Egypt* (University of

Chicago Press, 1978), pp. 12–13. Waterbury, *Egypt of Nasser and Sadat*, pp. 272–77, has tempered Binder's claims, but affirms that rural notables form an influential lobby in Egyptian politics.

91. Fu'ad Mursi, *Hadha al-Infitah al-Iqtisadi* (Cairo: Dar al-Thaqafa al-Jadida, 1984), p. 250–51.

92. Waterbury, *Egypt of Nasser and Sadat*, p. 280.

93. The best account of Sadat's early policies is John Waterbury, *Egypt: Burdens of the Past/Options for the Future* (Indiana University Press, 1978).

94. Mansi, *al-Musharaka al-Siyasiyya*, pp. 78–80; Muhammad Abd al-Hamid Abu Zayd, *Nizam al-'Umad bayn al-Ibqa' wal-Ilgha'* (Cairo: Dar al-Thaqafa al-'Arabiyya, 1984), p. 70.

95. Salah al-Din Mansi Muhammad, *al-Wujud al-Siyasi lil-Fallahin* (Cairo: Dar Nafi', 1984), pp. 35–37.

96. Ibid., p. 65.

97. Waterbury, *Egypt of Nasser and Sadat*, p. 285.

98. Huda Khalil, "75 'Amman 'ala Nidal al-Fallahin al-Ta'awuniyyin fi Misr," *al-Ahali*, December 14, 1983.

99. Waterbury, *Egypt of Nasser and Sadat*, p. 295.

100. Dethier, *Trade, Exchange Rate*, vol. 1, p. 195, and vol. 2, p. 224; and Joachim von Braun and Hartwig de Haen, *The Effects of Food Price and Subsidy Policies on Egyptian Agriculture* (Washington: International Food Policy Research Institute, 1983), p. 10.

101. Maury E. Bredahl, *Macroeconomic Policy and Agricultural Development: Concepts and Case Studies of Egypt, Morocco and Jordan* (University of Missouri, College of Agriculture, 1985), p. 6; and Dethier, *Trade, Exchange Rate*, vol. 1, pp. 254–55.

102. Harold Alderman and Joachim von Braun, "Egypt's Food Subsidy Policy: Lessons and Options," *Food Policy*, vol. 11 (August 1986), p. 224.

103. Harold Alderman and Joachim von Braun, *The Effects of the Egyptian Food Ration and Subsidy System on Income Distribution and Consumption* (Washington: International Food Policy Research Institute, 1984), p. 48.

104. The best account of the evolution of emigration policy is Ali E. Hillal Dessouki, "The Shift in Egypt's Migration Policy: 1952–1978," *Middle Eastern Studies*, vol. 18 (January 1982), pp. 53–68.

105. For an analysis of the successive waves of migration, see Nazli Choucri, "The Hidden Economy," *World Development*, vol. 14 (June 1986), p. 698.

106. Ann Mosely Lesch, "Egyptian Labor Migration: Economic Trends and Government Policies," *UFSI Reports, Africa*, no. 38 (1985), p. 7.

107. The difference of magnitude between recorded and actual remittances is discussed in detail in chap. 6.

108. David G. Becker, "'Bonanza Development' and the 'New Bourgeoisie': Peru Under Military Rule," in David G. Becker and others, *Postimperialism: International Capitalism and Development in the Late Twentieth Century* (Boulder, Colo.: Lynne Rienner, 1987), pp. 63–105.

109. For a critical assessment of these effects, see Saad Eddin Ibrahim,

"Oil, Migration, and the New Arab Social Order," in Malcolm H. Kerr and El Sayed Yassin, eds., *Rich and Poor States in the Middle East* (Boulder, Colo.: Westview Press, 1982), pp. 17–70.

110. Galal A. Amin and Elizabeth Awny, *International Migration of Egyptian Labour* (Ottowa: International Development Research Centre, May 1985), p. 113.

111. Ann Mosely Lesch, "The Impact of Labor Migration on Urban and Rural Egypt," *UFSI Reports, Africa*, no. 39 (1985), pp. 7–8.

112. Ibid., pp. 8–9.

113. Usama Rashid, "Man Yahmi al-Ard al-Zira'i?" *al-Ahali*, September 19, 1984.

114. Lesch, "Impact of Labor Migration," pp. 6–7.

115. Simon Commander and Aly Abdullah Hadhoud, "From Labour Surplus to Labour Scarcity? The Agricultural Labour Market in Egypt," *Development Policy Review*, vol. 2 (June 1986), pp. 164–65. A great deal of information about rural wages in Egypt is available. For benchmark studies see Bent Hansen, "Employment and Wages in Rural Egypt," *American Economic Review*, vol. 59 (1969), pp. 298–313; Robert Mabro, "Industrial Growth, Agricultural Under-Employment and the Lewis Model. The Egyptian Case, 1937–1965," *Journal of Development Studies*, vol. 3 (July 1967), pp. 322–51; and Hassan Youssef Aly and Richard Grabowski, "Technological Change and Surplus Labor in Egyptian Agriculture, 1952–1972," *Journal of Agricultural Economics*, vol. 35, (January 1984), pp. 109–16.

116. Commander, "Land Management and Constraints," p. 4.

117. Richard H. Adams, Jr., review of Samir Radwan and Eddy Lee's *Agrarian Change in Egypt, Journal of Development Studies*, vol. 23 (January 1987), pp. 313–14.

118. James F. Toth, review of Simon Commander's *The State & Agricultural Development in Egypt since 1973*, in *Middle East Journal*, vol. 42 (Autumn 1988), pp. 687–88.

119. Richard H. Adams, Jr., "Development and Structural Change in Rural Egypt, 1952 to 1982," *World Development*, vol. 13 (June 1985), p. 708.

120. This "consuming village" argument is best stated in Muhammad Abu Mandur, "al-Tashawwuh al-'Amm wa-Makhatir al-Mustaqbal," *AI*, March 26, 1984, pp. 24–37. Also see Gum'a Abduh Qasim, "al-Qarya al-Misriyya al-Istihlakiyya," *AI*, July 11, 1983, pp. 26–27.

121. Muhammad Abu Mandur, "al-Qarya al-Misriyya fi 'Asr al-Infitah wal-Naft," *Arab Researcher*, vol. 5 (October 1985), p. 53.

122. Gunter Mayer, "Socioeconomic Structure and Development of Small-Scale Manufacturing in Old Quarters of Cairo," paper presented at the annual meeting of the Middle East Studies Association, Baltimore, November 15–17, 1987.

123. Galal Amin, "al-Qita' al-Maghlub 'ala Amrihi," *AI*, April 5, 1982, pp. 22–23.

124. A string of estimable authors, from Karl Marx to Karl Wittfogel, have argued that control over irrigation works gives any regime in Cairo despotic

342 Notes (pages 91–96)

power vis-à-vis the rest of society; see Perry Anderson, *Lineages of the Absolutist State* (London: New Left Books, 1974), pp. 462–549. Most students of irrigation systems in the Middle East have disputed this thesis; see Helen Anne B. Rivlin, *The Agricultural Policy of Muhammad 'Ali in Egypt* (Harvard University Press, 1961) and Robert Fernea, *Shaykh and Effendi: Changing Patterns of Authority among the El Shabana of Southern Iraq* (Harvard University Press, 1970).

125. *The Challenge of World Poverty* (Vintage Books, 1970), p. 208.

126. James C. Scott, *Weapons of the Weak: Everyday Forms of Peasant Resistance* (Yale University Press, 1985), p. 29. For an application (and critique) of Scott's model using Egyptian examples, see Brown, *Peasant Politics*.

127. "'Adad Sukkan Misr bi-Jihaz al-Ihsa' Am 'Adad Sukkan Misr bil-Sa'a al-Sukkaniyya?" *AI*, June 5, 1989, pp. 46–47.

128. "Egypt: The Missing Farmland," *Middle East Economic Digest*, December 23, 1988, p. 23.

CHAPTER 4

1. For a critique of the conventional image of the bourgeoisie, see Immanuel Wallerstein, "The Bourgeois(ie) as Concept and Reality," *New Left Review*, no. 167 (1988), pp. 91–106. For an illuminating discussion of business groups in developing countries, see Nigel Harris, "New Bourgeoisies?" *Journal of Development Studies*, vol. 24 (January 1988), pp. 237–49.

2. David Vogel, "Why Businessmen Distrust Their State: The Political Consciousness of American Corporate Executives," *British Journal of Political Science*, vol. 8 (1978), pp. 45–78.

3. For Muhammad Ali's economic policies see Helen Anne B. Rivlin, *The Agricultural Policy of Muhammad 'Ali in Egypt* (Harvard University Press, 1961); Roger Owen, *The Middle East in the World Economy, 1800–1914* (London: Methuen, 1981), pp. 64–76; and Kenneth M. Cuno, "Landholding, Society and Economy in Rural Egypt, 1740–1850: A Case Study of al-Daqahliyya Province," Ph.D. dissertation, University of California at Los Angeles, 1985, pp. 358–549.

4. Robert L. Tignor, *State, Private Enterprise, and Economic Change in Egypt, 1918–1952* (Princeton University Press, 1984), p. 24.

5. For a lively account of the nineteenth century financial frauds perpetrated against Egypt, see David S. Landes, *Bankers and Pashas* (Harvard University Press, 1958).

6. Owen, *Middle East*, p. 223.

7. Tignor, *State, Private Enterprise*, pp. 27–37.

8. The most valuable account of why *dirigisme* prevails in late-developing

countries like Egypt is Alexander Gerschenkron, *Economic Backwardness in Historical Perspective* (Harvard University Press, 1962).

9. The best account of Bank Misr in English is Eric Davis, *Challenging Colonialism: Bank Misr and Egyptian Industrialization, 1920–1941* (Princeton University Press, 1983).

10. Tignor, *State, Private Enterprise*, p. 78. The capitulations were a series of tariff preferences that Western powers had enforced on Egypt since the mid-nineteenth century.

11. For a description of these lobbies and their programs, see Marius Deeb, *Party Politics in Egypt: The Wafd and Its Rivals, 1919–1939* (London: Ithaca Press, 1979), pp. 21–34.

12. Robert Tignor, "Equity in Egypt's Recent Past: 1945–1952," in Gouda Abdel-Khalek and Robert Tignor, eds., *The Political Economy of Income Distribution in Egypt* (New York: Holmes and Meier, 1982), pp. 20–54 and 110–11. The cost of these tariffs, of course, was borne by Egyptian consumers; local prices for wheat and corn were twice as high as international prices and provoked serious riots in 1938. The wheat import duty was finally abolished in 1950, but other restraints continued until Nasser abolished them in 1961.

13. Mohamed Mansour, "An Economic Analysis of the World Market for Egyptian Cotton," Ph.D. dissertation, Oregon State University, 1984.

14. See John Waterbury, *The Egypt of Nasser and Sadat: The Political Economy of Two Regimes* (Princeton University Press, 1983), pp. 60–82.

15. Anouar Abdel-Malek, *Egypt: Military Society* (Random House, 1968), supplied the classic discussion of the growth of ties between the army regime and the local bourgeoisie in a system of state capitalism. For a more recent study of the same trend, with lavish empirical details, see Samia Sa'id Imam, *Man Yamlik Misr?!* (Cairo: Dar al-Mustaqbal al-'Arabi, 1986), pp. 83–122.

16. John Waterbury, "Corruption, Political Stability and Development: Comparative Evidence from Egypt and Morocco," *Government and Opposition*, vol. 11 (Autumn 1976), pp. 439–40.

17. James M. Buchanan, Robert D. Tollison, and Gordon Tullock, eds., *Toward a Theory of the Rent-Seeking Society* (Texas A & M University Press, 1980), p. 3. During the 1950s and 1960s most development economists agreed that in the Third World, market forces alone did not lead to a socially desirable pattern of investment; see Tibor Scitovsky, "Two Concepts of External Economies," in A.N. Agarwala and S.P. Singh, eds., *The Economics of Underdevelopment* (Oxford University Press, 1958), pp. 295–308; and Ragnar Nurkse, *Problems of Capital Formation in Underdeveloped Countries* (Oxford University Press, 1967), pp. 4–31.

18. Once controversial, the continuity between Nasser's economic policies and Sadat's is now a well-established hypothesis. See Marie-Christine Aulas, "Sadat's Egypt: A Balance Sheet," *MERIP Reports*, no. 107 (July–August 1982), pp. 6–18; and Esmail Hosseinzadeh, "How Egyptian State Capitalism Reverted to Market Capitalism," *Arab Studies Quarterly*, vol. 10 (1988), pp. 299–318.

19. John Waterbury, *Egypt: Burdens of the Past/Options for the Future* (Indiana University Press, 1978), pp. 235–36.

20. For an analysis, see Maurice P. Martin, "The October Paper," *CEMAM Reports* (1974), pp. 55–64.

21. For evaluations of the overall impact of *infitah*, see Rodney Wilson, "The Developmental Impact of Egypt's Import Liberalisation," *Middle Eastern Studies*, vol. 22 (October 1986), pp. 481–504; and Jeswald W. Salacuse, "Foreign Investment and Legislative Exemptions in Egypt: Needed Stimulus or New Capitulations?" in Laurence O. Michalak and Jeswald W. Salacuse, eds., *Social Legislation in the Contemporary Middle East* (Berkeley: Institute of International Studies, 1986), pp. 241–61.

22. The idea of rent seeking was pioneered in an influential essay by Anne O. Krueger, "The Political Economy of the Rent-Seeking Society," *American Economic Review*, vol. 64 (June 1974), pp. 291–303. Dr. Krueger, one of the most insightful neoclassical economists to have studied development questions, has held powerful positions in the World Bank and her ideas have influenced that institution's dealings with Egypt.

23. For the wider effects of rent seeking, see the essays in Buchanan, Tollison, and Tullock, *Toward a Theory of the Rent-Seeking Society*.

24. In particular, the report by ERA 2000, "Further Mechanization of Egyptian Agriculture," prepared for U.S. Agency for International Development, Gaithersburg, 1979.

25. Jennifer Bremer, *New Lands Concepts Paper II: Rethinking an AID Assistance Strategy for the New Lands of Egypt* (Washington: Development Alternatives, 1981), p. 7.

26. Carl H. Gotsch and Wayne M. Dyer, "Rhetoric and Reason in the Egyptian 'New Lands' Debate," *Food Research Institute Studies*, vol. 18 (1982), pp. 130–31. Also see "Egypt: Desert Dreams," *Economist*, May 12, 1984, p. 39.

27. The Abis project was pioneered by a U.S. government agency, the Egyptian-American Rural Improvement Services Organization. The New Valley experimented with extending cultivation to a series of oases in the desert west of the Nile.

28. Sarah P. Voll, "Egyptian Land Reclamation Since the Revolution," *Middle East Journal*, vol. 34 (Spring 1980), pp. 133 and 135.

29. Mustafa al-Gabali, "Taqyim al-Tajriba al-Misriyya fi Istislah al-Aradi," *l'Egypte Contemporaine*, vol. 76 (April 1985), pp. 41–67.

30. Bremer, *New Lands Concepts Paper II*, p. 37.

31. Robert Springborg, "Patrimonialism and Policy Making in Egypt: Nasser and Sadat and the Tenure Policy for Reclaimed Lands," *Middle Eastern Studies*, vol. 15 (1979), pp. 49–69.

32. "Egypt: Desert Dreams," pp. 39–40.

33. "La Istithna'at fi Istislah al-Aradi," *al-Ahram al-Iqtisadi*, March 21, 1988, p. 45. (Hereafter *AI*.)

34. Gamal Fadil, "al-Islah al-Mafqud fi al-Istislah," *AI*, February 27, 1984,

pp. 27–29; and Alan Mackie, "All Change, But Only Very Slowly, on the Nile," *Euromoney*, July 1981, p. 99.

35. "I'fa' Daribi 10 Sanawat li-Istislah al-Aradi," *al-Ahram*, July 14, 1984.

36. "The Billionaires," *Fortune*, October 12, 1987, p. 125.

37. Karim Mahmud, "Sharikat Uthman La'abat Dawran Asasiyyan fi Fawzihi bi-Mansab al-Naqib," *al-Sha'b*, March 15, 1983. In 1974 Uthman officially retired from Arab Contractors so that he could join Sadat's cabinet. He now claims that he has no stock in that firm and that his personal wealth is quite modest. No one believes him. When he retired from Arab Contractors he retained the title of honorary chairman for life. He effectively controls the company through his brother Husayn, who became chairman on his retirement, and a dozen other relatives who pack the firm's board.

38. Uthman Ahmad Uthman, *Safahat min Tajribati* (Cairo: al-Maktab al-Misri al-Hadith, 1981), pp. 583–84.

39. "al-Lubi al-Iqtisadi wal-Ghazw min al-Dakhil," *al-Shira'*, April 29, 1985, pp. M2-M3.

40. Judith Miller, "How a Controversial Contractor Built an Egyptian Empire," *New York Times*, May 19, 1985.

41. For an abbreviated list of Uthman's holdings, see Imam, *Man Yamlik Misr?!*, pp. 294–95. For his entry into food production, see Uthman's autobiography, *Safahat*, pp. 607–14.

42. For an update on the soft drink situation in Egypt, including comments by Uthman's son, Isma'il, the chairman of Schweppes Egypt, see Tony Walker, "Egypt's Soft Drink Makers Lose Their Fizz," *Financial Times*, January 7, 1989.

43. Uthman describes the logic of his proposal, in glowing patriotic terms, in *Safahat*, pp. 623–24.

44. Neamine M. Refaat Abdel Aziz, "Management and the Role of Leadership in a Land Reclamation and Cultivation Project: 'El Salihiya,'" Master's thesis, American University of Cairo, 1987.

45. Anne Charnock, "The Greening of Egypt," *New Scientist*, January 23, 1986, pp. 44–48.

46. Abdel Aziz, "Management and the Role of Leadership."

47. Gunter Meyer, "Effects of the 'New Valley' Project Upon the Development of the Egyptian Oases," *Applied Geography and Development*, vol. 15 (1980), p. 96.

48. Imad Ghunayyim, "al-Zahira al-Uthmaniyya fi Iqtisad Misr," *AI*, October 3, 1983, pp. 20–23.

49. "Qalu wa-Naqul 'an Mashru' al-Salihiyya," *al-Sha'b*, May 4, 1983.

50. Abdel Aziz, "Management and the Role of Leadership."

51. "Qalu wa Naqul."

52. "Egypt Also Turns to Desert Farming to Solve Its Food Shortages," *International Management*, May 1983, p. 50.

53. "Egypt: Desert Dreams," p. 40.

54. Mackie, "All Change," p. 95.

55. Kate Gillespie, *The Tripartite Relationship* (Praeger, 1984), p. 126, cited in Clement Henry Moore, "Money and Power: The Dilemma of the Egyptian Infitah," *Middle East Journal*, vol. 40 (Autumn 1986), p. 636. The same official added, "In our opinion, they are just another inefficient public company which wants to stay the same under the guise of being private." This judgment derives from a typical and consequential American misunderstanding, the belief that only public sector companies seek rents.

56. Yusuf al-Qadi, "Madha Yahduth fi Mashru' al-Salihiyya?" *AI*, July 9, 1984, p. 11.

57. "Uthman Ahmad Uthman: Lastu Thalith Aghniya al-'Alam wa-Hadha Huwa al-Dalil," *al-Majalla*, March 9–15, 1988, pp. 33–36.

58. For a pioneering study of plasticulture technology and its social effects, see Sharif S. Elmusa, "A Multilevel Analysis of the Characteristics, Determinants, and Impact of Technological Change in East Jordan Valley Agriculture (1950–1980): A Study in Development and Dependence," Ph.D. dissertation, M.I.T., May 1986.

59. Imam, *Man Yamlik Misr?!*, pp. 126–27.

60. For a typical leftist analysis, interpreting Egyptian development in terms of power struggles between productive and unproductive wings of the bourgeoisie, see Mahmoud Hussein, *Class Conflict in Egypt: 1945–1970* (New York: Monthly Review, 1973), pp. 15–61.

61. Robert Springborg, "Agrarian Bourgeoisie, Semiproletarians, and the Egyptian State: Lessons for Liberalization," Macquarie University, 1990, pp. 13–15.

62. For a history of business lobbying in this period, see Marius Deeb, *Party Politics in Egypt: the Wafd and Its Rivals, 1919–1939* (London: Ithaca Press, 1979).

63. For the role of intermarriage in stitching together Egypt's political and economic elites, see Malak Zaalouk, *Power, Class and Foreign Capital in Egypt: The Rise of the New Bourgeoisie* (London: Zed Books, 1989), pp. 128–36.

64. The mechanisms of *shilla* and *duf'a* have been admirably analyzed by Robert Springborg, "Patterns of Association in the Egyptian Political Elite," in George Lenczowski, ed., *Political Elites in the Middle East* (Washington: American Enterprise Institute, 1975), pp. 83–107.

65. Samir A. Makdisi, "Observations on Investment Behavior in Arab Countries," in Michael Czinkota and Scot Marciel, eds., *U.S.-Arab Economic Relations: A Time of Transition* (Praeger, 1985), p. 185.

66. For comparative studies of patronage in Middle Eastern governments, and some important clues about how it varies over time, see the excellent essays in Ernest Gellner and John Waterbury, eds., *Patrons and Clients in Mediterranean Societies* (London: Duckworth, 1977).

67. Mohamed Heikal, *Autumn of Fury* (Random House, 1983), pp. 177–79.

68. For background, see Giacomo Luciani, "Allocation vs. Production

States: A Theoretical Framework," in Giacomo Luciani, ed., *The Arab State* (University of California Press, 1990), pp. 65–84.

69. Diaa Bekheet, "Bribery Trial Places Official Corruption in Spotlight," *Middle East Times*, September 6–12, 1987.

70. Quoted in Hanna Batatu, *The Old Social Classes and the Revolutionary Movements of Iraq* (Princeton University Press, 1978), p. 318.

71. Sa'id Abd al-Khaliq, "al-Harb al-Khaffiyya li-Tasfiyat al-Ajhiza al-Raqabiyya li-Salih al-Fasad," *al-Wafd*, April 17, 1986.

72. For a detailed description of the economic pressures on civil servants, see Arnold Hottinger, "Survival and Inefficiency in Egypt," *Swiss Review of World Affairs*, February 1984, pp. 24–27.

73. Thomas W. Lippman, *Egypt after Nasser* (Paragon, 1989), pp. 86–87.

74. For definitions of patronage and corruption, see Arnold J. Heidenheimer, ed., *Political Corruption: Readings in Comparative Analysis* (New Brunswick, N.J.: Transaction Books, 1978), pp. 31–64.

75. The Egyptian authorities are still trying to recover some of Ismat Sadat's ill-gotten gains; in February 1988 they ordered $8 million of his assets impounded. See *Middle East Economic Digest*, February 6, 1988, p. 12. (Hereafter *MEED*.) For details on Sadat's other relatives, see Amanda Mitchison, "Corruption in Egypt," *New African*, December 1983, p. 20.

76. Heikal, *Autumn of Fury*, p. 193.

77. Gamal Fadil, "al-Tanmiya al-Sha'biyya min 'Asa Musa ila al-Intiqadat!" *AI*, November 21, 1983, pp. 32–33.

78. Abd al-Qadir Shuhayb, "Haqiqat Mashru'at al-Tanmiya al-Sha'biyya!" *al-Sha'b*, January 4, 1983, p. 8.

79. For typical panegyrics, see "'Ala Tariq al-Tanmiya al-Sha'biyya 13 Mashru'an wa-Bankan Wataniyyan bi-Ra'smal 21 Milyun Junayh fi Asyut," *al-Musawwar*, October 30, 1981, pp. 76–77.

80. Abd al-Qadir Shuhayb, "Jara'im bi-Ism al-Tanmiya al-Sha'biyya," *al-Sha'b*, January 25, 1983.

81. For examples, see the articles by Abd al-Qadir Shuhayb, particularly "Adrar Mashru'at al-Tanmiya al-Sha'biyya," *al-Sha'b*, January 11, 1983.

82. Abd al-Qadir Shuhayb, "Ayna Dhahabat Qurud al-Amn al-Ghidha'i?" *al-Sha'b*, January 18, 1983.

83. Abd al-Qadir Shuhayb, "al-Muqawilun al-'Arab wal-Tanmiya al-Sha'biyya," *al-Sha'b*, February 1, 1983.

84. Nahal Shukri, "Lajnat al-Tanmiya bil-Hizb al-Watani Taqirr: Sharika Ra'smaluha 100 Milyun Junayh," *al-Ahram*, September 18, 1984.

85. Three-quarters of all engineers in Egypt belong to the Syndicate, a powerful body which combines the functions of professional association and union; see Clement Henry Moore, *Images of Development: Egyptian Engineers in Search of Industry* (M.I.T. Press, 1980), p. 21. For Uthman's control of the Syndicate, see Mahmud, "Sharikat Uthman."

86. "al-Lubi al-Iqtisadi."

87. For discussion of the conditions under which corruption actually augments the power of a regime, see J.S. Nye, "Corruption and Political Development: A Cost-Benefit Analysis," reprinted in Heidenheimer, ed., *Political Corruption*, pp. 564–78.

88. Personal networks in Morocco did perform this function; see John Waterbury, "Corruption, Political Stability and Development: Comparative Evidence From Egypt and Morocco," *Government and Opposition*, vol. 11 (1976), pp. 426–45. On the logic of political machines, see William L. Riordon, *Plunkitt of Tammany Hall* (E.P. Dutton, 1963). For a case where a party more or less successfully administered patronage networks, see Yahya M. Sadowski, "Ba'thist Ethics and the Spirit of State Capitalism," in Peter J. Chelkowski and Robert J. Pranger, eds., *Ideology and Power in the Middle East* (Duke University Press, 1988), pp. 160–84.

89. Shuhayb, "Adrar Mashru'at."

90. Abd al-Qadir Shuhayb, "Nata'ij Hazila li-Mashru'at al-Tanmiya al-Sha'biyya," *al-Sha'b*, February 22, 1983.

91. Adil Ibrahim, "Tamwin al-Hukuma: Kayf Yatasarrab ila al-Suq al-Sawda?" *AI*, (c. 1984), pp. 28–31.

92. Gamal Fadil, "Aradi al-Dawla bila Himaya!" *AI*, August 20, 1984, pp. 21–23.

93. Adil Ibrahim, "Waqa'i' Khatira lil-Ta'addi 'ala Aradi al-Dawla," *AI*, October 8, 1984, pp. 46–47. Also see the series of articles by Izzat Ali, beginning with "Mafia al-Istila' 'ala al-Aradi!" *AI*, September 10, 1984, pp. 22–27.

94. *Innahu Kana min al-Mufsidin*; Qur'an, sura 28, aya 4. For the ideology of Egypt's radical Islamic movements in this period, see Gilles Kepel, *The Prophet and Pharoah: Muslim Extremism in Egypt* (London: Al Saqi Books, 1985).

95. "Inaugural Address," Cairo Domestic Service, October 14, 1981, in Foreign Broadcast Information Service, *Daily Report: Near East & South Asia*, October 15, 1981, p. D6. (Hereafter FBIS, *Near East*.)

96. Assem Abdel-Mohsen, "Sword of Justice," *Middle East*, April 1983, pp. 17–18.

97. For an assessment of the strengths and failures of the anticorruption drive, see Sabri Abu Majd, "Interview with Prime Minister Fu'ad Muhyi al-Din," FBIS, *Near East*, October 21, 1983, pp. D4-D6.

98. For a full account of the Ismat Sadat case, see Abdallah Imam, *Qadiyat Ismat Sadat: Muhakamat 'Asr* (Cairo: Ruz al-Yusuf, 1983).

99. Abdel-Mohsen, "Sword of Justice," pp. 17–18.

100. Amnesty International, *Egypt: Human Rights Violations* (London, 1983).

101. Yahya Sadowski, "Egypt's Islamist Movement: A New Political and Economic Force," *Middle East Insight*, vol. 5 (November–December 1987), p. 39.

102. For a detailed description of how Mubarak intended to win the

collaboration of the political opposition, see "Mubarak Interview in 5 Nov at-Tadamun," in FBIS, *Near East*, November 4, 1983, pp. D1-D8.

103. See Abdel Monem Said Aly, "Democratization in Egypt," *American-Arab Affairs*, no. 22 (Fall 1987), pp. 11–27.

104. Nemat Shafik, "Private Investment in Egypt under the Infitah," (Oxford University, November 1988), p. 9.

105. See the series of articles by Imani Qandil, including "wa Marratan Ukhra: Man Hum Rijal al-A'mal wa Ayna Jama'at al-Masalih al-Ukhra?" *AI*, January 6, 1986, pp. 18–20; "al-Qarar 119 wa-Humum San' al-Siyasa al-Iqtisadiyya," *AI*, April 14, 1986, pp. 16–17; and "al-Ghuraf al-Tijariyya..al-Fa'iliyya wa-Qadaya al-Mustaqbal," *AI*, November 9, 1987, pp. 30–33.

106. The old Wafd defended business interests, but also sought wide-ranging state intervention to strengthen the national economy; see Tignor, *State, Private Enterprise*, pp. 79–81 and 147–51.

107. Wahid Abd al-Magid, "al-Asas al-Ijtima'i li-Hizb al-Wafd al-Jadid. 2: Mafhum al-'Adala al-Ijtima'iyya fil-Fikr al-Wafdi al-Jadid," *AI*, April 18, 1988, pp. 32–38.

108. Said Aly, "Democratization in Egypt," pp. 18–22.

109. For an introduction to the Tagammu', see Raymond A. Hinnebusch, "The National Progressive Unionist Party: the Nationalist-Left Opposition in Post-Populist Egypt," *Arab Studies Quarterly*, vol. 3 (1981), pp. 325–51.

110. See the scathing criticism of NDP in al-Sayyid Zahra, "Ma Huwa Nasib al-Hizb al-Watani min al-Dimuqratiya?" *al-Ahali*, May 23, 1984.

111. Robert Bianchi, *Unruly Corporatism: Associational Life in Twentieth-Century Egypt* (Oxford University Press, 1989), pp. 15–16.

112. Rabi' Abu al-Khayr, "al-Ma'raka al-Intikhabiyya," *al-Musawwar*, May 1984, pp. 20–25 and 60–65; "Limadha Lam Tusawwit al-Qahira," *al-Yamama*, June 6, 1984.

113. Sawsan al-Jayyar, "Intikhabat al-Fallahin 'Mas'ala 'A'iliyya'," *Ruz al-Yusuf*, April 23, 1984.

114. These overtures were not totally original; Sadat too had used his powers of patronage to woo rural notables.

115. Yusuf Wali may have understood earlier than most the regime's potential to curry a rural constituency. A document entitled "Seven Point Foundation of the Agricultural Sector," written in 1982 soon after Yusuf Wali took charge of the Agriculture Ministry, opens with the statement: "The rural sector and the farmers in particular, will always remain the backbone of the political power supporting the philosophy of the National Democratic party."

116. "al-Ra'is Mubarak Yantaqid Nuwwab al-Hizb al-Watani," *al-Ahali*, June 19, 1985; "Istib'ad Mustafa al-Sa'id min Amanat al-Hizb al-Hakim," *al-Ahali*, October 23, 1985.

117. Markaz al-Dirasat al-Siyasiyya wal-Istratijiyya bil-Ahram, *al-Taqrir al-Istratiji al-'Arabi 1986* (Cairo: al-Ahram, 1987), pp. 380–83.

118. Markaz al-Dirasat al-Siyasiyya wal-Istratijiyya bil-Ahram, *al-Taqrir*

al-Istratiji al-'Arabi 1985 (Cairo: al-Ahram, 1986), pp. 338–42; and "Shahr 'Asal Jadid bayn Wizarat al-Maliya wa-Rijal al-'A'mal," *AI*, April 11, 1983, pp. 24–27.

119. Qandil, "wa Marratan Ukhra," p. 19.

120. Markaz al-Dirasat, *al-Taqrir al-Istratiji al-'Arabi 1986*, p. 382.

121. Markaz al-Dirasat al-Siyasiyya wal-Istratijiyya *bil-Ahram, al-Taqrir al-Istratiji al-'Arabi 1987* (Cairo: al-Ahram, 1988), pp. 343–48.

122. All from *al-Wafd*, January 16, February 13, and March 27, 1986.

123. Musbah Qutb, "Qira'a fi Awraq Jumhuriyat Zaki Badr," *al-Ahali*, March 4, 1987.

124. Ahmad al-Jarallah, "Mubarak Interviewed on Abu Ghazalah, Other Issues," *Arab Times*, April 20–21, 1989, in FBIS, *Near East*, April 25, 1989, p. 8.

125. Sa'd al-Din Ibrahim, "Fi Taba'i' al-Fasad," *AI*, December 5, 1988, p. 10.

126. For similar cases see Paul M. Lubeck, ed., *The African Bourgeoisie: Capitalist Development in Nigeria, Kenya, and the Ivory Coast* (Boulder, Colo.: Lynne Rienner, 1987); Janet MacGaffey, *Entrepreneurs and Parasites: The Struggle for Indigenous Capitalism in Zaire* (Cambridge University Press, 1987); and Catherine Boone, "The Making of a Rentier Class: Wealth Accumulation and Political Control in Senegal," *Journal of Development Studies*, vol. 26 (April 1990), pp. 425–49.

127. Political economists have debated endlessly in recent years whether the coordination of businessmen and bureaucrats that characterizes successful development programs is the product of an "autonomous state" which imposes coordination on businessmen, or of a "relatively autonomous state" which businessmen use to reconcile disputes among contradictory sectoral interests. Much of this debate revolves around metaphysical claims that the power of either the state or businessmen predominates "in the final analysis." For most practical purposes, the two sides of the debate both underline the common need for coordination. For intelligent summaries of the contending positions in this debate, see Chalmers A. Johnson, *MITI and the Japanese Miracle: The Growth of Industrial Policy, 1925–1975* (Stanford University Press, 1982); and Harvey B. Feigenbaum, *The Politics of Public Enterprise: Oil and the French State* (Princeton University Press, 1985).

128. This argument was popularized by Peter Evans in *Dependent Development: The Alliance of Multinational, State and Local Capital in Brazil* (Princeton University Press, 1979). Also see Dietrich Rueschemeyer and Peter B. Evans, "The State and Economic Transformation: Toward an Analysis of the Conditions Underlying Effective Intervention," in Peter B. Evans, Dietrich Rueschemeyer, and Theda Skocpol, eds., *Bringing the State Back In* (Cambridge University Press, 1985), pp. 44–77.

129. The term is borrowed from Claudia Rosett, "Crony Capitalism, Aquino-Style," *Wall Street Journal*, February 7, 1990.

130. The classic statement of this argument, and still one of the most interesting essays on the politics of the Third World, is Michal Kalecki,

"Observations on Social and Economic Aspects of 'Intermediate Regimes,'" in *Essays on Developing Economies* (Atlantic Highlands, N.J.: Humanities Press, 1976), pp. 30–37.

CHAPTER 5

1. "Mubarak Outlines Economic Plans in Party Speech," in Foreign Broadcast Information Service, *Daily Report: Near East & South Asia*, January 28, 1982, p. D1. (Hereafter FBIS, *Near East*.)

2. Uthman Muhammad Uthman, "Di'am Raghif al-'Aysh wa-'Ajiz al-Mizaniyya," *al-Ahali*, June 23, 1982.

3. Yusuf Wali, "Mazahir al-Khalal fi al-Siyasa al-Zira'iyya 'Ayn'?" *al-Ahram al-Iqtisadi*, July 9, 1984, pp. 15–17. (Hereafter *AI*.)

4. Mahmud al-Tuhami, "Wazir al-Zira'a Ya'tarif: 3000 Milyun Dular Hajm al-Fajwa al-Ghidha'iyya," *Ruz al-Yusuf*, April 5, 1982.

5. Ibid.

6. The debt figure is from "Debtor Countries Face Tough 1989," *Middle East Economic Digest*, December 23, 1988, p. 18. (Hereafter *MEED*.) The petroleum figure is from World Bank, *Egypt: Country Economic Memorandum* (Washington, January 5, 1989), vol. 2: annexes, p. 51.

7. Egypt's agricultural exports are discussed in chap. 7.

8. "Man Hum al-Wuzara?" *al-Ahram*, January 4, 1982; and *AI*, May 9, 1988, p. 88.

9. "Wazir al-Zira'a al-Misri Dr. Yusuf Wali li-'al-Shira'": Nakhsha Ittisal al-Qamh bil-Siyasa," *al-Shira'*, January 14, 1985, p. M2.

10. See "First Among the Worst," *Euromoney*, September 1986, p. 95.

11. Karam Yahya and Sayyid Abd al-Magid, "Kayf Yukhrij al-Iqtisad al-Misri min Haql Ilgham al-Saba'inat," *al-Ahali*, May 26, 1982.

12. "Siyasat al-Tanmiya al-Zira'iyya bi-Jumhuriyat Misr al-'Arabiyya," *al-Dirasat al-I'lamiyya lil-Sukkan wal-Tanmiya wal-Ta'mir*, April–June 1982, p. 27.

13. Hasan Salluma, "Wazir al-Zira'a Yatlub Ilgha' Di'am al-Mahasil al-Zira'iyya," *al-Ahram*, February 9, 1982.

14. See Mahmud Dawud, "al-Tarkib al-Mahsuli fi Misr: Kayf Yajib an Yakun?" *al-Ahram*, December 28, 1981.

15. Husayn Shahbun, "Awwal Hadith li-Wazir al-Zira'a Yuhaddid fihi Malamih al-Siyasa al-Zira'iyya al-Jadida," *al-Ahram*, January 10, 1982.

16. Abd al-Wahhab Hamid, "al-'Alaqa bayn al-Malik wal-Musta'jir wa Mustaqbal al-Zira'a," *AI*, May 27, 1985, p. 36.

17. Yusuf Wali, "al-Malamih al-Ra'isiyya li-Injazat Qita' al-Zira'a," *AI*, September 2, 1985, p. 71.

18. Fawzi Abd al-Latif and Mahmud al-Marsafi, "Adwa' 'ala Injazat al-Qita' al-Zira'i khilal 'Amayn," *al-Musawwar*, November 4, 1983, p. 62.

19. In 1988 Wali was still repeating the claims about success in attaining

self-sufficiency in lentils that he made in 1982; see "Briefs," *AI*, July 18, 1988, p. 95.

20. "Taqrir Duwali Yu'akkid: Tadahwar Mu'addal Numuw al-Natij al-Zira'i fi Misr,"*AI*, April 27, 1987, p. 12.

21. By this time yields had begun to improve generally, and for certain crops ranked only behind California in productivity. See "Misr Tahtall al-Martaba al-Thaniya fi Mutawassit Intajiyyat Feddan al-Aruzz," *AI*, November 23, 1987, p. 10.

22. Gamal Abd al-Wahhab, "Hatta fi Luqmat al-'Aysh Na'tamid 'ala Amrika," *al-Ahali*, June 22, 1983.

23. Hamid, "al-'Alaqa bayn al-Malik," pp. 34–35.

24. These studies were conducted as part of the Agricultural Development Systems—Egypt Project, a program sponsored by AID with headquarters at Davis, which commissioned reports from a consortium of Egyptian and American universities. These reports (nearly 150 in all) form a goldmine of information on Egypt's agricultural potential.

25. Abd al-Wahhab, "Hatta fi Luqmat al-'Aysh."

26. Shahbun, "Awwal Hadith."

27. "Youssef Wally on Agriculture in Egypt," *Business Monthly*, vol. 4 (January 1988), p. 4.

28. Tony Walker, "Paying the Price for Neglect," *Financial Times*, June 5, 1985; and "Rice Self-Sufficiency: An Ambitious Plan," *Middle East Times*, June 18–24, 1988.

29. Interview with President Husni Mubarak by Abd al-Aziz al-Masa'id, *al-Ra'y al-'Amm*, April 4, 1987, in FBIS, *Near East*, April 7, 1987, p. D2.

30. The Hansen Institute of San Diego, California, continues to sponsor annual joint conferences of Egyptian and Israeli agricultural experts. Regrettably, these exchanges rarely focused on the part of Israel's experience that Egypt most needed to emulate—Tel Aviv's sophisticated overseas marketing system.

31. Muhammad al-Shirbini, "Hal Tusaytar Isra'il 'ala al-Istithmar fi Misr?" *al-Wafd*, October 9, 16, and 30, 1986. Also see Ali Khamis, "Mukhattat Sahyuni li-Tajwi' Badu al-Sahra' al-Gharbiyya," *al-Wafd*, March 5, 1987.

32. Wali's relationship with the Americans antedated his tenure as minister; he had taken charge of the ministry's contacts with foreign aid agencies under Mahmud Dawud in 1979.

33. Mahmud Hamid and Karam Yahya, "al-Taqrir Yad'am Masalih Kibar al-Mullak al-Zira'iyyin: Hal Nahnu fi Haja ila Khibra Ajnabiyya li-Hall Mushkilat al-Zira'a?" *al-Ahali*, August 25, 1982.

34. U.S. Embassy, *Status Report: United States Economic Assistance to Egypt* (Cairo, April 1987), p. 55.

35. The logic for the new AID strategy drew heavily on the thinking of the World Bank's Berg Report. It was partially implemented by Peter McPherson, whom Ronald Reagan appointed director of AID, and was institutionalized by his successor, Alan Woods. See U.S. Agency for International Development, *Development and the National Interest, U.S. Economic Assistance into the*

21st Century (Washington: U.S. Agency for International Development, February 17, 1989).

36. "al-Duktur Yusuf Wali Yu'lin fi Iftitah Mu'tamar Tasdid al-Qurud al-Zira'iyya," *AI*, October 26, 1987, p. 13.

37. "Wazir al-Zira'a al-Misri," p. M5.

38. Robert Springborg, *Mubarak's Egypt* (Boulder, Colo.: Westview Press, 1989), pp. 156 and 167.

39. Wali, "Mazahir al-Khalal," pp. 15–16.

40. Jean-Jacques Dethier, "Agricultural Prices in Egypt: Issues, Policies, and Perspectives," paper prepared for National Workshop on Agricultural Price and Marketing Policies in Egypt at Cairo, April 11–16, 1987, p. 5.

41. Denis J. Sullivan, "American Economic Aid to Egypt, 1975–87," Ph.D. dissertation, University of Michigan, 1987, pp. 196–99.

42. Harold Alderman, Joachim von Braun, and Sakr Ahmed Sakr, *Egypt's Food Subsidy and Rationing System: A Description* (Washington: International Food Policy Research Institute, 1982), p. 15.

43. Peter Kemp, "Egypt Relaxes State Controls in Bid to Raise Output," *MEED*, May 16–22, 1987, p. 32.

44. For the background of the negotiations see Rida Hilal, *Sina'at al-Taba'iyya* (Cairo: Dar al-Mustaqbal al-'Arabi, 1987).

45. Adil Husayn, *al-Iqtisad al-Misri min al-Istiqlal ila al-Taba'iya, 1974–79* (Beirut: Dar al-Wahda, 1981), vol. 2, p. 290. Chapter 8 of this invaluable work contains a detailed analysis of the Dickie Memorandum, outlining the IMF's recommendations for Egypt.

46. "Misr 1977: Sunduq al-Naqd al-Duwali Daghata wal-Hukuma Qarrarat wa Taraja'at," *al-Majalla*, October 19–25, 1988, p. 25.

47. Karima Kurayyim, "al-Infitah La Yubarrir Ilgha' al-Di'am," *AI*, October 15, 1984, p. 32.

48. Mohamed Heikal, *Autumn of Fury* (Random House, 1983), p. 92.

49. Boaz Shoshan, "Grain Riots and the 'Moral Economy,'" *Journal of Interdisciplinary History*, vol. 10 (Winter 1980), pp. 459–78.

50. Ahmed Abdalla, *The Student Movement and National Politics in Egypt, 1923–1973* (London: Al Saqi Books, 1985), pp. 149–75.

51. On industrial unrest in the 1970s, see Ghali Shoukri, *Egypt: Portrait of a President, 1971–1981* (London: Zed Press, 1981), pp. 239–42; on the 1980s, see "Khalfiyat al-Ahdath al-Damiya fi Masani' Hulwan," *al-Shira'*, August 21, 1989, pp. M2–M3, and "Egypt: Mubarak Loses First Round in Prices Battle," *MEED*, October 5, 1984, p. 7.

52. Dirk J. Vandewalle, "Reforming the Subsidy System in Egypt," *Institute of Current World Affairs*, May 1986, p. 7. For an analysis of the riots and their causes, see Sa'd al-Din Ibrahim, "'Ala Hawamish al-Ahdath al-'Unfiyya fi Misr," *al-Shira'*, April 7, 1986, pp. M8-M9.

53. For a valuable analysis of other IMF-triggered equity riots, see David Seddon, "Politics and the Price of Bread in Tunisia," in Alan Richards, ed., *Food, States, and Peasants* (Boulder, Colo.: Westview Press, 1986), pp. 201–23.

54. Husayn Abd al-Razzaq, *Misr fi 18 wa 19 Yanayir* (Cairo: Dar al-Kalima, 1979), pp. 81–82.

55. Egyptians in the 1970s believed that the social gap between the rich and the rest of society was widening. Studies of social inequality suggest that actually between 1974–75 and 1981–82 "there [was] a significant improvement in the income distribution pattern." See Karima Korayem, *The Impact of Economic Adjustment Policies on the Vulnerable Families and Children in Egypt* (Cairo: Dar El Alam El Arabi, 1987), p. 42. Yet the public perception may not actually have been wrong. The forces that maintained equity—worker remittances, the growth of the hidden economy—were almost serendipitous. They were not the result of government policies, which were often skewed to favor the rich.

56. See Robert Tignor, "Equity in Egypt's Recent Past: 1945–1952," in Gouda Abdel-Khalek and Robert Tignor, eds., *The Political Economy of Income Distribution in Egypt* (New York: Holmes & Meier, 1982), pp. 20–54.

57. Grant M. Scobie, *Food Subsidies in Egypt: Their Impact on Foreign Exchange and Trade* (Washington: International Food Policy Research Institute, 1983), p. 12. "In 1966 cards based on civil records were issued for four items: kerosene, oil, sugar, and tea. Other subsidized items were made available in 1967 without strict rations..During seven years of the 1960s consumer prices for wheat exceeded world prices." Alderman, von Braun, and Sakr, *Egypt's Food Subsidy and Rationing System*, p. 13.

58. Scobie, *Food Subsidies in Egypt*, p. 56.

59. Grant M. Scobie, *Government Policy and Food Imports: The Case of Wheat in Egypt* (Washington: International Food Policy Research Institute, 1981), p. 72.

60. Scobie, *Food Subsidies in Egypt*, p. 59.

61. John Waterbury, *Egypt: Burdens of the Past/Options for the Future* (Indiana University Press, 1978), p. 120.

62. Kurayyim, "al-Infitah La Yubarrir," p. 34.

63. Alderman, von Braun, and Sakr, *Egypt's Food Subsidy and Rationing System*, p. 10.

64. Nadia Khouri-Dagher, "The Answers of Civil Society to a Defaulting State: A Case Study around the Food Question in Egypt," paper delivered at the annual meeting of the Middle East Studies Association, Baltimore, November 14–17, 1987, p. 3.

65. See figure 5-3.

66. Uthman, "Di'am Raghif al-'Aysh."

67. The committee was chaired by Atif Sidqi, who became prime minister four years later, in 1986.

68. "al-Bada'il al-Matruha li-Muwajahat Mushkilat al-Di'am," *AI*, October 8, 1984, p. 52.

69. Alderman, von Braun, and Sakr, *Egypt's Food Subsidy and Rationing System*, p. 19.

70. Mansur Fahmi and Muhammad Uthman, "Hal Haqqaq al-Di'am al-Ishba' al-Matlub lil-Mustahlik," *AI*, January 16, 1984, pp. 24–25.

71. Sonia M. Aly and Dyaa K. Abdou, "Could Food Stamps be an Alternative to the Food Distribution System in Egypt?" Economics Working Paper 159 (Davis, Calif.: Agricultural Development Systems-Egypt Project, n.d.), pp. 19–22. The basic idea of such systems is that the poor are given coupons which they may use, like cash, on any genuine food item. The great advantage of this approach is that it would eliminate the system of multiple pricing, which should lead to more allocative efficiency. The great disadvantage is that it would create an incentive to resell or counterfeit food coupons. Given the endemic corruption of the Egyptian bureaucracy, it was decided that the danger outweighed the potential benefits.

72. Gawdat Abd al-Khaliq, "Nadwa: Ab'ad Qadiyat al-Di'am," *l'Egypte Contemporaine*, vol. 72 (April 1981), p. 260.

73. For background, see Alderman, von Braun, and Sakr, *Egypt's Food Subsidy and Rationing System*, pp. 19–27; and Harold Alderman and Joachim von Braun, *The Effects of the Egyptian Food Ration and Subsidy System on Income Distribution and Consumption* (Washington: International Food Policy Research Institute, July 1984), pp. 9–22.

74. Khouri-Dagher, "The Answers of Civil Society," p. 16.

75. Springborg, *Mubarak's Egypt*, p. 81.

76. Vandewalle, "Reforming the Subsidy System," p. 9.

77. "al-Bada'il al-Matruha," p. 48.

78. Ali Lutfi, "Waraqat 'Amal 'ala Tarshid al-Di'am," *l'Egypte Contemporaine*, vol. 72 (April 1981), pp. 37–38.

79. "Egypt's New Man Confronts Old Problems," *Financial Times*, November 11, 1986; and "al-Muhawala al-Thalitha li-Ibram Ittifaq bayn al-Hukuma al-Misriyya wal-Sanduq al-Duwali," *al-Majalla*, December 17, 1986, pp. 36–39.

80. For background, see Uthman, "Di'am Raghif al-'Aysh;" and Ramzi Zaki, "Hal Tusallih Ziyadat al-Ujur ka-Badil 'an al-Di'am?" *l'Egypte Contemporaine*, vol. 72 (April 1981), pp. 247–51.

81. Tharwat Surur, "al-Khabbazun Yuraddun 'ala al-Khubara': al-Di'am li-Khubz al-Baladi, La li-Khubz al-Aghniya'," *al-Ahali*, November 23, 1983; and Kamal al-Din Husayn, "Raghif al-'Aysh," *Mayu*, April 4, 1983.

82. Foreign Agricultural Service, *Annual Grain and Feed Report: Egypt* (U.S. Department of Agriculture, March 27, 1986), p. 3.

83. John Parker, "Egypt's Agricultural Trade Policy Strives to Serve Consumers" (Foreign Agricultural Service, U.S. Department of Agriculture, January 6, 1987), p. 6.

84. Hasan Sallumah, "Reducing Size of Subsidized Bread," *al-Ahram*, December 3, 1988, in FBIS, *Near East*, December 7, 1988, p. 10–11.

85. MENA, "Government Offers Higher Prices to Wheat Farmers," May 25, 1989, in FBIS, *Near East*, May 26, 1989, p. 17; and "Wali Interviewed on Agriculture, Party Affairs," *al-Anba'*, June 4, 1989, in FBIS, *Near East*, June 6, 1989, p. 10.

86. FBIS, *Near East*, December 7, 1988, p. 10; and *al-Akhbar*, April 14, 1989, in FBIS, *Near East*, April 18, 1989, p. 11.

87. "'Strict' Price Controls Placed on Foodstuffs," *al-Ahram*, May 4, 1989, in FBIS, *Near East*, May 8, 1989, p. 9.

88. "Give us Our Daily Bread Cheap," *Economist*, October 6, 1984, p. 41.

89. Amin Radwan, "Potential for Serious Problems," *al-Safir*, October 1, 1988, in FBIS, *Near East*, October 5, 1988, pp. 10–12.

90. "Mubarak: 'Not Possible' to Abolish Subsidies," *MENA*, November 18, 1986, in FBIS, *Near East*, November 18, 1986, p. D1.

91. International Monetary Fund, "Arab Republic of Egypt: Recent Economic Developments" (May 10, 1988), p. 1.

92. Harold Alderman and Joachim von Braun, "Egypt's Food Subsidy Policy: Lessons and Options," *Food Policy*, vol. 11 (August 1986), p. 227.

93. Abd al-Wahhab, "Hatta fi Luqmat al-'Aysh."

94. Hamid, "al-'Alaqa bayn al-Malik," p. 37.

95. "al-Saytara 'ala al-As'ar wa-Himayat al-Mustahlik wa-Muharabat al-Jasha'," *Mayo*, May 20, 1985.

96. Muhammad Hilmi Yasin suggests a pattern of periodic crises or shortages; see "al-Dukhul al-Tufayliyya fi Tijarat al-Khudar wal-Fakiha," *al-Tali'a*, vol. 9 (1973), pp. 35–39.

97. U. S. Agency for International Development, *Country Development Strategy Statement: Annex H, Selected GOE Policy Changes and Implications for the Future, 1983* (Washington, April 1984), Appendix II, p. 6; and "al-Tas'ira . . . fi al-Mizan!" *Mayo*, May 6, 1985.

98. "Wazir al-Zira'a: As'ar al-Khudar wal-Fakiha sa-Tankhafid Natijat Ilgha' al-Wusata'," *al-Ahram*, March 23, 1985.

99. Yasin, "al-Dukhul al-Tufayliyya," p. 37.

100. Muhammad Abd al-Qaddus, "Irtifa' Januni fi As'ar al-Khudar wal-Fakiha," *al-Wafd*, May 16, 1985; and Hasan Badawi, "As'ar al-Khadrawat Tartafi' ila al-Di'f," *al-Ahali*, October 2, 1985.

101. Badawi, "As'ar al-Khadrawat."

102. Zaynab Ibrahim, "Qararna 'Awdat al-Tas'ira lil-Mughalah fi As'ar al-Khudar," *Mayo*, June 3, 1985.

103. Ra'fat Amin, "Ilgha' Tas'ir al-Khudar wal-Fakiha: li-Salih Man? Ziyadat al-As'ar Mu'akkada wal-Qarar li-Salih al-Tujjar Faqat," *al-Ahram*, May 18, 1985.

104. Zaynab Ibrahim, "al-Tujjar Yu'ayyidun Naql al-Suq ila Matar Imbaba wal-Haykstip," *Mayo*, July 22, 1985.

105. Izzat Ali, "'Awdat al-Hayat bi-Shaklin Hadhrin ila al-Aswaq," *al-Ahali*, October 9, 1985.

106. R. Fraenkel, "Report of Visit to Rood El Farig Market" (Cairo: U.S. AID, April 28, 1982).

107. For the role of the wholesalers in the countryside, see Yasin, "al-Dukhul al-Tufayliyya," pp. 35–42; and Nu'man al-Zayyati, "Imbaraturiyat Suq al-Khudar Tusaytir 'ala al-As'ar," *AI*, April 11, 1988, pp. 16–18.

108. "Ma'idat al-Qahira," *al-Majalla*, August 12–18, 1987, p. 52.

109. Mustafa al-Sa'id, "al-Tujjar Yarfa'un al-As'ar bi-Mu'addalat Ha'ila wal-Hukuma Tarfa' Yaddaha," *al-Ahali*, August 3, 1983.

110. In 1983 the wholesalers had also used their monopoly to raise prices despite an increase of food and vegetable supplies; see Dr. Atwa Ahmad, cited in Ra'fat Amin, "Ilgha' Tas'ir al-Khudar wal-Fakiha: li-Salih Man? al-As'ar Tartafi'a Raghm Fa'id al-Intaj," *al-Ahram*, May 15, 1985.

111. Kirby S. Moulton, "Importer Perspectives on Egyptian Export Trade," in "Papers and Proceedings: Second Economics Policy Workshop: Agricultural Marketing in Egypt," Economics Working Paper 30 (Davis, Calif.: Agricultural Development Systems-Egypt Project, June 1981), p. 8.

112. Alan Richards, "The Agricultural Crisis in Egypt," *Journal of Development Studies*, vol. 16 (1980), pp. 312–13.

113. Calculated from figures in Nabil T. Habashy, "Economic Aspects and Estimation of Post Harvest Losses in Some Horticulture Crops," Economics Working Paper 64 (Davis, Calif.: Agricultural Development Systems-Egypt Project, March 1982), pp. 4–5, 7, 10 and 11. About 95 percent of all potatoes, tomatoes, and grapes produced makes it off the farm; about 92 percent of the original total survives wholesaling, with only 85 percent being passed along at full price; 84 percent of the original crop is sold at retail level, 79 percent at full price.

114. For the evolution of agricultural marketing in Egypt, see Barbara K. Larson, "The Rural Marketing System of Egypt over the Last Three Hundred Years," *Comparative Studies in Society and History*, vol. 27 (July 1985), pp. 494–530.

115. Sahar Diya' al-Din, "Tujjar al-Jumla Yattahimun Tujjar al-Tajzi'a bil-Mughalah fi Raf' al-As'ar," *al-Wafd*, June 26, 1986; and Muhammad al-Shirbini, "Qanun al-'Ard wal-Talab Yunhar Amam Jasha' Tujjar al-Tajzi'a," *al-Wafd*, June 6, 1985.

116. Hasan 'Ashur, "3 Wuzara' wa 3 Muhafizin Yu'lin al-Khamis al-Qadim Maw'idan al-Tahdid al-Aswaq al-Badila li-Suq Rawd al-Faraj," *AI*, August 12, 1985, pp. 28–29.

117. Yasin, "al-Dukhul al-Tufayliyya," p. 37.

118. Sana' Tabbala, "Ijra'at Hamma lil-Saytara 'ala al-As'ar," *Mayo*, September 16, 1985.

119. Abd al-Azim Darwish, "Tarah Luhum wa-Khudar Idafiyya li-Tathbit As'ariha," *al-Ahram*, June 7, 1985.

120. Ali Isma'il and Muhammad Sa'd, "Wizarat al-Tamwin Taghmud 'Aynha 'an Kibar al-Tujjar wa-Rijal al-Hukm al-Mahalli," *al-Ahali*, September 25, 1985.

121. Badawi, "As'ar al-Khadrawat."

122. Ali, "'Awdat al-Hayat."

123. Ra'fat Amin, "Ilgha' Tas'ir al-Khudar wal-Fakiha: li-Salih Man?" *al-Ahram*, a five-part series, May 14–20, 1985.

124. The crisis at Rawd al-Farag also supplied ammunition for Wali in his campaign to remove government subsidies on consumer goods. In 1987 an internal debate erupted in the NDP about a government proposal to eliminate subsidies on broad beans and lentils. One member, the head of the national association of physicians, noted that these two crops formed the basic supply

of protein for the poor. Wali argued in defense of the government position, claiming that "the subsidies on broad beans benefit no one except for the six merchants who monopolize trade in broad beans so that the subsidy does not reach its intended beneficiaries." See "Nuwwab al-Hizb al-Watani Ya'tariduna 'ala Raf' al-Di'am 'an al-Ful wal-'Adas," *AI*, June 15, 1987, p. 13.

125. "Mubarak Acceptance Speech for Second Term," October 12, 1987, in FBIS, *Near East*, October 16, 1987, p. 19.

126. Nu'man al-Zayyati, "Imbaraturiyat Suq al-Khudar." Also see "Youssef Wally on Agriculture in Egypt," pp. 14–15.

127. Mahmud Shakir, "Yawm Dakhil Imbaraturiyat Rawd al-Faraj," *al-Wafd*, May 24, 1988.

128. *MEED*, December 12–18, 1987, p. 10.

129. Usama Saraya, "Misr Tastati' Tahqiq 100% min al-Iktifa' al-Dhati min al-Qamh wa Laysa 70% Faqat khilal al-'Amayn al-Qadimayn," *AI*, July 27, 1987, pp. 12–13.

130. *MEED*, September 1, 1989, p. 11; John Parker, "Egypt: Wheat," *USDA Market Fundamentals*, April 28, 1989, p. 11.

131. Edward Hoyt, "Pricing to Encourage Production," *Business Monthly*, vol. 4 (January 1988), p. 18.

132. Abd al-Rahman Aql, "Hal Takfi al-Maikana Wahduha lil-Tatwir?" *al-Ahram*, May 1, 1985.

133. "Price Increases for Agricultural Produce," MENA, September 30, 1989, in FBIS, *Near East*, October 3, 1989, p. 16.

134. Hoyt, "Pricing to Encourage Production," p. 18.

135. Foreign Agricultural Service, *Annual Situation Report: Egypt, 1987, 1988*, and *1989* (U.S. Department of Agriculture); and *MEED*, December 8, 1989, p. 24, and December 22, 1989, p. 12.

136. Andrew Watson, "The Reform of Agricultural Marketing in China since 1978," *China Quarterly*, vol. 113 (March 1988), pp. 1–28.

137. Nicholas R. Lardy, "Agricultural Reforms in China," *Journal of International Affairs*, vol. 39 (Winter 1986), p. 94.

138. Ashur, "3 Wuzara' wa 3 Muhafizin," p. 29.

139. E. Lee Feller, *Food Distribution Technology, A Critical Oversight in Economic Development: Focus Egypt* (Coldwater, Mich.: November 1986), p. 16.

140. Feller thought that the most appropriate solution for Egypt was development of wholesaler-sponsored voluntary franchised chains. He recognized that existing Egyptian retail firms were too small, undercapitalized, and traditional to be able to form a modern retailing cooperative on their own. Instead he hoped that the Egyptian government would encourage the formation of new joint-venture firms that specialized in wholesale marketing and that the new wholesalers would then sponsor the creation of a retail cooperative as a way of breaking into markets controlled by traditional wholesalers. His report, ibid., is filled with details on how such a system would work.

141. Wheeler McMillen, *Feeding Multitudes* (Danville, Ill.: Interstate Publishers, 1982).

142. "al-Tamatim min al-Majnuna ila al-Mahayyara," *AI*, August 29, 1988, p. 11.

143. Jennifer Bremer, "Privatization of Agricultural Input Supply: Constraints and Opportunities for Reform," report prepared for U.S. AID (Robert Nathan and Associates, February 11, 1986), p. I-7.

144. Alderman, von Braun, and Sakr, *Egypt's Food Subsidy and Rationing System*, p. 31.

145. Hamid, "al-'Alaqa bayn al-Malik," p. 35.

146. George R. Gardner and John B. Parker, *Agricultural Statistics of Egypt, 1970–1984* (Washington: U.S. Department of Agriculture, August 1985), p. 78.

147. Gamal Abd al-Wahhab, "Fi Imbaraturiyat al-Dawajin," *al-Ahali*, November 16, 1983.

148. Alderman, von Braun, and Sakr, *Egypt's Food Subsidy and Rationing System*, p. 35.

149. Gardner and Parker, *Agricultural Statistics*, p. 26.

150. For an overview of government supports to poultry breeders, see John Freivalds, "Developing Egypt's Poultry Industry: Opportunity vs. Bureaucracy," *Agribusiness Worldwide*, February–March 1982, pp. 48–55.

151. Rida Hilal, "al-Haqiqa al-Gha'iba fi Jarimat I'dam al-Bayd wal-Dawajin," *AI*, June 24, 1985, pp. 20–22.

152. "Poultry Sector Outlook Brightens," *Business Monthly*, vol. 4 (January 1988), p. 22.

153. Jean-Jacques Dethier, *Trade, Exchange Rate, and Agricultural Pricing Policies in Egypt*, vol. 2 (Washington: World Bank, 1989), pp. 62 and 108.

154. Lucie Wood Saunders and Soheir Mehenna, "Village Entrepreneurs: An Egyptian Case," *Ethnology*, vol. 25 (January 1986), pp. 85–86.

155. Jay Sjerven, "Ismailia Misr Poultry Sets Example for Private Sector Initiative in Egypt," *Agribusiness Worldwide*, November–December 1986, p. 6.

156. Gardner and Parker, *Agricultural Statistics*, p. 76.

157. Abd al-Magid Salah al-Din, "al-Waqi' al-Murr wal-Mustaqbal al-Muzlim li-Sina'at al-Dawajin," *AI*, April 18, 1988, p. 20.

158. "al-Suq al-Sawda' Tal'ab bil-I'laf!" *AI*, December 12, 1983, p. 18; and Hilal, "al-Haqiqa al-Gha'iba," p. 21.

159. Hilal, "al-Haqiqa al-Gha'iba," p. 21.

160. Foreign Agricultural Service, "Annual Grain and Feed Report: Egypt," March 1986, p. 13.

161. Husayn Shahbun and Abd al-Fattah Ibrahim, "Mashru'at Tanmiyat al-Tharwa al-Hayawaniyya Tat'aththar," *al-Ahram*, June 23, 1985.

162. This account draws on the special report on the corn and poultry crisis prepared by the Ministry of Agriculture in June 1985. For the text of the report, see Hasan Salluma, "al-Fasl al-Akhira fi Ma'sat I'dam 4 Malayin Katkut Hayy!" *al-Ahram*, June 24, 1985.

163. Salah Muntasir, "Mujarrad Ra'y: I'dam al-Katakit," *al-Ahram*, June 11, 1985.

164. Darwish, "Tarah Luhum."

165. "Hasan Salluma, "al-Tawassu' fi al-Tasni' al-Zira'i wal-I'laf," *al-Ahram*, January 19, 1985; and Yusuf Wali, "Wazir al-Zira'a Yarudd: Man al-Mas'ul fi I'dam al-Katakit," *AI*, July 1, 1985, pp. 56–60.

166. Abd al-Magid al-Shuwaydfi, "Wazir al-Zira'a fi al-Sharqiyya: Rash al-Qutn bil-Ta'irat li-Muwajahat Shiddat al-'Isaba," *al-Ahram*, June 20, 1985; and Wali, "Wazir al-Zira'a Yarudd," p. 60.

167. "Asaf Yaguri Mallak fi Misr," *al-Shira'*, October 3, 1988, p. 12.

168. "al-Bada'il al-Matruha," *AI*, October 8, 1984, p. 52.

169. Abd al-Wahhab, "Fi Imbaraturiyat al-Dawajin."

170. "4155 Mazra'at Dawajin Yuhaddiduha al-Tawaqquf li-Naqs al-I'laf," *al-Ahram*, June 12, 1985.

171. "Ta'dil Qawanin al-Dara'ib li-Muntiji al-Dawajin," *al-Ahram*, November 18, 1984.

172. Hilal, "al-Haqiqa al-Gha'iba," p. 22.

173. "4155 Mazra'at Dawajin."

174. Mirvat al-Husri, "Wali wa Rijal al-'A'mal fi Munaqashat Sakhina Sakhina," *AI*, February 17, 1986, p. 25.

175. "Ittihadat al-Muntijin: Khatwa Wara' Ziyadat al-Intaj," *AI*, March 14, 1988, p. 57.

176. Mirvat al-Sayyid, "Muja'a fi 'Alaf al-Dawajin," *al-Wafd*, May 22, 1986.

177. Hani El Banna, "Poultry Farms Fall Victim to Abundance and Archaic Laws," *Middle East Times*, September 13–19, 1987.

178. Foreign Agricultural Service, *Annual Situation Report: Egypt, 1988*, p. 6.

179. al-Sayyid, "Muja'a."

180. Foreign Agricultural Service, *Annual Situation Report: Egypt, 1987*, p. 18.

181. Ibid., *1988*, p. 11.

182. El Banna, "Poultry Farms Fall Victim."

183. Sjerven, "Ismailia Misr Poultry," pp. 6–10.

184. Ibid., p. 8.

185. "Poultry Sector Outlook Brightens," p. 22.

186. "According to Deputy Prime Minister and Minister of Agriculture Dr. Youssef Wali:" *AI*, January 18, 1988, p. 96.

187. El Banna, "Poultry Farms Fall Victim."

188. Ibid.

189. Speech by President Husni Mubarak at Mit Birah village on the occasion of Farmers Day, September 8, 1988, in FBIS, *Near East*, September 13, 1988, pp. 14ff.

190. In game theory, the prisoner's dilemma is a situation in which uncertainty may make the parties to a decision choose not to collaborate, even though cooperation promises the best long-term outcome for all; see R. Duncan Luce and Howard Raiffa, *Games and Decisions* (Wiley, 1957).

191. Faruq Abd al-Magid, "Niqabat Mihniyya," *AI*, June 18, 1990, p. 63.

192. The best study of the "agrarian bourgeoisie" is Robert Springborg,

"Agrarian Bourgeoisie, Semiproletarians, and the Egyptian State: Lessons for Liberalization," *Middle East Journal* (forthcoming).

193. Springborg, *Mubarak's Egypt*, p. 263.

194. Robert Bianchi, *Unruly Corporatism: Associational Life in Twentieth-Century Egypt* (Oxford University Press, 1989), p. 173.

195. Seddon, "Politics and the Price of Bread," pp. 201–23; Pamela Dougherty, "Jordan Faces Up to Its Double Trouble," *MEED*, June 16, 1989, pp. 10–11; and Robert A. Mortimer, "Algeria After the Explosion," *Current History*, April 1990, pp. 161–64 and 180–82.

CHAPTER 6

1. See George J. Viksnins and Michael T. Skully, "Asian Financial Development: A Comparative Perspective of Eight Countries," *Asian Survey*, vol. 27 (May 1987), pp. 535–51; and William E. James, Seiji Naya, and Gerald M. Meier, *Asian Development: Economic Success and Policy Lessons* (University of Wisconsin Press, 1989), pp. 59–88.

2. Edward S. Shaw, *Financial Deepening in Economic Development* (Oxford University Press, 1973), p. 3. The other classic work on this subject is Ronald I. McKinnon, *Money and Capital in Economic Development* (Brookings, 1973).

3. See Yoon-je Cho and Deena Khatkhate, *Lessons of Financial Liberalization in Asia: A Comparative Study*, World Bank Discussion Paper 50 (Washington: World Bank, 1989); and Christine Kessides and others, eds., *Financial Reform in Socialist Economies* (Washington: World Bank, 1989).

4. For one of the most recent experiments, see Pamphil Kweyuh, "Kenya's Loan Lifeline," *South*, June 1990, pp. 22–23. For a quick description of one of the World Bank's favorite reform projects, see World Bank, "Improving Rural Financial Markets in Indonesia," *World Development Report, 1986* (Oxford University Press, 1986), p. 100.

5. World Bank, *World Development Report 1989* (Oxford University Press, 1989), pp. 180–81.

6. Jean-Jacques Deschamps, "Analysis of the Credit and Institutional Aspects of the Agricultural Production Credit Project," report prepared for USAID/Cairo, Egypt (Washington: Development Alternatives, February 1986), p. A-3.

7. For a discussion of how the General Organization for Agricultural and Cooperative Credit worked, see Hassan Ali El-Tobgy, *Contemporary Egyptian Agriculture*, 2nd ed. (Cairo: Ford Foundation, 1976), pp. 86–91.

8. Deschamps, "Analysis," p. II-12.

9. For the 1960s and 1970s, see Samir Radwan, *Agrarian Reform and Rural Poverty: Egypt, 1952–1975* (Geneva: International Labour Office, 1977), p. 67; for the 1980s, Deschamps, "Analysis," p. II-4.

10. John Waterbury, *The Egypt of Nasser and Sadat: The Political Economy of Two Regimes* (Princeton University Press, 1983), pp. 288–89.

11. "Bunuk al-Qura La Takhdum al-Qadiya al-Zira'iyya," *al-Ahali*, August 17, 1983.

12. Sharif al-Abd, "al-Ta'amul ma'a Bank al-I'timan Yuhaddid al-Nashat al-Zira'i wa-Yusallib al-Zira'iyyin Huquqahum," *al-Ahram al-Iqtisadi*, December 11, 1989, pp. 46–47. (Hereafter *AI*.)

13. This complaint was inspired by the work of Dale W Adams, a development expert who wrote a global critique of the iniquities of subsidized agricultural lending. See "A Critique of Traditional Agricultural Credit Projects and Policies," *Journal of Development Economics*, vol. 8 (1981), pp. 347–66; and J. D. Von Pischke, Dale W Adams, and Gordon Donald, eds., *Rural Financial Markets in Developing Countries: Their Use and Abuse* (Johns Hopkins University Press, 1983).

14. Deschamps, "Analysis," pp. II-3 and II-4; Jennifer Bremer, "Privatization of Agricultural Input Supply: Constraints and Opportunities for Reform," report prepared for U.S. AID (Robert Nathan Associates, February 11, 1986), p. II-1.

15. Jay Sjerven, "Small Farmers' Project Opens New Vista for Egyptian Agricultural Sector," *Agribusiness Worldwide*, July–August 1986, p. 10.

16. Despite laudatory official evaluations senior AID officials in Cairo remained skeptical of, even hostile to, the project. They suspected that the Egyptians had used statistics to overstate the achievements of the program in hopes of winning additional American funding.

17. Ralph J. Edwards, "Technology Transfer Aspects for Design of the Agricultural Production Credit Project," report prepared for U.S. AID/Cairo, Egypt (Washington: Development Alternatives, February 18, 1986), p. 6.

18. Ibid.; Deschamps, "Analysis."

19. Deschamps, "Analysis," p. IV-5.

20. Bremer, "Privatization," p. I-7.

21. U. S. Agency for International Development, *Status Report: United States Economic Assistance to Egypt* (Cairo, September 1988), p. 57.

22. Deschamps, "Analysis," p. IV-1.

23. The term was coined by McKinnon, in *Money and Capital*, pp. 68–88.

24. International Monetary Fund, "Arab Republic of Egypt: Recent Economic Developments" (Washington, May 10, 1988), p. 100.

25. Ibid.

26. Nabil Mohareb, "Toward Egyptian Money and Capital Markets—Part I: Recent Economic Measures," *Middle East Executive Reports*, vol. 9 (December 1986), pp. 10–13.

27. Martin French, "Clobbered by Cairo Irregulars," *Euromoney*, June 1987, pp. 81–87.

28. "Bank Lending Controls Relaxed," *Middle East Economic Digest*, September 16, 1988, p. 19. (Hereafter *MEED*.)

29. Clement Henry Moore, "Arab Financial Reforms: Bankers as Midwives of Civil Societies?" paper presented at Social Science Research Council

conference on Retreating States and Expanding Societies, Aix-en-Provence, France, March 25, 1988, p. 12.

30. This concept was popularized by Milton Friedman, "Government Revenue from Inflation," *Journal of Political Economy*, vol. 79 (July–August 1971), pp. 846–56.

31. Makram Muhammad Ahmad, "Sidqi on Public Sector, IMF, Sectarian Strife," *al-Musawwar*, May 4, 1990, in Foreign Broadcast Information Service, *Daily Report: Near East & South Asia*, May 7, 1990, pp. 13–14. (Hereafter FBIS, *Near East.*)

32. World Bank, *World Development Report 1990* (Oxford University Press, 1990), p. 178.

33. U.S. Embassy, *Egyptian Economic Trends* (Cairo, March 1989), pp. 2 and 6–8.

34. World Bank, *World Development Report 1989*, p. 63; and International Monetary Fund, *International Financial Statistics July 1990* (Washington, 1990), p. 208, line 14.

35. Valerie R. Bencivenga and Bruce D. Smith, "Deficits, Inflation, and the Banking System in Developing Countries: The Optimal Degree of Financial Repression," Working Paper 214 (Rochester Center for Economic Research, Rochester University, January 1990); and Ronald I. McKinnon and Donald J. Mathieson, "How to Manage a Repressed Economy," *Princeton Essays in International Finance*, 145 (December 1981), pp. 1–30.

36. See in *World Development Report 1989*, pp. 32–33.

37. For an overview of Egyptian banking during the *infitah*, see Clara Caselli, *L'internationalisation bancaire en egypte* (Milan: Giuffre Editore, 1982). Modern banking has a long history in Egypt; see Robert L. Tignor, "The Introduction of Modern Banking into Egypt, 1855–1920," *Asian and African Studies*, vol. 15 (1981), pp. 103–22.

38. David Butter, "Egypt's Banks Pull Through the Recession," *MEED*, March 14, 1987, p. 9.

39. Clement Henry Moore, "Money and Power: The Dilemma of the Egyptian Infitah," *Middle East Journal*, vol. 40 (Autumn 1986), p. 638.

40. "State-owned Banks See Assets Increase," *MEED*, January 12, 1990, pp. 20–22.

41. See S. Ahmad and others, "Fiscal Implications of the Open Door Policy" (Washington: World Bank, 1985), cited in Nemat Shafik, "Private Investment in Egypt under the Infitah," paper presented to the Middle East Studies Association, November 1988, pp. 6–7.

42. For recent developments, see Mahmud Salim, "Khatwa Uwla li-Iqamat Suq Awraq Maliya fi Misr," *al-Majalla*, January 9, 1990, pp. 38–39.

43. Mohareb, "Toward Egyptian Money and Capital Markets," pp. 10–13.

44. Anthony Walker, "Stricter Discipline on New Lending," *Financial Times*, October 23, 1986.

45. One of the main criticisms made of the policy of *infitah* was that foreign firms seemed largely interested in investing in banking, rather than in industry or "productive" enterprises. Clement Henry Moore noted that "of the £E 2.1

billion capitalized in in-country projects by the end of 1983, 54 per cent was concentrated in banking and related financial services, whereas only 23 per cent went to industry." "Money and Power," p. 639.

46. Michael Field, "Reforms Follow IMF Deal," *Financial Times*, November 25, 1987.

47. Rosamund McDougall, "Back to the Good Old Basics," *Banker*, July 1988, pp. 33–39; and Victor Mallet, "Egypt: Sadat's Open Door Closes," *Financial Times*, April 4, 1990.

48. "Analysis: Egyptian American Bank," *MEED*, February 24, 1989, p. 4.

49. Mallet, "Egypt;" and David Butter, *Egypt: Remaking the Arab Connection*, MEED Profile number 2 (London: Middle East Economic Digest, 1989), p. 60.

50. Assem Abdul Mohsen, "Who Benefits from Cairo's Banking Bonanza," *Middle East*, October 1981, pp. 66–70.

51. Shafik, "Private Investment," p. 7.

52. Muhammad Haykal, Egypt's leading journalist, quotes the higher figure; see MENA, October 3, 1987, in FBIS, *Near East*, October 5, 1987, p. 11. Most economists, including authorities at the IMF, prefer a figure closer to $50 billion. The Egyptian government has launched a major campaign to get expatriates to reinvest their money in Egypt, offering them the same tax holidays and other benefits extended to foreign capital. But, even though Egyptian television regularly stages interviews with businessmen who have returned and prospered, most of those with money abroad still have trouble identifying attractive investments. See Mahmud Mu'awwad, Abd al-Gawwad Ali, and Sharif al-Abd, "Misr Turrahib bi-'Awdat al-Amwal al-Misriyya min al-Kharij lil-Musharaka fi al-Tanmiya," *al-Ahram* [International Edition], January 10, 1988; and "Limadha Yastathmir al-Misriyyun Amwalahum fil-Kharij?" *al-Majalla*, September 2–8, 1987, pp. 34–35.

53. Shirley Christian, "Argentina's Bustling Underground," *New York Times*, January 23, 1989.

54. Tony Walker, "Egypt to Lift Interest Rates Today," *Financial Times*, May 15, 1989.

55. For an introduction to IMF thinking on financial development, see Warren L. Coats, Jr., and Deena R. Khatkhate, eds., *Money and Monetary Policy in Less Developed Countries: A Survey of Issues and Evidence* (New York: Pergamon, 1980).

56. *International Monetary Fund, Annual Report, 1989* (Washington: IMF, 1989), pp. 62–63. Under a standby arrangement, the Fund supplies credit for up to three years to countries having trouble meeting their foreign obligations.

57. Alan A. Tait, *Value-Added Tax: International Practice and Problems* (Washington: International Monetary Fund, 1988).

58. For a discussion of the complex mechanisms by which Egypt kept its exchange rate overvalued, see Giacomo Luciani, "Multiple Puzzle: Egypt's Exchange Rate Regime Controversy," *Journal of Arab Affairs*, vol. 5 (Fall 1986), pp. 111–30. The Egyptian pound was significantly devalued during the

May 1987 IMF-sponsored reforms; but within two years, inflation inside Egypt had resulted in the need for a further devaluation.

59. For an IMF justification of devaluation, see Azizali F. Mohammed, "IMF Never Proposes A 'Shock' Treatment," *Wall Street Journal*, July 13, 1990. The Fund's critics, in Egypt and elsewhere, charged that devaluation fueled inflation. Fund experts replied that the price rises accompanying devaluation were not really inflation, but just a necessary price adjustment. The distinction between inflation and necessary price adjustment, however, was lost on the average Egyptian who found that after devaluation he was spending more and enjoying it less. For a sample of the Egyptian-IMF dialogue on this point, see Majid Atiyah, "Interview with Dr. Abd al-Shakur Sha'lan," *al-Musawwar*, June 30, 1989, in FBIS, *Near East*, July 6, 1989, pp. 5–7. For evidence of the growth of doubts within the Washington development community about the efficacy of devaluation, see Riccardo Faini and Jaime de Melo, "Adjustment, Investment and the Real Exchange Rate in Developing Countries," *Economic Policy*, October 1990, pp. 492–519.

60. "Mufawadat Misriyya ma'a Sunduq al-Naqd wal-Bank al-Duwali," *al-Yawm al-Sabi'*, January 8, 1990, p. 24.

61. For a statement reflecting government thinking on this subject, see Mustafa Amin, "Fikra," *al-Akhbar*, April 27, 1989, in FBIS, *Near East*, May 1, 1989, p. 12.

62. Tony Walker, "Egypt: Toward Exchange Rate Reform," *Banker*, no. 136 (December 1986), pp. 99–100.

63. David Butter, "Flushing Out the Bad Debts," *MEED*, October 20, 1989, p. 8.

64. For an official history of conditional lending at the IMF, see Manuel Guitian, *Fund Conditionality: Evolution of Principles and Practices* (Washington: International Monetary Fund, 1981); for a more critical analysis of the topic, see Miles Kahler, "Orthodoxy and Its Alternatives: Explaining Approaches to Stabilization and Adjustment," in Joan M. Nelson, ed., *Economic Crisis and Policy Choice: The Politics of Adjustment in the Third World* (Princeton University Press, 1990), pp. 33–62.

65. David Butter, "IMF Deal Gives Egypt New Lease of Life," *MEED*, July 14, 1989, pp. 4–5; Max Rodenbeck, "Setback for Cairo over IMF Deal," *Financial Times*, July 20, 1990.

66. "IMF Talks to Resume in June," *MEED*, June 2, 1989, p. 9; and "Budget Deficit Comes Down to IMF Target," *MEED*, June 16, 1989, p. 14.

67. "Deposit Rate Increased to Attract Savings," *MEED*, May 26, 1989, pp. 29–30.

68. Butter, "IMF Deal," pp. 4–5; "Economy Minister Drops Hint on Interest Rate Hike," *MEED*, December 22, 1989, p. 11.

69. "Washington Talks Fail to Break IMF Deadlock," *MEED*, October 13, 1989, pp. 14–15.

70. "Economy Minister Drops Hint," p. 11; "World Bank/IMF Talks Enter Critical Phase," *MEED*, February 2, 1990, p. 14.

366 Notes (pages 219–22)

71. "Price Rises Presage Tough Budget," *MEED*, May 18, 1990, pp. 12–13; *MEED*, March 9, 1990, p. 23; and "Ijra'at Iqtisadiyya Jadida fi Misr," *al-Yawm al-Sabi'*, January 22, 1990, p. 24.

72. Peter Norman and William Dawkins, "Debt Forgiveness Rewards Egypt for Support in Gulf," *Financial Times*, January 23, 1991; and Clyde Farnsworth, "Egypt's Reward: Forgiven Debt," *New York Times*, April 10, 1991. In the final months of 1990, the United States, Saudi Arabia, and other Arab Gulf states forgave $14 billion of Egyptian debts. American Secretary of State James Baker promised publicly to lobby the IMF on Egypt's behalf. This eased the economic pressure on Egypt, but a final agreement with the Fund still proved elusive. See David Lennon, "Egypt's Debt Burden Eased by $14bn," *Financial Times*, January 24, 1991; William Schmidt, "Baker Tells Cairo He'll Put in a Good Word with the I.M.F.," *New York Times*, March 12, 1991; and "IMF Seeks Further Reform Measures," *MEED*, March 22, 1991, p. 9.

73. Alberto Giovannini, "Savings and the Real Interest Rate in LDCs," *Journal of Development Economics*, vol. 18 (August 1985), pp. 197–217. For a devastating outline of the perils of financial liberalization, see Carlos Diaz-Alejandro, "Good-Bye Financial Repression, Hello Financial Crash," *Journal of Development Economics*, vol. 19 (September–October 1985), pp. 1–24.

74. "ROSCAs intermediate in the most basic way. A small number of individuals, typically six to forty, form a group and select a leader who periodically collects a given amount (a share) from each member. The money collected (the fund) is then given in rotation to each member of the group." World Bank, *World Development Report, 1989*, p. 114. In Egypt, ROSCAs are known as *gam'iyyat al-iddikhar*.

75. A. Shakour Shaalan, "The Impact of Macroeconomic Policies on Investment," in Said El-Naggar, ed., *Investment Policies in the Arab Countries* (Washington: International Monetary Fund, 1990), pp. 28–29.

76. See S. Van Wijnbergen, "Interest Rate Management in LDCs," *Journal of Monetary Economics*, vol. 12 (1983), pp. 433–52; and Edward F. Buffie, "Financial Repression, the New Structuralists, and Stabilization Policy in Semi-Industrialized Economies," *Journal of Development Economics*, vol. 14 (April 1984), pp. 305–22.

77. "When the Pips Refuse to Squeak," *Economist*, March 4, 1989, p. 34; Matt Moffett, "Off-the-Books Growth Is Fueling Mexico, But Underground is a Two-Edged Sword," *Wall Street Journal*, October 4, 1989; Richard House, "Hidden Boom in Brazil," *South*, October 1989, pp. 40–41; and "China: So Taxing," *Economist*, April 8, 1989, pp. 40–41.

78. Midhat Hasanayn, "al-Iqtisad al-Sirri fi Misr," *AI*, December 15, 1985, p. 16.

79. Mahmoud Abdel-Fadil, *The Political Economy of Nasserism: A Study in Employment and Income Distribution Policies in Urban Egypt, 1952–72*, Occasional Paper 52 (Cambridge University Press, 1980), pp. 93–94 and fig. 6.1, p. 95.

80. "250 Alfan Yatasawwilun Yawmiyyan fi al-Qahira," *al-Shira'*, April 11, 1988, pp. M6–8.

81. The ILO has sponsored a number of excellent studies of informal activities in Egypt, including *Craftswomen in Kerdassa, Egypt: Household Production & Reproduction* (Geneva: International Labour Organisation, 1984).

82. See the essays collected in S. V. Sethuraman, ed., *The Urban Informal Sector in Developing Countries: Employment, Poverty and Environment* (Geneva: International Labour Organisation, 1981).

83. For a definition of the parallel economy which may also clarify some of the dimensions of the hidden economy discussed here, see David L. Lindauer, "Parallel, Fragmented, or Black? Defining Market Structure in Developing Economies," *World Development*, vol. 17 (December 1989), pp. 1871–80.

84. Nazli Choucri, "Dimensions of National Security: The Case of Egypt," research paper prepared for the World Resources Institute (Washington, March 1987), pp. 7–16 and 7–17.

85. "The Hidden Economy in Egypt and Its Relationship to Current and Future Economic and Political Stability," (Washington: Hitachi Foundation, January 1989), p. 6.

86. Rodney Wilson, "The Developmental Impact of Egypt's Import Liberalisation," *Middle Eastern Studies*, vol. 22 (October 1986), p. 498.

87. Ibid., pp. 483–84.

88. *Country Development Strategy Statement: Egypt FY 1985, Annex D: Selected GOE Policy Changes 1974–82, and Implications for the Future* (Washington: Agency for International Development, February 1983), p. 3. The import rationalization committees were later dissolved and a wide-ranging reduction of tariffs executed in 1986.

89. Kate Gillespie and William A. Stoever, "Investment Promotion Policies in Sadat's Egypt: Lessons for Less-developed Countries," *Journal of Arab Affairs*, vol. 7 (Spring 1988), pp. 19–48.

90. John Parker, "Egypt's Agricultural Trade Policy Strives to Serve Consumers" (Foreign Agricultural Service, U.S. Department of Agriculture, January 6, 1987); and "al-Lubi al-Iqtisadi wal-Ghazw min al-Dakhil," *al-Shira'*, April 29, 1985, pp. M2-M3.

91. Samir Mu'awwad, "al-Ra'smaliya: al-Bur Sa'idiyya," *AI*, May 25, 1987, pp. 10–13.

92. Luciani, "Multiple Puzzle."

93. Nigel Harris, *The End of the Third World: Newly Industrializing Countries and the Decline of Ideology* (Penguin Books, 1986), pp. 30–54; and Keith Griffin, *Alternative Strategies for Economic Development* (Macmillan in association with the OECD Development Center, 1989).

94. See Azizali F. Mohammed, "IMF Never Proposes a 'Shock' Treatment," *Wall Street Journal*, July 13, 1990.

95. For an overview of these problems, see Giacomo Luciani, "Multiple Puzzle."

96. For an analysis of the contribution black markets can make to national development, with some details on the Egyptian case, see Tariq Banuri, "Black Markets, Openness, and Central Bank Autonomy," *WIDER Working Papers*, no. 62 (Helsinki: World Institute for Development Economics Research, August 1989).

97. David Shirreff, "Why the Black Market Thrives," *Euromoney*, May 1984, p. 186.

98. Hasanayn, "al-Iqtisad al-Sirri."

99. "Shira' al-'Aqarat wal-Ma'adin al-Nadira Akthar Ribhan lil-Mustathmir," *al-Majalla*, December 24, 1986, pp. 30–31.

100. Abdel-Fadil, *Political Economy of Nasserism*, p. 21.

101. Gunter Meyer, "Socioeconomic Structure and Development of Small-Scale Manufacturing in Old Quarters of Cairo," paper presented at the annual meeting of the Middle East Studies Association, Baltimore, November 14–17, 1987, p. 6.

102. Michael Hofman, "The Informal Sector in an Intermediate City: A Case in Egypt," *Economic Development and Cultural Change*, vol. 9 (January 1986), pp. 263–77.

103. Wilson, "Developmental Impact," pp. 494–95 and 501.

104. Gunter Meyer, "Industrial Expansion in the New Desert Cities in Egypt," paper presented at the annual meeting of the Middle East Studies Association of North America, Beverly Hills, Calif., November 3–5, 1988, pp. 2–4.

105. Piet van den Akker, "Savings Clubs (Jam'iyyat Iddikhar): The Egyptian Experience," *Development: Seeds of Change* (1987: 2/3), pp. 145–47.

106. William Ollard, "Egypt: Laying the Basis for a Free Market," *Euromoney*, February 1985, pp. 108–15.

107. In practice, *musharaka* differs from the payment of interest in that dividends paid under *musharaka* must be directly linked to both the profits and losses of the institution holding the deposits, so that depositors share in its risks. *Musharaka* operations resemble those of mutual funds in the West.

108. For an introduction to contemporary Islamic banking, see Mohsin S. Khan and Abbas Mirakhor, "Islamic Banking: Experiences in the Islamic Republic of Iran and Pakistan," IMF Working Paper WP/89/12 (Washington, January 30, 1989). For a wider background on the relation between Islamic ideologies and finance, see Maxime Rodinson, *Islam and Capitalism* (University of Texas Press, 1978).

109. "190 Sharika Rasmiyya Ta'mal fi Tawzif al-Amwal," *al-Ahali*, March 4, 1987; and Mahmud Abd al-Fadil, *al-Khadi'a al-Maliya al-Kubra* (Cairo: Dar al-Mustaqbal al-'Arabi, 1989), p. 14.

110. For an articulation of this philosophy by one of the more genuinely pious directors of an IMMC, see Abd al-Latif al-Sharif, "..Hadhihi Ru'yati li-Qadaya al-Tanmiya," *al-Sha'b*, March 8, 1988.

111. Bahman Roshan, "Faisal Islamic Bank of Egypt: An Assessment," *Arabia*, November 1985, pp. 63–64; and Samir Mustafa Mitwalli, "Madha Taqulu Mizaniyat al-Bunuk al-Islamiyya?" *AI*, October 26, 1987, pp. 32–35.

112. See the moving account of Muhammad Shibl, "If They Enter a Company They Ruin It!," *al-Ahrar*, July 4, 1988, in FBIS, *Near East*, July 20, 1988, p. 10.

113. David Butter, "Egyptian Banking and Finance," *MEED*, June 3, 1988, pp. 87–92.

114. French, "Clobbered by Cairo Irregulars," p. 83.

115. "9 Sharikat li-Tawzif al-Amwal Tastanzif Wafr al-Muwatinin," *al-Shira'*, July 25, 1988, pp. M7-M10.

116. Butter, "Egyptian Banking and Finance," pp. 91–92.

117. This is according to depositions presented to the Capital Markets Authority under application of the new Investment Law. "Al-Sharif Leads the Way in Islamic Firms Overhaul," *MEED*, November 18, 1988, p. 14. These figures are probably low, since they do not include the numbers for Sharif's depositors, and the declared value of Rayyan's deposits was thought to be conservative.

118. Husayn Sha'lan, "Misr: al-Hukuma fi Mawqi' Aqwa wal-Mudi' Huwa al-Khasir al-Akbar," *al-Yawm al-Sabi'*, November 7, 1988, p. 22.

119. Abd al-Fadil, *al-Khadi'a al-Maliya al-Kubra*, p. 16; and Butter, "Egyptian Banking and Finance," p. 92.

120. Butter, "Egyptian Banking and Finance," p. 92.

121. Mahmud Abd al-Fadil and Gihan Diyab, "Ab'ad wa-Mukawwanat 'al-Iqtisad al-Khafi' wa-Harakat al-Amwal al-Sawda' fil-Iqtisad al-Misri (1974–1984)," *l'Egypte Contemporaine*, vol. 76 (April 1985), pp. 5–40; and Roy, "Hidden Economy," pp. 30 and 32.

122. Hernando de Soto, *The Other Path: The Invisible Revolution in the Third World* (Harper and Row, 1989), p. 243.

123. Mahmud Abd al-Fadil, "al-Tawzif al-Siyasi li-Sharikat Tawzif al-Amwal," *AI*, July 18, 1988, pp. 26–29.

124. "Bank Credit Ceiling Abolished," *MEED*, September 2, 1988, p. 20.

125. "Central Bank Goes Slow on Private Debt Issue," *MEED*, May 6, 1988, p. 5.

126. For testimony on the influence of the Association of Banks, see "al-Lubi al-Iqtisadi."

127. Margaret Hughes, "Clamps Ease But Pain Fades Slowly," *Financial Times*, June 5, 1985; and Muhammad Abd al-Qaddus, "al-Hukuma Tataraja' 'an al-Qararat al-Iqtisadiyya," *al-Wafd*, January 24, 1985.

128. For this debate, see Rida Hilal, "Junun al-Dular," *AI*, April 6, 1987, pp. 19–21.

129. Yahya Sadowski, "The Sphinx's New Riddle: Why Does Egypt Delay Economic Reform?" *American-Arab Affairs*, no. 22 (Fall 1987), p. 38.

130. Rida Hilal, "al-Qararat al-Jadida Tastab'id Tujjar al-Umla," *AI*, May 18, 1987, p. 12.

131. *MEED*, August 8, 1987, p. 11.

132. David Butter, "Turning Point for Egypt's Banks," *MEED*, June 3, 1988, p. 87.

133. Tony Walker, "Credit Standing Slips Badly," *Financial Times*, June 27, 1988.

134. "Black Market Currency Dealers Make a Comeback," *MEED*, December 5, 1987, p. 5.

135. Butter, "Turning Point."

136. Tony Walker, "Egypt Money Markets in Turmoil," *Financial Times*, March 20, 1989.

137. Gamal Shawqi, "Paper Reports on Foreign Currency Crisis," *al-Wafd*, September 25, 1989, p. 1, in FBIS, *Near East*, September 28, 1989, p. 15.

138. Izzat Ibrahim, *al-Musawwar*, November 18, 1988, in FBIS, *Near East*, November 23, 1988, pp. 13–14.

139. French, "Clobbered by Cairo Irregulars," pp. 81–87.

140. The best investigation of the politics of Islamic Funds is Abd al-Fadil, "al-Tawzif al-Siyasi li-Sharikat Tawzif al-Amwal"; also see FBIS, *Near East*, November 23, 1988.

141. John Kifner, "Islamic Fundamentalism in a Troubled Egypt," *New York Times*, July 12, 1987.

142. For the extent of IMMC political influence, see "Sha'i'at Khatf wa-Itlaq Nar wa-Satw 'ala Mahallat al-Dhahab," *al-Majalla*, September 14–20, 1988, pp. 38–41.

143. Abd al-Fadil, *al-Khadi'a al-Maliya al-Kubra*, p. 5.

144. Mahmud Salim, "Ihdharu min al-Sharikat allati Ta'ti Arbahan 'Aliyatan 'ala Istithmaratkum," *al-Majalla*, March 1–7, 1989, p. 41.

145. Abd al-Fadil, *al-Khadi'a al-Maliya al-Kubra*, pp. 87–89.

146. FBIS, *Near East*, November 23, 1988.

147. Butter, "Turning Point," p. 92.

148. Abd al-Fadil, *al-Khadi'a al-Maliya al-Kubra*, p. 35.

149. "al-Sa'd Yahtakir 'Fiat' wal-Sharif 'al-Blastik' wal-Rayyan 'ala Hafat al-Iflas," *al-Shira'*, December 5, 1988, p. M6.

150. Abd al-Fadil, *al-Khadi'a al-Maliya al-Kubra*, pp. 22–25 and 46–49.

151. Ibid., pp. 69–70.

152. Ibid., p. 39; and Ayman al-Sayyad and Siham Abd al-Al, "Muhakamat al-Rayyan: Lughz al-Dhahab al-Makhba'," *al-Majalla*, March 13, 1990, p. 16.

153. "Sharikat Tawzif al-Amwal wa-Tuham bil-Ihtiyal," *al-Majalla*, June 22–28, 1988, pp. 35–38.

154. Muhammad Khalifa, "'al-Rayyan' Tashtari 'al-Hilal' bi-25 Milyun Junayh," *al-Majalla*, March 2, 1988, pp. 36–37.

155. *Money: Whence It Came, Where It Went* (Houghton Mifflin, 1975), p. 85.

156. Abd al-Qadir Shuhayb, "Milyunan Misri fi Intizar Nihayat Azmat Sharikat Tawzif al-Amwal," *al-Majalla*, May 25–31, 1988, pp. 40–41.

157. Tony Walker, "Egypt: A Mountain to Climb," *Financial Times*, September 27, 1989.

158. Abd al-Fadil, *al-Khadi'a al-Maliya al-Kubra*, p. 83.

159. French, "Clobbered by Cairo Irregulars," pp. 81–82.

160. David Butter, "Egypt: Islamic Companies Law Sparks Debate," *MEED*, January 9, 1988, p. 9.

161. David Butter, "Crunch Time for Investors," *MEED*, August 5, 1988, p. 7. For speculation about the background of the government's campaign, see Shuhayb, "Milyunan Misri."

162. "Islamic Investment Companies Feel the Squeeze," *MEED*, May 27, 1988, p. 3.

163. Butter, "Crunch Time," p. 7.

164. Tony Walker, "Islamic Investment Groups in Egypt Defer Deals," *Financial Times*, May 23, 1988.

165. "Sharikat al-Amwal Tuhaddid bil-Sidam," *al-Yawm al-Sabi'*, June 13, 1988, p. 7.

166. "Sha'i'at Khatf," p. 39.

167. Rosamund McDougall, "Pyramid Selling by the Nile," *Banker*, July 1988, pp. 40–41.

168. Ahmad al-Suyufi, "The Government Backs Down in Face of Threats by Investment Companies," *al-Sha'b*, July 19, 1988, in FBIS, *Near East*, July 21, 1988, p. 15.

169. Tony Walker, "Egypt Surprised by Growth of Islamic Investment Houses: Sector Faces Uncertainty," *Financial Times*, October 24, 1988.

170. Ibid.

171. "Crisis of Investment Companies Entered Phase of Realization," *al-Sharq al-Awsat*, July 24, 1988, cited in FBIS, *Near East*, July 26, 1988, p. 7.

172. "Egypt Depositors Protest," *New York Times*, July 18, 1988.

173. "Misr: Ashab al-Wada'i' Yuthirun Qadaya Jadida," *al-Majalla*, October 12–18, 1988, pp. 8–9.

174. Husayn Sha'lan, "Misr: Suqut Dawlat 'al-Rayyan'," *al-Yawm al-Sabi'*, November 21, 1988, pp. 22–23.

175. "Badr, Al-Hoda Misr Submit Financial Details," *MEED*, December 2, 1988, p. 15.

176. David Butter, "The Missing Millions," *MEED*, November 25, 1988, p. 8.

177. "Muhammad Rashad Nabih lil-'Majalla': Amwal al-Mudi'in Turadd Khilal 10 Ashhur," *al-Majalla*, June 12, 1990, p. 20; and "In Brief," *MEED*, June 8, 1990, p. 22.

178. "Al-Sharif Opens Its Books," *MEED*, January 13, 1989, p. 21.

179. "Al-Sharif Leads the Way in Islamic Firms Overhaul," *MEED*, November 18, 1988, p. 14.

180. "Day of Reckoning Approaches for Investment Companies," *MEED*, October 28, 1988, p. 13.

181. "In Brief," *MEED*, June 22, 1990, p. 14.

182. Salah Muntasir, "Uktubir Cites Mubarak on Rayyan Issue," *Uktubir*, December 4, 1988, in FBIS, *Near East*, December 6, 1988, p. 5.

183. "New Law Tests Islamic Investors," *MEED*, October 14, 1988, p. 44.

184. "We Didn't Lose a Penny," *Middle East*, January 1988, p. 24; and

"Al-Rayyan Picks Danes for Dairy Complex," *MEED*, February 20, 1988, p. 5.

185. Yusuf al-Qaʻid, "Misr: al-Nizam al-Masrafi fi Khatr," *al-Mustaqbal*, November 3, 1984; and Moore, "Money and Power," pp. 642 and 644–45.

186. Imam Ahmed, "Egypt's Central Bank Clamps Down on Corruption," *Middle East Times*, August 23–29, 1987.

187. Waterbury, *Egypt of Nasser and Sadat*, pp. 149–50.

188. World Bank, *World Development Report 1989*, p. 1.

189. Mahabub Hossain, *Credit for Alleviation of Rural Poverty: The Grameen Bank in Bangladesh*, Research Report 65 (Washington: International Food Policy Research Institute; in collaboration with Bangladesh Institute of Development Studies, February 1988).

190. Flora Lewis, "The Right to Credit," *New York Times*, September 26, 1990.

191. "Patching Up Poverty," *Economist*, August 20, 1988, p. 70.

CHAPTER 7

1. "Mubarak Discusses IMF, Reforms on Farmers Day," Cairo Domestic Service, September 8, 1988, in Foreign Broadcast Information Service, *Daily Report: Near East & South Asia*, September 13, 1988, p. 16. (Hereafter FBIS, *Near East*.)

2. David Butter, "IMF Deal Gives Egypt New Lease of Life," *Middle East Economic Digest*, July 14, 1989, p. 4. (Hereafter *MEED*.)

3. Lionel Barber, "The Twelve Apostles of Development," *International Economy*, vol. 3 (September–October 1989), p. 63.

4. *MEED*, February 17, 1989, p. 15.

5. David B. Ottaway, "U.S. Withholds $230 Million From Egypt," *Washington Post*, March 8, 1989.

6. "U.S. Thaws Aid to Egypt," *Washington Post*, August 18, 1989.

7. See the series of articles on IMF riots in *al-Majalla*: "Ahdath al-Khubz," October 19–25, 1988, pp. 18–25, and "Kawabis al-Sunduq al-Duwali," May 3–9, 1989, pp. 12–19.

8. Patrick E. Tyler, "Heading to U.S., Says PLO Backs Peace Plan," *Washington Post*, September 24, 1989.

9. Julian Ozanne, "Tanzania Stays Faithful to Its African Socialism," *Financial Times*, June 14, 1990. This quotation is from a critique of Tanzania's reform efforts, but identical language has been used in IMF and AID sermons to Egyptian officials.

10. World Bank, *World Development Report 1989*, (Washington: World Bank, 1989), p. 166; and Michael Holman, "Even 'Model Pupils' Are Not Proving the Case for Adjustment," *Financial Times*, November 22, 1989.

11. World Bank, Country Economics Department, *Adjustment Lending: An Evaluation of Ten Years of Experience* (Washington: World Bank, 1988);

and *Sub-Saharan Africa from Crisis to Sustainable Growth: A Long-Term Perspective Study* (Washington: World Bank, 1989).

12. International Monetary Fund, External Relations Department, *Ten Common Misconceptions About the IMF* (Washington, 1989), p. 8.

13. Tony Walker, "Pace of Cairo Reform Tries IMF," *Financial Times*, December 6, 1988.

14. "Timetable Slips on New IMF Deal," *MEED*, June 9, 1989, p. 5.

15. "Washington Talks Fail to Break IMF Deadlock," *MEED*, October 13, 1989, pp. 14–15.

16. Butter, "IMF Deal," pp. 4–5; "Budget Deficit Comes Down to IMF Target," *MEED*, June 16, 1989, p. 14; and "Economy Minister Drops Hint on Interest Rate Hike," *MEED*, December 22, 1989, p. 11.

17. "Budget Deficit Comes Down to IMF Target," p. 14. Also see Butter, "IMF Deal," pp. 4–5.

18. Ronald I. McKinnon, *The Order of Economic Liberalization: Lessons from Chile and Argentina*, Carnegie-Rochester Conference Series on Public Policy, no. 17 (1982), pp. 165–72; and Keith Griffin, *Alternative Strategies for Economic Development* (Macmillan, 1989), pp. 50–59.

19. Sadiq Ahmed, *Public Finance in Egypt*, World Bank Staff Working Papers no. 639 (Washington: World Bank, 1984); and Jorgen R. Lotz, "Taxation in the United Arab Republic," *IMF Staff Papers*, vol. 13 (March 1966), pp. 121–53.

20. There was a handful of Egyptian economists, particularly on the left, who believed the tax apparatus could be modernized and expanded. See Isma'il Sabri Abdallah, "Burnamijna al-Iqtisadi Waqi'i wa-Mumkin al-Tanfidh," *al-Ahali*, May 9, 1984; and "25 Alf Milyuner fi Misr . . . Hal Yadfa'un al-Dara'ib?" *al-Wafd*, June 20, 1985.

21. For major statements by this school, see T. N. Srinivasan, "Neoclassical Political Economy, the State and Economic Development," *Asian Development Review*, vol. 3 (1985), pp. 38–58; and Deepak Lal, "The Political Economy of Economic Liberalization," *World Bank Economic Review*, vol. 1 (1987), pp. 273–99.

22. For the classic statement of this argument, see Janos Kornai, *Contradictions & Dilemmas: Studies on the Socialist Economy & Society* (M.I.T. Press, 1986), pp. 33–50.

23. Lal, "Political Economy," p. 293.

24. Robert D. Tollison, "Rent Seeking: A Survey," *Kyklos*, vol. 35 (1982), pp. 575–602; Robert D. Tollison, "Is the Theory of Rent-Seeking Here to Stay?" in Charles K. Rowley, ed., *Democracy and Public Choice* (Oxford: Blackwell, 1987), pp. 143–57; and Gordon Tullock, "Rent Seeking," in John Eatwell, Murray Milgate, and Peter Newman, eds., *The New Palgrave: A Dictionary of Economics* (Macmillan, 1987), vol. 4, pp. 147–49.

25. Michael Lipton, "Agriculture, Rural People, the State and the Surplus in Some Asian Countries: Thoughts on Some Implications of Three Recent Approaches in Social Science," *World Development*, vol. 17 (October 1989), p. 1562.

26. This is a two hundred-year-old argument with deep roots in the liberal tradition; see James D. Savage, *Balanced Budgets and American Politics* (Cornell University Press, 1988), pp. 85–120.

27. Indeed, analyses of rent seeking and arguments in favor of budget constraints have a common origin in the "public choice" school of political economy. For a survey of this literature, see James M. Buchanan and Robert D. Tollison, eds., *The Theory of Public Choice-II* (University of Michigan Press, 1984), particularly Geoffrey Brennan and James M. Buchanan, "Towards a Tax Constitution for Leviathan," pp. 71–89. For a fruitful attempt to trace the links between rent-seeking behavior and budget deficits, see Mancur Olson, *The Rise and Decline of Nations: Economic Growth, Stagflation, and Social Rigidities* (Yale University Press, 1982).

28. Joseph White and Aaron Wildavksy, *The Deficit and the Public Interest: The Search for Responsible Budgeting in the 1980s* (University of California Press and the Russell Sage Foundation, 1989). pp. 110–11.

29. See the quotations from Senator Patrick Moynihan in William Schneider, "The Political Legacy of the Reagan Years," in Sidney Blumenthal and Thomas Byrne Edsall, eds., *The Reagan Legacy* (New York: Pantheon Books, 1988), pp. 51–52. Entitlements is a common pseudonym for a form of rent.

30. The major statement propounding AID's newfound neoclassical doctrine is *Development and the National Interest: U.S. Economic Assistance into the 21st Century* (Washington: U.S. Agency for International Development, February 17, 1989).

31. "The most important questions about the role of the state are not How Big? or How Much? but What Kind? What Comparative Advantage? How Can State Performance Be Improved?" Tony Killick, *A Reaction Too Far: Economic Theory and the Role of the State in Developing Countries* (London: Overseas Development Institute, 1989), p. 8. Killick provides an excellent account of how the neoclassical economists tend to confuse the size of the state with its perniciousness.

32. Horticultural crops typically required a larger initial investment. An orchard of oranges does not start producing fruit until four years after it is planted. Thus, only the more prosperous and skilled farmers could afford to specialize in horticulture.

33. Many, however, feared that the shift to fodder production was a misallocation of resources resulting from government distortions of the market; subsidized cereals raised the demand for meat while nontariff barriers made imports expensive and raised the price that local livestock owners could charge.

34. Much of the EC's trade was between its members; while trade in fresh vegetables grew by 40 percent in the late 1970s and early 1980s, third countries (not members of the EC) only managed to increase their share by 17 percent. Maury E. Bredahl and Edward B. Hogan, *The Common Agricultural Policy: Macroeconomic Forces and Horticultural Trade* (University of Missouri, College of Agriculture, 1985), pp. ix-x.

35. Nurul Islam, *Horticultural Exports of Developing Countries: Past*

Performances, Future Prospects, and Policy Issues (Washington: International Food Policy Research Institute, April 1990), p. 9.

36. See Bela Balassa, *The Newly Industrializing Countries in the World Economy* (New York: Pergamon, 1981).

37. See Muhammad Khalifa, "al-Tasdir Asbaha Qadiya fi Misr," *al-Majalla*, March 25–31, 1987, pp. 40–41.

38. "The Promotion of Egyptian Exports of Horticulture Crops," Fourth Economics Policy Workshop (Davis, Calif.: Agricultural Development Systems—Egypt Project, March 29–30, 1982), pp. 18–19.

39. Abd-El-Raheem M. Hashem, *Egyptian Food System Development: Simulation of Alternative Strategic Plans for Egyptian Food Security*, Ph.D. dissertation, Kansas State University, 1986, p. 169.

40. "Promotion of Egyptian Exports," pp. 31 and 33.

41. Youssef Walley and others, *Strategy for Agricultural Development in the Eighties for the Arab Republic of Egypt*, International Development Series Report 9 (Iowa State University, June 1982), pp. 61–62.

42. Izzat Ali, "al-Mawalih: Hadith al-Fursa al-Da'i'a," *al-Ahram al-Iqtisadi*, August 1, 1988, p. 26. (Hereafter *AI*.)

43. Robert Springborg, *Mubarak's Egypt* (Boulder, Colo.: Westview Press, 1989), p. 80.

44. Izzat Ali, "Wa-Faqadna Fursa Dhahabiyya fi Tasdir al-Basal," *AI*, July 16, 1984, pp. 14–17.

45. Maury E. Bredahl, *Macroeconomic Policy and Agricultural Development: Concepts and Case Studies of Egypt, Morocco and Jordan* (University of Missouri, College of Agriculture, 1985), pp. 19–21.

46. Muhammad al-Shirbini and Mirvat al-Sayyid, "al-Tasdir Yuhtudir," *al-Wafd*, October 31, 1985.

47. For the growing political influence of the Conference see Khalifa, "al-Tasdir Asbaha Qadiya fi Misr," pp. 40–41.

48. Ali, "al-Mawalih," pp. 22–25.

49. Izzat Ali, "al-Majlis al-Sila'i lil-Burtuqal wal-Maham al-Matruha," *AI*, August 29, 1988, pp. 64–68.

50. "Madha Hadatha lil-Khudrawat al-Misriyya?" *al-Ahali*, January 19, 1983. For additional details, see "Sadiratuna al-Zira'iyya.. Limadha Tatanaqas?" *AI*, March 2, 1981, p. 6.

51. From Wizarat al-Zira'a, al-'Alaqat al-Kharijiyya, *Dirasa 'an Tanmiyat al-Sadirat al-Misriyya min al-Khudar wal-Fakiha ila Duwal al-'Alam* (Cairo: Wizarat al-Zira'a, 1988), reviewed in *AI*, September 12, 1988, pp. 86–87.

52. "Namw al-Sadirat al-Sina'iyya bi-Nisbat 11% wal-Zira'iyya bi-Nisbat 18% ma'a 'Adam Ziyadat al-Waridat Illa bi-Nisbat 7%," *AI*, July 25, 1988, p. 11.

53. Joachim von Braun, in "Promotion of Egyptian Exports," pp. 10–11.

54. Islam, *Horticultural Exports*, p. 82.

55. Other foreign agribusinesses with large-scale projects were FMC Corp. and Ralston Purina; see David Butter, *Egypt: Remaking the Arab Connection* (London: Middle East Economic Digest, July 1989), pp. 55–56.

56. Waheed Ali Megahed, Mohamed Saied Zayed, and Mossaad El-Sayed Ragab, *Domestic Marketing Channels for Tomatoes*, Economics Working Paper 178 (Davis, Calif.: Agricultural Development Systems—Egypt Project, July 1983), p. 1.

57. According to National Cooperative Business Association, "Egyptian Food Distribution Systems: An Assessment and Recommended Plan of Action" [1987]. AID has probed the prospect that joint ventures with American firms might supply Egyptian entrepreneurs with the capital and expertise necessary to modernize agricultural marketing.

58. Wheeler McMillen, *Feeding Multitudes* (Danville, Ill.: Interstate Publishers, 1982); and Robert West Howard, *The Vanishing Land* (Ballantine, 1985), pp. 136–39.

59. The World Bank has shown some interest in nudging the commodity councils in the direction of becoming producer cooperatives, lending them millions of dollars to develop common processing facilities; see *MEED*, April 21, 1989, p. 12.

60. M.A. Elsentericy and F.A. Fahmy, "An Empirical Study of the Export Channels for Egyptian Fresh Tomatoes," *Annals of Agricultural Science, Ain-Shams University*, vol. 31 (1986), pp. 837–957 (in Arabic), cited in *World Agricultural Economics and Rural Sociology Abstracts*, vol. 29 (April 1987), p. 250.

61. Calculated from figures in Nabil T. Habashy, "Economic Aspects and Estimation of Post Harvest Losses in Some Horticulture Crops," Economics Working Paper 64 (Davis, Calif.: Agricultural Development Systems—Egypt Project, March 1982).

62. "Madha Hadatha lil-Khudrawat al-Misriyya?"

63. Usama Ahmad Salih, "al-Halaqa al-Mafquda fi Taraju' Sadirat al-Burtuqal," *AI*, August 29, 1988, pp. 70–73.

64. Kamal Gaballah, "Milyar Junayh Sanawiyyan Faqid Khudar wa-Fakiha fi Misr," *AI*, February 19, 1990, p. 38.

65. "al-Batatis al-Misriyya: Hal Takhsar al-Suq al-Urubbiyya al-Mushtaraka," *AI*, October 1, 1984, p. 12.

66. Ibid.

67. Tuhami Muntasar, "Batatis al-Tasdir fi Khatar," *al-Wafd*, January 23, 1986. A similar problem plagued potato exports in 1989; see *MEED*, March 3, 1989, p. 23.

68. For a description of internal transportation systems, see Cheryl McQueen, *Marketing in Egypt* (U.S. Department of Commerce, International Trade Administration, December 1981), pp. 28 and 33–34.

69. Mahmoud Nafadi, "Experts Advise More Effective Use of Nile as Transportation Channel," *Middle East Times*, September 29–October 3, 1987.

70. Phil Finnegan, "Egypt: Making the Trains Run at All," *8 Days*, August 22, 1981, p. 48.

71. Clive Daniels, *Egypt in the 1980s: The Challenge* (London: Economist Intelligence Unit, 1983), pp. 188–89.

72. Finnegan, "Egypt," p. 48; also see "Freight Service Planning and Marketing: A Case Study of the Egyptian Railways," *MENA Economic Weekly*, vol. 25 (July 4, 1986), pp. 5–9.

73. See Islam, *Horticultural Exports*, p. 10. Private Egyptian exporters might be able to enforce their own quality and health codes; but historical experience suggests that this task too will probably be left to the state.

74. Shahira al-Rafi'i, "al-Ikhtiraq al-Misri lil-Suq al-Urubbiyya," *AI*, December 21, 1987, p. 31.

75. For a good general history see Brian E. Hill, *The Common Agricultural Policy: Past, Present and Future* (London: Methuen, 1984).

76. For the workings of the CAP in horticulture, see Bredahl and Hogan, *Common Agricultural Policy*, pp. 16–55.

77. The major study of the effects of community expansion is Reimar V. Alvensleben, Hans-Cristoph Behr, and Hans-Harald Jahn, "Prospective Effects of the EC-Enlargement of the Markets for Fruit and Vegetables" (Institut für Gartenbausökonomie der Universität Hannover, June 1984).

78. Bredahl and Hogan, *Common Agricultural Policy*, p. 57.

79. For official Egyptian recognition of the importance of economic ties with Europe, see "Hawl Dirasat Majlis al-Shura lil-'Alaqat: al-Siyasa wal-Iqtisadiyya ma'a al-Suq al-Urubbiyya," *AI*, March 7, 1988, pp. 12–13.

80. Bredahl and Hogan, *Common Agricultural Policy*, p. 55; and "al-Batatis al-Misriyya," p. 12.

81. al-Rafi'i, "al-Ikhtiraq al-Misri," p. 31.

82. Bredahl and Hogan, *Common Agricultural Policy*, pp. 43–44.

83. Joachim von Braun and Hartwig de Haen, "Egypt and the Enlargement of the EEC: Impact on the Agricultural Sector," *Food Policy*, February 1982, p. 48.

84. See Max Rodenbeck, "Double Blow," *Middle East International*, March 17, 1989, pp. 14–15; and Alan Cowell, "Mubarak, in Europe, Stresses Role as Peace Broker," *New York Times*, September 28, 1988.

85. Islam, *Horticultural Exports*, p. 10.

86. "Triple Detente," *Economist*, July 14–20, 1990, pp. 27–29; and Paul L. Montgomery, "Europeans In Accord On Farms," *New York Times*, November 7, 1990.

87. Ali, "al-Majlis al-Sila'i," pp. 64–68.

88. White and Wildavksy, *Deficit and the Public Interest*, p. 103.

89. See Cheryl Payer, ed., *Commodity Trade of the Third World* (Macmillan, 1975). For recent conditions, see Nicholas D. Kristof, "Raw Material Prices Recover," *New York Times*, September 15, 1987.

90. Some scholars have argued that the volatility of agricultural prices inexorably strips title to land away from less productive (or less lucky?) farmers and concentrates it in the hands of their more successful neighbors. This concentration of landholding, however, does not mean large-scale farms are universally the most efficient unit of agricultural production. International comparisons suggest that small farms actually achieve higher yields per unit of land; see World Bank, *The Assault on World Poverty—Problems of Rural*

Development, Education, and Health (Johns Hopkins University Press, 1975), pp. 215–16.

91. Clyde H. Farnsworth, "Nations Agree to Cut Tariffs on 3d-World Tropical Items," *New York Times,* December 6, 1988; and "False Security," *Economist,* December 17–23, 1988, p. 71.

92. Clyde H. Farnsworth, "Farm Issue is Clouding Trade Talks," *New York Times,* December 5, 1988; and Paul Lewis, "U.S. Assailed on Freer Farm Trade," *New York Times,* March 8, 1988.

93. "Old MacDonald in the Way," *Economist,* June 30–July 6, 1990, p. 67.

94. David Rapp, *How the U.S. Got Into Agriculture and Why It Can't Get Out* (Washington: Congressional Quarterly, 1988), p. 165; also see Sam Nakagama, "In Japan, Farm Supports Prop Up More than Farms," *New York Times,* July 13, 1990.

95. Robert J. Samuelson, "Farm Folly," *Washington Post,* December 28, 1988; "Milking the Sacred Cow," *Economist,* December 2–8, 1989, pp. 85–86; and Hill, *Common Agricultural Policy.*

96. Rapp, *How the U.S. Got Into Agriculture,* p. xii. For background see Carol S. Kramer, ed., *The Political Economy of U.S. Agriculture* (Washington: Resources for the Future, 1989); Mark Ritchie and Kevin Ristau, "U.S. Farm Policy," *World Policy Journal,* vol. 4 (Winter 1986–87), pp. 113–34; and Harriet Friedmann, "The Political Economy of Food: The Rise and Fall of the Postwar International Food Order," *American Journal of Sociology,* vol. 88 (1982), pp. S248-S286.

97. "Agricultural Disarmament," *Economist,* October 8–14, 1988, p. 15.

98. For an attempt, see James Duncan Shaffer, "A Market Alternative to Farm Price Support Programs: Full Participation Markets in Contracts for Future Delivery," Discussion Paper FAP 89–02 (Washington: Resources for the Future, May 1989).

99. "'A'idat Misr min al-Qutn 340 Milyun Dular," *al-Mustaqbal,* May 28, 1988, p. 29; and Mohamed Mansour, "An Economic Analysis of the World Market for Egyptian Cotton," Ph.D. dissertation, Oregon State University, 1984, p. 1.

100. Wizarat al-Zira'a, al-'Alaqat al-Zira'iyya al-Kharijiyya, *Dirasa 'an al-Qutn fi Misr wal-'Alam* (Cairo: Wizarat al-Zira'a, 1984) reviewed in *AI,* October 29, 1984, pp. 56–57; and Eric Monke and Lester D. Taylor, "Government Policy and International Trade in Cotton," Economics Working Paper 113 (Davis, Calif.: Agricultural Development Systems—Egypt Project, December 1982), p. 9.

101. Muhammad Shamil Abaza, "Tasa'ulat . . . Hawla al-Siyasa al-Qut-niyya al-Misriyya," *AI,* June 1, 1981, pp. 13–14. For a period in the 1960s when the United States, the world's largest exporter of cotton, had constructed an elaborate system of minimum prices, world cotton prices were relatively stable. But this "safety net" disappeared in the 1970s.

102. Robert L. Tignor, *State, Private Enterprise, and Economic Change in Egypt, 1918–1952* (Princeton University Press, 1984), p. 129. One subsidy, by the way, bred another. The obligation to buy local extra-long staple cotton

made Egyptian textile firms less competitive. To compensate industrialists, the state inaugurated a program of higher tariffs, direct subsidies, and officially sanctioned monopolies.

103. Marius Deeb, *Párty Politics in Egypt: The Wafd and Its Rivals, 1919–1939* (London: Ithaca Press, 1979), pp. 22–29.

104. Marius Deeb, "Large Landowners and Social Transformation in Egypt," in Tarif Khalidi, ed., *Land Tenure and Social Transforation in the Middle East* (Beirut: American University of Beirut, 1984), p. 429.

105. Mansour, "Economic Analysis," p. 22; and E. M. H. Lloyd, *Food and Inflation in the Middle East, 1940–45* (Stanford University Press, 1956), pp. 119–24.

106. Yusuf Hanna, "Matlub Nazra Jadida li-Sharikat al-Qutn," *AI*, August 29, 1988, pp. 60–62.

107. Jean-Jacques Dethier, *Trade, Exchange Rate, and Agricutural Pricing Policies in Egypt*, vol. 1 (Washington: World Bank, 1989), pp. 191–97.

108. Monke and Taylor, "Government Policy," p. 9.

109. Nazira al-Afandi, "Dhahabna al-Abyad wal-Suq al-'Alamiyya lil-Qutn," *AI*, September 19, 1988, pp. 57–58.

110. Mansour, "Economic Analysis," pp. 7 and 15–17.

111. Dethier, *Trade, Exchange Rate*, vol. 1, pp. 182–84.

112. Eric A. Monke, Dennis C. Cory, and Donald G. Heckerman, "Surplus Disposal in World Markets: An Application to Egyptian Cotton," *American Journal of Agricultural Economics*, vol. 69 (August 1987), p. 573.

113. Sultan Abu Ali, "Fadihat Tas'ir al-Qutn," *AI*, December 14, 1981, p. 19.

114. Adil Muhammad Lahita, "al-Qutn al-Misri Yasqut 'an 'Ushrihi," *AI*, April 20, 1990, p. 15.

115. Yusuf Hanna, "Madha Yantazir al-Qutn al-Misri?" *AI*, October 16, 1989, p. 72.

116. Yusuf Hanna, "al-Qutn fi Khatar," *AI*, August 5, 1985, pp. 62–63.

117. For background, see "The Future of Cotton in the Egyptian Economy," Economics Working Paper 114 (Davis, Calif.: Agricultural Development Systems—Egypt Project, December 18–19, 1982), p. 4.

118. Even the Berg Report, *Accelerated Development in Sub-Saharan Africa: An Agenda for Action* (Washington: World Bank, 1981), ignored the effect of relative prices; so did the study by Khalid Ikram, *Egypt, Economic Management in a Time of Transition* (Johns Hopkins University Press, 1980).

119. Foreign Agricultural Service, "Egypt: Annual Cotton Report," (Cairo: U.S. Embassy, June 20, 1986), p. 3.

120. Yusuf Hanna, "Madha Yahduth fi Sharikat Tasdir al-Aqtan," *AI*, March 6, 1989, p. 66.

121. Egyptian officials are increasingly receptive to these proposals. See the remarks of Ahmad Shuman reported in Yusuf Hanna, "Ayna Mawqa' al-Qutn 'ala Kharitat Iqtisad Misr?" *AI*, September 18, 1989, pp. 24–27.

122. *MEED*, May 12, 1989, p. 13.

123. Gamal Abd al-Wahhab, "Hatta fi Luqmat al-'Aysh Na'tamid 'ala Amrika," *al-Ahali*, June 23, 1983.

124. M. Raqaa El Amir, Saad Nassar, and Ahmed A. Hafez Mohammed, "Some Remarks on the Institutional Framework of the Rice Industry in Egypt," Economics Working Paper 51 (Davis, Calif.: Agricultural Development Systems—Egypt Project, November 1981), p. 5.

125. Tony Walker, "The Nile Thirsts for Life," *Financial Times*, November 30, 1987.

126. Patrick E. Tyler, "Egyptian Food Crisis Feared As Waters of Nile Drop," *Washington Post*, March 25, 1987; and Isam Rif'at, "Khitab Jaffaf ila Misr," *AI*, December 21, 1987, pp. 8–9 and 13.

127. Ayman al-Sayyad, "al-Nil Yuhaddid Misr," *al-Majalla*, March 16–22, 1988, p. 34.

128. Azza Husseini, "Report Criticizes 'Massive' Waste of Irrigation Water in Agriculture," *Middle East Times*, May 10–30, 1987.

129. The best introduction to water problems in the United States is Marc Reisner, *Cadillac Desert* (Penguin, 1986). Interestingly, despite the claims of Karl Wittfogel, oriental despotism (the creation of absolute central power to deal with hydraulic problems) was not a major force in Egyptian history. Traditionally, irrigation along the Nile took the form of basin systems which could be built and maintained by individual villages. Only in the nineteenth century did Egyptians begin to switch to canal irrigation and require central supervision of the construction of long-distance channels.

130. Montague Keen, "New Channels for the Waters of the Nile," *Ceres: The FAO Review*, vol. 20 (November–December 1987), pp. 16–20.

131. Scot E. Smith, "Drought and Water Management: The Egyptian Response," *Journal of Soil and Water Conservation*, vol. 41 (September–October 1986), pp. 297–300; "Irrigation Minister Radi On Nile Water Level," in FBIS, *Near East*, February 3, 1988, p. 12; and "A Silverish Lining to Sudan's Clouds," *Economist*, August 27, 1988, pp. 74–75.

132. Amru Abd al-Hadi Nasif, "al-Fayadan Ba'd al-Jaffaf," *al-Shira'*, November 28, 1988, pp. M4-M5; and Alan Cowell, "Nile Gives Abundantly as Doomsday Recedes," *New York Times*, December 20, 1988.

133. See Smith, "Drought and Water Management," and Keen, "New Channels."

134. *MEED*, November 10, 1989, p. 17.

135. Angus Hindley, "Tension Flows from an Ebbing Nile," *MEED*, May 25, 1990, pp. 4–5.

136. Mancur Olson, Jr., *The Logic of Collective Action; Public Goods and the Theory of Groups* (Harvard University Press, 1965), is the locus classicus. For a description of the resulting inequities, see Claus Offe, *Disorganized Capitalism* (M.I.T. Press, 1985), pp. 170–220.

137. For background, see Kenneth M. Cuno, "The Origins of Private Ownership of Land in Egypt: A Reappraisal," *International Journal of Middle East Studies*, vol. 12 (1980), pp. 245–75.

138. For a beautiful description of this evasion, and its consequences for

political life in rural areas, see Yusuf al-Qa'id, *al-Harb fi Barr Misr* (Beirut: Dar Ibn Rushd, 1978).

139. Alain De Janvry, *The Agrarian Question and Reformism in Latin America* (Johns Hopkins University Press, 1981), provides an excellent account of the mechanisms of change in land regimes and the diverse courses societies may choose to follow. Also, see John S. Saul, *The State and Revolution in Eastern Africa* (New York: Monthly Review Press, 1979), pp. 297–338.

140. Egypt's problems in devising a functional system of landed property rights are typical of developing societies; for comparable cases see David Feeny, "The Development of Property Rights in Land," in Robert H. Bates, ed., *Toward a Political Economy of Development* (University of California Press, 1988), pp. 272–99.

141. Roel Meijer, "Contemporary Egyptian Historiography of the Period 1936–1942: A Study of Its Scientific and Political Character," Ph.D. dissertation, Amsterdam, 1985, pp. 8–10.

142. John Waterbury, *The Egypt of Nasser and Sadat: The Political Economy of Two Regimes* (Princeton University Press, 1983), p. 266.

143. Mamduh Mihran and Asim Rashwan, "Ta'dil Qanun al-'Ijar al-Zira'i?" *al-Musawwar*, March 11, 1983, p. 24.

144. Mahmud Murad, "As'ila Matruha Hawla: Raf' al-Ijar, Tawrith al-'Aqd, Man' al-Ta'jir min al-Batin," *al-Ahram*, May 24, 1985.

145. Abd al-Wahhab Hamid, "al-'Alaqa bayn al-Malik wal-Musta'jir wa Mustaqbal al-Zira'a," *AI*, May 27, 1985, p. 36.

146. For a review of the categories employed here, see table 3–3.

147. Waterbury, *Egypt of Nasser and Sadat*, p. 269.

148. Ibid., p. 283.

149. Mohaya A. Zaytoun, "Income Distribution in Egyptian Agriculture and Its Main Determinants," in Gouda Abdel-Khalek and Robert Tignor, eds., *The Political Economy of Income Distribution in Egypt* (New York: Holmes & Meier, 1982), p. 277.

150. For an excellent analysis of the 1975 data, see Iliya Harik, *Distribution of Land, Employment and Income in Rural Egypt* (Cornell University, Rural Development Committee, December 1979).

151. Waterbury, *Egypt of Nasser and Sadat*, pp. 270–72. Waterbury's critique was thoughtful and informative, a mine of information on the inadequacies of Egypt's agricultural statistics. He was correct (see below) in his suspicion that rich peasants and capitalist farmers would not commit "class suicide."

152. Amal Allam, "Bi-Raghm Ziyadat al-Misahat al-Ma'ruda Ma Zala al-Talb 3 Ad'af al-'Ard!" *al-Wafd*, February 5, 1987.

153. Elizabeth Taylor-Awny, "Labor Shortage in Egyptian Agriculture: A Crisis for Whom?" in Teodor Shanin, ed., *Peasants and Peasant Societies* (Oxford: Basil Blackwell, 1987), pp. 166–73; and Elizabeth Taylor, "Peasants or Proletarians? The Transformation of Agrarian Production Relations in Egypt," in B. Munslow and H. Finch, *Proletarianisation in the Third World* (London: Croom Helm, 1984), pp. 164–88.

154. See Nicholas S. Hopkins, *Agrarian Transformation in Egypt* (Boulder, Colo.: Westview Press, 1987).

155. Muhammad Abu Mandur al-Dib, "al-'Alaqa bayn al-Malik wal-Musta'jir fi al-Zira'a al-Misriyya," *al-Tali'a*, June 1975, p. 80.

156. Mihran and Rashwan, "Ta'dil," p. 26.

157. Aryan Nasif, "al-Haqq.. wal-Batil fi al-'Alaqa al-Ijariyya al-Zira'iyya," *al-Ahali*, August 4, 1982.

158. Mihran and Rashwan, "Ta'dil," p. 24; and Mahmud Abd al-Fadil, "Mustaqbal al-Zira'a wal-Mas'ala al-Zira'iyya fi Misr," *al-Ahali*, December 28, 1983.

159. al-Dib, "al-'Alaqa bayn al-Malik wal-Musta'jir," p. 78.

160. Sharif al-Abd, "al-'Alaqa al-Zira'iyya al-Mutawazina bayn al-Malik wal-Musta'jir Kayf?" *al-Ahram*, December 26, 1982.

161. Sharif al-Abd, "Nizam al-'Ijarat al-Zira'iyya Yahtaj ila I'adat Nazar," *al-Ahram*, December 25, 1982; and Mihran and Rashwan, "Ta'dil," p. 26.

162. Wahid Abd al-Magid, "al-Usus al-Ijtima'iyya li-Hizb al-Wafd al-Jadid: Mawqif al-Hizb min al-'Alaqat al-Ijariyya fi al-Zira'a wal-Iskan," *AI*, May 23, 1988, pp. 62–65.

163. Muhammad Nu'man, "al-'Alaqa bayn Malik wa-Musta'jir al-Ard al-Zira'iyya," *al-Ahali*, February 2, 1983.

164. Ibid.

165. Mahmud Murad, "al-Ard liman Yazra'ha.. wa-Lakin?" *al-Ahram*, May 31, 1985.

166. Muhammad Sulayman, "Mashakil al-Zira'a fi Misr: Hiwar 7 Sa'at Bayn al-Hukuma wal-Mu'arada," *al-Ahali*, September 15, 1982.

167. Prosterman spelled out his conclusion in Roy L. Prosterman and Jeffrey M. Riedinger, *Land Reform and Democratic Development* (Johns Hopkins University Press, 1987), an impassioned yet rigorous appeal for U.S. support of land reform efforts worldwide.

168. Roy Prosterman and Tim Hanstad, "Aide Memoire on Our Discussion of Registered Tenants" (Seattle, Wash.: University of Washington, March 22, 1988), pp. 5–11.

169. Mirvat al-Husri, "Wali wa Rijal al-'A'mal fi Munaqashat Sakhina Sakhina," *AI*, February 17, 1986, pp. 24–25.

170. Sulayman, "Mashakil al-Zira'a fi Misr," *al-Ahali*, September 15, 1982.

171. Mihran and Rashwan, "Ta'dil," p. 26.

172. al-Abd, "Nizam al-Ijarat al-Zira'iyya;" and Abd al-Fadil, "Mustaqbal al-Zira'a."

173. Nasif, "al-Haqq.. wal-Batil."

174. Abdel Monem Said Aly, "Democratization in Egypt," *American-Arab Affairs*, no. 22 (Fall 1987), p. 18.

175. "Sarakhat li-Ashab al-Khamsa al-Afdina fa-Aqall wa-Muqtarahat li-Alladhina la Yaktafun bil-Surakh," *al-Ahram*, September 28, 1984.

176. "Tahdid al-'Ijar Wafqan li-Mustawa al-As'ar," *al-Ahram*, April 6, 1985.

177. Muhammad Abu Mandur, "al-'Alaqa bayn al-Malik wal-Musta'jir fi

al-Zira'a al-Misriyya," *al-Ahram*, April 11, 1985; and Muhammad Iraqi, "Ba'd al-Sayf . . . Yabda' al-Hujum," *al-Ahali*, September 4, 1985.

178. Hamid, "al-'Alaqa bayn al-Malik," p. 36; and Iraqi, "Ba'd al-Sayf."

179. al-Husri, "Wali wa Rijal al-'A'mal," p. 25.

180. Murad, "As'ila Hawla;" and Prosterman and Hanstad, "Aide Memoire."

181. See Richard H. Adams, Jr., *Development and Social Change in Rural Egypt* (Syracuse University Press, 1986), pp. 89–90; and Nu'man, "al-'Alaqa bayn al-Malik wa-Musta'jir."

182. Abd al-Fadil, "Mustaqbal al-Zira'a."

183. Mihran and Rashwan, "Ta'dil," p. 24.

184. The 1977 property estimates, which showed that rich peasants controlled a declining share of the land area, surprised many observers. For nearly a century this class had steadily augmented its holdings. Waterbury suggested that the 1977 estimates were probably flawed; see *Egypt of Nasser and Sadat*, pp. 270–71. The 1982 cadastre seems to have proven him right; for its figures see Robert Springborg, "Rolling Back Agrarian Reforms in Egypt" (Macquarie University, September 1989). Selections from the Springborg article were published as "Rolling Back Egypt's Agrarian Reform," *Middle East Report*, vol. 20 (September–October 1990), pp. 28–30.

185. Springborg, "Rolling Back Agrarian Reforms."

186. Ibid., p. 27.

187. Simon Commander and Aly Abdullah Hadhoud, "From Labour Surplus to Labour Scarcity? The Agricultural Labour Market in Egypt," *Development Policy Review*, vol. 4 (June 1986), pp. 171–75.

188. Ibid.

189. Jamal Kamal, *al-Jumhuriya*, November 9, 1989, in FBIS, *Near East*, November 15, 1989, pp. 10–11.

190. "Responsible Iraqi Source Confirms: Instructions Have Been Issued to Resolve Egyptians' Remittances Issue," *al-Sharq al-Awsat*, November 14, 1989, in FBIS, *Near East*, November 15, 1989, p. 13.

191. Alan Cowell, "Egyptian Laborers Are Fleeing Iraq," *New York Times*, November 15, 1989.

192. Abd al-Nabi Abd al-Sattar, "Paper Expects 'Breakthrough'," *al-Wafd*, November 12, 1989, in FBIS, *Near East*, November 14, 1989, p. 25.

193. *MEED*, November 17, 1989, p. 14.

194. Nabil Zaki, "Reporter Details Iraq-Egypt 'Crisis'," *al-Akhbar*, November 22, 1989, in FBIS, *Near East*, November 27, 1989, p. 7.

195. "Economy Feels the Strain as Workers Stream Home," *MEED*, August 31, 1990, p. 10.

196. Cairo, MENA, "Official on Economic Effects of Gulf Situation," September 5, 1990, and "254,993 Returned from Iraq, Kuwait Since 2 Aug," in FBIS, *Near East*, September 6, 1990, p. 18, and September 14, 1990, pp. 6–7.

197. "Ba'd Azmat al-Khalij: Milyar Dular Khasa'ir Misr al-Siyahiyya," *al-Majalla*, December 5–11, 1990, p. 13.

198. "Gulf Crisis Losses Put at $3.6 Billion," *MEED*, September 28, 1990, p. 19.

199. Simon Brindle, "Egypt: Forever in Debt to You," *Middle East*, January 1991, pp. 29–30. For an overview of the Gulf crisis's impact on Egypt, see Mahmud Salim, "al-Ghazw al-'Iraqi Yuhaddid al-Iqtisad al-Misri," *al-Majalla*, September 12–18, 1990, pp. 40–43.

200. Hence the title of Stockman's book, *The Triumph of Politics: The Inside Story of the Reagan Revolution* (New York: Avon, 1987).

201. For a detailed criticism of the taxation system in Egypt, see Abdallah, "Burnamijna al-Iqtisadi," and Uthman Muhammad Uthman, "Di'am Raghif al-'Aysh wa-'Ajiz al-Mizaniyya," *al-Ahali*, June 23, 1982.

202. For an introduction to their ideas, see Joseph E. Stiglitz, *Economics of the Public Sector* (Norton, 1988); and S. Wellisz and R. Findlay, "The State and the Invisible Hand," *World Bank Research Observer*, vol. 3 (January 1988).

203. P.T. Bauer, *Economic Analysis and Policy in Underdeveloped Countries* (London: Duke University Press, 1957), pp. 108–09.

204. Henry David Thoreau, "Civil Disobedience," in Carl Bode, ed., *The Portable Thoreau* (Viking, 1947), p. 109. Of course, in the same sentence Thoreau argued that actually "that government is best which governs not at all."

205. United Nations Development Program, *Human Development Report 1990* (Oxford University Press, 1990), p. 136. The adult literacy rate in Egypt at the end of this period was lower than that in many patently poorer countries such as Ethiopia, Zaire, Rwanda, Uganda, Ghana, Madagascar, Kampuchea, Kenya, China, and Zambia.

206. Nigel Harris, *The End of the Third World: Newly Industrializing Countries and the Decline of Ideology* (Penguin, 1986), p. 147.

207. See Demetris Papageorgiou, Armeane M. Choksi, and Michael Michaely, *Liberalizing Foreign Trade in Developing Countries: The Lessons of Experience* (Washington: World Bank, 1990).

208. See Chalmers Johnson, "The Taiwan Mode," in James C. Hsiung, ed., *The Taiwan Experience, 1950–1980* (Praeger, 1981), pp. 9–18.

CHAPTER 8

1. Tony Killick, *A Reaction Too Far: Economic Theory and the Role of the State in Developing Countries* (London: Overseas Development Institute, 1989), p. 30.

2. Alan Cowell, "2¢ Loaf is Family Heartbreak in Egypt," *New York Times*, July 9, 1990.

3. Miles Kahler, "Orthodoxy and Its Alternatives: Explaining Approaches to Stabilization and Adjustment," in Joan M. Nelson, ed., *Economic Crisis and Policy Choice* (Princeton University Press, 1990), p. 55; and Joan M. Nelson, "The Politics of Long-Haul Economic Reform," in Joan M. Nelson,

ed., *Fragile Coalitions: The Politics of Economic Adjustment* (New Brunswick, N.J.: Transaction Books, 1989), pp. 9–10. Readers with an interest in Egypt might pay special attention to John Waterbury, "The Political Management of Economic Adjustment and Reform," in Ibid., pp. 39–56.

4. "The Best of All Monopoly Profits . . . " *Economist*, August 11, 1990, p. 67.

5. Steven Greenhouse, "A Thorny East Bloc Issue: Replacing Hated Managers," *New York Times*, December 12, 1989; and Craig R. Whitney, "When Communist Bosses Become Capitalist Ones," *New York Times*, July 13, 1990.

6. See Stephen Engelberg, "Marxist Functionaries Prosper in New Poland," *New York Times*, July 19, 1990; "Enter Comrade Capitalist," *Economist*, August 26, 1990, pp. 36–37; and Barry Newman, "Poland Has Plenty of One Thing: Crooks," *Wall Street Journal*, April 9, 1991.

7. For an example, see Ronald I. McKinnon, *The Order of Economic Liberalization: Financial Control in the Transition to a Market Economy* (forthcoming).

8. For the democratic argument, see Anders Aslund, "Moscow's New Power Center," *New York Times*, April 19, 1991. On the concept of "developmental dictatorship," see Richard L. Sklar, "Democracy in Africa," *African Studies Review*, vol. 26 (September 1983), pp. 11–24. For Soviet interest in the models of Chile and South Korea, see Jerry F. Hough, *The Struggle for the Third World: Soviet Debates and American Options* (Brookings, 1986).

9. The key studies are Stephen Haggard and Robert Kaufman, "The Politics of Stabilization and Structural Adjustment," in Jeffrey D. Sachs, ed., *Developing Country Debt and Economic Performance*, vol. 1 (University of Chicago Press, 1989), pp. 209–54; and Nelson, *Fragile Coalitions*. Also see the economic studies by Gustav Ranis, "The Role of Institutions in Transition Growth: The East Asian Newly Industrializing Countries," *World Development*, vol. 17 (September 1989), pp. 1443–53. Also see Robert Wade, "What Can Economics Learn from East Asian Success?" in The American Academy of Political and Social Science, *Annals*, vol. 505 (September 1989), pp. 68–79.

10. Alice H. Amsden, *Asia's Next Giant: South Korea and Late Industrialization* (Oxford University Press, 1989), p. 8.

11. See World Bank, *World Development Report 1989* (Oxford University Press, 1989), pp. 180–81, 184–85; and *World Development Report 1990* (Oxford University Press, 1990), pp. 194–95, and 200–01; Peter S. Heller and Jack Diamond, *International Comparisons of Government Expenditure Revisited: The Developing Countries, 1975–86* (Washington: International Monetary Fund, April 1990); and Robert Wade, *Governing the Market: Economic Theory and the Role of Government in East Asian Industrialization* (Princeton University Press, 1990).

12. Joseph Grunwald and Kenneth Flamm, *The Global Factory* (Brookings, 1985); and Jeffrey D. Sachs, "External Debt and Macroeconomic Performance in Latin America and East Asia," in William C. Brainard and George L. Perry, eds., *Brookings Papers on Economic Activity 2* (1985), pp. 523–73.

13. Anne Krueger, 1987, cited in *Development and the National Interest: U.S. Economic Assistance into the 21st Century* (Washington: U.S. Agency for International Development, February 17, 1989), p. 51.

14. The emphasis on "good government," as opposed to regime type, was already evident in the work of Lloyd G. Reynolds, one of the first experts to argue that political reform was the key to economic development; "The Spread of Economic Growth to the Third World: 1850–1980," *Journal of Economic Literature*, vol. 21 (September 1983), p. 976.

15. On Indonesia, see Lincoln Kaye, "A Change of Customs," *Far Eastern Economic Review*, April 25, 1985, pp. 118–20; and Eugene B. Mihaly, "Indonesia: A New Dragon?" *World Today*, August–September 1990, pp. 162–64. On Mexico, see "Doing the Impossible Takes a Little Longer," *Economist*, June 9, 1990, p. 43; and Gary Hector, "Why Mexico Is Looking Better," *Fortune*, January 15, 1990, pp. 135–37.

Index